PROLOG

GYNECOLOGY AND SURGERY

FIFTH EDITION

CRITIQUE BOOK

ORTHO·McNEIL

Ortho–McNeil Pharmaceutical is pleased to provide *PROLOG: Gynecology and Surgery,* Fifth Edition to future specialists in obstetrics and gynecology. Recognizing the importance of high-quality education, Ortho–McNeil is privileged to introduce this valuable educational resource.

THE AMERICAN COLLEGE OF OBSTETRICIANS AND GYNECOLOGISTS · WOMEN'S HEALTH CARE PHYSICIANS ·

1951

ISBN 1-932328-01-7

12345/87654

The American College of Obstetricians and Gynecologists
409 12th Street, SW
PO Box 96920
Washington, DC 20090-6920

Contributors

PROLOG Editorial and Advisory Committee

CHAIR

Ronald T. Burkman, Jr, MD
  Chair, Department of Obstetrics and
    Gynecology
  Baystate Medical Center
  Springfield, Massachusetts
  Deputy Chair and Professor
  Department of Obstetrics and
    Gynecology
  Tufts University School of Medicine
  Boston, Massachusetts

MEMBERS

Major Peter E. Nielsen, MD
  Obstetrics–Gynecology Residency
    Program Director
  Maternal–Fetal Medicine
  Department of Obstetrics and
    Gynecology
  Madigan Army Medical Center
  Gig Harbor, Washington
Louis Weinstein, MD
  Professor and Chair
  Department of Obstetrics and
    Gynecology
  Medical College of Ohio
  Toledo, Ohio
Sterling B. Williams, MD
  Vice President, Education
  The American College of Obstetricians
    and Gynecologists
  Washington, DC

PROLOG Task Force for *Gynecology and Surgery,* Fifth Edition

COCHAIRS

Diane M. Hartmann, MD
  Associate Dean of Graduate Medical
    Education
  Associate Professor of Obstetrics and
    Gynecology
  University of Rochester School of
    Medicine and Dentistry
  Rochester, New York
Joseph S. Sanfilippo, MD, MBA
  Professor of Obstetrics, Gynecology,
    and Reproductive Sciences
  Magee-Womens Hospital
  University of Pittsburgh School of
    Medicine
  Pittsburgh, Pennsylvania

MEMBERS

Martin Gimovsky, MD
  Vice Chair and Program Director
  Director, Division of Maternal–Fetal
    Medicine
  Department of Obstetrics and Gynecology
  Newark Beth Israel Medical Center
  Newark, New Jersey
Ira M. Golditch, MD
  Clinical Professor of Obstetrics and
    Gynecology
  Obstetrics, Gynecology, and Reproductive
    Sciences
  University of California, San Francisco
    School of Medicine
  San Francisco, California
John F. Greene, MD
  Associate Professor
  Residency Program Director,
    Obstetrics–Gynecology
  University of Connecticut
  Assistant Director, Women's Health
  Hartford Hospital
  Hartford, Connecticut

Continued on next page

PROLOG Task Force for *Gynecology and Surgery,* Fifth Edition
(continued)

Vicki L. Handa, MD
  Assistant Professor
  Gynecologic Specialties
  Johns Hopkins University School of
    Medicine
  Baltimore, Maryland
John H. Mattox, MD
  Chair and Program Director
  Clinical Professor, Gynecology and
    Community Medicine
  Obstetrics and Gynecology
  Good Samaritan Regional Medical
    Center
  Phoenix, Arizona
Holly E. Richter, PhD, MD
  Associate Professor
  Medical/Surgical Gynecology
  Obstetrics and Gynecology
  University of Alabama at Birmingham
  Birmingham, Alabama
Thomas E. Snyder, MD
  Associate Professor
  General Gynecology/Reconstructive
    Surgery
  Department of Obstetrics and
    Gynecology
  University of Kansas
  Kansas City, Kansas
Joel I. Sorosky, MD
  Professor and Director
  Division of Gynecologic Oncology
  Department of Obstetrics and
    Gynecology
  University of Iowa Hospitals
  Iowa City, Iowa

Cyril O. Spann Jr, MD
  Professor, Gynecologic Oncology
  Emory University School of Medicine
  Atlanta, Georgia
Albert George Thomas, MD
  Associate Professor
  Obstetrics, Gynecology, Reproductive
    Science
  Mount Sinai School of Medicine
  New York, New York

ACOG STAFF
Sallye B. Brown, RN, MN
  Director, Educational Development and
    Testing
  Division of Education
Christopher T. George, MA
  Editor, PROLOG

Note: This PROLOG unit was developed under the direction of the PROLOG Advisory Committee and the Task Force for *Gynecology and Surgery*, Fifth Edition. Any discussion of unapproved uses of products is clearly cited.

Current guidelines state that participants in continuing medical education (CME) activities should be made aware of any affiliation or financial interest by the contributors that may affect the development of the unit. The advisory committee and task force members declare that neither they nor any business associate nor any member of their immediate families has financial interest or other relationships with any manufacturer of any products or any providers of any of the services discussed in this publication except for **Joseph S. Sanfilippo, MD**, who has received research funds from Eli Lilly and Company, Wyeth Pharmaceuticals, and Pfizer Inc.; **Albert George Thomas, MD**, who is on the speaker's bureau for Ortho-McNeil Pharmaceutical, Inc., Berlex Laboratories, Inc, Pfizer Inc. (formerly Upjohn-Pharmacia), and Wyeth Pharmaceuticals and is a consultant for GlaxoSmithKline; **John H. Mattox, MD**, who is on the speaker's bureau for Wyeth Pharmaceuticals, Ortho-McNeil Pharmaceutical, Inc., and Solvay Pharmaceuticals, Inc., has received research support from Solvay Pharmaceuticals, Inc., and is a member of the advisory board for Ortho-McNeil Pharmaceutical, Inc.; and **Ronald T. Burkman Jr, MD**, who has received grant support from Ortho-McNeil Pharmaceutical, Inc., for educational programs and research, has been a consultant for Upjohn-Pharmacia, and has received grand rounds support from Ortho-McNeil Pharmaceutical, Inc., Wyeth Pharmaceuticals, Organon Inc, and Berlex Laboratories, Inc.

Preface

Purpose

PROLOG (Personal Review of Learning in Obstetrics and Gynecology) is a voluntary, strictly confidential, self-evaluation program. It is designed to enable physicians to assess their current knowledge and to review current concepts within the specialty. The content is carefully selected and presented in multiple-choice questions that are clinically oriented. The questions are designed to stimulate and challenge physicians in areas of medical care that they confront in their practices or when they work as consultant obstetrician–gynecologists.

PROLOG provides the American College of Obstetricians and Gynecologists with a means of identifying the educational needs of the Fellowship. Individual scores are reported only to the participant; however, cumulative performance data obtained for each PROLOG unit help determine the direction for future educational programs offered by the College.

Continuing medical education credits may be earned by participation in the PROLOG self-evaluation process. In addition, PROLOG serves as a valuable study tool, reference guide, and means of attaining up-to-date knowledge in the specialty.

Process

PROLOG offers the most advanced knowledge available in 5 areas of the specialty: obstetrics, gynecology and surgery, reproductive endocrinology and infertility, gynecologic oncology and critical care, and patient management in the office. A new PROLOG unit is produced annually, addressing 1 of those subject areas. *Gynecology and Surgery*, Fifth Edition, is the second unit in the fifth 5-year series of PROLOG.

Each unit of PROLOG represents the efforts of a special task force of subject experts under the supervision of an editorial and advisory committee. PROLOG sets forth current information as viewed by recognized authorities in the field of women's health. This educational resource does not define a standard of care, nor is it intended to dictate an exclusive course of management. It presents recognized methods and techniques of clinical practice for consideration by obstetrician–gynecologists for incorporation into their practices. Variations of practice that take into account the needs of the individual patient, resources, and the limitations that are special to the institution or type of practice may be appropriate.

Each unit of PROLOG is presented as a 2-part set, with performance information and cognate hour credit available to those who choose to send their answer sheets for confidential scoring.

The first part of the PROLOG set is the Question Book, which contains educational objectives for the unit, multiple-choice questions, and a computer-scored answer sheet. Participants can work through the book at their own pace, choosing to use PROLOG as a closed- or open-book assessment. Return of the answer sheet for scoring is encouraged but voluntary.

The second part of PROLOG is the Critique Book, which reviews the educational objectives and questions set forth in the Question Book and contains a discussion, or critique, of each question. The critique provides the rationale for correct and incorrect options. Current, accessible references are listed for each question. ACOG Fellows may request additional literature searches, as well as information about ACOG publications, by contacting the Resource Center, PO Box 96920, Washington, DC 20090-6920, telephone (202) 863-2518.

Participants who return their answer sheets for credit will receive a Performance Report indicating their answers and their correct score percentage. A data package will be sent and will offer participants a means of comparing their scores with the scores of a sample group of other participants. Please allow 1 month to process answer sheets.

Fellows who submit their answer sheets for scoring will be credited automatically with 25 cognate hours of Formal Learning in the ACOG Program for Continuing Professional Development. For the Physician's Recognition Award of the American Medical Association, 25 category 1 credit hours may be reported.

Credit for PROLOG *Gynecology and Surgery*, Fifth Edition, is initially available through December 2006. During that year, the unit will be reevaluated. If it is determined that content in the unit remains current, credit will be extended for an additional 3 years. PROLOG is planned and produced in accordance with the Standards for Enduring Materials of the Accreditation Council for Continuing Medical Education.

Conclusion

PROLOG was developed specifically as a personal study resource for the practicing obstetrician–gynecologist. It is presented as a self-assessment mechanism that, with its accompanying performance information, should assist the physician in designing a personal, self-directed learning program. The many quality resources developed by the College, as detailed each year in the ACOG *Publications and Educational Materials Catalog*, are available to help fulfill the educational interests and needs that have been identified. PROLOG is not intended as a substitute for the certification or recertification programs of the American Board of Obstetrics and Gynecology.

PROLOG Objectives

PROLOG is a voluntary, strictly confidential, personal continuing education resource that is designed to be both stimulating and enjoyable. By participating in PROLOG, obstetrician–gynecologists will be able to do the following:

- Review and update clinical knowledge
- Recognize areas of knowledge and practice in which they excel, be stimulated to explore other areas of the specialty, and identify areas requiring further study
- Plan continuing education activities in light of identified strengths and deficiencies
- Compare and relate present knowledge and skills with those of other participants
- Obtain continuing medical education credit, if desired
- Have complete personal control of the setting and of the pace of the experience

The obstetrician–gynecologist who completes *Gynecology and Surgery*, Fifth Edition, will be able to do the following:

- Associate history, as well as signs and symptoms, with clinical diagnoses of specific gynecologic and general medical conditions
- Select appropriate laboratory tests and procedures and then analyze the results to make specific diagnoses
- Use an efficacious and cost-effective program of office management for each selected diagnosis
- Understand fundamental concepts of physiology and pathophysiology
- Apply epidemiologic principles to the health care of women
- Counsel patients regarding the extent of their medical problems, including benefits and risks of treatment as well as alternatives
- Apply professional medical ethics to the practice of obstetrics and gynecology
- Incorporate appropriate legal, risk management, and office management guidelines and techniques into clinical practice

Gynecology and Surgery, Fifth Edition, includes the following topics:

SCREENING AND DIAGNOSIS
Abnormal Pap test results
Adolescent abnormal uterine bleeding
Altered mental status after hysterectomy
Appendicitis
Asymptomatic bacteriuria in a geriatric patient
Cervical cancer screening
Cervicitis and postcoital bleeding
Chronic pelvic pain
Depression
Ectopic pregnancy: evaluation with serum markers
Evaluation of postmenopausal bleeding
Factor V Leiden mutation
Geriatric patient–polypharmacy–drug reactions and interactions
Initial assessment of sexual molestation
Liquid-based Pap tests
Pain diagnosis
Premenarcheal pelvic mass
Premenopausal adnexal masses
Pulmonary embolus, myocardial infarction, and septic shock
Retroperitoneal hematoma
Screening for cystic fibrosis carrier status

Straddle injury
Stress incontinence
Tamoxifen citrate (Nolvadex) for breast cancer prevention
Urethral diverticulum in adults
Urethritis
Urge incontinence
Urinary system physiologic changes in older women
Use of drugs for urinary retention
Use of gonadotropin-releasing hormone agonists prior to hysterectomy
Uterine leiomyoma
Vessel injury during laparoscopic trocar placement
Vulvar abscess

SURGICAL MANAGEMENT
Adhesion prevention at laparotomy
Bladder injury repair
Bowel injury at laparoscopy
Hidradenitis suppurativa
Incisional hernias in minimally invasive procedures
Menorrhagia treated by endometrial ablation
Pelvic mass intraoperative consultation
Rectovaginal fistula
Supracervical hysterectomy
Surgical abortion
Surgical alternatives to hysterectomy
Surgical management of stress incontinence
Urethral diverticulum in adults
Vaginal vault prolapse
Vulvar intraepithelial neoplasia
Wound dehiscence and evisceration

PATHOPHYSIOLOGY
Hysteroscopic complications
Risk of deep vein thrombosis with selective estrogen receptor modulators
Von Willebrand's disease and other hematologic disorders at menarche

EPIDEMIOLOGY
Benefits of hormone therapy
Breast cancer risks
Cystic fibrosis
Risk reduction for ovarian cancer
Treatment outcome with hormone therapy

GENETICS
Cystic fibrosis carrier status
Genetic factors associated with endometriosis

COUNSELING
Advice to a patient on complications of supracervical hysterectomy
Contraceptive choice for a *BRCA*-positive woman
Contraception options for a patient with history of thrombosis
Emergency contraception
Insomnia at perimenopause
Ovary removal at hysterectomy
Sexual dysfunction as a side effect of selective serotonin reuptake inhibitors
Smoking cessation strategies

A subject matter index appears at the end of the Critique Book.

PROLOG

Gynecology and Surgery

FIFTH EDITION

1

Femoral nerve injury during laparoscopic surgery

A 34-year-old nulligravid woman who is 1.73 m (68 in.) tall and who weighs 54.5 kg (120 lb) undergoes extensive laparoscopic dissection and fulguration of pelvic endometriosis for chronic pelvic pain. Several hours after surgery, she reports numbness, but no pain, on the left antero-medial thigh. As she attempts to stand, she falls to the floor when her leg buckles. A physical examination reveals weakness of the left musculus quadriceps femoris and complete absence of the knee jerk reflex. The most appropriate next step in management of this patient case is

(A) isometric and isotonic quadriceps exercises
* (B) consultation with a neurologist
(C) observation
(D) surgical exploration
(E) galvanic muscle stimulation

The most frequent cause of iatrogenic injury to the femoral nerve, the largest branch of the lumbar plexus, is gynecologic surgery. The injury usually results from nerve compression associated with the use of self-retaining retractors. Femoral neuropathy also may result from improper patient positioning during surgery. Specifically, extreme flexion of the thigh with abduction and external rotation of the hip in an exaggerated lithotomy position can injure the femoral nerve, especially with the use of "candy cane" stirrups. When the patient is in this position, the nerve may become acutely angulated and twisted beneath the taut inguinal ligament as it enters the thigh, resulting in injury from compression, traction, or ischemia. Rarely, suture transfixation, surgical transection, or hematoma compression may injure the femoral nerve. The true incidence of nerve injury is unknown.

Nerve compression or ischemia causes most femoral nerve injuries associated with laparoscopic surgery in the lithotomy position. Most of these injuries resolve with conservative therapy without residual effects. Although recovery usually starts within a few weeks and is complete within 8–10 weeks, neurologic deficits may take as long as 4–6 months to resolve. A small percentage of patients require either an orthotic device or ambulatory support for persistent leg weakness.

Studies have shown that thin patients with a body mass index of 20 kg/m² or less who remain in the lithotomy position for 4 hours or longer are at risk for development of femoral nerve injury. Smoking within 30 days of the procedure, probably because of its vasoconstrictive effect, is an added risk factor for persistent neuropathy that lasts at least 3 months. Neuropathy may occur even with careful placement, padding, and strapping of the lower extremities in lithotomy positions.

Approximately 95% of patients with postoperative femoral nerve injury have sensory changes that include cutaneous anesthesia or dysesthesia of the anterior and medial thigh and anteromedial leg and foot. Motor defects, which occur in most instances, include limitation of leg extension from loss of quadriceps femoris function and reduction of thigh flexion from loss of sartorius and pectineus function. A diminished or absent knee jerk response is the most reliable objective sign of quadriceps hypotonia.

In the patient described, the most appropriate next step in treatment would be consultation with a neurologist as soon as possible to confirm the diagnosis and determine a course of therapy. Electromyographic studies may be beneficial, especially if direct trauma, such as transection of the femoral nerve, is suspected. Radiologic examination can be performed to rule out a hematoma or foreign body, particularly in patients with appreciable pain or a previous history of bleeding diathesis. Nerve compression from a hematoma usually requires immediate surgical evacuation or percutaneous drainage to prevent permanent nerve damage. Immediate surgical exploration is indicated in patients with suspected femoral nerve transection or ligation; these patients commonly report pain. End-to-end anastomosis of the transected nerve provides good results when performed shortly after the injury. Early physical therapy, including galvanic muscle stimulation, will help retard atrophy of the involved muscles. When the quadriceps muscle begins to regain strength, isometric and isotonic exercises of increasing intensity and frequency will build muscle strength and endurance. Because prompt treatment is indicated after the diagnosis of femoral nerve injury, observation without treatment would be inappropriate. In women with regional anesthesia, the diagnosis of femoral nerve injury may be more difficult.

Chan JK, Manetta A. Prevention of femoral nerve injuries in gynecologic surgery. Am J Obstet Gynecol 2002;186:1–7.

Walsh C, Walsh A. Postoperative femoral neuropathy. Surg Gynecol Obstet 1992;174:255–63.

Warner MA, Martin JT, Schroeder DR, Offord KP, Chute CG. Lower-extremity motor neuropathy associated with surgery performed on patients in a lithotomy position. Anesthesiology 1994;81:6–12.

2

Physician responsibility for follow-up

A young woman presents to the emergency department with abdominal pain and irregular vaginal bleeding. The results of a pregnancy test are positive. Ultrasonography findings are consistent with an ectopic pregnancy, and you are concerned about possible rupture of the ectopic pregnancy. You call a representative of the woman's health care plan and are informed that her coverage has lapsed. The most appropriate next step is

  (A) to arrange for examination in your clinic the following morning
  (B) to tell the patient to return to the emergency department in 24 hours
  (C) to obtain a social services consultation
* (D) to hospitalize the patient for definitive care
  (E) to transfer the patient to the nearest public hospital as soon as possible

Regardless of financial implications, patients should receive care that is appropriate to their clinical presentation. Despite the financial and regulatory pressures to which physicians increasingly are subjected, the patient's well-being must remain the highest priority.

Beneficence requires physicians to act in the best interests of patients. Physicians have a duty to provide sound advice and to take actions directed at promoting the well-being of patients. Moreover, the best interest of the patient should prevail over a physician's self-interest or the interests of third parties.

In the situation here, this ethical guideline precludes the less effective and potentially dangerous referral of care to an alternative provider based on the patient's insured status. Because the situation calls for emergency admission and treatment, deferral of care in any capacity is not an option. Refusal or deferral of care, particularly when the safety of the individual is a significant concern, is subject to multiple government guidelines, such as the Emergency Medical Treatment and Labor Act. The same reasoning applies to the referral of patients for financial reasons. Nevertheless, there are limited circumstances under which a clinician may refuse to treat. Physicians may refuse to provide care when the treatment demanded is ethically wrong, medically inappropriate, or futile. In addition, clinicians have a right to refuse to provide care that violates their personal or professional standards.

Federal requirements for patient screening and transfer. In: American College of Obstetricians and Gynecologists. Guidelines for women's health care. Washington, DC: ACOG; 1996. p. 193–8.

Lo B. Ethical issues in clinical medicine. In: Braunwald E, Fauci AS, Kasper DL, Hauser SL, Longo DL, Jameson JL, editors. Harrison's principles of internal medicine. 15th ed. New York (NY): McGraw-Hill; 2001. p. 5–8.

McCullough LB, Chervenak FA. Ethical challenges in the managed practice of obstetrics and gynecology. Obstet Gynecol 1999;93:304–7.

Physician responsibility under managed care: patient advocacy in a changing health care environment. In: American College of Obstetricians and Gynecologists. Ethics in obstetrics and gynecology. Washington, DC: ACOG; 2002. p. 64–8.

Spencer EM. Economics, managed care and patient advocacy. In: Fletcher JC, Lombardo PA, Marshall MF, Miller FG, editors. Introduction to clinical ethics. 2nd ed. Frederick (MD): University Publishing Group; 1997. p. 239–54.

3

Fecal incontinence

A 28-year-old primiparous woman undergoes an uncomplicated vaginal delivery. At her 6-week postpartum visit, she reports frequent incontinence of stool. She explains that the incontinence bothers her a good deal, and she requests help with this problem. Examination reveals an intact rectovaginal septum but decreased anal sphincter tone. The most appropriate next step is

      (A) overlapping anal sphincteroplasty
      (B) anal manometry
      (C) electromyographic (EMG) biofeedback
  * (D) endoanal ultrasonography
      (E) pudendal nerve terminal motor latency test

Childbirth may be complicated by injury to the anal sphincter. Lacerations of the external anal sphincter (third- and fourth-degree perineal lacerations) occur with 5–6% of spontaneous vaginal deliveries. However, occult sphincter injuries are common. For example, postpartum endoanal ultrasonography suggests that 28–35% of primiparous women sustain unrecognized sphincter injuries at the time of vaginal delivery.

Not all postpartum anal incontinence is due to sphincter injury, however. Among women who reported anal incontinence 8 weeks after vaginal delivery, only 45% had sphincter defects detected on endoanal ultrasonography. In addition, not all women with sphincter injuries are incontinent. Among women with a postpartum sphincter defect detected by endoanal ultrasonography, only 37% reported anal incontinence. The symptom of anal incontinence is 68% sensitive and 79% specific for anal sphincter defect. Thus, the symptom of anal incontinence is not pathognomonic for a sphincter defect. Other causes of fecal incontinence include pudendal nerve injury, peripheral neuropathies (eg, diabetes mellitus), neurologic diseases (eg, multiple sclerosis), gastrointestinal diseases (eg, irritable bowel syndrome), and drug effects. Figure 3-1, which illustrates the anatomy of the anal canal and rectum, shows the physiologic mechanisms important to continence and defecation.

The diagnosis of an anal sphincter defect should be suspected in this case but confirmed before proceeding with surgical intervention. If sphincter injury is present postpartum and the patient is incontinent, surgery is preferred and will provide continence in approximately 80% of patients. In the case described, the first step is to determine if an anatomic defect is present. Endoanal ultrasonography is the most appropriate method for the diagnosis of occult sphincter defects. This imaging technique provides a 360-degree view of the internal and external anal sphincter complex (Figs. 3-2 and 3-3). Magnetic resonance imaging (MRI) also has been used to image the anal sphincter complex but is more expensive; a role for MRI has yet to be established in the management of anal incontinence.

Electromyographic (EMG) biofeedback may be most useful for women who have anal sphincter weakness without an anatomic sphincter defect. Anal sphincter weakness and atrophy can result from obstetric pudendal nerve injuries or other peripheral neuropathies. Incontinent women who should be considered for EMG biofeedback include women with limited sphincter defects and women who are poor surgical candidates. In addition, EMG biofeedback can serve as an adjunct to surgery.

Anal manometry can provide objective evidence of sphincter weakness and can be used to assess sensory function. However, this test would not provide additional useful information about this patient because weakness of the sphincter complex is evident from the physical examination.

Neurophysiologic testing can identify women with pudendal neuropathies (eg, pudendal nerve terminal motor latencies). Stretch injuries to the pudendal nerve can occur during childbirth and may complicate 75–80% of obstetric sphincter lacerations. In women with known sphincter defects, neurophysiologic testing may provide useful information for preoperative counseling. Anal sphincteroplasty may be less successful among women with pudendal neuropathy, and, therefore, a pudendal nerve terminal motor latency test may identify the best candidates for surgical correction of anal sphincter defects. However, the value of this test and its interpretation remain controversial.

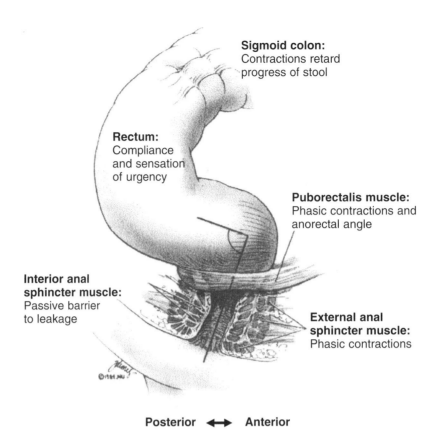

Sigmoid colon:
Contractions retard
progress of stool

Rectum:
Compliance
and sensation
of urgency

Puborectalis muscle:
Phasic contractions and
anorectal angle

**Interior anal
sphincter muscle:**
Passive barrier
to leakage

**External anal
sphincter muscle:**
Phasic contractions

Posterior ◄──► Anterior

FIG. 3-1. Anatomy of the anal canal and rectum showing the physiologic mechanisms important to continence and defecation. (Reprinted from Gastrointestinal disorders: behavioral and physiological basis for treatment, Whitehead WE, Schuster MM. p. 233. Copyright 1985, with permission from Elsevier.)

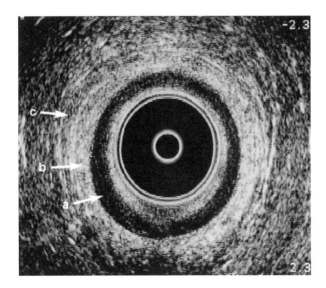

FIG. 3-2. Endoanal ultrasonography image from a normal volunteer (mid-anal canal). (**a**) Internal sphincter. (**b**) Longitudinal muscle. (**c**) External anal sphincter. (Reproduced with permission from Rottenberg GT, Williams AB. Pictorial review: endoanal ultrasound. Br J Radiol 2002;75:484.)

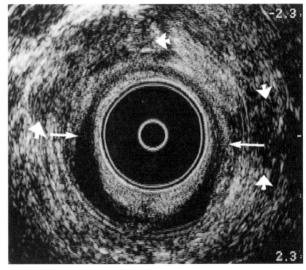

FIG. 3-3. Endoanal ultrasonography image from woman with an obstetric injury. There is a defect in the external anal sphincter between the 9-o'clock and 12-o'clock positions and between the 2-o'clock and 3-o'clock positions (arrowheads). There is also a disruption of the internal anal sphincter (arrows). (Reproduced with permission from Rottenberg GT, Williams AB. Pictorial review: endoanal ultrasound. Br J Radiol 2002;75:486.)

Abramowitz L, Sobhani I, Ganansia R, Vuagnat A, Benifla JL, Darai E, et al. Are sphincter defects the cause of anal incontinence after vaginal delivery? Results of a prospective study. Dis Colon Rectum 2000; 43:590–6 [discussion 596–8].

Cook TA, Mortensen NJ. Management of faecal incontinence following obstetric injury. Br J Surg 1998;85:293–9.

Faltin DL, Boulvain M, Irion O, Bretones S, Stan C, Weil A. Diagnosis of anal sphincter tears by postpartum endosonography to predict fecal incontinence. Obstet Gynecol 2000;95:643–7.

Handa VL, Danielsen BH, Gilbert WM. Obstetric anal sphincter lacerations. Obstet Gynecol 2001;98:225–30.

Stoker J, Halligan S, Bartram CI. Pelvic floor imaging. Radiology 2001;218:621–41.

Sultan AH, Kamm MA, Hudson CN, Thomas JM, Bartram CI. Anal-sphincter disruption during vaginal delivery. N Engl J Med 1993; 329:1905–11.

Whitehead WE, Wald A, Norton NJ. Treatment options for fecal incontinence. Dis Colon Rectum 2001;44:131–42 [discussion 142–4].

4

Current Procedural Terminology coding and history documentation

You review with a new colleague the *Current Procedural Terminology* (CPT) coding so that she will better understand your billing process as required by Medicare. In your discussion of the history component, you explain to her that there are basically four types of history: problem-focused, expanded problem-focused, detailed, and comprehensive. A comprehensive history requires documentation of

* (A) the chief complaint
  (B) 4 elements of the history of present illness or 3 chronic or inactive conditions
  (C) 10 elements of review of systems
  (D) 2 or 3 elements of past, family, and social history, depending on whether the patient is a new or established patient

In the United States, the CPT is the standard coding system for reporting physician services. Coding these procedures provides a universal language to determine a level of service, including the complexity of the management provided by the physician. The codes and the descriptions of their meanings are copyrighted by the American Medical Association.

It is critical that physicians and every member of all of their staffs understand how the CPT coding process

works. The coding calls for precise definitions for every category of office visit, including level of history, level of the examination, and level of medical decision making. All visits except preventive visits require that the chief complaint or complaints be documented. The remainder of the options are not required as documentation for a comprehensive history (see Table 4-1).

A visit for a new patient starts with CPT code 99201, and the number increases as the visit becomes more

TABLE 4-1. *Current Procedural Terminology* (CPT) Coding for Patient History

Level of History	Chief Complaint	History of Present Illness CPT	History of Present Illness Medicare	Review of Systems CPT	Review of Systems Medicare	Past, Family, Social CPT	Past, Family, Social Medicare
Problem-focused	Required and documented	Brief	1–3 elements	Not required		Not required	
Expanded problem-focused	Required and documented	Brief	1–3 elements	Problem-pertinent	1 system	Not required	
Detailed	Required and documented	Extended	4+ elements or 3+ chronic or inactive conditions	Extended	2–9 systems	Pertinent	1 of 3 elements
Comprehensive	Required and documented	Extended	4+ elements or 3+ chronic or inactive conditions	Complete	10 systems	Complete	2 of 3 elements

Modified from American College of Obstetricians and Gynecologists. CPT coding in obstetrics and gynecology—2002. Washington, DC: ACOG; 2001. p.16.

complex. The CPT requirements for the ambulatory visit require documentation of the previously described 3 components or documentation of time spent counseling the patient. Code selection can be based on time only if face-to-face counseling takes up more than 50% of the encounter. An expanded problem-focused visit, CPT code 99242, requires 30 minutes of face-to-face time to enable billing on time. As the CPT code increases to denote the level of visit, the number of history elements and time also increase.

Although requests for changes in CPT codes are reviewed each year, final revisions require several years to be listed in the CPT book. It is incumbent on the physician to know the currently required year of CPT coding.

In general, following the Medicare requirements for office visits will satisfy the requirements of health care insurers, but differences may exist. Inaccurate coding or provision of insufficient information delays payment and, in a worst-case scenario, could be interpreted as fraudulent billing.

The American College of Obstetricians and Gynecologists (ACOG) has a six-step process in its review of code proposals to be presented to the CPT editorial panel. The editorial panel adds new or revised codes in January of each year. Other resources include the *International Classification of Diseases Clinical Modification* diagnostic coding, the ACOG coding guidebook entitled *Frequently Asked Questions in Obstetric and Gynecologic Coding*, and coding workshops available to physicians.

American College of Obstetricians and Gynecologists. CPT coding in obstetrics and gynecology—2002. Washington, DC: ACOG; 2000.

American College of Obstetricians and Gynecologists. Frequently asked questions in obstetric and gynecologic coding. Washington, DC: ACOG; 2002.

American Medical Association. CPT: current procedural terminology—2001. Chicago (IL): AMA; 2000.

Health Care Financing Administration and World Health Organization. International classification of diseases 10th revision clinical modification (ICD-10-CM). Washington, DC: US Government Printing Office; 1991.

5

Hidradenitis suppurativa

A 34-year-old woman presents to your office with nodular and pustular vulvar and axillary lesions that have been present for 10 years and intermittently and spontaneously drain (Fig. 5-1). Prior gastrointestinal tract evaluation was negative for Crohn's disease. The most appropriate treatment for this patient is

    (A) antibiotics
    (B) skinning vulvectomy
    (C) retinoic acid
*   (D) surgical excision

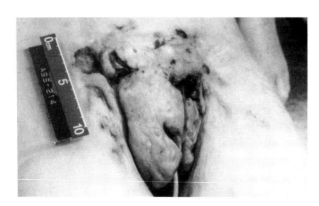

FIG. 5-1. Hidradenitis suppurativa. (Groginsky EM, Olson JK, Lallas TA, Buekers TE, Potts S, Sorosky JI. A case of severe hidradenitis suppurativa contributing to a death and a review of the literature. J Lower Genital Tract Dis 1999;3:69. With permission of Blackwell Publishing.)

Hidradenitis suppurativa is a chronic infection of the skin and subcutaneous tissues. The differential diagnosis of this condition includes Crohn's disease of the vulva, folliculitis, and granulomatous sexually transmitted diseases. The gynecologist helps treat this disorder when the lesions involve the mons pubis, the genitocrural folds, and buttocks.

Chronic hidradenitis suppurativa results from progressive inflammation and tissue damage associated with recurrent deep folliculitis in the axillary, periareolar, and perianal regions—areas where apocrine glands are located. Hidradenitis suppurativa occurs most often in the second to fourth decades of life. Patients generally have a poor quality of life because this dermatologic condition is both painful and associated with a malodorous discharge. Although the estimated incidence is approximately 1 in

300, most cases are not severe. Predisposing factors include the following:

- Obesity
- Diabetes mellitus
- Perianal antiperspirant use
- Androgen excess
- Poor hygiene
- Smoking

The pathophysiology of hidradenitis suppurativa appears to be follicular hyperkeratosis with plugging and dilation of the follicle. Once occlusion of the gland occurs, bacteria trapped by the keratin plug multiply, resulting in cellulitis and abscess formation. With disease progression, spontaneous abscess occurs through cutaneous tracts. The wound does not heal, and recurring infections result. The sequelae of this process are chronic draining sinuses, intertwining cutaneous fistulaes, and fibrosis. The malodorous discharge can have negative social and psychologic effects that lead to frustration with the medical establishment and avoidance of social and interpersonal relationships. Vulvar squamous cell carci-

noma occurs in as many as 5% of individuals with hidradenitis suppurativa.

Medical therapies in the very early stages of hidradenitis suppurativa include the long-term use of antibiotics, antiandrogens, retinoic acid, and cyclosporin. Because of the extensive disease and chronic scarring, this patient's condition will not respond to medical management, so surgical excision is recommended. Skinning vulvectomy would not remove the subcutaneous tissue where the chronic draining sinuses, intertwining cutaneous fistulae, and fibrosis are located. Human immunodeficiency virus (HIV) positivity is not related to hidradenitis suppurativa.

Droegemueller W. Postoperative counseling and management. In: Stenchever MA, Droegemueller W, Herbst AL, Mishell DR Jr, editors. Comprehensive gynecology. 4th ed. St. Louis (MO): Mosby; 2001. p. 772–821.

Endo Y, Tamura A, Ishikawa O, Miyachi Y. Perianal hidradenitis suppurativa: early surgical treatment gives good results in chronic or recurrent cases. Br J Dermatol 1998;139:906–10.

Groginsky EM, Olson JK, Lallas TA, Buekers TE, Potts S, Sorosky JI. A case of severe hidradenitis suppurativa contributing to a death and a review of the literature. J Lower Genital Tract Dis 1999;3:67–70.

von der Werth JM, Jemec GB. Morbidity in patients with hidradenitis suppurativa. Br J Dermatol 2001;144:809–13.

6

Liquid-based Pap tests

A 25-year-old sexually active woman comes to your office as a new patient for her annual gynecologic examination. She reports having multiple sexual partners and a low-grade squamous intraepithelial lesion treated by cryosurgery 2 years ago. The most appropriate method for evaluating her normal-appearing cervix is

        (A) human papillomavirus (HPV) testing
*   (B) a liquid-based Pap test
        (C) colposcopy
        (D) direct visualization of the cervix after application of acetic acid

The Pap test is the best example of a successful screening test for the prevention of cancer. Its early positive impact resulted in widespread implementation without the results of formal clinical trials. The sensitivity of the conventional Pap test is variable, with false-negative rates of 6–55% in various series. Modifications of the Pap test have been developed in an effort to improve detection of premalignant cytologic changes.

In this case, the patient has risk factors for the development of cervical cancer, including multiple sexual partners and a prior history of dysplasia. The best option for evaluation of her normal-appearing cervix is the liquid-based Pap test, which has been shown in multiple

studies to have a higher sensitivity than the conventional Pap test for the detection of dysplastic lesions.

Human papillomavirus testing would not be appropriate prior to the performance of a cytologic screening test. Such testing may be beneficial in the triage of cases of atypical squamous cells of undetermined significance (ASC-US). Recently, results from the Atypical Squamous Cells of Undetermined Significance/Low-Grade Squamous Intraepithelial Lesions Triage Study (ALTS) trial have suggested that screening of Pap tests that have detected ASC-US for the presence of oncogenic HPV subtypes is the most cost-effective follow-up method. If the results of screening are negative, the patient can be followed conservatively. If the screening results are positive, the patient should undergo colposcopy.

Because of its cost and patient discomfort, colposcopy would not be the recommended screening test prior to obtaining the cytology results. It would be the next step in evaluation if the cytology findings were abnormal.

Direct visualization of the cervix after the application of dilute acetic acid is not an accepted screening method at this time. Colposcopic examination after the application of dilute acetic acid may be indicated based on cytology results.

Cervical cytology screening. ACOG Technology Assessment in Obstetrics and Gynecology No. 2. American College of Obstetricians and Gynecologists. Obstet Gynecol 2002;100:1423–7.

Montz FJ, Farber FL, Bristow RE, Cornelison T. Impact of increasing Papanicolaou test sensitivity and compliance: a modeled cost and outcomes analysis. Obstet Gynecol 2001;97:781–8.

Papillo JL, Zarka MA, St. John TL. Evaluation of the ThinPrep Pap test in clinical practice. A seven-month, 16,314-case experience in northern Vermont. Acta Cytol 1998;42:203–8.

Stoler MH. Advances in cervical screening technology. Mod Pathol 2000;13:275–84.

7

Vulvar cyst

A 14-year-old adolescent presents with a large cystic mass in the floor of the terminal end of the urethra (Fig. 7-1). The most likely diagnosis is

    (A) Bartholin's cyst
* (B) Skene's duct cyst
    (C) inclusion cyst
    (D) urethral diverticulum
    (E) fibroma

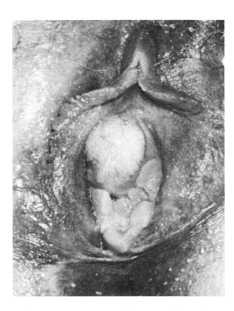

FIG. 7-1. Skene's duct cyst. (Reprinted from Benign diseases of the vulva and vagina, 4th ed., Kaufman RH, Faro S, Friedrich EG Jr, Gardner HL, editors. p. 242. Copyright 1994, with permission from Elsevier.)

Masses in the vulvar region are a fairly common gynecologic finding. Anatomic location and knowledge of its embryologic origins are key to making the proper diagnosis. In this case, the age of the patient and the location of the cystic mass point to the diagnosis of a Skene's duct cyst.

Congenital cysts arise from vestigial remnants of embryologic development. Skene's duct cysts are urogenital sinus derivatives. The cyst wall usually contains transitional columnar squamous epithelium, stratified columnar squamous epithelium, or both; foci of squamous epithelium occasionally are observed (Fig. 7-2). Treatment of Skene's duct cysts in children consists of partial excision with marsupialization of the cyst wall. In adults, the treatment of choice is total excision of the cyst, because the lesion often is accompanied by chronic inflammation.

Bartholin's gland cysts occur in a posterolateral part of the introitus and are not found prior to the onset of sexual activity. They are caused predominantly by infection. Most Bartholin's cysts are unilocular. The treatment is incision and drainage in acute cases, along with placement of a Word catheter, or marsupialization or excision, especially in recurrent cases.

Inclusion cysts are the most common cystic masses of the vagina. They usually are found in the posterior or lateral walls of the lower third of the vagina. These cysts most commonly result from birth trauma or previous vaginal surgery. Inclusion cysts usually contain a thick, pale yellow, oily substance. The majority of these cysts do

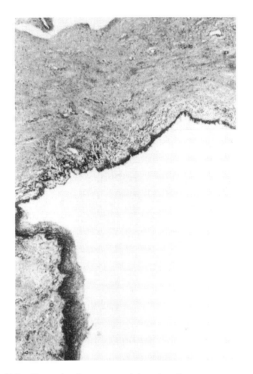

FIG. 7-2. Skene's duct cyst. Islands of squamous, transitional, and columnar epithelium are present (hematoxylin and eosin stain). (Reprinted from Benign diseases of the vulva and vagina, 4th ed., Kaufman RH, Faro S, Friedrich EG Jr, Gardner HL, editors. p. 242. Copyright 1994, with permission from Elsevier.)

not cause symptoms. If they do cause pain or dyspareunia, the optimal treatment is excision.

Urethral diverticula, which may be difficult to distinguish from Skene's duct cysts on first inspection, occur in 3–4% of women during their lifetime. Diverticulae usually are central suburethral masses rather than masses lateral to the distal urethra. The majority of diverticula occur in women aged 30–50 years. Congenital, inflammatory, and traumatic causes are possible, but most urethral diverticulae are caused by infection. During examination, milking of the urethra may result in the expression of pus from the urethral meatus. Excretory urography or cystourethroscopy may be necessary to distinguish between a Skene's duct cyst and a urethral diverticulum. The surgical management is diverticulectomy if the diverticulum is located in the proximal or middle third of the urethra, or marsupialization if it is located in the distal third of the urethra.

Fibromas are the most common benign solid tumors of the vulva. They occur in all age groups, and almost always in the midline and anterior vulva. They may be found up to the level of the clitoris. Fibromas are generally firm and freely mobile. They tend to be very slow growing. If the diagnosis is in doubt or the tumor causes discomfort, it should be widely excised. The defect then may be closed primarily.

Droegemueller W. Benign gynecologic lesions: vulva, vagina, cervix, uterus, oviduct, ovary. In: Stenchever MA, Droegemueller W, Herbst AL, Mishell DR Jr, editors. Comprehensive gynecology. 4th ed. St. Louis (MO): Mosby; 2001. p. 479–530.

Ishigooka M, Hayami S, Hashimoto T, Tomaru M, Yaguchi H, Sasagawa I, et al. Skene's duct cyst in adult women: report of two cases. Int Urol Nephrol 1995;27:775–8.

Phupong V, Aribarg A. Management of Skene's duct cysts in newborn girls. BJU Int 2000;86:562.

Skene's duct cysts. In: Kaufman RH, Faro S, Friedrich EG Jr, Gardner HL, editors. Benign diseases of the vulva and vagina. 4th ed. St. Louis (MO): Mosby–Year Book; 1994. p. 241–2.

8

Prophylactic antibiotics at abdominal hysterectomy

You schedule a vaginal hysterectomy for a 45-year-old healthy patient who has experienced an anaphylactic reaction to penicillin. She has no cervicitis or evidence of bacterial vaginosis. The Pap test results are normal. The best antibiotic strategy to employ to prevent serious morbidity secondary to infection in this patient is the administration of

      (A) no antibiotics, because she is at low risk
      (B) intravenous metronidazole in the recovery room
*   (C) intravenous metronidazole prior to surgical incision
      (D) intravenous cephalosporin prior to surgical incision

The use of prophylactic antibiotics prior to a surgical procedure can significantly decrease the risk of postoperative surgical site infection. For example, a single dose of an antibiotic (usually a first-generation cephalosporin) administered prophylactically to the low-risk patient has been shown to be effective in preventing serious infections after hysterectomy. Figure 8-1 shows the effect of prophylaxis on the probability of infection in hysterectomy patients, according to duration of operation and operative approach. A number of studies have demonstrated the utility of various antibiotic regimens in preventing serious posthysterectomy morbidity and the cost-effectiveness of such regimens. Thus, evidence supports the prophylactic use of single-dose antibiotics in the hysterectomy patient.

For antibiotic prophylaxis to be effective, the patient must not be infected at the time of the operation. It is prudent to administer the antibiotic before making the surgical incision, because the theoretical purpose of prophylaxis is to obtain a tissue level of antibiotic before introducing the bacterial inoculum into the surgical site. Antibiotics given after organisms are introduced are less effective with increased time from infection to antibiotic administration. In one study, antibiotic administration was not protective if 3 hours had elapsed after bacterial inoculation.

Intravenous metronidazole administered prior to the presurgical incision would be appropriate therapy to achieve antimicrobial levels in this patient who is allergic to penicillin. Physicians should avoid indiscriminate antibiotic use in the absence of postoperative infection because of the possibility of selection of resistant bacterial strains. In this case, the use of cephalosporins in a patient with a previous history of an anaphylactic reaction to penicillin is contraindicated because of the cross-reactivity.

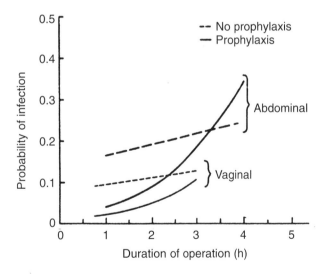

FIG. 8-1. Effect of prophylaxis on the probability of infection in hysterectomy patients, according to duration of operation and operative approach. The estimated probabilities of infection, with and without prophylaxis, are shown for each type of hysterectomy, as a function of the duration of the operation, in a 40-year-old private patient. (Shapiro M, Munoz A, Tager IB, Schoenbaum SC, Polk BF. Risk factors for infection at the operative site after abdominal or vaginal hysterectomy. N Engl J Med 1982;307:1664. Copyright © 1982 Massachusetts Medical Society. All rights reserved.)

American College of Obstetricians and Gynecologists. Antibiotic prophylaxis for gynecologic procedures. ACOG Practice Bulletin 23. Washington, DC: ACOG; 2001.

Davey PG, Parker SE, Crombie IK, Jaderberg M. The cost effectiveness of amoxicillin/clavulanic acid as antibacterial prophylaxis in abdominal and gynaecological surgery. Pharmacoeconomics 1995;7:347–56.

Hemsell DL, Johnson ER, Hemsell PG, Nobles BJ, Little BB, Heard MC. Cefazolin is inferior to cefotetan as single-dose prophylaxis for women undergoing elective total abdominal hysterectomy. Clin Infect Dis 1995;20:677–84.

Korn AP, Grullon K, Hessol N, Lin P, Siopak J. Does vaginal cuff closure decrease the infectious morbidity associated with abdominal hysterectomy? J Am Coll Surg 1997;185:404–7.

Mittendorf R, Aronson MP, Berry RE, Williams MA, Kupelnick B, Klickstein A, et al. Avoiding serious infections associated with abdominal hysterectomy: a meta-analysis of antibiotic prophylaxis. Am J Obstet Gynecol 1993;169:1119–24.

Shapiro M, Munoz A, Tager IB, Schoenbaum SC, Polk BF. Risk factors for infection at the operative site after abdominal or vaginal hysterectomy. N Engl J Med 1982;307:1661–6.

9

Use of drugs for urinary retention

A 57-year-old woman undergoes a Burch retropubic urethropexy for stress urinary incontinence. She presents 4 weeks after the operation with complaints of urinary frequency, urgency, and a feeling of incomplete bladder emptying. Results of a urine dipstick test are negative for leukocyte esterase, and a postvoid residual volume is 200 mL. The best next step in her management is

    *   (A) intermittent self-catheterization
       (B) surgical revision
       (C) use of bethanechol chloride (Urecholine)
       (D) use of tamsulosin hydrochloride (Flomax)
       (E) use of oxybutynin chloride (Ditropan)

Voiding dysfunction, including having the inability to empty the bladder totally or a poor urinary stream, occurs in as many as 25% or more of women after surgery for urinary incontinence. Increased voiding dysfunction has been noted with the pubovaginal sling procedure because it is more obstructive than the retropubic procedures (ie, Burch or Marshall–Marchetti–Krantz procedure). Postoperative voiding dysfunction or urinary retention is usually transient and best treated with the use of an indwelling catheter or intermittent self-catheterization until the resumption of complete bladder emptying. Self-catheterization can be performed using a commercially available reusable soft plastic catheter. In a survey conducted by the American Urogynecological Society, practitioners were queried about the management of cases of prolonged urinary retention after antiincontinence procedures. Among the respondents, 30% allowed 3–6 months for resumption of spontaneous voiding before performing surgical revision, and 90% performed multichannel urodynamic evaluation before the revision. Resumption of spontaneous voiding occurs in 33–100% of patients after urethrolysis. Intermittent self-catheterization would be preferred over the placement of an indwelling Foley catheter to avoid chronic irritation of the urethra and the risk of infection. This can be performed with the use of a soft commercially available plastic catheter.

Various other nonsurgical treatments have been used to facilitate bladder emptying after surgery (eg, cholinergic bethanechol chloride [Urecholine] and α-blocking drugs such as tamsulosin hydrochloride [Flomax]), but most have limited effect. Cholinergic drugs, which promote micturition, appear to be more effective in treating post-surgical anesthetic effects on the bladder than in treating postsurgical retention after a surgical procedure for incontinence. The use of α-blocking agents to manage postoperative voiding problems in women shows marginal benefits.

The use of benzodiazepines has been advocated for this indication; however, no randomized data support their use. Intravesical prostaglandin treatment also has been described. A small double-blind placebo-controlled study to evaluate the effect of intravesical prostaglandin $F_{2\alpha}$ on women with postoperative retention after surgery for urinary stress incontinence suggests a short-lived effect.

Anticholinergic agents such as oxybutynin chloride (Ditropan) and tolterodine tartrate (Detrol) show efficacy in the treatment of postoperative bladder spasm or detrusor instability, but they may aggravate postoperative urinary retention.

Chaliha C, Stanton SL. Complications of surgery for genuine stress incontinence. Br J Obstet Gynaecol 1999;106:1238–45.

Nguyen JK, Glowacki CA, Bhatia NN. Survey of voiding dysfunction and urinary retention after anti-incontinence procedures. Obstet Gynecol 2001;98:1011–17.

Stanton SL, Cardozo LD, Kerr-Wilson R. Treatment of delayed onset of spontaneous voiding after surgery for incontinence. Urology 1979; 13:494–6.

Tammela T. Prevention of prolonged voiding problems after unexpected postoperative urinary retention: comparison of phenoxybenzamine and carbachol. J Urol 1986;136:1254–7.

Tammela T, Kontturi M, Käär K, Lukkarinen O. Intravesical prostaglandin $F_{2\alpha}$ for promoting bladder emptying after surgery for female stress incontinence. Br J Urol 1987;60:43–6.

Watson AJ, Currie I, Jarvis GJ. A prospective placebo controlled double blind randomised study to investigate the use of Indoramin to prevent post-operative voiding disorders after surgical treatment for genuine stress incontinence. Br J Obstet Gynaecol 1999;106:270–2.

10

External genital mutilation

You are caring for a 24-year-old Sudanese woman who underwent female circumcision at age 10 years. A common gynecologic complication that accompanies this procedure is

       (A) menometrorrhagia
*   (B) recurrent vaginitis
       (C) vulvar cancer
       (D) miscarriage

Female circumcision or female genital mutilation (FC/FGM) is a culturally determined ritual that has been practiced on an estimated 130 million women and girls worldwide. Because of global immigration patterns, physicians in the United States and Canada will increasingly encounter women who have been circumcised.

In 1995, the World Health Organization developed a classification system for FC/FGM (Box 10-1; Figs. 10-1–10-4 [see color plate]). Box 10-2 provides instructions on recording the types of FC/FGM. Figure 10-5 illustrates labia minora infibulation (see color plate). In certain cultures, FC/FGM is considered to be a powerful marker of a woman's belonging to the community and an affirmation of her identify. For many women in these cultures, to be circumcised is to be normal. Arguments in favor of FC/FGM used by proponents of the procedure are shown in Box 10-3.

Female genital mutilation, especially infibulation, may cause a number of health complications that stem from interference of the drainage of urine and menstrual blood—for example, recurrent vaginitis. Other examples

---

BOX 10-1

World Health Organization Classification System for Female Circumcision/Female Genital Mutilation

- Type I: Clitoridectomy, ie, excision of prepuce and partial or total clitoridectomy
- Type II: Excision, ie, removal of clitoris, accompanied by partial or total excision of the labia minora
- Type III: Infibulation, ie, removal of the clitoris, labia minora, and labia majora. Raw surfaces are reapproximated, generally by tying legs together until they heal as a "hood of skin" that covers the urethra and most of the vagina. A small opening to allow passage of urine and menstrual blood is preserved.
- Type IV: Other, ie, any other form of genital manipulation, including cutting, burning, stretching, or applying chemicals

Data from World Health Organization. Female genital mutilation: report of a WHO Technical Working Group, Geneva, 17–19 July 1995. Geneva: World Health Organization, 1996. (WHO Report no. WHO/FRH/WHD/96.10).

BOX 10-2

Recording Types of Female Circumcision/Female Genital Mutilation

- The extent of cutting or damage to the genitals and surrounding area may vary within each type.
- Clinical examination is necessary to establish type and extent of cutting.
- Do not record type on basis of patient knowledge. Patient may be unaware of the exact degree of cutting.
- Conditions under which the procedures are done usually are not conducive to accurate cutting. The end result on one woman may have features of different types of female circumcision and female genital mutilation.

Toubia N. Caring for women with circumcision: a technical manual for health care providers. New York: RAINBO, Research Action and Information Network for Bodily Integrity of Women; 1999. Copyright © 1999 RAINBO.

BOX 10-3

Arguments Used in Favor of Female Circumcision/Female Genital Mutilation

- Reinforces a woman's place in her given society
- Establishes eligibility for marriage
- Initiates a girl into womanhood
- Enhances a husband's sexual pleasure
- Safeguards the woman's virginity

Toubia N. Caring for women with circumcision; a technical manual for health care providers. New York: RAINBO, Research Action and Information Network for Bodily Integrity of Women; 1999. Copyright © 1999 RAINBO.

of the complications caused by FC/FGM are dysmenorrhea, chronic pelvic infections and pain, infertility, chronic urinary tract infections, urinary stones, slow urinary stream incontinence, and dyspareunia. Box 10-4 provides information on counseling for FC/FGM.

U.S. federal law and Canadian law prohibit the circumcision of any woman younger than 18 years. Thus, persons who perform FC/FGM on young women in Canada or the United States may be subject to criminal penalty.

American College of Obstetricians and Gynecologists. Female circumcision/female genital mutilation: clinical management of circumcised women. Washington (DC): ACOG; 1999.

Baker C, Gilson G, Vill M, Current L. Female circumcision: obstetric issues. Am J Obstet Gynecol 1995;164:1616–8.

Female genital mutilation. American Academy of Pediatrics Committee on Bioethics. Pediatrics 1998;102:153–6.

Toubia N. Caring for women with circumcision; a technical manual for health care providers. New York (NY): Research Action and Information Network for Bodily Integrity of Women; 1999.

BOX 10-4

Counseling for Female Circumcision/ Female Genital Mutilation

Counseling Around Defibulation
- Discuss technique and counsel against reinfibulation in a session prior to that of the procedure unless it is an emergency.
- Obtain informed consent, allowing time for consultation with family members.
- Postoperative care: Include sitz baths and local creams.
- Prepare patient for emotional reactions to new physical state.

Counseling Against Reinfibulation
- Explain the medical problems resulting from the obstruction of infibulation.
- Allow time for emotional processing and family consultation unless it is an emergency.
- Reinfibulation is illegal in some countries (eg, United Kingdom) but not in the United States; if patient insists on reinfibulation, provide alternatives (such as partial stitching, referral, or denial of service), depending on your own ethical choice.

Toubia N. Caring for women with circumcision: a technical manual for health care providers. New York: RAINBØ, Research Action and Information Network for Bodily Integrity of Women; 1999. Copyright © 1999 RAINBØ.

11

Treatment outcome with hormone therapy

A 60-year-old healthy woman is considering combination hormone therapy (HT), 0.625 mg conjugated equine estrogen (CEE) plus 2.5 mg medroxyprogesterone acetate (MPA), for the next 5–6 years to prevent osteoporosis. Which of the following possible complications of her use of HT poses the highest absolute risk to her?

      (A) Coronary heart disease
      (B) Breast cancer
      (C) Colorectal cancer
*   (D) Venous thromboembolism
      (E) Stroke

Many clinicians find it difficult to interpret observational epidemiologic or clinical trial studies in a manner that patients can understand. Most observational studies and some clinical trials report data as a relative risk, ie, the ratio of the observed events in a group exposed to a risk divided by the events experienced by a group not exposed to the risk factor. The incidence rates used in the numerator and denominator can be calculated directly in cohort studies and clinical trials, whereas case–control studies estimate the relative risk mathematically but do not provide incidence rates.

Unfortunately, the relative risk estimate does not give the type of data that most patients want—the likelihood that they will experience an event within a given period of time. For example, as Box 11-1 shows, in a particular study one might note that the relative risk for some

adverse event for women exposed to a certain risk factor is 10, which to many women might seem an unacceptable risk. However, if the baseline rate in a population of women not exposed to the risk factor is 1 event per 1 million woman–years, the attributable or absolute risk for women exposed to the risk factor would be only 9 additional events per 1 million woman–years, a risk that may be quite acceptable to some women. Conversely, low relative risks for commonly occurring adverse events may be of much greater public health significance.

Many women who are trying to decide whether to initiate or continue HT find it difficult to assess their true risk of disease. However, clinical trial data from the Women's Health Initiative do provide information that women can use to estimate better the risks and benefits associated with a decision to continue or initiate combined continuous HT. Table 11-1 lists relative risk estimates, reported as hazard ratios for certain events, along with absolute risks per 10,000 woman–years based on data from this study. It is important to recognize that the data provide information only on the continuous use of 0.625 mg CEE plus 2.5 mg MPA taken in combination daily. Furthermore, other important factors, such as effect on vasomotor changes and quality of life, were not reported in the initial publication. Finally, the results need to be interpreted with caution because approximately 40% of study subjects in both the HT arm and the placebo arm stopped using their study drugs during the course of the study. However, even with these possible limitations in mind, one can ascertain that venous thromboembolism carries the highest absolute risk compared with the other risk factors listed for this patient. Most important, this clinical trial was the first to confirm previously reported observational data for this and other risk factors. In addition, women who used this form of HT experienced a reduction in risk for colorectal cancer, not an increased risk. In addition, this study demonstrated a reduced risk of osteoporotic fractures of the spine and hip.

BOX 11-1

Relative Risk Versus Attributable Risk

Relative risk = incidence in the exposed group/incidence in the unexposed group.

Attributable risk = incidence in the exposed group – incidence in the unexposed group.

Example: The incidence of an adverse event in a group of women exposed to a risk factor is 10 events per 1 million woman–years, whereas the incidence of the same event in a group of unexposed women is 1 event per 1 million woman–years.

Relative risk = 10 events per 1 million woman–years/1 event per 1 million woman–years.

Relative risk = 10.

Attributable risk = (10 events per 1 million woman–years) – (1 event per 1 million woman–years).

Attributable risk = 9 more events per 1 million woman–years due to the exposure.

TABLE 11-1. Hazard Ratios with 95% Confidence Intervals (CI) and Absolute Risk of Certain Health Events for Women Who Take Continuous 0.625 mg Conjugated Equine Estrogen Plus 2.5 mg Medroxyprogesterone Acetate

Health Event	Hazard Ratio (95% CI)	Outcome Rates per 10,000 Woman–Years		Absolute Risk– Benefit per 10,000 Woman–Years
		Treated	Placebo	
Coronary heart disease	1.29 (1.02–1.63)	37	30	7
Stroke	1.41 (1.07–1.85)	29	21	8
Breast cancer	1.26 (1.00–1.59)	38	30	8
Pulmonary embolism	2.13 (1.39–3.25)	20	12	8
Venous thromboembolism	2.11 (1.58–2.82)	34	16	18
Hip fracture	0.66 (0.45–0.98)	10	15	5
Colorectal cancer	0.63 (0.43–0.92)	10	16	6

CI, confidence interval.

Adapted from Writing Group for the Women's Health Initiative Investigators. Risks and benefits of estrogen plus progestin in healthy postmenopausal women: principal results from the Women's Health Initiative randomized controlled trial. JAMA 2002;288:321–33. Copyright © 2002 American Medical Association. All rights reserved.

American College of Obstetricians and Gynecologists. Response to the Women's Health Initiative: study results by the American College of Obstetricians and Gynecologists. Washington, DC: ACOG; 2003.

Rossouw JE, Anderson GL, Prentice RL, LaCroix AZ, Kooperberg C, Stefanick ML, et al. Risks and benefits of estrogen plus progestin in healthy postmenopausal women: principal results from the Women's Health Initiative randomized controlled trial. JAMA 2002;288:321–33.

12

Premenopausal adnexal masses

A 29-year-old woman with regular menses at monthly intervals visits your office for an annual examination. A rectovaginal examination reveals a firm mass in the cul-de-sac that is slightly tender to palpation. Transvaginal ultrasonography identifies a complex adnexal mass measuring 3 cm × 4 cm. The CA 125 level is within normal limits. The most appropriate next step in evaluation is

    (A) magnetic resonance imaging (MRI) of the pelvis
    (B) pelvic computed tomography (CT) scan
*   (C) transvaginal ultrasonography in 2–3 months
    (D) diagnostic laparoscopy

It has been estimated that 5–10% of women in the United States will undergo a surgical procedure for a suspected ovarian neoplasm during their lifetime. Although 13–21% of these women will be found to have a malignant ovarian neoplasm, most adnexal masses, particularly if discovered during the reproductive years, are benign. The factors to be considered in making a therapeutic decision include age, symptoms, physical examination, ultrasonography findings, tumor markers, and family history.

The differential diagnosis of an adnexal mass varies with the patient's age. Premenarcheal girls and postmenopausal women are at high risk for malignancy compared with reproductive-aged women. In the latter group,

the differential diagnosis varies, and both benign and malignant tumors of genital and extragenital origin may occur. A differential diagnosis in women of reproductive age may include pregnancy, leiomyomata, functional and neoplastic ovarian masses, and endometriosis.

In cases in which the cyst has no septations or solid components, the risk of malignancy is less than 1%. A complex adnexal mass increases the risk of malignancy, but the risk is still low in a patient of this age.

Routine screening using the CA 125 tumor marker is not recommended in any age group. However, the CA 125 level is elevated in approximately one half of women with early epithelial cancer and, therefore, it is a good test in this patient with a complex mass, and especially in the menopause age group. Indicators for surgery for adnexal masses are noted in Box 12-1.

Ultrasonography in combination with CA 125 testing has been shown to be more accurate than MRI or CT scan for diagnosis and determination of which adnexal masses may be safely followed or explored. Laparoscopy may be used for diagnosis and therapy of adnexal masses but would not be the next step in the evaluation of this patient.

DiSaia PJ, Creasman WT. Clinical gynecologic oncology. 6th ed. St. Louis (MO): Mosby; 2002. p. 259–66.

Jermy K, Luise C, Bourne T. The characterization of common ovarian cysts in premenopausal women. Ultrasound Obstet Gynecol 2001; 17:140–4.

Menon U, Jacobs IJ. Tumor markers and screening. In: Berek JS, Hacker NF, editors. Practical gynecologic oncology. 3rd ed. Philadelphia (PA): Lippincott Williams & Wilkins; 2000. p. 39–51.

Milad MP, Cohen L. Preoperative ultrasound assessment of adnexal masses in premenopausal women. Int J Gynaecol Obstet 1999; 66:137–41.

13

Vessel injury during laparoscopic trocar placement

You are performing operative laparoscopy to remove an ovarian cyst. After placement of the umbilical port camera, you are unable to visualize either the medial umbilical ligament or the inferior epigastric vessels. No adhesions are present. To avoid inferior epigastric vessel injury, you recommend placement of the lateral port

(A) through the middle of the rectus muscle halfway between the symphysis and umbilicus
(B) medial to the rectus muscle at the level of the iliac crest
(C) 3 cm superior to the symphysis and 12 cm lateral to the midline
(D) 3 cm superior to the symphysis and 5 cm lateral to the midline
* (E) 5 cm superior to the pubis and 8 cm lateral to the midline

Injury to the inferior epigastric vessels at the time of laparoscopy can cause significant morbidity and require laparotomy for control in severe cases. The laparoscopist can avoid injury by paying careful attention to anatomic landmarks (Fig. 13-1). One study reported that 45% of clinicians chose a lateral puncture site within 1 cm of the inferior epigastric vessel when asked to demonstrate on a model.

The inferior epigastric artery branches from the external iliac artery and courses superiorly and medially to enter the rectus sheath. In the rectus muscle it eventually anastomoses with the superior epigastric, which is a branch of the internal thoracic artery. At a level more than 5 cm superior to the symphysis, the inferior epigastric vessels consistently are within 7 cm of the midline. The lateral border of the rectus muscle at these levels is more than 7 cm from the midline. These vessels may be slightly more lateral in the obese patient than in the average-sized patient.

To avoid injury to the inferior epigastric vessels during placement of the lateral ports, the best approach is to use the laparoscope to identify the vessels as they course along the parietal peritoneum. The lateral port then can be placed under direct visualization laterally or medially to the vessels. Another approach is to identify the medial umbilical ligament and place the trocar medial to this structure because the inferior epigastric vessels consistently are lateral to this structure. The difficulty with the latter approach is that the port site may be too medial for surgery on the adnexa. Sometimes the identification of these structures anterior to the peritoneum may not be possible, so alternative strategies must be used.

If the lateral port sites are placed at least 5 cm superior to the symphysis and 8 cm lateral to the midline, which is lateral to the rectus, the inferior epigastric vessels should not be injured. At this level, the inferior epi-

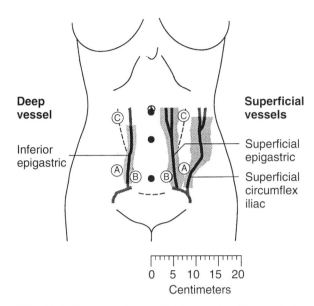

Deep vessel

Inferior epigastric

Superficial vessels

Superficial epigastric

Superficial circumflex iliac

0 5 10 15 20
Centimeters

FIG. 13-1. Deep and superficial vessels of the anterior abdominal wall, front view. Shown as black vessels with gray shadows are mean ± standard deviations for data from computed tomographic scans. Vessels shown without standard deviations are extrapolated locations. Dashed lines indicate the relative location of the rectus abdominis muscle lateral margin and the symphysis pubis; solid circles, standard sites for midline laparoscopic trocar placement; lettered circles, recommended locations for lateral trocar placement ([**A**] ideal location for lateral trocars 5 cm above the symphysis, 8 cm from the midline; [**B**] alternate location for lateral trocars 3 cm above the symphysis, 4 cm from the midline; and [**C**] location for trocars near the level of the umbilicus, 8 cm from the midline). (Reprinted from Am J Obstet Gynecol, Vol 171, Hurd WW, Bude RO, DeLancey JO, Newman JS. The location of abdominal wall blood vessels in relationship to abdominal landmarks apparent at laparoscopy. p. 644. Copyright 1994, with permission from Elsevier.)

gastric vessels should course posteriorly to, or in the body of, the rectus muscle. Care still should be taken, however, to avoid the external iliac vessels; injury to them could have catastrophic consequences. The best way to avoid these vessels is by introducing the lateral port into the peritoneal cavity under direct visualization in a controlled fashion. A point 12 cm lateral to the midline would place the port site at the anterior axillary line; this site might be too lateral and dangerous because it would be directly anterior to the sidewall. A point 5 cm lateral to the midline would effectively place the trocar through the point at highest risk of injury to the vessel. A point medial to the rectus at the level of the iliac crest is, in effect, the umbilicus or within 2 cm in the midline. This site would not be useful, because the umbilical port has already been placed. Some authors recommend using a conical rather than a pyramidal trocar tip to further decrease the likelihood of injury to the inferior epigastric vessels.

In the event of injury, bleeding from the epigastric vessels can be controlled by several methods. A Foley

catheter can be placed through the sheath, the bulb distended, and traction applied for tamponade of the vessels on the parietal peritoneal surface. The disadvantage of this method is that the surgical procedure cannot be continued through that port site.

Another method is to use fulguration with the electrocautery device. The potential disadvantage is that the surgeon may not be able to grasp the vein and artery with the bipolar instrument, and uncontrolled bleeding and hematoma formation may result. Several suturing techniques have been used, including needle suturing with subsequent intracorporeal or extracorporeal knot tying. For surgeons not skilled with laparoscopic suturing maneuvers, other methods have been described to control bleeding, with the knots tied down and allowed to remain externally over gauze (Figs. 13-2–13-5). The suture can be removed 6–8 hours later at the surgeon's discretion.

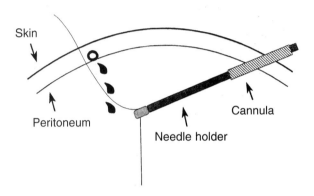

Skin

Peritoneum

Cannula

Needle holder

FIG. 13-2. A straight-needle suture is pushed through the abdominal wall below and lateral to the damaged vessel and is pulled through the contralateral cannula using a laparoscopic needle holder. (Chatzipapas KI, Magos AL. A simple technique of securing inferior epigastric vessels and repairing the rectus sheath at laparoscopic surgery. Obstet Gynecol 1997;90:305.)

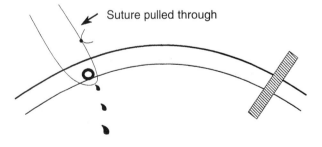

Suture pulled through

FIG. 13-3. A second suture is inserted below and medial to the vessel and is also pulled through the contralateral cannula. (Chatzipapas KI, Magos AL. A simple technique of securing inferior epigastric vessels and repairing the rectus sheath at laparoscopic surgery. Obstet Gynecol 1997;90:305.)

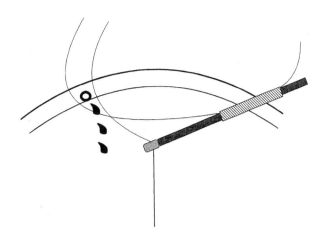

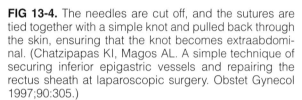

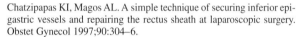

FIG 13-4. The needles are cut off, and the sutures are tied together with a simple knot and pulled back through the skin, ensuring that the knot becomes extraabdominal. (Chatzipapas KI, Magos AL. A simple technique of securing inferior epigastric vessels and repairing the rectus sheath at laparoscopic surgery. Obstet Gynecol 1997;90:305.)

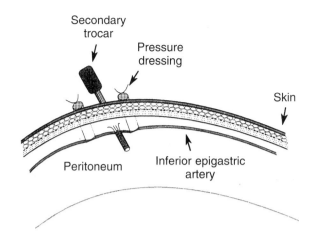

FIG. 13-5. The knot is cut off, and the suture is tied over a pressure dressing. The procedure is repeated above the damaged vessels to secure hemostasis. (Chatzipapas KI, Magos AL. A simple technique of securing inferior epigastric vessels and repairing the rectus sheath at laparoscopic surgery. Obstet Gynecol 1997;90:305.)

Chatzipapas KI, Magos AL. A simple technique of securing inferior epigastric vessels and repairing the rectus sheath at laparoscopic surgery. Obstet Gynecol 1997;90:304–6.

Gostout B. Laparoscopy. In: Webb M, editor. Mayo Clinic manual of pelvic surgery. Philadelphia (PA): Lippincott Williams & Wilkins; 2000. p. 193–210.

Hurd WW, Bude RO, DeLancey JO, Newman JS. The location of abdominal wall blood vessels in relationship to abdominal landmarks apparent at laparoscopy. Am J Obstet Gynecol 1994;171:642–6.

Pring DW. Inferior epigastric haemorrhage, an avoidable complication of laparoscopic clip sterilization. Br J Obstet Gynaecol 1983; 90:480–2.

14

Lifestyle stress

A 31-year-old single mother tells you during her well-woman examination that she has noted unexpected recent weight loss and malaise. On obtaining her history, you learn that she was treated several times over the past 2 years for dysmenorrhea and menorrhagia without improvement. The best next step in management would be to

    (A) prescribe a selective serotonin reuptake inhibitor (SSRI)
    (B) order magnetic resonance imaging (MRI) of the abdomen and pelvis
    (C) test fasting levels of follicle-stimulating hormone (FSH) and luteinizing hormone (LH)
 * (D) administer a screening questionnaire for depression
    (E) refer the patient for nutrition counseling

Depression is a common disorder with widespread symptomatology that affects 1 in 5 women. Its recognition and prompt treatment should be part of the care obstetrician–gynecologists provide as primary care physicians.

Criteria for diagnosis of a major depressive episode are shown in Box 14-1. The presence of 5 or more of these signs and symptoms daily for a 2-week period confirms the diagnosis of clinical depression. Depression also may be manifested in various physical symptoms (Box 14-2). Women are 2–3 times more likely to experience clinical depression than men. A number of factors may predispose women to depression:

- Physical or sexual abuse
- Socioeconomic deprivation
- Lifestyle stress due to multiple roles
- Genetic predisposition
- Early childhood loss of a parent
- Life cycle events

Life cycle events such as perinatal loss, infertility, pregnancy, and menopause are of particular risk to women. Such events may precipitate a major depressive episode.

Depression is a common reason for psychiatric hospitalization in the United States. With recognition and proper treatment, the signs and symptoms of clinical depression may be mitigated in weeks. When a major depressive episode is untreated, it lasts approximately 9 months. Suicidal and homicidal ideation is present in a minority of severely affected individuals.

Depression has a biologic basis and a behavioral component. Thus, treatment includes both modulation of neurotransmitter activity and behavioral-based therapy. A decrease in serotonin activity, combined with an abnormality in norepinephrine regulation, calls for pharmacotherapy. Drugs commonly used block the reuptake of both serotonin and norepinephrine (tricyclic antidepressants) or just that of serotonin. Psychotherapy is aimed at promoting insight and providing support as a means to

---

BOX 14-1

Criteria for Diagnosis of a Major Depressive Episode

At least 5 of the following 9 symptoms must be present for at least 2 weeks to fulfill the definition of major depressive episode, and at least one of the symptoms must be either depressed mood or loss of interest or pleasure.

1. Depressed mood most of the day, nearly every day
2. Markedly decreased interest or pleasure in activities
3. Significant appetite or weight change
4. Insomnia or hypersomnia nearly every day
5. Observable psychomotor retardation or agitation nearly every day
6. Fatigue or loss of energy nearly every day
7. Feelings of worthlessness or inappropriate guilt nearly every day
8. Diminished ability to think, concentrate, or make decisions
9. Recurrent thoughts of death or suicide

The symptoms must represent a change from the patient's previous level of functioning.

American Psychiatric Association. Diagnostic and statistical manual of mental disorders, 4th ed., Text Revision. Washington, DC: APA; 2000. p. 327. Adapted with permission from the Diagnostic and Statistical Manual of Mental Disorders, Fourth Edition. Copyright © 1994 American Psychiatric Association.

---

remedy the various behavioral effects of depression. Behaviors that indicate a need for psychotherapy may include helplessness, unexpressed anger, and unresolved grief.

The diagnosis may be expedited by the use of a screening questionnaire, such as the Zung self-rating depression scale (see Appendix 1). This questionnaire should be employed prior to instituting specific treatment such as SSRIs. In the presence of a normal pelvic examination, imaging studies such as an MRI or tests of serum levels of FSH and LH are not warranted as initial steps in management. Referral for nutritional counseling may be helpful but should be reserved for a later time.

American Psychiatric Association. Diagnostic and statistical manual of mental disorders: DSM-IV. 4th ed. Washington, DC: APA; 1994.

Campbell J, Kub JE, Rose L. Depression in battered women. J Am Womens Assoc 1996;51:106–10.

Stotland N. Common psychiatric problems. In: Berek JS, Adashi EY, Hillard PA, editors. Novak's gynecology. 12th ed. Baltimore (MD): Williams & Wilkins; 1996. p. 299–332.

Zung WW. A self-rating depression scale. Arch Gen Psychiatry 1965;12:63–70.

15

Designated health care surrogate

A patient should appoint an agent who will have legal authority to make decisions regarding her medical care if she becomes incapacitated and unable to express her wishes regarding her health care. The proper instrument to express her decision is

    (A) a living will
    (B) a durable power of attorney
    (C) a verbal contract
*   (D) an advance health care directive that appoints a health care agent and includes instructions regarding the patient's wishes

When a patient becomes unable to make decisions in regard to her health care, controversies and conflicts can arise among her family members and friends and the physicians who care for her. Such disagreements have led to laws and ethical guidelines relating to decisions made on behalf of incompetent patients. Several types of documents are available to enable individuals to prepare for situations in which they become unable to make decisions about their health care. An advance health care directive is a written instrument in which the individual appoints a health care agent and in which she can write instructions in regard to her health care wishes (eg, not to receive treatment that will prolong the dying process in the case of terminal illness). The instrument gives the agent the legal authority to make decisions about medical care in the event the individual becomes unable to make decisions for herself. The agent and the physician who cares for the patient must comply with the instructions of the directive. Because the advance directive appoints a trusted individual to participate actively in the decisions regarding care of the patient and also includes written instructions regarding the patient's wishes, it is the most effective instrument for care of the patient when the person is incapacitated and cannot make decisions for herself.

The advance health care directive allows an individual to do more than can be done with the traditional living will, which only states a desire not to receive life-sustaining treatment in the event of terminal illness or permanent unconsciousness. In contrast to the living will, the advance directive allows an individual to state her wishes about refusing or accepting life-sustaining treatment in any situation in which she is unable to make these decisions, not just if she is in a coma or is terminally ill. A living will, unlike an advance directive, does not permit an individual to appoint a health care agent. A durable power of attorney for health care, which is a legally recognized document for appointing a health care agent, is not as comprehensive as an advance directive in that it does not permit an individual to give instructions about her own health care.

A verbal contract between an individual and her designated surrogate may provide some information about the individual's health care wishes if there is no written document to provide this information, but it is the least reliable method for communicating a person's wishes for her health care to the physicians responsible for providing care. Furthermore, a verbal contract does not clearly identify who has the authority to speak for the patient as the proxy or health care agent. Because there is fairly widespread agreement on the need for sufficient evidence to be available in order to support a particular substituted judgment, patients should be encouraged to designate in writing a single proxy or agent, which gives that individual priority over other friends and relatives. A single designated surrogate can resolve situations in which several relatives disagree about care that should be provided when a patient is comatose or incompetent.

A notarized written statement by an individual, including desires about the goals and types of medical care she does or does not want to receive and her desires concerning life support in the event of profound illness, should be honored by the providers of health care. The advance health care directive is the most legally recognized comprehensive format to ensure that an individual's health care wishes will be known and considered when appropriate.

A number of states have requirements for advance directives. In addition, the *Code of Federal Regulations* requires that hospitals maintain written policies and procedures concerning advance directives with respect to all adults receiving medical care. Hospitals must provide written information concerning an individual's right to make decisions about such medical care, including the right to accept or refuse medical or surgical treatment and the right to formulate, at the individual's option, advance directives.

Alpers A, Lo B. Avoiding family feuds: responding to surrogate demands for life-sustaining interventions. J Law Med Ethics 1999;27: 74–80.

Fischer GS, Alpert HR, Stoeckle JD, Emanuel LL. Can goals of care be used to predict intervention preferences in an advance directive? Arch Intern Med 1997;157:801–7.

Tonelli MR. Substituted judgment in medical practice: evidentiary standards on a sliding scale. J Law Med Ethics 1997;25:22–9.

16
Risk reduction for ovarian cancer

A 30-year-old obese nulligravid woman visits your office for her annual gynecologic examination. Because her mother died from ovarian cancer, she is concerned about her risk of getting the disease. The most appropriate prophylactic approach to reduce her future risk of developing epithelial ovarian cancer is the use of

    (A) medroxyprogesterone acetate
*   (B) oral contraceptives
    (C) tamoxifen citrate (Nolvadex) for 5 years
    (D) a progestin-releasing intrauterine device (Mirena)

Epithelial ovarian cancer is the leading cause of death from gynecologic malignancies in the United States. Approximately 1 in 70 women in the United States will develop ovarian cancer in their lifetime. Most cases are diagnosed in advanced stages and have a poor prognosis. Ovarian cancer accounts for more deaths than all other gynecologic cancers combined. Current screening techniques are neither sensitive nor specific enough to detect early cancer as part of a screening program in the general population. Therefore, prevention of the disease is crucial.

This patient has 2 risk factors for the development of ovarian cancer: a positive family history of the disease and nulliparity. With 1 first-degree relative with ovarian cancer, the risk of the patient's dying of the same disease is approximately 3 times that of the general population.

Studies have shown a 40–50% decrease in risk of epithelial ovarian cancer in oral contraceptive users. Protection appears to continue for a 10–15-year period after discontinuation of oral contraceptives, although

some studies have indicated a lifetime risk reduction. Hospital and population studies reveal that the risk continues to decrease as years of oral contraceptive use increase, although there seems to be little additional protection beyond 6 years of use.

Women with mutations in the *BRCA1* or *BRCA2* gene have a higher lifetime risk of developing epithelial ovarian cancer; the risk is approximately 45% in women with *BRCA1* mutations and 25% in women with *BRCA2* mutations. Recent studies suggest that oral contraceptive use may reduce risk in these populations.

Few data support the use of medroxyprogesterone acetate for the prevention of ovarian cancer. Tamoxifen citrate (Nolvadex) has been shown to be effective in the prevention of the development of breast cancer, but no evidence exists that tamoxifen helps to prevent ovarian cancer. No studies to date have demonstrated an association between the use of a progestin-releasing intrauterine device and the prevention of epithelial ovarian cancer.

American College of Obstetricians and Gynecologists. Prophylactic oophorectomy. ACOG Practice Bulletin 7. Washington, DC: ACOG; 1999.

Epithelial ovarian cancer. In: DiSaia PJ, Creasman WT. Clinical gynecologic oncology. 6th ed. St. Louis (MO): Mosby; 2002. p. 289–350.

Nahhas WA. Ovarian cancer. Current outlook on this deadly disease. Postgrad Med 1997;102:112–20.

Narod SA, Risch H, Moslehi R, Dorum A, Neuhausen S, Olsson H, et al. Oral contraceptives and the risk of hereditary ovarian cancer. Hereditary Ovarian Cancer Clinical Study Group. N Engl J Med 1998;339:424–8.

17

Retroperitoneal hematoma

A 44-year-old thin woman with a body mass index (BMI) lower than 25 kg/m^2 has arrived in the recovery room after undergoing a 1½-hour operative laparoscopy for pelvic pain. She has had numerous previous surgeries, including abdominal hysterectomy, subsequent laparotomy for bilateral salpingo-oophorectomy, and appendectomy. Dense omental abdominal wall adhesions were released with the use of cautery and sharp transection. Pelvic and upper abdominal findings were otherwise unremarkable. Initial vital signs in the recovery room include blood pressure of 100/60 mm Hg and pulse rate of 95 beats per minute. After 5 minutes, her blood pressure decreases to 60 mm Hg, and her pulse rate increases to 120 beats per minute. She has increasing abdominal pain and distention. An initial fluid bolus has no effect. The most appropriate management course at this time is

        (A) blood transfusion
        (B) a second intravenous fluid bolus
        (C) another laparoscopic evaluation
*   (D) exploratory laparotomy
        (E) intravenous analgesia

Retroperitoneal and other vascular injuries are the most serious complications of closed laparoscopic surgical procedures, but they occur infrequently (2.6–11.0 per 1,000 operative laparoscopies). Patients at risk for these injuries include very thin or obese patients with a BMI higher than 30 kg/m^2 and patients with a history of multiple previous laparotomies.

The most common site of vascular injury is the inferior epigastric vessels on placement of a secondary port site. Because of the increasing abdominal distention in this patient, however, another vascular injury site should be suspected. Most other vessel injuries occur secondary to the blind placement of the Veress needle. Factors that increase the risk of perforation or laceration with the Veress needle include the following:

- The presence of bowel adhesions
- Lateral displacement of the needle during insertion, especially where adhesions are present
- A needle insertion angle that is too steep
- Uncontrolled sudden entry of the needle

The patient should be in a horizontal position so that the sacral promontory and sacral curve can be identified easily (Fig. 17-1). Veress needle injuries may be arterial or venous and may involve the aorta or common iliac arteries or common iliac veins (Fig. 17-2). Venous injury may be more likely because the left common iliac vein is the lowest vascular structure in the midline and is relatively thin walled compared with the arterial vessels. The aortic bifurcation is at or below the level of the umbilicus in many cases, and the left common iliac vein may cross the midline below the umbilicus. The margin of error may be especially small in thin patients (Fig. 17-3). The signs of venous injury, however, may be subtle, especially in the setting of a pneumoperitoneum and the decreased venous pressure from Trendelenburg's position. Furthermore, a retroperitoneal hematoma may pack a large vessel injury, and only as the pressure gradients return to normal may bleeding ensue, leading to hypovolemic shock.

Immediate laparotomy is necessary to manage this patient's hemodynamic instability. Observation, further fluid bolus, intravenous analgesia, or blood transfusion for primary treatment of these symptoms in the recovery room would be inappropriate; however, these measures should be initiated on the patient's return to the operating room. A second laparoscopic evaluation would be difficult in light of the potential for a substantial hemoperitoneum. A vascular surgeon should be present at the time of laparotomy.

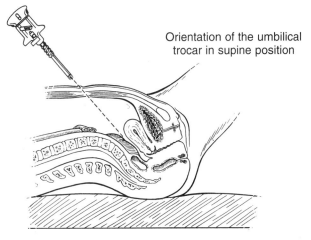

Orientation of the umbilical
trocar in supine position

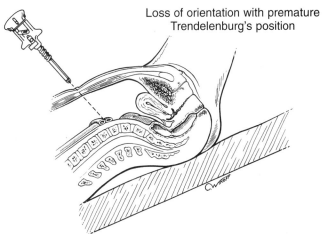

Loss of orientation with premature
Trendelenburg's position

FIG. 17-1. The patient must be horizontal so that the sacral promontory and sacral curve are clearly identified and the operator is not disoriented by premature Trendelenburg's positioning. (Nezhat CR, Nezhat FR, Luciano AA, Siegler AM, Metzger DA, Nezhat C. Operative gynecologic laparoscopy: principles and techniques. New York [NY]: McGraw-Hill; 1995. p. 290. With permission of The McGraw-Hill Companies.)

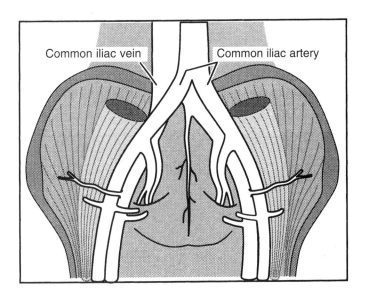

Common iliac vein   Common iliac artery

FIG. 17-2. Relationship of the iliac arteries and veins. (Reprinted from Management of perioperative complications in gynecology, Baker VV, Deppe G, editors. Kost ER, Mutch DG, Hemorrhage. p. 49. Copyright 1997, with permission from Elsevier.)

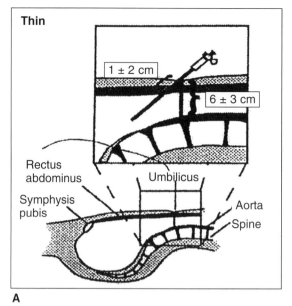

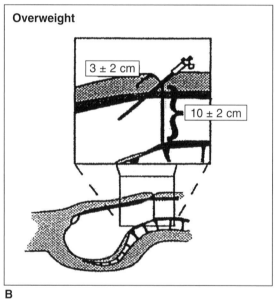
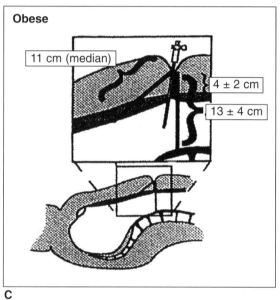

FIG. 17-3. Representative sagittal views of patients in 3 groups: (**A**) thin (ie, nonobese), (**B**) overweight, and (**C**) obese. (Modified from Hurd WH, Bude RO, DeLancey JO, Gauvin JM, Aisen AM. Abdominal wall characterization with magnetic resonance imaging and computed tomography: the effect of obesity on the laparoscopic approach. From J Reprod Med 1991;36:473–6.)

Hulka J, Peterson HB, Phillips JM, Surrey MW. Operative laparoscopy: American Association of Gynecologic Laparoscopists' 1993 membership survey on operative laparoscopy. J Am Assoc Gynecol Laparosc 1995;2:133–6.

Hurd WH, Bude RO, DeLancey JO, Gauvin JM, Aisen AM. Abdominal wall characterization with magnetic resonance imaging and computed tomography: the effect of obesity on the laparoscopic approach. J Reprod Med 1991;36:473–6.

Nezhat CR, Nezhat FR, Luciano AA, Siegler AM, Metzger DA, Nezhat C. Operative gynecologic laparoscopy: principles and techniques. New York (NY): McGraw-Hill; 1995. p. 287–310.

Peterson HB, Hulka JF, Phillips JM. American Association of Gynecologic Laparoscopists' 1988 membership survey on operative laparoscopy. J Reprod Med 1990;35:587–9.

18

Irregular perimenopausal bleeding

A 43-year-old woman had regular menses until approximately 6 months ago. Since that time, she has had bleeding at intervals of 1–2 weeks that has varied significantly in amount of flow. She reports marked mood swings and irritability. A pelvic examination reveals an enlarged, irregular uterus of approximately 8 weeks of gestational size. She neither smokes nor has a history of coagulopathy or cardiovascular disease. An endometrial biopsy shows proliferative endometrium. The patient desires effective birth control and currently is using only condoms. The most appropriate next step in management is

        (A) a copper-containing intrauterine device (IUD)
        (B) dilation and curettage (D&C) and hysteroscopy
        (C) continuous norethindrone acetate
   *   (D) low-dose oral contraceptives

Perimenopausal women may experience many troublesome symptoms, including irregular menses, mood changes, and occasional hot and cold flushes similar to those of menopause. In addition, the potential for pregnancy, although diminished, is not eliminated. Indeed, 51% of pregnancies in women older than 40 years are unplanned, and of these, 65% result in abortion.

The current patient presents with a classic history of dysfunctional bleeding. Her uterine enlargement and menstrual irregularity raise the possibility of an intrauterine abnormality that may contribute to the bleeding history.

Copper-containing IUDs may provide the birth control protection the patient desires, and newer levonorgestrel-containing IUDs reduce menstrual flow. However, some women who use IUDs experience irregular bleeding, which is the most common reason for the removal of these devices; thus, an IUD, which may exacerbate bleeding, would not be the first therapeutic choice in this patient.

Performance of a D&C and hysteroscopy to evaluate a patient with irregular bleeding is a reasonable choice. However, it would not be the next step in management for this patient. The previously performed endometrial biopsy should be considered effective to rule out a neoplasm, and the cost of an outpatient procedure may not be justified until other conservative measures have been attempted.

Continuous norethindrone acetate in a moderate to high dose may control dysfunctional bleeding reasonably well. However, continued irregular bleeding from induced endometrial atrophy may occur.

Low-dose oral contraceptives offer the best choice among the suggested options. These oral contraceptives provide cycle control, contraception, and additional benefits (eg, a lower incidence of several gynecologic and nongynecologic malignancies, preservation of bone density, and possible improvement in acne).

Although contraceptive efficacy is the same here as for younger women, ovulatory suppression may be incomplete. This problem is not often important because women in this age group who take oral contraceptives may be more compliant than a younger population. However, it is important to recognize that pregnancy may occur with inconsistent use.

Significant benefits of oral contraceptive use in women older than 40 years are cycle control and suppression of dysfunctional bleeding. An early study in women who took oral contraceptives with 50 μg of estrogen found decreased mean blood loss of 53% among patients who had both enlarged and normal-sized uteri. A randomized, multicenter trial in women who took 35 μg estrogen triphasic norgestimate demonstrated that control of dysfunctional bleeding was better in the treated group than in the control group.

Although the incidence of thrombophlebitis and thromboembolism is increased in women who take oral contraceptives, recent data show no significant risk of ischemic or hemorrhagic stroke in young healthy women or nonsmoking women regardless of age. Two case–control studies suggest that women with classic aura-associated or peripheral neurologic migraines who use oral contraceptives may be at higher risk for stroke. However, the dose of oral contraceptives used was not specified. For women who have common nonaura or focal neurologic symptom migraines, oral contraceptives usually may be prescribed safely.

A collaborative study analyzed the risk of breast cancer and low-dose oral contraceptives. The overall relative risk in users was 1.07, a slight but statistically significant elevation. Breast neoplasms in oral contraceptive users were noted to be more localized and to have fewer metastases compared with breast neoplasms among women who had not used oral contraceptives. Studies that have examined the incidence of benign breast disease have shown a decreased risk in oral contraceptive users compared with nonusers. The risk decreased with long-term use prior to, but not after, the first pregnancy.

Several other health benefits appear to be related to use of oral contraceptives. Evidence suggests that oral contraceptives are associated with a lower incidence of various conditions such as colorectal, endometrial, and ovarian cancer, as well as Alzheimer's disease. Colorectal cancer is currently the third leading cause of morbidity and mortality in both men and women. The Nurses Health Study demonstrated a 40% lower risk of colorectal cancer among women who used oral contraceptives 96 months or longer compared with women who did not use oral contraceptives.

Burkman RT, Collins JA, Shulman LP, Williams JK. Current perspectives on oral contraceptive use. Am J Obstet Gynecol 2001;185:S4–S12.

Collaborative Group on Hormonal Factors in Breast Cancer. Breast cancer and hormonal contraceptives: collaborative reanalysis of individual data on 53,297 women with breast cancer and 100,239 women without breast cancer from 54 epidemiological studies. Lancet 1996;347: 1713–27.

Davis A, Godwin A, Lippman J, Olson W, Kafrissen M. Triphasic norgestimate-ethinyl estradiol for treating dysfunctional uterine bleeding. Obstet Gynecol 2000;96:913–20.

Fernandez E, La Vecchia C, Franceschi S, Braga C, Talamini R, Negri E, et al. Oral contraceptive use and risk of colorectal cancer. Epidemiology 1998;9:295–300.

Petitti DB, Sidney S, Bernstein A, Wolf S, Quesenberry C, Ziel HK. Stroke in users of low-dose oral contraceptives. N Engl J Med 1996;335:8–15.

Teichmann AT, Brill K, Albring M, Schnitker J, Wojtynek P, Kustra E. The influence of the dose of ethinylestradiol in oral contraceptives on follicle growth. Gynecol Endocrinol 1995;9:299–305.

Westhoff C, Britton JA, Gammon MD, Wright T, Kelsey JL. Oral contraceptive and benign ovarian tumors. Am J Epidemiol 2000;152:242–6.

19

Vulvar vestibulitis

Twice in the past year a 24-year-old woman has come to your office and reported vulvar discomfort. Results of her Pap test have been normal, and cultures for sexually transmitted diseases have been negative. The patient calls today to report vaginal burning without discharge. Further questioning reveals that vaginal entry during intercourse or on insertion of a tampon is accompanied by pain. You instruct the patient to avoid over-the-counter preparations and to come to your office for evaluation. Inspection of the vulva reveals mild erythema of the vestibular area. The best option to establish the diagnosis is

      (A) biopsy of the erythematous introital area
      (B) fungal culture of area
      (C) viral culture of area
*   (D) cotton-tipped swab touch test to the vestibule to localize the pain

Vulvodynia is defined by the International Society for the Study of Vulvovaginal Diseases as chronic vulvar discomfort, especially characterized by burning, stinging, irritation, or rawness. The condition can be divided into two major groups: 1) organic causes and 2) essential, dysesthetic causes. In the latter group, no specific cause can be attributed to the symptom of vulvar burning.

The largest subset of patients with vulvodynia have vulvar vestibulitis syndrome (VVS), characterized by exquisite pain of the vulvar vestibule. Diagnostic hallmarks of this entity include severe pain on vestibular touch or attempted vaginal entry, tenderness to pressure localized within the vulvar vestibule, and physical findings confined to vestibular erythema of various degrees. The typical patient has had this disorder for months or years and has seen many doctors in desperation for a cure that remains elusive. Interpersonal relationships are likely to have been strained, as coitus becomes impossible because of severe entry dyspareunia. Some patients relate onset to a surgical or gynecologic event, whereas others note a relationship with the menstrual cycle and may describe intermittent swelling. Theories of causation include hypersensitization to *Candida* species, generalized allergies, and subclinical human papillomavirus (HPV) infection. In addition to dyspareunia, patients report burning pain on tampon insertion, as well as persistent, spontaneous vaginal burning with or without persistent vaginal discharge.

On examination of the vestibule, foci of erythema may be obvious, often with noticeable hyperemia around the openings of the Bartholin's and Skene's ducts (Fig. 19-1). Rarely, one may note shallow ulcers present in the vestibule adjacent to the hymenal ring (Fig. 19-2). A significant number of patients with VVS also report dysuria and urinary frequency, which suggests that both problems represent disorders of urogenital sinus–derived epitheli-

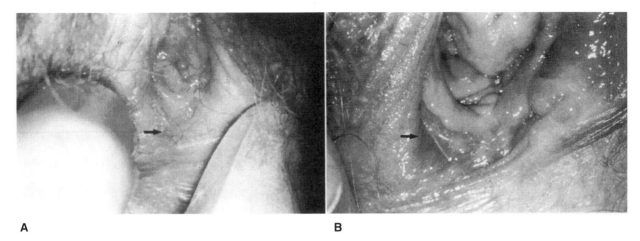

A   B

FIG. 19-1. Vestibulitis. (**A**) Hyperemic area at the 6-o'clock position. (**B**) Hyperemic area prominent around opening of Bartholin's duct. (Reprinted from Benign diseases of the vulva and vagina, 4th ed., Kaufman RH, Faro S, Friedrich EG Jr, Gardner HL, editors. p. 302. Copyright 1994, with permission from Elsevier.)

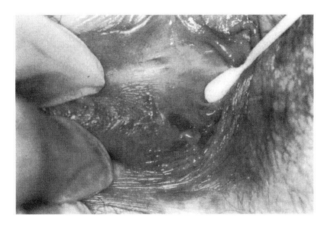

FIG. 19-2. Vestibulitis. A superficial ulcer is seen on the vestibule. (Reprinted from Benign diseases of the vulva and vagina, 4th ed., Kaufman RH, Faro S, Friedrich EG Jr, Gardner HL, editors. p. 302. Copyright 1994, with permission from Elsevier.)

um. The area must be examined carefully with 3–5% acetic acid to elicit the presence of acetowhite changes that may suggest HPV. When the areas near vestibular gland openings or clefts are pressed with a cotton-tipped swab, the burning pain is elicited (Fig. 19-3). A cotton-tipped swab is used on the vestibule to determine the exact location of the pain. The cotton-tipped swab touch test provokes an inappropriate perception of pain (hyperesthesia) or allodynia, or the perception of a different sensation than that applied (ie, burn instead of touch).

Because the cause of VVS is unknown, there is no ideal treatment. Conservative measures are not usually effective. Occasional spontaneous remissions do occur. This fact, coupled with the placebo effect, make it difficult to assess new treatments without randomized controlled trials. Surface electromyographic biofeedback and group cognitive–behavioral therapy compared favorably with vestibulectomy in treating dyspareunia result-

ing from VVS in a randomized comparison of these 3 modalities. Biofeedback is thought to reduce pain by training patients to reduce the instability and hypertonicity of the pelvic floor muscles that may be responsible for vulvar pain.

Vulvar biopsy should be performed only in the presence of a mass or suspected malignant lesion. The erythema characteristic of VVS is diffuse and nonspecific, so it is not useful in establishing a diagnosis. Indeed, a reevaluation of criteria for diagnosing VVS found erythema to be a less useful diagnostic criterion. Fungal or viral cultures in the absence of focal findings would not be helpful in diagnosing VVS.

Tricyclic antidepressants have had some usefulness as a treatment of VVS. However, because of potential adverse effects with indiscriminate use, these drugs should be dispensed only if a diagnosis has been established.

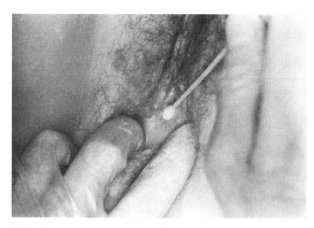

FIG. 19-3. Gentle palpation of the vulvar vestibule elicits painful response. (Reprinted from Benign diseases of the vulva and vagina, 4th ed., Kaufman RH, Faro S, Friedrich EG Jr, Gardner HL, editors. p. 302. Copyright 1994, with permission from Elsevier.)

Bergeron S, Binik YM, Khalife S, Pagidas K, Glazer HI. Vulvar vestibulitis syndrome: reliability of diagnosis and evaluation of current diagnostic criteria. Obstet Gynecol 2001;98:45–51.

Bergeron S, Binik YM, Khalife S, Pagidas K, Glazer HI, Meana M, et al. A randomized comparison of group cognitive–behavioral therapy, surface electromyographic biofeedback, and vestibulectomy in the treatment of dyspareunia resulting from vulvar vestibulitis. Pain 2001; 91:297–306.

Droegemueller W. Benign gynecologic lesions: vulva, vagina, cervix, uterus, oviduct, ovary. In: Stenchever MA, Droegemueller W, Herbst AL, Mishell DR, editors. Comprehensive gynecology. 4th ed. St. Louis (MO): Mosby; 2001. p. 479–530.

Mariani L. Vulvar vestibulitis syndrome: an overview of non-surgical treatment. Eur J Obstet Gynecol Reprod Biol 2002;101:109–12.

Miscellaneous vulvar disorders. In: Kaufman RH, Faro S, Friedrich EG Jr, Gardner HL, editors. Benign diseases of the vulva and vagina. 4th ed. St. Louis (MO): Mosby–Year Book; 1994. p. 299–305.

20

Straddle injury

A 7-year-old girl presents in the emergency department with an injury to the perineum. She is bleeding actively, and you are told she fell on the crossbar of her brother's bicycle. The history you obtain from the patient and the history from her caretaker mother are inconsistent in regard to the details of the event. The child has been in good health up to the present. On examination, there are no bruises over the skin. The general physical examination is unremarkable. Examination of the external genitalia notes a defect involving the fourchette and extending into the perirectal area. The anal orifice is intact. The best next step is

        (A) observation in the emergency department
        (B) laparoscopy
   *   (C) examination under anesthesia
        (D) ultrasonography of the pelvis

The exact incidence of genital trauma in the pediatric or adolescent patient is difficult to assess. Most reports in the literature are anecdotal case reports or are the result of small series related to child sexual abuse. In a study of 4,450 female pediatric patients in the Pennsylvania Trauma Outcome Study database, a total of 338 girls were noted to have blunt perineal trauma. Motor vehicle accidents were responsible for the majority of these cases, followed by falls and bicycle-related injuries, especially if the child was younger than 9 years. Sexual assaults were more common in patients younger than 5 years. A detailed history is the appropriate place to start the evaluation. Inconsistencies between the history obtained from a caretaker and from the child may raise the possibility of sexual abuse.

The external genitalia have an excellent blood supply, and minor injuries can bleed profusely, especially with laceration of the vagina, hymen, and adjacent structures. Observation in the emergency department would not be the best next step in treating this patient, because active bleeding is present. The extent of trauma cannot be discerned adequately unless the patient undergoes examination under anesthesia. Examination under anesthesia will allow assessment of the perineum, vagina, and anal area to determine if there are any lacerations that require repair. The urethra is vulnerable to trauma and laceration, and it, too, must be inspected carefully.

Vulvar injuries are often deceleration injuries, most commonly secondary to straddle injuries (eg, falling on a balance bar or on the crossbar of a bicycle). Falls while playing at a playground or getting in or out of a bathtub or pool also have been associated with straddle injuries. Under this circumstance, the vagina, urethra, and hymen are frequently spared because of the overlying labia protecting these structures. However, the external genitalia of the pediatric patient are less well protected than the genitalia of the adult or adolescent. Bruising, abrasions, and hematoma in the area are the most common injuries. Lacerations are unusual unless the patient fell on a sharp object. Blunt trauma frequently spares the urethra and the hymen. Straddle injuries with their blunt trauma effects—ie, bruising and crush injuries—are to be distinguished from penetrating injuries.

Vulvar hematomas can be painful enough to result in the child's refusing to urinate. Associated periurethral swelling also may prohibit urination. Clinicians must distinguish between hematomas that have minimal distortion of anatomy and can be treated conservatively with analgesics and ice applied to the perineum on the one hand and hematomas that are more extensive and require examination under anesthesia and often primary repair on the other hand. It is important to establish that the child can void, because vulvar injuries, especially those that involve the periurethral area, can cause urethral spasm. A Foley catheter is often necessary when urination is a problem. Bladder drainage should be continued until the swelling subsides. In addition, perineal tears also can cause dysuria in the absence of direct injury to the urethra. This cause of dysuria is best treated with phenazopyridine (Pyridium) for 2–3 days until the abrasions have resolved. Sitz baths are also helpful in relieving pain. If pain persists, the possibility of a pelvic fracture must be evaluated. Large hematomas may dissect into the loose areolar tissue along the vaginal wall and the fascial planes overlying the pubic symphysis and lower abdominal wall. The expanding hematoma can result in pressure necrosis of the overlying skin. Evacuation of the hematoma relieves pain and prevents necrosis and secondary infection.

Large vulvar hematomas are best incised at the medial mucosal surface near the vaginal orifice. The wound should be irrigated and all devitalized tissue removed.

Ligation of bleeding vessels and placement of absorbable mattress sutures usually control bleeding. A closed drainage system (eg, Jackson-Pratt or Blake drain) facilitates removal of blood, reduces pain, and lowers the incidence of secondary infection.

As stated, perineal injuries can involve the rectum and anus. In a series of cases of anorectal trauma in pediatric patients, the authors noted that most injuries were due to sexual abuse.

Most vaginal injuries are the result of an object penetrating the vagina through the hymenal opening and producing a laceration or a tear of the hymenal ring. These injuries often occur in association with a fall on a sharp object. Hymenal trauma, although uncommon, can occur and usually is associated with penetrating injuries. No treatment usually is required, because bleeding often is minimal. Injury to the upper vagina must be considered with hymenal trauma. The thin vaginal mucosa is of limited distensibility and thus is lacerated easily. Penile penetration is directed toward the posterior vaginal wall, and the hymen tears usually are noted between the 4-o'clock and 8-o'clock positions. With deeper penetration, the rectovaginal septum may be torn, with extension into the rectum. A retroperitoneal hematoma, although infrequent, can result secondary to laceration of a major vessel in the pelvic floor. In all such cases of vaginal injury, examination under anesthesia may be required if assessment cannot be completed in an outpatient setting.

Some pediatric patients may present in shock because of blood loss. Child protective services must be contacted if any suspicion of abuse arises. Proper documentation on the record must reflect this discussion. If this report is not made and the child returns with more profound injuries, the initial treating physician may incur liability.

Because of the acute nature of the injury, ultrasonography of the pelvis would not be the best next step. Screening for sexually transmitted diseases and forensic evaluation should be undertaken whenever abuse is suspected. Laparoscopy is usually not necessary unless blunt trauma involving the abdomen is suspected.

Black CT, Pokorny WJ, McGill CW, Harberg FJ. Ano-rectal trauma in children. J Pediatr Surg 1982;17:501–4.

Gray MJ, Norton P, Treadwell K. Tampon-induced injuries. Obstet Gynecol 1981;58:667–8.

Holland AJ, Cohen RC, McKertich KM, Cass DT. Urethral trauma in children. Pediatr Surg Int 2001;17:58–61.

Merritt DF, Rimza ME, Muram D. Genital injuries in pediatric and adolescent girls. In: Sanfilippo JS, Muram D, Dewhurst J, Lee PA, editors. Pediatric and adolescent gynecology. 2nd ed. Philadelphia (PA): WB Saunders; 2001. p. 539–49.

Muram D. Genital tract injuries in the prepubertal child. Pediatr Ann 1986;15:616–20.

Scheidler MG, Schultz BL, Schall L, Ford HR. Mechanisms of blunt perineal injury in female pediatric patients. J Pediatr Surg 2000;35: 1317–9.

Tarman GJ, Kaplan GW, Lerman SL, McAleer IM, Losasso BE. Lower genitourinary injury and pelvic fractures in pediatric patients. Urology 2002;59:123–6.

21

Proper procedure for cardiopulmonary resuscitation

A second person arrives at the scene of active ongoing cardiopulmonary resuscitation (CPR) that is being performed on a woman by a single rescuer. The proper basic life support technique is to maintain compressions and breaths in a ratio of

     (A) 5:1
*   (B) 10:1
     (C) 10:2
     (D) 15:2

Health care providers should understand, and be prepared to practice, basic techniques of life support under any circumstances. The goal of resuscitation is to maintain adequate cerebral perfusion until cardiopulmonary function has been restored or additional help arrives. Resuscitation of adults should follow this sequence:

1. Assessment of unresponsiveness

2. Activation of emergency medical services

3. Provision of basic life support

Additionally, the appropriate use of defibrillators should be considered. Early use of defibrillators in cases of specific cardiac arrhythmias has demonstrated substantial improvement in outcome.

In 2-person CPR, 1 person is positioned at the victim's side and performs chest compressions. The second person, who is stationed at the victim's head, keeps the airway open and monitors the carotid pulse to assess the effectiveness of chest compressions.

Rescue breathing is dependent on an open airway. When a victim loses consciousness, the muscles of the jaw and neck relax. The tongue then may fall back and block the airway. Tilting the head back and lifting the jaw upward safely restores the airway. If there is reason to believe that the victim has sustained a neck injury, opening the airway by only lifting the jaw will prevent worsening the injury.

The person at the victim's head provides rescue breathing. The rate of chest compressions should be 100 compressions per minute. After 15 compressions, 2 breaths are provided. Each rescue breath should take a full 2 seconds. The victim exhales after the first breath, and with the first compression of the next cycle of chest compressions exhales the second breath. Rescue breathing may be mouth to mouth or mouth to nose. If the victim's chest does not rise with a rescue breath, the rescuer should reopen the airway and then attempt to give rescue breaths.

The rate, as well as the number, of compressions and breaths is the same for both 1-person and 2-person adult

CPR. After the patient is intubated, the rate of compressions and breathing will change to 5:1 regardless of whether there are 1 or 2 rescuers. A 5:1 ratio also is employed for infants and children, regardless of whether they are intubated. The ratio of compressions to breaths is 3:1 for a newborn.

Ahya SN, Flood K, Paranjothi S, Schaiff RA, editors. The Washington manual of medical therapeutics. 30th ed. Philadelphia (PA): Lippincott Williams & Wilkins; 2001. p. 181–94.

American Heart Association. Fundamentals of BLS for healthcare providers: American Heart Association fighting heart disease and stroke. Dallas (TX): American Heart Association; 2001.

American Heart Association Emergency Cardiac Care Committee and Subcommittees. Guidelines for cardiopulmonary resuscitation and emergency cardiac care. JAMA 1992;268:2171–298.

Myerburg RJ, Castellanos A. Cardiovascular collapse, cardiac arrest, and sudden cardiac death. In: Braunwald E, Fauci AS, Kasper DL, Hauser SL, Longo DL, Jameson JL, editors. Harrison's principles of internal medicine. 15th ed. New York (NY): McGraw-Hill; 2001. p. 228–33.

22

Surgical management of stress incontinence

You are counseling a 55-year-old woman regarding surgical management of stress urinary incontinence. She specifically asks about the tension-free vaginal tape (TVT) sling operation. You tell her that the most common perioperative complication of this procedure is

      (A) long-term urinary retention
      (B) unplanned laparotomy
      (C) mesh erosion
 *   (D) bladder perforation
      (E) hemorrhage

The TVT sling operation was first described in 1996. In this operation, a small vaginal incision is used to insert a polypropylene mesh tape under the midurethra (see Fig. 22-1). The tape is inserted with specially designed curved needles. The sling is placed without significant tension and is not sewn in place. Although frequently performed with the patient under general regional anesthesia, this procedure also can be performed with the patient under intravenous sedation. Appropriate candidates for this procedure include women with stress urinary incontinence and urethral hypermobility. Limited data support its use in women with prior urethropexy, women with evidence of intrinsic urethral sphincter deficiency, and patients with a well-supported bladder neck.

In published studies, the TVT sling procedure results in objective cure of stress incontinence in 80–100% of women, although follow-up generally has been limited to less than 24 months. Perioperative complications occur in

approximately 9% of cases. The most common complication is bladder perforation (4–6%), which can be recognized intraoperatively by cystoscopy. Bladder perforation can be managed with postoperative bladder drainage and rarely leads to sequelae. Voiding difficulties after insertion of the TVT sling are common, but urinary retention lasting more than 1 week occurs in fewer than 3% of cases. Other, less common complications include unintended laparotomy; significant intraoperative bleeding; mesh erosion; and injuries to vessels, nerves, and intestine.

Other options for surgical management of stress urinary incontinence include retropubic urethropexies (ie, Burch colposuspension or the Marshall–Marchetti–Krantz procedure) and traditional suburethral sling procedures. Retropubic urethropexies and suburethral slings have high cure rates (75–88% at 4 years) and a low incidence of serious complications.

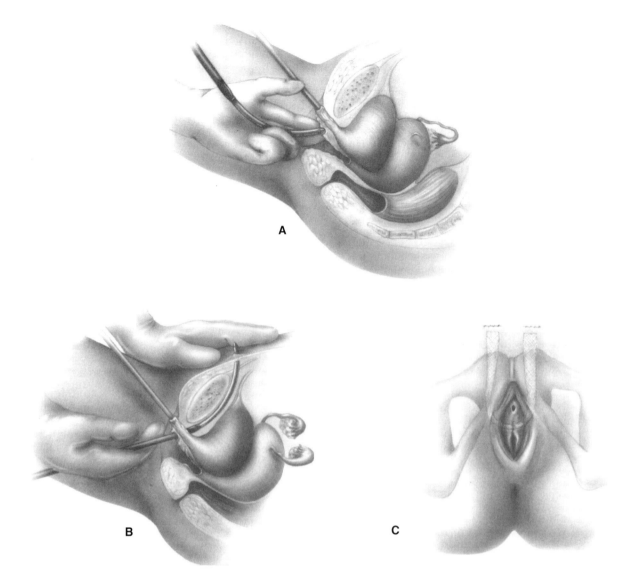

FIG. 22-1. In the tension-free vaginal tape (TVT) sling operation, a small vaginal incision is used to insert a polypropylene mesh tape under the midurethra using specially designed curved needles. The sling is placed without significant tension and is not sewn in place. (**A**) The tip of the needle is angulated laterally, and the endopelvic fascia is perforated just behind the inferior surface of the pubic symphysis. (**B**) After perforation of the rectus fascia, a hand is used to palpate the needle tip suprapubically and to guide the needle to the abdominal incision. (**C**) The incisions are closed. The completed procedure allows fixation of the tape below the midurethra with the ends just below the skin level. (Kohli N, Miklos JR, Lucente V. Tension-free vaginal tape: a minimally invasive technique for treating female SUI. Contemp Ob/Gyn 1999;44:145–7. Figures copyright © V. Montegrande & Co., Inc., 1999.)

Bezerra CA, Bruschini H, Cody DJ. Suburethral sling operations for urinary incontinence in women (Cochrane Review). In: The Cochrane Library, Issue 2, 2003. Oxford: Update Software.

Klutke JJ, Klutke CG. The tension-free vaginal tape procedure: innovative surgery for incontinence. Curr Opin Obstet Gynecol 2001; 13:529–32.

Klutke C, Siegel S, Carlin B, Paszkiewicz E, Kirkemo A, Klutke J. Urinary retention after tension-free vaginal tape procedure: incidence and treatment. Urology 2001;58:697–701.

Leach GE, Dmochowski RR, Appell RA, Blaivas JG, Hadley HR, Luber KM, et al. Female Stress Urinary Incontinence Clinical Guidelines Panel summary report on surgical management of female stress urinary incontinence. The American Urological Association. J Urol 1997;158: 875–80.

Tamussino KF, Hanzal E, Kolle D, Ralph G, Riss PA. Tension-free vaginal tape operation: results of the Austrian registry. Obstet Gynecol 2001;98:732–6.

23

Factor V Leiden mutation

A 23-year-old woman requests a prescription for an oral contraceptive. She has no current health problems. She had an uncomplicated delivery last year. She informs you that her mother was treated for deep vein thrombosis (DVT) and pulmonary embolism. The patient's body mass index is 23 kg/m², and her general examination findings are normal. The most likely cause of thrombophilic disorder to be identified with screening is

       (A) antiphospholipid antibodies
       (B) protein C deficiency
       (C) protein S deficiency
  * (D) Factor V Leiden mutation
       (E) hyperhomocystinemia

It has long been known that a woman's risk of developing DVT increases when oral contraceptives are taken. Whereas it is clear that the risk increases with tablets containing at least 50 µg ethinyl estradiol (EE), it is not evident that the risk is significantly lessened with the use of tablets containing 20 µg EE compared with 30 µg EE. The overall risk of DVT in women who use the higher-dose EE has been estimated at 30–40 events per 100,000 women-years, approximately 3 times the rate experienced by nonusers of oral contraceptives and roughly half the rate experienced by pregnant women.

Over the past decade, research has increased our knowledge of inherited and acquired thrombophilic states, including how to identify women at risk. Approximately 50–60% of patients with a potentially inheritable thrombophilic disorder will not experience a thrombotic event until a precipitating factor occurs (eg, use of oral contraception, pregnancy, trauma, immobilization, or surgery). The following hypercoagulable states have been identified:

* Factor V Leiden mutation
* Prothrombin gene mutation G20210A
* Antiphospholipid antibody syndrome
* Protein S deficiency
* Protein C deficiency
* Antithrombin III deficiency
* Hyperhomocystinemia

The presence of thrombophilic disorders should be suspected when a prior family member has had a thrombotic event. Factor V Leiden is the most likely mutation and varies with ethnic background. Among inpatients who experienced a documented thrombosis, a Factor V Leiden mutation was found in 40–70% of the individuals and a prothrombin gene mutation in 30–80%. It is important to note that the assays for both of these conditions are reliable during an acute episode of thrombosis, as well as in the presence of anticoagulation. Box 23-1 lists diagnostic tests for thrombophilia.

Antiphospholipid syndrome is an acquired hypercoagulable state and can manifest itself as a venous or arterial thrombosis. It has been associated with unexplained idiopathic thrombocytopenia, recurrent pregnancy loss, intrauterine growth restriction, and early preeclampsia. Screening for the presence of antiphospholipid antibodies and protein C and protein S deficiency should be considered in patients with these clinical problems in spite of the low prevalence.

Hyperhomocystinemia may be acquired or inherited and is associated with increased risk of venous thrombosis. It also has been associated with early thrombus formation in coronary artery disease. The relative incidence is low. Comprehensive routine screening prior to initiation of birth control is not cost-effective.

BOX 23-1

Diagnostic Tests for Thrombophilia

Highest Priority
* Increased resistance to activated protein C
* Factor V Leiden mutation
* Prothrombin gene mutation
* Increased factor VIII
* Increased homocysteine
* Presence of lupus anticoagulant

Intermediate Priority
* Decreased protein C
* Decreased protein S
* Decreased antithrombin III
* Increased anticardiolipin antibodies

Modified from Seligsohn U, Lubetsy A. Genetic susceptibility to venous thrombosis. N Engl J Med 2001;344: 1222–31.

American College of Obstetricians and Gynecologists. Prevention of deep vein thrombosis and pulmonary embolism. ACOG Practice Bulletin 21. Washington, DC: ACOG; 2000.

Seligsohn U, Lubetsky A. Genetic susceptibility to venous thrombosis. N Engl J Med 2001;344:1222–31.

24

Pelvic mass intraoperative consultation

A general surgical colleague requests an intraoperative consultation. She has operated on a 14-year-old nulligravid adolescent girl for presumed appendicitis. She found the patient to have a twisted right ovarian solid mass measuring 8 cm × 5 cm. A salpingo-oophorectomy has been performed. Frozen section analysis reveals a malignant ovarian germ cell tumor. Your intraoperative evaluation reveals no gross evidence of disease. The most appropriate next step is

  (A) total abdominal hysterectomy and contralateral salpingo-oophorectomy
  (B) closing the abdomen and waiting for the final pathology report
  * (C) surgical staging with preservation of the uterus and contralateral tube and ovary
  (D) wedge resection of the remaining ovary

Less than 5% of all ovarian cancers are germ cell tumors. However, in children and adolescents, more than 60% of ovarian neoplasms are germ cell tumors, and about one third of these tumors are malignant. Malignant germ cell tumors usually occur in adolescents and younger women; the median age is 20 years. These aggressive tumors are usually curable with appropriate surgery and chemotherapy. It is unusual during the initial diagnosis and treatment to have to completely remove the reproductive organs. Therefore, total abdominal hysterectomy with contralateral salpingo-oophorectomy is an inappropriate treatment. Subsequent childbearing after conservative surgery and chemotherapy is an important goal, because the majority of women with germ cell tumors have early-stage disease and an excellent prognosis.

Malignant germ cell tumors have a rapid growth rate, and most women present with an abdominal or pelvic mass or pain, depending on the size of the mass and the age of the patient. Approximately 10% of patients present with acute abdominal pain, generally due to intracapsular hemorrhage, torsion, or rupture. As in the patient described, the initial symptoms of germ cell tumors can be misdiagnosed as acute appendicitis.

Malignant germ cell tumors spread by intraperitoneal surface dissemination or via the lymphatic system. Therefore, surgical staging to evaluate both these routes of spread is necessary. Surgical staging with a unilateral oophorectomy or salpingo-oophorectomy is the surgical treatment of choice. Surgical staging includes pelvic and paraaortic lymph node sampling; peritoneal washings from the pelvis and the tumor surface; omental sampling; evaluation of both hemidiaphragms with biopsies or cytology; biopsies of adhesions or suspicious areas; and

peritoneal sampling of the surface of the bladder, pelvic cul-de-sac, and paracolic gutters. Staging also includes meticulous inspection of the small and large bowel and visualization of the liver, gallbladder, stomach, pancreas, kidneys, and spleen. Dysgerminomas have a predilection for lymphatic spread, and lymph node assessment will guide subsequent chemotherapy. Surgical staging will identify women with stage IIIC disease (ie, patients with lymph nodes positive for disease). This staging will allow selection of appropriate chemotherapy in women with advanced-stage disease and prevent the administration of chemo-therapy to women with stage I disease.

Closing the abdomen and waiting for the final pathology report will mandate either a second surgical procedure or selection of chemotherapy based on incomplete data. Malignant germ cell tumors are highly curable with combination chemotherapy, usually bleomycin sulfate, etoposide, and cisplatin (Platinol). Because these tumors have a rapid growth rate, chemotherapy generally is administered immediately, even when staging is incomplete. Accurate surgical staging at the time of surgery will prevent either overtreatment or the need to select a regimen using incomplete information.

Germ cell tumors are generally unilateral. Dysgerminomas are bilateral in 10–15% of cases. At surgery, bilaterally enlarged ovaries usually are observed. Wedge resection of a normal-appearing ovary offers little diagnostic information. Additional ovarian surgery increases the possibility of adhesive disease and the potential for decreased fertility. Therefore, if the contralateral ovary is normal in size, shape, and consistency, it should be inspected carefully but not be bivalved, and biopsy should not be performed. Gynecologists should understand the steps involved in staging ovarian cancer and, if necessary, ask for assistance with the technical aspects of the surgical procedures.

DiSaia PJ, Creasman WT. Clinical gynecologic oncology. 6th ed. St. Louis (MO): Mosby; 2002. p. 351–77.

Hurteau JA, Williams SJ. Ovarian germ cell tumors. In: Rubin SC, Sutton GP, editors. Ovarian cancer. 2nd ed. Philadelphia (PA): Lippincott Williams & Wilkins; 2001. p. 371–82.

Talerman A. Germ cell tumors of the ovary. In: Kurman RJ, editor. Blaustein's pathology of the female genital tract. 5th ed. New York (NY): Springer; 2002. p. 967–1033.

25

Lichen sclerosus in the pediatric patient

In a pediatric patient, for which one of the following conditions (shown in Fig. 25-1) would you prescribe clobetasol propionate and inquire about the possibility of sexual abuse?

(A) Vulvar adhesions
* (B) Lichen sclerosus
(C) Embryonal rhabdomyosarcoma
(D) Müllerian agenesis

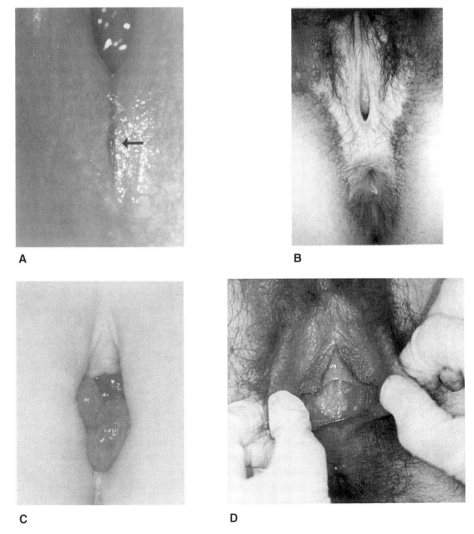

FIG. 25-1. (Emans SJ, Laufer MR, Goldstein DP. Pediatric and adolescent gynecology. 4th ed. Philadelphia [PA]: Lippincott–Raven; 1998.)

The condition for which you would prescribe clobetasol propionate and inquire about the possibility of sexual abuse is lichen sclerosus. Lichen sclerosus is an inflammatory skin disease in adults and children that can cause itching and soreness. It is most commonly diagnosed in the anogenital area, but 15–20% of the time it is found on other areas of the body. The possible causes are trauma, autoimmunity, and infection. Koebner's phenomenon occurs when scarring, secondary to friction, and trauma induce the skin lesions typical of the disorder. Parietal cell and thyroid autoantibodies have been identified in patients with the disease but are not necessarily associated with severity. Alopecia areata, vitiligo, and cicatricial pemphigoid are skin disorders commonly found in these patients, and such diseases as diabetes mellitus also are common. In girls, infective organisms commonly seen in uncomplicated cases are streptococcus and *Escherichia coli*, along with organisms causing diseases associated with abuse (ie, *Candida* species, *Gardnerella vaginalis*, and human papillomavirus).

Other common symptoms include dyspareunia and urinary discomfort. It is important for the practitioner to remember that some patients may be asymptomatic. Gross examination may reveal ivory-colored papules, plaques, fissuring, erosions, and hyperkeratosis. Biopsy in children is usually not necessary, because the association with cancer in children is negligible to absent. In adults, however, as many as 4–5% may have an associated squamous cell carcinoma. The disease is a hypotrophic dystrophy characterized by flattening of rete pegs, a band of monocytic infiltrate in the subdermal layer, hyalinization of the subdermal tissues, and keratinization. Estrogen, testosterone, and progesterone treatments have fallen out of favor.

The treatment is 1–2% hydrocortisone cream. If the patient fails to respond, topical clobetasol propionate, a potent corticosteroid, should be administered twice a day, followed by a taper. A 30-g tube should last for 3 months. Surgery is indicated only if the clitoris is buried, the labia are fused, or the vaginal introitus has become stenosed. Rarely, if ever, is surgery indicated in the pediatric age group.

Lichen sclerosus in the pediatric age group has been linked to sexual abuse. Trauma to the genital area can result in Koebner's phenomenon and subsequent lichen sclerosus. Vulvar and perianal bruising, erosion, and fissures on a background of pallor suggest the potential of abuse. The diagnosis of lichen sclerosus, however, should not imply sexual abuse.

Labial adhesions are thought to occur as a result of local irritation and scratching. Examination reveals a thin, avascular line of fusion in the midline. Most children are asymptomatic, but difficulty with urination or menstruation can occur. The treatment is the application of estrogen cream, zinc oxide, or a weak corticosteroid for 10–14 days. If this treatment is ineffective, the gentle use of a lubricated cotton-tipped swab or sound may break down the membrane.

Most genital tumors found in adults rarely occur in children. A very unusual tumor specific to children is embryonal carcinoma of the vagina (sarcoma botryoides). It most often originates from the upper vagina or cervix and arises from undifferentiated mesenchymal tissue. Tumor spread is rapid, and extension is through the subvaginal tissues. On gross examination, these tumors have a grapelike appearance. The management is generally chemotherapy followed by surgery, irradiation, or both. The survival rate is reported as high as 90%.

Müllerian agenesis is failure of the upper vagina and uterus to form. This abnormality, also termed the Mayer–Rokitansky–Kuster–Hauser syndrome, presents as a blind vagina. The patient is infertile, and treatment is by progressive vaginal dilation or a surgical vaginoplasty procedure to restore sexual function. All patients with müllerian anomalies should have an assessment of the urinary system to determine if a renal anomaly is present.

Edwards S, Handfield-Jones S, Gull S. National guideline on the management of vulval conditions. Int J STD AIDS 2002;13:411–5.

Mroueh J, Muram D. Common problems in pediatric gynecology: new developments. Curr Opin Obstet Gynecol 1999;11:463–6.

Powell JJ, Wojnarowska F. Lichen sclerosus. Lancet 1999;353:1777–83.

Warrington S, de San Lazaro C. Lichen sclerosus et atrophicus and sexual abuse. Arch Dis Child 1996;75:512–6.

26
Breast cancer risks

A 59-year-old woman has been undergoing hormone therapy (HT) of 0.625 mg conjugated equine estrogen (CEE) plus 2.5 mg medroxyprogesterone acetate (MPA) for the past 5 years. Her history reveals hypertension and type 2 diabetes mellitus, which are controlled with medications. Breast cancer was recently diagnosed in a great-aunt. Which of the following poses the greatest risk of breast cancer for this patient?

  (A) Family history of breast cancer
  (B) Current history of hypertension
  (C) Current history of diabetes mellitus
* (D) Use of HT

Breast cancer is diagnosed in nearly 200,000 women each year in the United States. Risk assessment for this disease is important because it allows clinicians to make decisions on when to begin screening, how often to screen, whether the use of medications such as HT carries any risk, and whether the use of prophylactic medications such as tamoxifen citrate (Nolvadex) is warranted.

To assist clinicians in risk assessment for a given patient, investigators have developed prediction models. Two of the more widely used models are the Gail model and the Claus model.

The Gail model incorporates age, number of first-degree relatives with breast cancer, age at menarche, age at first live birth, and the number of breast biopsies into its risk prediction. An overall risk score is developed from these categories and then is multiplied by an adjusted population risk of breast cancer to determine an individual's risk. The Claus model incorporates more information about family history of breast cancer but excludes other risk factors from its calculations. Of the two models, the Gail model appears to be the more accurate for women undergoing routine mammographic studies, whereas the Claus model is more applicable for women with at least one first- or second-degree relative with breast cancer. For the patient under discussion, because her relative with breast cancer was neither first nor second degree, family history does not contribute significantly to her risk of breast cancer. Although age at menopause and other risk factors consistently have been associated with breast cancer, hypertension and diabetes mellitus have not been shown to be consistent risk factors in most studies.

The role of HT as a risk factor for breast cancer has been debated for years. It appears that current use of HT for 4 years or longer carries a relative risk of 1.3–1.4 for breast cancer compared with women who do not use HT. However, the absolute risk is relatively modest. In the Women's Health Initiative, a recently completed randomized clinical trial, the absolute risk for breast cancer for women who used CEE plus MPA was 8 cases per 10,000 women–years. Hormone therapy was not associated with an increased risk of breast cancer prior to 4 years of use. However, one cannot assume that shorter duration of HT use carries no risk, because in most instances breast cancer has a latency period of several years from development of a new lesion until detection. Furthermore, a growing amount of information suggests that use of estrogen alone (as opposed to estrogen in combination with a progestin, ie, usually MPA in the United States) carries less risk for breast cancer among HT users. Unfortunately, except for women who have undergone hysterectomy, the tradeoff is an increased risk of endometrial cancer when estrogen is used in an unopposed fashion. Thus, for this patient, use of combination HT poses the greatest potential risk for breast cancer.

Armstrong K, Eisen A, Weber B. Assessing the risk of breast cancer. N Engl J Med 2000;342:564–71.

Breast cancer and hormone replacement therapy: collaborative reanalysis of data from 51 epidemiological studies of 52,705 women with breast cancer and 108,411 women without breast cancer. Collaborative Group on Hormonal Factors in Breast Cancer. Lancet 1997;350: 1047–59.

Ross RK, Paganini-Hill A, Wan PC, Pike MC. Effect of hormone replacement therapy on breast cancer risk: estrogen versus estrogen plus progestin. J Natl Cancer Inst 2000;92:328–32.

Rossouw JE, Anderson GL, Prentice RL, LaCroix AZ, Kooperberg C, Stefanick ML, et al. Writing Group for the Women's Health Initiative Investigators. Risks and benefits of estrogen plus progestin in healthy postmenopausal women—principal results from the Women's Health Initiative randomized controlled trial. JAMA 2002;288:321–33.

Schairer C, Lubin J, Troisi R, Sturgeon S, Brinton L, Hoover R. Menopausal estrogen and estrogen-progestin replacement therapy and breast cancer risk. JAMA 2000;283:485–91.

Weiss LK, Burkman RT, Cushing-Haugen KL, Voigt LF, Simon MS, Daling JR, et al. Hormone replacement therapy regimens and breast cancer risk. Obstet Gynecol 2002;100:1148–58.

27

Screening tests for lesbians

Your new patient is a healthy 52-year-old woman who has not sought medical care in 5 years. She is 1.65 m (65 in.) tall, weighs 81.6 kg (180 lb), and, except for smoking 1 pack of cigarettes per day, has an unremarkable medical history. She has been in a monogamous lesbian relationship for 3 years and reports no problems. Which of the following screening tests is most appropriate, based on her risk factors?

      (A) Test for chlamydial infection
*   (B) Pap test
      (C) Chest radiography
      (D) Rapid plasma reagin (RPR) test

Approximately 4–10% of women in the United States identify themselves as lesbians. Research suggests that lesbians seek medical care less frequently than do heterosexual women. Reasons for this behavior include fear of interaction with health care professionals and misconceptions about disease risk.

Health professionals can put lesbian patients at ease in several ways. Brochures about lesbian health issues can be displayed in visible locations in the office or health center. Patient intake forms should inquire about the partner with whom the patient lives and whether the patient has sex with men, women, or both. When gathering the history of a lesbian, ask about her relationships using questions similar to ones you ask heterosexual patients. Sample questions, therefore, include the following:

- How long have you and your partner been together?
- What does your partner do for a living?
- Does your partner have any children?

As yet, there are no definitive data to indicate whether midlife lesbians have a higher incidence of chronic diseases than do their heterosexual peers. It does appear, however, that as a group, lesbians have a higher prevalence of risk factors that might affect the development of such diseases (see Box 27-1).

Most lesbians have had heterosexual intercourse at some point in their lives, but the overall frequency of such encounters may be considerably lower than for heterosexual women. Nevertheless, screening for sexually transmitted diseases should be performed using the same guidelines in both groups of women. Testing for chlamydial infection and syphilis by means of an RPR test is not necessary in this asymptomatic patient at this time. Despite the fact that this woman is a smoker, screening chest radiography is not warranted. Both annual chest radiography

---

BOX 27-1

Risk Factors for Chronic Disease in Lesbians Compared with Heterosexual Women

- Nulliparity or fewer pregnancies
- Limited use of hormonal contraceptives
- Higher prevalence of obesity
- Higher rates of alcohol consumption and cigarette smoking

---

and sputum cytology have failed to show a survival advantage for lung cancer patients.

Screening studies of lesbians who have reported no prior sex with men have identified human papillomavirus (HPV) and abnormal Pap test findings. This finding most likely is due to the fact that 70–80% of women who have sex with women also have had male sexual partners in the past, which allows for the acquisition of HPV during their own or their partner's history of heterosexual intercourse. Current recommendations for Pap test screening for women who have sex with women are the same as the recommendations for heterosexual women. This patient's smoking history is a risk factor for cervical cancer.

Carroll NM. Optimal gynecologic and obstetric care for lesbians. Obstet Gynecol 1999;93:611–3.

Cochran SD, Mays VM, Bowen D, Gage S, Bybee D, Roberts SJ, et al. Cancer-related risk indicators and preventive screening behaviors among lesbians and bisexual women. Am J Public Health 2001;91: 591–7.

Gruskin EP, Hart S, Gordon N, Ackerson L. Patterns of cigarette smoking and alcohol use among lesbians and bisexual women enrolled in a large health maintenance organization. Am J Public Health 2001;91: 976–9.

Marrazzo JM, Stine K, Koutsky LA. Genital human papillomavirus infection in women who have sex with women: a review. Am J Obstet Gynecol 2000;183:770–4.

28

Substance abuse in physicians

You are told by a hospital staff nurse that for the past several months, a physician in your department has arrived late for work and has become irritable and short-tempered with the nursing staff. This week, two other nurses tell you that the physician appeared to have alcohol on his breath and that they are concerned about his interactions with patients. The most appropriate initial step for you to take is

(A) to tell the physician that you will file a report with the department chair
(B) to evaluate the credibility of the nursing complaints
(C) to report the physician to the National Practitioner Data Bank
(D) to report the physician to the state medical board
* (E) to report your concerns to the hospital's chief of staff or physician well-being committee

An impaired physician is unable to fulfill personal or professional responsibilities. The impairment may be caused by drug dependency, alcoholism, physical illness, or psychiatric illness. It is estimated that the risk of addiction in physicians closely approximates that of the general population and that 15% of physicians will be impaired at some point in their career. Substance abuse disorders are treatable illnesses and, like other psychiatric or biobehavorial conditions, may be regarded as disabilities under federal law.

As part of its obligation to protect patients from harm, and as required by the Joint Commission on Accreditation of Healthcare Organizations, the medical staff must implement a process to identify and manage matters of individual physician health that is separate from the credentialing and disciplinary functions. Furthermore, the process must educate the medical staff about illness and impairment recognition issues specific to physicians. Many hospitals create a practitioner well-being committee to perform this function. Such a mechanism will assist impaired physicians in matters related to health, chemical dependency, mental illness, or behavior.

The hospital's response to an impaired physician will depend on the circumstances of the case. In many instances, hospitals and medical staffs require physicians with substance abuse problems to enter into, and successfully complete, a supervised rehabilitation program. In some cases, it may be appropriate to restrict or revoke the physician's privileges until the successful completion of rehabilitation. Rather than discipline, the intent is support, assistance, and rehabilitation until the physician is fully productive again.

The most appropriate initial step is to report your concerns regarding your colleague to the hospital's chief of staff or physician well-being committee. The committee typically assists in obtaining evaluation and rehabilitation services, monitors the progress of physicians through the

rehabilitation or treatment program, and provides an informal confidential access point for persons who voluntarily seek counsel and assistance. A quarterly summary of the committee's general activities, without mention of specific physician names, should be reported to the hospital's medical executive committee.

According to the American Medical Association's Code of Ethics, physicians have an ethical obligation to report a peer who is impaired or who has a behavioral problem that may adversely affect his or her patients or practice of medicine to a hospital well-being committee, a hospital administrator, or an external program for impaired physicians. A timely and appropriate referral may save a physician's life and can help ensure patient quality of care.

Although you could report your colleague to the department chair, voluntary compliance by the impaired physician with counseling and rehabilitation as required by the well-being committee usually obviates the need for reporting to the department chair or the medical executive committee. Failure to comply with well-being committee requirements, failure to resolve the case, or a determination by the well-being committee that patient safety or quality of care is at risk (ie, the physician is providing unsafe treatment) will result in the committee's notification of the medical staff leadership (eg, the department chair or the medical executive committee). Any adverse action by the department chair or medical executive committee that involves credentialing and peer review actions, such as limitation, reduction, or loss of clinical privileges or medical staff membership, necessitates notification of the state medical board. Medical professional liability insurance carriers must file with the state medical boards reports on settlement judgments and arbitration awards. The state boards, in turn, report these settlements to the National Practitioner Data Bank. Similarly, only adverse clinical actions, not entry into a counseling and treatment program, are reported to the National Practitioner Data Bank by the state medical board.

It is not your responsibility to evaluate the credibility of the nursing complaints about your colleague; instead, it is the responsibility of the well-being committee to evaluate the credibility of any complaint, concern, or allegation about a physician.

Avery DM, Daniel WD, McCormick MB. The impaired physician. Prim Care Update Ob Gyns 2000;7:154–60.

Boisaubin EV, Levine RE. Identifying and assisting the impaired physician. Am J Med Sci 2001;322:31–6.

Joint Commission on Accreditation of Healthcare Organizations. 2002 Hospital accreditation standards. Oakbrook Terrace (IL): JCAHO; 2002. p. 290.

29

Asymptomatic microscopic hematuria

A 44-year-old woman with a 20-pack-per-year smoking history has had 3 urinary tract infections successfully treated by antibiotic therapy over the past 6 months. On a follow-up office visit, urinalysis shows 10–20 erythrocytes per high-power field without evidence of leukocytes or bacteria. Intravenous pyelography (IVP) is performed and the findings reported to be normal. The most appropriate next step in the evaluation of this patient is

*   (A) cystoscopy
       (B) renal ultrasonography
       (C) spiral computed tomography (CT) scan
       (D) another microscopic urinalysis in 6 months

Asymptomatic microscopic hematuria commonly is discovered on urinalysis. Studies estimate the prevalence to be 0.2–16%. Blood in the urine may originate from any site along the urinary tract. Causes range from minor findings that do not require treatment to malignant lesions. The goal in the evaluation of any patient with asymptomatic microscopic hematuria is to detect urologic disease at an early stage, when it is amenable to cure and before it causes significant morbidity.

Although the recommendation is controversial, the American Urologic Association consensus panel has defined asymptomatic microscopic hematuria as 3 or more red blood cells per high-power field on microscopic evaluation of the urinary sediment from 2 of 3 properly collected midstream clean-catch samples. High-risk patients with any degree of hematuria should be considered for a complete evaluation.

In this patient, risk factors for bladder cancer are smoking and age older than 40 years. Cystoscopy should be the next step in management and is considered the gold standard for the detection of a bladder tumor. The risk factors for cancer of the urinary tract are shown in Box 29-1. Patients older than 40 years and individuals at any age with risk factors should undergo outpatient cystoscopy at the initial assessment.

Imaging techniques are useful in the detection of renal cell carcinoma, transitional cell carcinoma of the renal pelvis or ureter, urolithiasis, and upper urinary tract infection. They are of limited use in the detection of bladder cancer.

BOX 29-1

Risk Factors for Malignancy of the Urinary Tract

- Smoking
- Age older than 40 years
- Occupational chemical exposure
- Analgesic or laxative abuse
- Pelvic irradiation
- Cyclophosphamide exposure

Adapted from Grossfeld GD, Litwin MS, Wolf JS Jr, Hricak H, Shuler CL, Agerter DC, et al. Evaluation of asymptomatic microscopic hematuria in adults: the American Urological Association best practice policy, I: definition, detection, prevalence, and etiology. Urology 2001;57: 599–603.

An IVP would not be effective in the detection of bladder cancer. Although IVP is useful for the detection of transitional cell cancers of the renal pelvis, it does not distinguish solid from cystic masses and has limited sensitivity in detecting renal masses smaller than 3 cm.

Renal ultrasonography has been increasingly used in addition to or in place of IVP. It is an excellent diagnostic modality in characterizing renal cysts. It is not sufficiently sensitive to detect small solid renal masses, however.

A spiral CT scan is the best imaging modality for evaluating urinary stones, renal or perirenal infection, and solid and cystic renal lesions. It is not reliable for the diagnosis of bladder lesions.

In this patient, who is at increased risk for malignancy, it would be inappropriate to repeat a urinalysis in 6 months.

Grossfeld GD, Carroll PR. Evaluation of asymptomatic microscopic hematuria. Urol Clin North Am 1998;25:661–76.

Grossfeld GD, Litwin MS, Wolf JS Jr, Hricak H, Shuler CL, Agerter DC, et al. Evaluation of asymptomatic microscopic hematuria in adults: the American Urological Association best practice policy, I: definition, detection, prevalence, and etiology. Urology 2001;57:599–603.

Grossfeld GD, Litwin MS, Wolf JS Jr, Hricak H, Shuler CL, Agerter DC, et al. Evaluation of asymptomatic microscopic hematuria in adults: the American Urological Association best practice policy, II: patient evaluation, cytology, voided markers, imaging, cystoscopy, nephrology evaluation, and follow-up. Urology 2001;57:604–10.

30

Cervicitis and postcoital bleeding

A 24-year-old sexually active woman taking oral contraceptives presents to her gynecologist with a 1-month history of daily spotting. She takes her oral contraceptives correctly and has 28-day cycles with 4 days of bleeding. The abnormal bleeding is aggravated by intercourse. A physical examination reveals a prominent ectropion and a mucopurulent discharge. The most appropriate test to confirm your diagnosis is

        (A) a pregnancy test
        (B) endovaginal ultrasonography
*   (C) chlamydial infection and gonorrhea testing
        (D) serum thyroid-stimulating hormone measurement

Abnormal bleeding is one of the most frequent problems encountered by gynecologists. It has multiple causes that range from hormonal disturbances to cancer. The most common causes of abnormal uterine bleeding in the reproductive-aged woman are complications of pregnancy (eg, threatened, incomplete, or missed abortion and ectopic pregnancy). In any case of abnormal bleeding in a reproductive-aged woman, even in a patient who uses oral contraceptives, a pregnancy test should be performed. In this patient, however, findings on physical examination suggest another cause of the bleeding.

Anatomic uterine and cervical lesions such as submucosal myomas, which can be detected by ultrasonography, can produce symptoms of prolonged and excessive bleeding. Cervical lesions such as ectropion, polyps, and cervicitis can cause irregular bleeding, particularly postcoital spotting. Mucopurulent cervicitis is an inflammatory condition diagnosed by the gross visualization of yellow mucopurulent material or the presence of 10 or more polymorphonucleocytes per high-power field on Gram stain of the endocervix (Fig. 30-1; see color plate). Approximately 40% of patients with sexually transmitted diseases have mucopurulent cervicitis, and more than 60% of these women are asymptomatic. Symptoms that suggest cervical infection include vaginal discharge, deep dyspareunia, and postcoital bleeding. The organism most commonly associated with mucopurulent cervicitis is *Chlamydia trachomatis*, but screening also should be done for *Neisseria gonorrhoeae*, because it frequently is associated with chlamydial infection.

Chlamydial and gonorrheal infections are the main preventable causes of cervicitis and pelvic inflammatory disease, which in turn are the most common causes of infertility and ectopic pregnancy in the United States. Yearly testing for these infections should be a regular part of health care for women and men younger than 25 years. This group includes adolescents; rates of both diseases are highest in 15- to 19-year-old women. A recent study estimated the prevalence of untreated gonorrheal and chlamydial infections in a general population setting using a ligase chain reaction assay from urine specimens. The study showed that the estimated number of undiagnosed chlamydial and gonorrheal infections in adults aged 18–35 years approached or exceeded the number of infections that were diagnosed and treated annually (8.3% versus 7.9%).

As this patient is being examined, it is appropriate to use a swab to obtain an endocervical sample for ligase chain reaction testing of *C trachomatis* and *N gonorrhoeae*. Studies show that the new DNA amplification assays, such as polymerase chain reaction and ligase chain reaction assays, are highly sensitive and specific when used on cervical and urine samples and exceed the sensitivity of culture. With these new testing kits, screening for chlamydial and gonorrheal infections is easier and more sensitive than using the culture technique. Box 30-1

BOX 30-1

Current Treatment Regimens for Chlamydial and Gonorrheal Mucopurulent Cervicitis

Chlamydia Mucopurulent Cervicitis
Azithromycin, 1 g orally in a single dose
   OR
Doxycycline, 100 mg orally twice a day for 7 d
Alternative regimens:
Erythromycin base, 500 mg orally 4 times a day for 7 d
Erythromycin ethylsuccinate, 800 mg orally 4 times a day for 7 d
Ofloxacin, 300 mg orally twice a day for 7 d
Levofloxacin, 500 mg orally once a day for 7 d

Gonorrhea Mucopurulent Cervicitis
Cefixime, 400 mg orally in a single dose
   OR
Ceftriaxone, 125 mg intramuscularly in a single dose
   OR
Ciprofloxacin, 500 mg orally in a single dose
   OR
Ofloxacin, 400 mg orally in a single dose
   OR
Levofloxacin, 250 mg orally in a single dose
   PLUS

If chlamydial infection is not ruled out
Azithromycin, 1 g orally
   OR
Doxycycline, 100 mg orally twice a day for 7 days

Modified from Sexually transmitted diseases treatment guidelines 2002. Centers for Disease Control and Prevention. MMWR Recomm Rep 2002;51(RR-6):45, 51, 52.

BOX 30-2

Current Treatment Regimens for Chlamydial and Gonorrheal Mucopurulent Cervicitis in Pregnancy

Chlamydia Mucopurulent Cervicitis
Erythromycin ethylsuccinate, 800 mg orally 4 times a day for 7 d
   OR
Erythromycin ethylsuccinate, 400 mg orally 4 times a day for 14 d
   OR
Azithromycin 1 g orally, single dose

Gonorrhea Mucopurulent Cervicitis
Pregnant women would not be treated with quinolones or tetracyclines. Pregnant women infected with *Neisseria gonorrhoeae* should be treated with a recommended or alternate cephalosporin (see Box 30-1).

Women who cannot tolerate a single, 2 g cephalosporin should receive a single dose of spectinomycin intramuscularly

---

Modified from Sexually transmitted diseases treatment guidelines 2002. Centers for Disease Control and Prevention. MMWR Recomm Rep 2002;51(RR-6):47, 48, 54.

---

shows current treatment regimens for gonorrheal and chlamydial infections, and Box 30-2 shows treatment regimens for pregnant women with these infections.

Current guidelines from the Centers for Disease Control and Prevention recommend repeated screening 3–4 months after a treatment regimen for chlamydial infection. The agency continues to recommend annual chlamydial screening for all sexually active women aged 24 years and younger, even if they are asymptomatic. Screening also is recommended for women older than 24 years at risk for the acquisition of chlamydial infection (eg, women with multiple or new sexual partners). Alternative treatments may be appropriate in areas of the country where resistant strains have been found.

A saline wet preparation also may be considered in this setting and most likely would identify the presence of polymorphonucleocytes. However, it would not definitively identify the presence of a chlamydial or gonorrheal infection. *Trichomonas* species may be found on a wet preparation, but trichomoniasis would not cause a mucopurulent cervicitis.

Hypothyroidism has been associated with menorrhagia and intermenstrual bleeding. A serum thyroid-stimulating hormone test should be performed when there is menorrhagia or other bleeding of unknown cause.

An endovaginal ultrasonographic examination would help identify organic causes of abnormal bleeding, such as intrauterine polyps or submucosal leiomyomata. In a patient with a 1-month history of abnormal bleeding with mucopurulent cervicitis, this diagnostic test would not be the most appropriate to perform initially.

Droegemueller W. Infections of the lower genital tract: vulva, vagina, cervix, toxic shock syndrome, HIV infections. In: Stenchever MA, Droegemueller W, Herbst AL, Mishell DR Jr, editors. Comprehensive gynecology. 4th ed. St. Louis (MO): Mosby; 2001. p. 641–705.

Howell MR, Quinn TC, Brathwaite W, Gaydos CA. Screening women for Chlamydia trachomatis in family planning clinics: the cost-effectiveness of DNA amplification assays. Sex Transm Dis 1998;25:108–17.

Sexually transmitted diseases treatment guidelines 2002. Centers for Disease Control and Prevention. MMWR Recomm Rep 2002;51(RR-6):1–78.

Turner CF, Rogers SM, Miller HG, Miller WC, Gribble JN, Chromy JR, et al. Untreated gonococcal and chlamydial infection in a probability sample of adults. JAMA 2002;287:726–33.

Van Dyck E, Ieven M, Pattyn S, Van Damme L, Laga M. Detection of Chlamydia trachomatis and Neisseria gonorrhoeae by enzyme immunoassay, culture and three nucleic acid amplification tests. J Clin Microbiol 2001;39:1751–6.

Wilansky DL, Greisman B. Early hypothyroidism in patients with menorrhagia. Am J Obstet Gynecol 1989;160:673–7.

31
Diethylstilbestrol exposure

A 44-year-old woman, para 3, currently undergoes twice-yearly vaginal and cervical surveillance for vaginal adenosis–related diethylstilbestrol (DES) exposure in utero. At a recent office visit, she asked about the risk of vaginal adenosis and other lower genital tract abnormalities in her 2 daughters. The most appropriate information to give this patient regarding her daughters' health risk is that there is

      (A) increased risk of cervical abnormalities
      (B) increased risk of infertility
*   (C) no increased risk of gynecologic abnormalities
      (D) increased risk of uterine adenocarcinoma
      (E) increased risk of breast cancer

Diethylstilbestrol is a synthetic nonsteroidal estrogen that was prescribed to millions of pregnant women between 1938 and 1971 in an attempt to prevent complications of pregnancy. It is the first known human transplacental carcinogen. Approximately 50% of all women exposed in utero will manifest reproductive tract problems. Vaginal adenosis is detected in more than 50% of women whose mothers received DES before 9 weeks of gestation. In utero exposure to DES has been associated with clear cell adenocarcinoma of the vagina and cervix, adenosis, abnormalities of the cervix and uterus, abnormalities of the testes, and possible infertility in men and women. Increased incidence of infertility, spontaneous abortion, and premature labor have been associated with DES syndrome, which is characterized by changes in the vagina (eg, adenosis), cervix (eg, ectropion, "hood," "coxcomb"), and uterus (eg, T-shaped, hypoplastic cavity).

In a study to evaluate the lower genital tract in daughters whose mothers were exposed to DES in pregnancy, the mothers' records were reviewed. It was found that 61.5% of the mothers exposed to DES during pregnancy demonstrated structural changes of the cervix, vaginal epithelial change consisting of adenosis, nonstaining vaginal epithelium after application of Lugol's solution, or white epithelium within the vagina. None of the daughters was found to have changes usually associated with DES exposure. These findings suggest that third-generation carryover effects of in utero DES exposure are unlikely.

Because of the increased risk of genital tract cancer in women exposed to DES, studies have looked at the increased risk of other types of cancer in women exposed to DES in utero. A modest association exists between DES exposure and breast cancer risk (relative risk = 1.27; 95% confidence interval 1.07–1.52). This risk was not exacerbated by a family history of breast cancer or by the use of oral contraceptives or hormone therapy. There is no evidence that DES was associated with risk of ovarian, endometrial, or other cancers. There are no data on the risk of these cancers in the daughters of DES-exposed women.

American College of Obstetricians and Gynecologists. Teratology. ACOG Educational Bulletin 236. Washington, DC: ACOG; 1997.

Kaufman RH, Adam E. Findings in female offspring of women exposed in utero to diethylstilbestrol. Obstet Gynecol 2002;99:197–200.

Titus-Ernstoff L, Hatch EE, Hoover RN, Palmer J, Greenberg ER, Ricker W, et al. Long-term cancer risk in women given diethylstilbestrol (DES) during pregnancy. Br J Cancer 2001;84:126–33.

Wingard DL, Cohn BA, Helmrich SP, Edelstein SL. DES awareness and exposure: the 1994 California Behavioral Risk Factor Survey. Am J Prev Med 1996;12:437–41.

32

Postoperative intestinal obstruction

A 54-year-old woman undergoes a lengthy total abdominal hysterectomy and bilateral salpingo-oophorectomy with lysis of adhesions. On postoperative day 2, the patient complains of nausea and vomits multiple times. Abdominal distention and tympany are noted. The oral liquid diet is discontinued, a nasogastric (NG) tube inserted, and administration of intravenous fluids continued. On postoperative day 6, nausea, vomiting, and abdominal distention persist. An abdominal plain radiograph shows loops of distended small bowel with multiple air–fluid levels. Findings of a computed tomography (CT) scan are consistent with complete small bowel obstruction. The most appropriate management for this patient is

* (A) exploratory laparotomy
(B) continuation of NG decompression
(C) placement of a long NG tube
(D) administration of intravenous antibiotics

The motility of the gastrointestinal tract usually is impaired temporarily after gynecologic surgery. The stomach and small bowel usually recover within 24–48 hours. However, the colon may require 3–5 days. Small bowel obstruction occurs in approximately 1–2% of patients. The mechanism of small bowel obstruction appears to be related to opening of the peritoneal cavity, manipulation of the contents, and prolonged procedures. The exact mechanism is unknown; however, the presence of extraluminal and intraluminal masses, adhesions from previous operative procedures, anesthesia, and postoperative narcotic use may be contributing causes. Adhesions, especially after multiple pelvic operations, appear to be responsible for more than 60% of bowel obstructions in the United States.

Ileus is defined as intestinal distention and slowing of passage of the intestine's content without demonstrable obstruction. A number of common causes are listed in Box 32-1. Symptoms may include mild, colicky abdominal pain. Signs include decreased or absent bowel sounds, abdominal distention, and tympany. Nausea and vomiting may or may not occur. Careful physical evaluation, with emphasis on abdominal and pelvic examinations, should be performed to detect a possible pelvic hematoma or abscess. Laboratory studies should include a complete blood count and electrolyte profile. Radiologic studies include plain radiology of the abdomen, both supine and upright, which usually shows dilated loops of small and large bowel and air–fluid levels. Free air may be noted on the upright radiograph for some 7–10 days postoperatively and usually is not indicative of perforated viscus.

Management of postoperative ileus consists of gastrointestinal decompression and maintenance of appropriate fluid and electrolytes. Simple nasogastric suction will decompress the stomach and remove swallowed air, which is the most common cause of gas in the small bowel. So-

called long tubes appear to have no therapeutic advantage. Adequate fluid and electrolyte replacement is important secondary to third-space loss through the bowel lumen and wall. Most cases of ileus will resolve spontaneously within several days, with resolution signaled by decreased abdominal distention, return of bowel sounds, and passage of stool or flatus. If no improvement is noted in 48–72 hours of conservative management, the patient should be reassessed for intraabdominal injury or infection.

Patients with complete small bowel obstruction initially may have increased bowel activity both above and below the point of obstruction. As a result, passage of diarrhea stool early in the course may be misleading to the unwary examiner. Proximal obstruction with vomiting causes dehydration and hypochloremia, hypokalemia, and metabolic alkalosis. More distal obstruction causes

---

BOX 32-1

Causes of Ileus

- Laparotomy
- Metabolic and electrolyte derangements (eg, hypokalemia, hyponatremia, hypomagnesemia, uremia, diabetic coma)
- Drugs (eg, opiates, psychotropic agents, anticholinergic agents)
- Intraabdominal inflammation
- Retroperitoneal hemorrhage or inflammation
- Intestinal ischemia
- Systemic sepsis
- Genitourinary tract injury

Modified from Evers BM. Small bowel. In: Townsend CM Jr, editor. Sabiston textbook of surgery: the biological basis of modern surgical practice. 16th ed. Philadelphia (PA): WB Saunders; 2001. p. 888.

less electrolyte disturbance; however, oliguria, azotemia, and hemoconcentration may accompany the dehydration. The jejunum and proximal ileum are sterile in the absence of obstruction; however, with obstruction, bowel flora may become dominated by organisms such as *Escherichia coli* and *Streptococcus fecalis*, leading to vomitus with a feculent character.

Diagnosis of complete obstruction by history, physical examination, and plain radiography is approximately 60% reliable. A CT scan is sensitive for diagnosis of complete small bowel obstruction and causes of obstruction, especially if abscess is involved. Contrast studies, including studies using barium and water-soluble media, have been used to diagnose the location and degree of obstruction. Most patients with complete obstruction require operative intervention. The operative approach should include lysis of adhesions, gentle handling of the bowel, reduction and repair of internal and abdominal wall hernias, and drainage of abscesses.

This patient presents with nausea and vomiting, temperature elevation, and leukocytosis indicative of complete obstruction that is unlikely to resolve without operative intervention. Continued NG suction or placement of a long NG tube will not be of predictable benefit to this patient. Although antibiotics are used as an adjunct to surgical management, administration of antibiotics alone would not be appropriate.

Clarke-Pearson DL, Nichols DH. Postoperative care and management of complications. In: Nichols DH, Clarke-Pearson DL. Gynecologic, obstetric, and related surgery. 2nd ed. St. Louis (MO): Mosby; 2000. p. 169–70.

Ellis H. The clinical significance of adhesions: focus on intestinal obstruction. Eur J Surg Suppl 1997;577:5–9.

Evers BM. Small bowel. In: Townsend CM Jr, editor. Sabiston textbook of surgery: the biological basis of modern surgical practice. 16th ed. Philadelphia (PA): WB Saunders; 2001. p. 873–916.

Feigin E, Seror D, Szold A, Carmon M, Allweis TM, Nissan A, et al. Water-soluble contrast material has no therapeutic effect on postoperative small-bowel obstruction: results of a prospective, randomized clinical trial. Am J Surg 1996;171:227–9.

Velasco JM, Vallina VL, Bonomo SR, Hieken TJ. Postlaparoscopic small bowel obstruction: rethinking its management. Surg Endosc 1998;12:1043–5.

33

Contraceptive choice for a *BRCA*-positive woman

A 25-year-old sexually active woman has used oral contraceptives for 3 years. Breast cancer has recently been diagnosed in her 60-year-old mother. No other family members have this disease. Your best answer to her question about whether she should continue to use oral contraceptives is that she should

(A) discontinue use, because they increase her risk of breast cancer
(B) discontinue use, because they increase her risk of ovarian cancer
* (C) continue use, because no overall increased risk of breast cancer has been established
(D) continue use after testing for *BRCA1* and *BRCA2* mutations

The relationship between the use of oral contraceptives and breast cancer incidence is controversial. The study with the largest number of cases is a reanalysis comparing 53,297 women with breast cancer and 100,239 women without the disease. No overall increased risk was observed among women with breast cancer diagnosed 10 or more years after cessation of oral contraceptive use. Current users of combined oral contraceptives were noted to have a slightly greater risk of localized disease. In addition, a family history of breast cancer was not associated with an increased risk of breast cancer in subjects who used oral contraceptives. These data thus are reassuring that in this case, if the patient continues to require adequate contraception to prevent unintended pregnancy, she would not be at increased risk of breast cancer.

Numerous well-established benefits have been associated with the use of oral contraceptives. One such important benefit has been an overall reduction in ovarian cancer risk of approximately 40% in current users.

An estimated 5–7% of all breast and ovarian cancers is attributable to inherited mutations in 2 highly penetrant autosomal-dominant susceptibility genes, *BRCA1* and *BRCA2*. Genetic testing for breast or ovarian cancer is indicated for a patient when multiple family members have breast or ovarian cancer or when a *BRCA* mutation has been discovered in the family. Testing of the general population is not recommended. *BRCA* is known to be a tumor–supressor gene, but its precise biologic functions are unclear. More than 600 mutations are possible in *BRCA1*, and 500 mutations are possible in *BRCA2*.

American College of Obstetricians and Gynecologists. Breast-ovarian cancer screening. ACOG Committee Opinion 239. Washington, DC: ACOG; 2000.

Breast cancer and hormonal contraceptives: collaborative reanalysis of individual data on 53,297 women with breast cancer and 100,239 women without breast cancer from 54 epidemiological studies. Collaborative Group on Hormonal Factors in Breast Cancer. Lancet 1996;347:1713–27.

Breast cancer and hormonal contraceptives: further results. Collaborative Group on Hormonal Factors in Breast Cancer. Contraception 1996;54 suppl:1S–106S.

Burke W. Oral contraceptives and breast cancer: a note of caution for high-risk women. JAMA 2000;284:1837–8.

Grabrick DM, Hartmann LC, Cerhan JR, Vierkant RA, Therneau TM, Vachon CM, et al. Risk of breast cancer with oral contraceptive use in women with a family history of breast cancer. JAMA 2000;284:1791–8.

Westhoff CL. Oral contraceptives and breast cancer-resolution emerges [editorial]. Contraception 1996;54 suppl:i–ii.

34

Magnetic resonance imaging of the reproductive tract

A sexually active 15-year-old adolescent girl presents with significant abdominal pain during menses. The pain involves both lower quadrants but is greater on the left. She has been in excellent health to date. The adolescent has been monitored on growth curves, which have been at the mean. Menarche occurred at 14½ years, and thelarche was 2 years earlier. An abdominal examination revealed normal bowel sounds and tenderness in the left lower quadrant, without the presence of rebound. On pelvic examination, 1 cervix was noted, and tenderness was elicited in the left lower quadrant. It was not possible to outline the pelvic organs completely. Recent tests for sexually transmitted diseases (STDs) and pregnancy proved negative. The most appropriate next step in management is

      (A) abdominal radiography
*   (B) pelvic ultrasonography
      (C) expectant management
      (D) magnetic resonance imaging (MRI)

The true incidence of müllerian anomalies is unknown but is believed to range between 0.1% and 3.8%. In the absence of an obvious diagnosis of an STD or pregnancy in this case, consideration should be given to a müllerian anomaly.

Embryologically, the steps of müllerian tract development include elongation, fusion, canalization, and septal resorption. At 6 weeks of gestation, the müllerian ducts are identified, and at 9 weeks elongation occurs to the level of the urogenital sinus. The uterovaginal canal is formed and inserts into the urogenital sinus at Müller's tubercle. Fusion of the ducts occurs from the caudal to the cephalic end up to the level of the uterine fundus. By 20 weeks of gestation, canalization and septum resorption occur.

The most appropriate next step in management of this patient, in light of the acute nature of her pain, is pelvic ultrasonography. This study will define the pelvic organs, including identification of a müllerian anomaly. Specific intervention can be planned based on ultrasonographic findings. Compared with MRI evaluation, ultrasonographic evaluation of anatomic müllerian tract defects is more cost-effective, and the anatomy frequently is defined better.

The American Fertility Society (now the American Society for Reproductive Medicine) devised a classification system for müllerian anomalies (Fig. 34-1). Incomplete canalization of the urogenital sinus leads to an imperforate hymen. The incidence is 0.1%, and it is usually an isolated finding. When it occurs in an infant, it is often noted when the patient cries (eg, when the practitioner performs a Valsalva maneuver). Distention also may be secondary to a mucocolpos in this age group. The mucocolpos can lead to urinary tract obstruction and infection. The patient with an imperforate hymen often presents with cyclic pelvic pain and a characteristic bluish hue to the hymen. Other presenting signs include dysuria, back pain, and dyschezia, in addition to amenorrhea. This patient does not manifest amenorrhea because there is a didelphic system with a hemivagina (see Fig. 34-2).

Imperforate hymen must be differentiated from low transverse septum in a postpubertal patient. When the latter is suspected, an MRI may help to delineate the anatomy. In addition, in a conscious patient, a Valsalva maneuver will produce a bulge with an imperforate hymen but not with a septum.

CLASSIFICATION OF MÜLLERIAN ANOMALIES

Patient's name _____ Date _____ Chart # _____

Age _____ G _____ P_____ Sp Ab _____ VTP_____ Ectopic_____ Infertile Yes _____ No_____

Other significant history (eg, surgery, infection)_____

_____

HSG _____ Sonography _____ Photography _____ Laparoscopy _____ Laparotomy_____

Examples

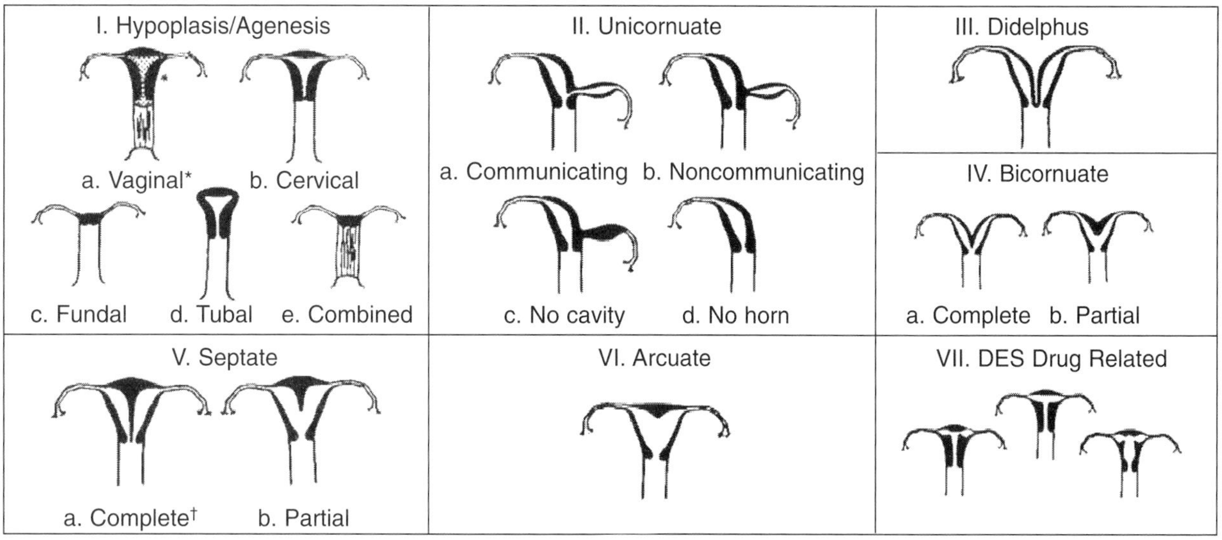

I. Hypoplasis/Agenesis
a. Vaginal*   b. Cervical
c. Fundal   d. Tubal   e. Combined

II. Unicornuate
a. Communicating   b. Noncommunicating
c. No cavity   d. No horn

III. Didelphus

IV. Bicornuate
a. Complete   b. Partial

V. Septate
a. Complete†   b. Partial

VI. Arcuate

VII. DES Drug Related

*Uterus may be normal or take a variety of abnormal forms.
† May have two distinct cervices.

Type of anomaly

Class I _____   Class V _____
Class II _____   Class VI _____
Class III _____   Class VII _____
Class IV _____

Treatment (surgical procedures) _____
_____
_____

Prognosis for conception and subsequent viable infant*
____ Excellent (>75%)   ____Good (50–75%)
____ Fair (25–50%)   ____Poor (<25%)

* Based on physician's judgment.

Recommended follow-up treatments _____
_____
_____

For additional supply contact:
American Society for Reproductive Medicine
1209 Montgomery Highway
Birmingham, AL 35216-2809
          Tel: 205-978-5000 • Fax: 205-978-5018

Property of
American Society for Reproductive Medicine

Additional findings_____
_____
_____
Vagina_____
Cervix _____

Tubes: Right_____ Left_____
Kidneys: Right _____ Left_____

Drawing
L   R

FIG. 34-1. American Fertility Society classification of müllerian anomalies. (Allen FS, Feste JR. Pelvic disease classifications. Fertil Steril 1989;51:199–201.)

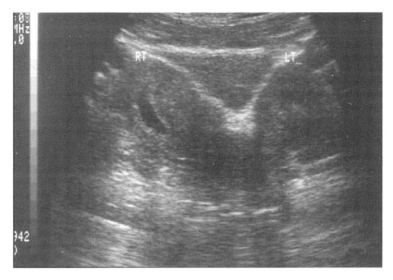

FIG. 34-2. Sonographic imaging of didelphic uterus. (Courtesy of J. Sumpkin and L. Hill, Magee-Womens Hospital, The University of Pittsburgh School of Medicine.)

Transverse vaginal septum occurs in 1 in 2,100 to 1 in 72,000 patients. It is believed to be sex-linked autosomal recessive in its transmission. It represents a vertical fusion disorder between the müllerian ducts and the urogenital sinus. The frequency of location is as follows: upper vagina, 46%; middle vagina, 40%; and lower vagina, 14%. Septa may be complete or incomplete. It may present before puberty with a fluid collection in a portion of the vagina. When extensive, compression of the ureters, rectum, and vena cava has been reported. Subsequent vaginal stenosis is possible, and thus vaginal reconstruction may be necessary.

In a patient who presents after puberty, signs and symptoms include cyclic lower abdominal pain, vaginal discharge, abnormal menstruation, and a pelvic mass. Inability to place a tampon and dyspareunia also may be noted. Associated congenital anomalies have been reported and include coarctation of the aorta, atrial septal defect, and malformations of the lumbar spine.

A patient with longitudinal vaginal septum is either asymptomatic or has cyclic pain, abnormal vaginal bleeding, or both. The cause is unknown but is believed to be associated with embryonic arrest of müllerian and metanephric ducts at 8 weeks of gestation. Often the problem is associated with uterus didelphys and an associated renal anomaly. Surgical treatment includes resection of the septum. In the presence of a didelphic system, successful pregnancy rates range from 37% to 40%. Although an MRI study is helpful in defining the anatomy, especially with respect to the presence or absence of a cervix, it is not always available on an urgent basis. It provides better resolution than computed tomography.

Vertical fusion defects result in a bicornuate, didelphic, or unicornuate uterus. Rudimentary horns may be associated with pelvic pain secondary to outflow tract obstruction when there is a functional endometrium. These noncommunicating horns are associated with pelvic pain and require resection through laparoscopy or laparotomy. Any surgical procedure should be preceded by appropriate anatomic assessment of the pelvic organs, initially using ultrasonography. A didelphic system may be associated with a hemivagina and blind vaginal pouch, as in the patient described. The patient may present with menses that are associated with pelvic pain. Resection of the vaginal septum relieves the outflow tract obstruction and pain.

In the case under discussion, neither laparoscopy nor laparotomy should be the next step, because it is useful to maximize preoperative knowledge prior to embarking on surgical intervention. Abdominal radiography, although helpful in some acute pain situations, would not be informative in this patient. In light of her acute pain, expectant management is inappropriate.

The American Fertility Society classifications of adnexal adhesions, distal tubal occlusion, tubal occlusion secondary to tubal ligation, tubal pregnancies, mullerian anomalies and intrauterine adhesions. Fertil Steril 1988;49:944–55.

Burgis J. Obstructive mullerian anomalies: case report, diagnosis, and management. Am J Obstet Gynecol 2001;185:338–44.

Candiani GB, Fedele L, Candiani M. Double uterus, blind hemivagina, and ipsilateral renal agenesis: 36 cases and long-term follow-up. Obstet Gynecol 1997;90:26–32.

Casey AC, Laufer M. Cervical agenesis: septic death after surgery. Obstet Gynecol 1997;90:706–7.

Gell JS, Bradshaw KD, Berga SL. Recognition and management of congenital reproductive anomalies. Curr Probl Obstet Gynecol Fertil 1998;21:68–96.

Tanaka YO, Kurosaki Y, Kobayashi T, Eguchi N, Mori K, Satoh Y, et al. Uterus didelphys associated with obstructed hemivagina and ipsilateral renal agenesis: MR findings in seven cases. Abdom Imaging 1998;23: 437–41.

35
Appendicitis

A 17-year-old high-school senior is referred to the emergency department by the school nurse because of malaise, decreased appetite, and abdominal pain. Further history indicates irregular menses. She is sexually active, but results of her pregnancy test are negative. The physical examination reveals lower right quadrant pain and rebound tenderness. The most appropriate next step is

    (A) laparoscopy
*   (B) computed tomography (CT) scan of the abdomen and pelvis
    (C) consultation with a gastroenterologist
    (D) administration of azithromycin and ciprofloxacin

The diagnosis and appropriate management of disease in most patients who present with acute right lower quadrant pain will depend primarily on the patient's history. The way in which the patient describes the pain, its relationship to movement, and its changing nature over time, as well as other specific gastrointestinal, genitourinary, or gynecologic symptoms, will determine the necessary diagnostic aids required to effect proper therapeutic intervention.

If the working diagnosis is uncertain, repeated interval history and physical examination over short periods of observation (1–2 hours) are helpful. This method is particularly useful when these observations can be made sequentially by the same individual.

The conditions responsible for acute right lower quadrant pain are primarily medical or surgical (see Box 35-1). Appendicitis is a common acute surgical condition with an age-related incidence that parallels that of the development of the lymphoid system; the incidence is greatest in early adulthood. There is a slightly higher rate of appendicitis in adolescent men than adolescent women, with a male-to-female ratio of 1.3:1.

The signs and symptoms of appendicitis may evolve dramatically over a 12–24-hour period. Anorexia is a consistent gastrointestinal sign and on occasion is accompanied by obstipation. Diffuse midepigastric pain, which frequently localizes to the right lower quadrant, is classically, although not invariably, described. Mild leukocytosis and low-grade fever also may occur.

Various imaging modalities may be helpful in diagnosis. A plain radiograph of the abdomen, although frequently obtained, is rarely of value. Ultrasonography has been explored as an option, but its diagnostic utility has been questioned because its efficacy has been described as overly user dependent. An important limitation of ultrasonography is its low sensitivity or specificity. A CT scan has been shown to be a more accurate approach, and it is particularly useful when there is a suspicion of abscess formation based on peritoneal signs. If a localized collection is present, a CT scan is a valuable aid in determining the feasibility of percutaneous drainage.

Radiologic evaluation should not delay or substitute for operative intervention when clinically indicated. Although laparoscopy could make the definitive diagnosis and provide for therapy, a short period of observation and further radiologic evaluation likely would increase the accuracy of diagnosis and the overall efficiency of surgical intervention.

Azithromycin and ciprofloxacin should not be administered on the basis of presumed pelvic inflammatory disease alone; the need for surgery should be excluded first. Consultation with a gastroenterologist is unlikely to be helpful upon the patient's initial hospitalization; it should be deferred until imaging studies and the rest of the workup are more complete.

BOX 35-1

Medical and Surgical Conditions That Cause Right Lower Quadrant Pain

- Acute pancreatitis
- Diverticulitis
- Acute ileitis
- Intussusception
- Crohn's disease
- Psoas abscess
- Pelvic inflammatory disease
- Omental torsion
- Mesenteric adenitis
- Liver abscess
- Cancer of the cecum
- Amebiasis
- Ascariasis
- Typhoid fever
- Appendicitis
- Ectopic pregnancy
- Meckel's diverticulitis
- Acute mesenteric occlusion
- Leaking aortic aneurysm

Reprinted from Surgical decision making, Norton LW, Eiseman B, Stiegmann GV, editors. Fiddian-Green RC, Acute right lower quadrant pain. p. 160–1. Copyright 2000, with permission from Elsevier.

Fiddian-Green RC. Acute right lower quadrant pain. In: Norton LW, Eiseman B, Stiegmann GV, editors. Surgical decision making. Philadelphia (PA): WB Saunders; 2000. p. 160–1.

Hale DA, Molloy M, Pearl RH, Schutt DC, Jaques DP. Appendectomy: a contemporary appraisal. Ann Surg 1997;225:252–61.

Kozar RA, Roslyn JJ. The appendix. In: Schwartz SI, Shires GT, Spencer FC, Daly JM, Fischer JE, Galloway AC, editors. Principles of surgery. 7th ed. Vol. 2. New York (NY): McGraw-Hill; 1999. p. 1383–94.

McQuaid KR. Alimentary tract. In: Tierney LM, McPhee SJ, Papdakis MA, editors. Current medical diagnosis and treatment 2002. New York (NY): Lange Medical Books/McGraw-Hill; 2002. p. 571–674.

Rao PM, Feltmate CM, Rhea JT, Schulick AH, Novelline RA. Helical computed tomography in differentiating appendicitis and acute gynecologic conditions. Obstet Gynecol 1999;93:417–21.

Silen W, editor. Cope's early diagnosis of the acute abdomen. 20th ed. New York (NY): Oxford University Press; 2000.

36

Urethral diverticulum in adults

A 55-year-old woman reports stress incontinence. Physical examination reveals a 2-cm tender anterior vaginal wall mass. Cystourethroscopy demonstrates a urethral diverticulum in the proximal urethra. Urodynamic studies are consistent with stress urinary incontinence. The most appropriate surgical management for this patient is

   (A) marsupialization of the diverticulum (Spence procedure)
   (B) transvaginal needle drainage
   (C) diverticulectomy
 * (D) diverticulectomy with urethropexy
   (E) urethral dilation

Symptoms of urethral diverticula may include incontinence, recurrent urinary tract infection, dysuria, dyspareunia, or urgency. The diagnosis may be suggested by a palpable tender anterior vaginal wall mass or expression of pus from the urethra. Stress incontinence is the presenting symptom in approximately 60% of women with diverticula. When incontinence is present, urodynamic evaluation is helpful in establishing a surgical plan.

Urethral diverticula are often multiple, so a thorough preoperative evaluation is mandatory. Diverticula can be identified with voiding cystourethrography, cystourethroscopy, or positive-pressure urethrography (Fig. 36-1). Voiding cystourethrography will identify the majority of diverticula. If the findings of voiding cystourethrography are normal and a diverticulum is suspected from clinical manifestations, cystourethroscopy or positive-pressure urethrography should be performed. Ultrasonography and magnetic resonance imaging may identify urethral diverticula in some cases, but they do not have an established role in the evaluation of suspected urethral diverticula.

Traditional surgical management of urethral diverticula includes transvaginal excision of the diverticulum sac with multilayered closure. Intraoperative urethroscopy may be helpful to identify the sac. Surgical principles include tension-free closure and meticulous hemostasis. In this patient with urodynamic stress urinary incontinence, simultaneous bladder neck suspension is appropriate. However, among continent women with urethral

diverticula, stress incontinence will occur de novo in up to 10% of patients undergoing diverticulectomy. Other potential complications of diverticulectomy include

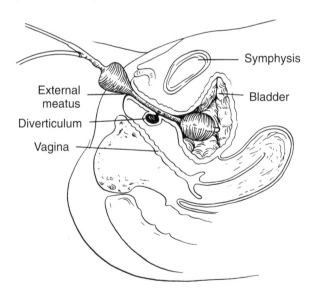

FIG. 36-1. Technique for positive-pressure urethrography to diagnose urethral diverticula. The double-balloon catheter, also known as the Tratner or Davis catheter, is in the urethra. With both balloons inflated, radiopaque dye can be instilled into the urethra, filling the urethral lumen and diverticulum sac. (Bent AE, Ostergard DR, Cundiff GW, Swift SE, editors. Ostergard's urogynecology and pelvic floor dysfunction. 5th ed. Philadelphia [PA]: Lippincott Williams & Wilkins; 2003. p. 254.)

recurrence, urinary tract infection, fistula formation, and stricture. Recurrent or persistent diverticula will occur in up to 14% of patients.

Marsupialization of a diverticulum, also known as the Spence procedure, is appropriate for very distal diverticula. This procedure would not be appropriate for a patient with urodynamic stress incontinence or any proximal diverticula.

Transvaginal needle drainage is not appropriate in this case. Needle drainage would not lead to resolution of the diverticulum and could cause superinfection.

Ganabathi K, Leach GE, Zimmern PE, Dmochowski R. Experience with the management of urethral diverticulum in 63 women. J Urol 1994;152:1445–52.

Hurt WG. Urethral abnormalities. In: Hurt WG, editor. Urogynecologic surgery. New York (NY): Raven Press; 1992. p. 157–68.

Jacoby K, Rowbotham RK. Double balloon positive pressure urethrography is a more sensitive test than voiding cystourethrography for diagnosing urethral diverticulum in women. J Urol 1999;162:2066–9.

Kim B, Hricak H, Tanagho EA. Diagnosis of urethral diverticula in women: value of MR imaging. AJR Am J Roentgenol 1993;161: 809–15.

Leach GE, Trockman BA. Surgery for fistulas and diverticulum. In: Walsh PC, Retik AB, Vaughan ED, Wein AJ, editors. Campbell's urology. 7th ed. Philadelphia (PA): WB Saunders; 1998. p. 1135–53.

Robertson JR. Urethral diverticula. In: Ostergard DR, Bent AE, editors. Urogynecology and urodynamics: theory and practice. 4th ed. Baltimore (MD): Williams & Wilkins; 1996. p. 361–70.

Summitt RL Jr, Stovall TG. Urethral diverticula: evaluation by urethral pressure profilometry, cystourethroscopy, and the voiding cystourethrogram. Obstet Gynecol 1992;80:695–9.

Wang AC, Wang CR. Radiologic diagnosis and surgical treatment of urethral diverticulum in women: a reappraisal of voiding cystourethrography and positive pressure urethrography. J Reprod Med 2000;45: 377–82.

37

Assisted reproductive technology

A 29-year-old woman visits your office for infertility treatment. She was treated on at least 2 occasions for acute pelvic inflammatory disease. She consulted her physician about 1 year ago for evaluation of infertility. On the basis of her history and the results of use of over-the-counter urinary luteinizing hormone detection kits, she was found to be ovulating. Her husband produced a normal semen sample. Because of an abnormal hysterosalpingogram, you perform a diagnostic laparoscopy and discover extensive pelvic adhesions and tuboovarian masses. Her current health insurance will pay for tubal reconstructive surgery but will not cover in vitro fertilization (IVF). The patient requests tubal reconstructive surgery. The most appropriate next step in management of this patient would be

(A) to perform tubal reconstructive surgery
(B) to have her prepare a letter requesting coverage for IVF
* (C) to prepare a letter requesting coverage for IVF
(D) to explain that there is nothing else that can be done
(E) to give her a referral for adoption

Indications for assisted reproductive technologies have broadened over the past 2 decades; the primary intent was to provide IVF for patients whose tubes have been destroyed by infection or prior surgery. Coverage for IVF varies by insurance plan and from region to region. Currently, some states (eg, Connecticut, Illinois, Massachusetts, New Jersey, New York, and Rhode Island) require insurers to cover this technology under specified conditions. In a healthy woman younger than 35 years with ovulatory cycles, normal ovarian reserve, and a partner with proven fertility, the take-home baby rate should be approximately 50%. Some facilities report higher results over 3 cycles of therapy.

Reconstructive tubal surgery in this case would require a major abdominal operation and a period of recovery with poor potential to achieve pregnancy. The patient would have a significant risk of tubal pregnancy should she conceive. The success of tubal repair may not be known for as long as 18 months after the operative procedure. During this time, the patient would have to pay costs associated with possible doctor visits and ovulation monitoring and handle frustration.

The patient's vulnerability and illness and the physician's implicit promise to help are the basis of the physician's obligation to act for the benefit of the patient. This basis succinctly defines the concept of fiduciary beneficence, one of the essential ingredients of the physician–patient relationship. It defines the role of the physician as a patient advocate. Although the patient could summarize her thoughts and submit them in writing to her insurance carrier, only her physician can adequately describe the specific medical details of her disease, the psychosocial issues surrounding this problem, her strong desire to have a child, and the rationale for the medical decision. The trust that a physician may enjoy not only from a single patient but also from society can be maintained only by the physician's commitment to serve as the patient's advocate. When a physician judges that the optimum treatment is not available under the patient's insurance coverage, the physician has a duty to act as an advocate for this coverage on the patient's behalf.

Child-free living or adoption is a viable option for specific couples. Nearly 70,000 children are adopted in the United States each year. A critical component in formulating plans for adoption is a frank discussion between the physician and the couple about their reasons for adoption, the type of adoption (eg, public or private agency) they prefer, and the degree of openness desired during the process. It is critical that the practitioner set aside a time to gather all the available information about adoption agencies, support groups, and laws specific to the state. It is strongly advised that couples attend seminars and support groups. Many couples have found it particularly helpful to meet with parents who have recently adopted a child. The American Society for Reproductive Medicine and other national agencies provide information about adoption.

Pellegrino ED, Thomasma DC. For the patient's good: the restoration of beneficence in health care. New York (NY): Oxford University Press; 1988.

Physician responsibility under managed care: patient advocacy in a changing health care environment. In: American College of Obstetricians and Gynecologists. Ethics in obstetrics and gynecology. Washington, DC: ACOG; 2002. p. 64–8.

Rodwin MA. Conflicts in managed care. N Engl J Med 1995;332: 604–7.

38

Wound dehiscence and evisceration

A 40-year-old woman has undergone a total abdominal hysterectomy and bilateral salpingo-oophorectomy through a vertical abdominal incision for symptomatic endometriosis. The fascia was closed with interrupted number 0 polyglycolic acid sutures. The patient's preoperative weight was 78 kg (172 lb). The surgery was uneventful, and she was discharged home on postoperative day 3. She presents to your office on postoperative day 10, reporting pink-tinged fluid draining from her incision. She is afebrile. On examination, the wound edges easily separate, and small bowel is noted in the subcutaneous tissue. The most appropriate treatment is closure of the fascia with

> (A) polyglycolic acid suture
> * (B polypropylene suture
> (C) polyglycolic acid mesh
> (D) polypropylene mesh
> (E) wire sutures

In most instances, the term *wound dehiscence* has been used to describe a wound separation that includes separation of the fascia. If the intestines protrude through the wound, it is called an *evisceration*. This uncommon complication occurs in less than 1% of patients who undergo abdominal surgery. If the skin edges do not separate and the fascial separation remains undetected, a large hernia eventually will develop. A number of factors increase the likelihood of wound dehiscence in nonirradiated women with benign disease (see Box 38-1), and these factors contribute to ischemia and necrosis of the fascia. Wound closure with an interrupted, Smead-Jones, or running technique does not influence the rate of fascial separation.

Fascial separation most commonly results from suture tearing through the fascia. Tearing can occur if too many sutures are placed too close together and tied too tightly.

Fascial sutures should be placed 1.5–2.0 cm from the fascial edge and 1 cm apart when closing a wound.

The classic sign of fascial separation is a serosanguinous discharge from the wound after the first few postoperative days. A wound infection is present in a large percentage of women who develop fascial separation. Because wound infection may occur several days before evisceration, the wound should be opened and the fascia examined to determine integrity. Fascial separation most commonly occurs after postoperative day 5.

After the diagnosis of evisceration is established, the wound should be covered with sterile saline–moistened towels, and the patient should be returned to the operating room immediately. The wound should be explored after anesthetics have been administered. The bowel should be inspected for viability. A broad-spectrum antibiotic (eg,

Factors That Increase the Likelihood of Wound Dehiscence in Nonirradiated Women With Benign Disease

- Wound infection
- Pulmonary disease
- Systemic infection
- Obesity
- Malnutrition
- Ileus
- Bowel obstruction
- Vomiting, coughing, or straining
- Corticosteroid use
- Prior surgical incision in the same site, excessive tension on the suture line, and sutures placed within 0.5 cm of the fascial edge

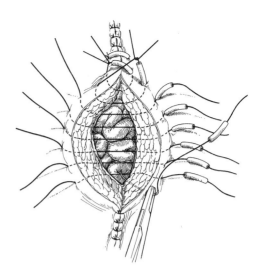

FIG. 38-2. Through-and-through closure of a wound evisceration using a number 2 permanent monofilament suture. If fascial edges are not widely separated or necrotic, a Smead-Jones closure can be used. (Reprinted from Gynecologic, obstetric, and related surgery, 2nd ed., Nichols DH, Clarke-Pearson DL. p. 231. Copyright 2002, with permission from Elsevier.)

cephalosporin) should be administered, and devitalized tissue should be sharply débrided. Several surgical techniques may be used for closure of the fascia. Most techniques use a large-bore permanent monofilament suture (eg, Prolene) that incorporates both the muscle and the fascia in the closure. Acceptable methods of closure are the interrupted, Smead-Jones, or running closure. The incision should be free of tension. Retention sutures, when used solely to close the fascia, should be placed at least 2–3 cm from the fascial edge and 2 cm apart (see Figs. 38-1 and 38-2). If the wound is infected or contam-

inated, the subcutaneous tissue is packed with saline-moistened gauze, and skin is not closed. Although the length of hospitalization and morbidity increase after fascial separation, the mortality remains low. Fascial separation and subsequent repair predispose the patient to later hernia development.

The experience with permanent mesh has been unsatisfactory because of an increased incidence of postoperative enterocutaneous fistula formation. Absorbable mesh of polyglycolic acid (eg, Dexon or Vicryl) is less likely to cause postoperative fistulae, but its use is associated with a higher incidence of hernia development.

The use of a permanent monofilament suture is recommended over an absorbable suture in repairing a fascial separation. These patients are at increased risk for the development of hernias, and a polyglycolic acid suture will hydrolyze and potentially increase the incidence of hernia formation. Wire sutures, which are more difficult to handle, have been replaced for the most part with the permanent monofilament suture.

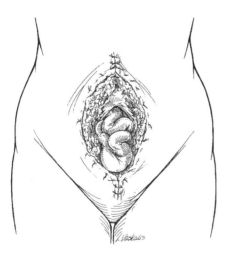

FIG. 38-1. Wound evisceration. The skin, fascia, and peritoneum have separated along most of the wound, exposing the underlying small intestine. (Reprinted from Gynecologic, obstetric, and related surgery, 2nd ed., Nichols DH, Clarke-Pearson DL. p. 231. Copyright 2002, with permission from Elsevier.)

Gallup DG. Opening and closing the abdomen and wound healing. In: Gershenson DM, DeCherney AH, Curry SL, Brubaker L, editors. Operative gynecology. 2nd ed. Philadelphia (PA): WB Saunders; 2001. p. 191–210.

Sutton G, Morgan S. Abdominal wound closure using a running, looped monofilament polybutester suture: comparison to Smead-Jones closure in historic controls. Obstet Gynecol 1992;80:650–4.

39

Medical abortion

A 26-year-old nulligravid woman requests a medical abortion. Vaginal probe ultrasonography confirms an intrauterine pregnancy at approximately 6 weeks and 2 days. The patient is scheduled to depart tomorrow for a long-planned 2-week overseas assignment. She has been a patient of yours for 3 years and is compliant and dependable. Her only medical problem is mild asthma. Findings from a complete blood count and chemistry testing are normal. She is Rh positive. The best next step in management is

      (A) mifepristone (Mifeprex) and misoprostol (Cytotec)
      (B) methotrexate sodium and misoprostol (Cytotec)
      (C) misoprostol (Cytotec) only
      (D) methotrexate sodium only
*   (E) recommendation of surgical abortion on her return

Medical abortions account for a greater proportion of all abortions. The advantage is that the patient does not undergo a surgical procedure and its inherent risks. The disadvantage is that the treatment takes place over days or weeks. Failures are treated with surgical abortion. Fortunately, efficacy rates are greater than 95% for a recommended mifepristone or methotrexate sodium regimen implemented at or before 49 days of gestation. A popular mifepristone regimen is an oral dose of 600 mg, followed by 400 μg of misoprostol in 48 hours. Efficacy rates for use up to 56 days of gestation are also quite high.

Mifepristone is a norethindrone derivative that competitively inhibits progesterone at the receptor level. This inhibition results in decidual breakdown and detachment of the blastocyst. The medication has no direct effect on trophoblastic cells. Although mifepristone alone can induce abortion, it most often is used in conjunction with a prostaglandin. The drug has not been associated with anomalies. It also causes cervical softening, causes the release of specific prostaglandins, and increases myometrium sensitivity to prostaglandin.

Misoprostol is a synthetic prostaglandin E_1 analogue that was developed primarily to treat gastric ulcers in patients taking nonsteroidal antiinflammatory drugs. It stimulates uterine contractions but has the effect of mild dilation on bronchioles. Therefore, its use is not contraindicated for patients with asthma. Peak serum levels are reached 34 minutes after oral administration and in 80 minutes by the vaginal route (a slightly more effective route). Serum concentrations are maintained longer with vaginal administration. Misoprostol has gastrointestinal adverse effects such as nausea, vomiting, and diarrhea, which usually are tolerated by patients. Congenital anomalies associated with misoprostol use include skull defects and limb abnormalities.

The passage of fetal tissue usually occurs within 4 hours of misoprostol ingestion. Although misoprostol can be self-administered at home, the U.S. Food and Drug Administration recommends that the drug be administered by a health care provider when mifepristone also is used. The patient is monitored, and if no expulsion of contents has occurred in 2 weeks, a suction curettage is recommended.

The use of methotrexate sodium as an abortifacient was popularized in the United States because of the initial unavailability of mifepristone. Methotrexate sodium is given in a dose of 50 mg/m^2 intramuscularly or a dose of 50 mg by mouth, followed by the administration of misoprostol 3–7 days later. Ultrasonography is performed 24–48 hours after the misoprostol dosing to check for viability. Methotrexate sodium arrests rapid cell division by blocking dihydrofolate reductase activity. It is used to manage early ectopic pregnancy, as well as gestational trophoblastic neoplasia. Complications at these low doses are rare but include nausea, vomiting, and diarrhea. Fetal anomalies can result, but most often they have been associated with higher doses. The disadvantage of the methotrexate sodium regimen is that passage of tissue may take longer, but the overall success rates are similar to mifepristone regimens. The use of misoprostol alone has been studied but has fallen out of favor because of decreased efficacy and increased adverse effects.

It is imperative that patients be available for care in the rare event of bleeding or severe pain. Nonsteroidal antiinflammatory drugs can be used and do not interfere with the action of misoprostol. Any patient who consents to a medical abortion should consent to a surgical abortion in the event of failure or bleeding. Bleeding is considered heavy if the patient soaks more than 2 maxipads per hour for 2 consecutive hours. The patient with such bleeding should contact the health care provider. Failed abortion rates using mifepristone or methotrexate sodium regimens are 1–2%, whereas failed abortion rates using surgical methods are a 10th of those rates. Infections are uncommon after medical abortion.

Practitioners must be aware that the administration of anti-D immune globulin is indicated if the patient is Rh negative. Other contraindications to medical abortion include possible ectopic pregnancy, chronic adrenal failure, allergies to medications used, and lack of access to emergency care.

Because this patient will be unavailable for emergency care for the next 2 weeks, surgical abortion could be considered on her return. The time recommended for medical abortion will be exceeded.

American College of Obstetricians and Gynecologists. Induced abortion. ACOG Patient Education Pamphlet AP043. Washington, DC: ACOG; 2001.

American College of Obstetricians and Gynecologists. Medical management of abortion. ACOG Practice Bulletin 26. Washington, DC: ACOG; 2001.

Paul M. Office management of early induced abortion. Clin Obstet Gynecol 1999;42:290–305.

Pymar HC, Creinin MD. Alternatives to mifepristone regimens for medical abortion. Am J Obstet Gynecol 2000;183 suppl:S54–S64.

40

The Health Insurance Portability and Accountability Act

The Health Insurance Portability and Accountability Act of 1996 (HIPAA) prohibits a health care provider, without a patient's authorization, from

* (A) disclosing personal health information to a third party
  (B) verbally discussing patient health information with other physicians during training rounds
  (C) using identifiable personal health information for medical research with institutional review board approval
  (D) providing patient information to an insurance company for payment purposes

The intent of HIPAA is to provide regulations to protect patients' privacy rights by preventing the misuse or disclosure of patients' health records. Health care entities that electronically transmit patient health information are required to implement these regulations. Covered entities include health care plans, health care providers (eg, hospitals, physicians, dentists, and therapists), third-party insurers, employers that maintain health records, life insurance companies, pharmacies, and medical equipment suppliers.

A company or individual who seeks or discloses protected health information in performing a service to, or on behalf of, a covered entity is considered a "business associate" of the covered entity. According to HIPAA, covered entities must have a written agreement in place with each business associate. Health care organizations are not automatically held responsible for their business associates' privacy violations. However, a health care organization must include provisions in its business associate contracts to require the business associate to report any privacy violations. Once the health care organization learns of a contract violation by its business associates, it must take reasonable steps to stop or fix the breach.

The privacy rule does not require a health care provider to get patient authorization before using or disclosing protected health information (PHI) for treatment, payment, or health care operations. An authorization gives a

provider permission to use PHI for specified purposes or to disclose such information to a third party identified by the patient. A HIPAA authorization contains federally mandated elements, including an expiration date or event, in addition to any applicable state law provisions.

According to the regulation, a health care organization is required to limit its use and disclosure of PHI to the minimum necessary to accomplish the intended purpose of the task or request. Compliance with the minimum necessary standard requires each organization to identify and classify those individuals within the organization who need access to the PHI and to establish policies and procedures for disclosure.

The protections provided in the privacy rule also cover oral communication of PHI. Health care providers are free to discuss PHI with one another in treatment settings, including during training rounds. These health care providers, however, should make sure that the PHI is not overheard by others.

Guidance in regard to the regulations provided by the Department of Health and Human Services has noted that audible verbal calling of patients' names in a waiting room is permitted. However, practices should work to limit unnecessary disclosure of PHI.

Information may be used for medical research without a patient's authorization if the health care organization gets a waiver of such authorization from its institutional review board or privacy board. After patient identification has been removed from health information, it also may be used for medical research purposes without patient authorization.

American College of Obstetricians and Gynecologists. Business associate relationships under the HIPAA privacy rule. HIPAA in Practice No. 3. Washington, DC: ACOG; 2002.

American College of Obstetricians and Gynecologists. Health Insurance Portability and Accountability Act (HIPAA) privacy manual: a how-to guide for your medical practice. 2nd ed. Washington, DC: ACOG; 2003.

American College of Obstetricians and Gynecologists. HIPAA privacy for small and mid-sized ob-gyn practices. HIPAA in Practice No. 1. Washington, DC: ACOG; 2002.

American College of Obstetricians and Gynecologists. Individual rights under the HIPAA privacy rule. HIPAA in Practice No. 4. Washington, DC: ACOG; 2003.

American College of Obstetricians and Gynecologists. Notice of privacy practices under the HIPAA privacy rule. HIPAA in Practice No. 2. Washington, DC: ACOG; 2002.

American College of Obstetricians and Gynecologists. Patient authorizations under the HIPAA privacy rule. HIPAA in Practice No. 5. Washington, DC: ACOG; 2003.

41

Emergency contraception

A 23-year-old woman, gravida 2, para 2, tells you that she had unprotected intercourse the previous night. She states that she does not desire another pregnancy at this time. The patient's menstrual cycle is regular every 30 days, and her last menstrual period was 2 weeks ago. She has no known medical illnesses, findings from the pelvic examination are normal, and a pregnancy test result is negative. The most appropriate next step in this patient's management is to prescribe

* (A) a combination estrogen–progestin
  (B) a long-acting injectable progestin
  (C) mifepristone (Mifeprex)
  (D) a high-dose estrogen
  (E) danazol (Danocrine)

Of the 3.5 million unintended pregnancies in the United States each year, approximately 40% end in birth, 13% end in miscarriage, and 45–50% end in abortion. It is believed that patient awareness and easy access to emergency contraception could prevent more than half of the unintended pregnancies and substantially decrease the abortion rate.

Emergency contraception using proven methods of birth control effectively prevents unintended pregnancy when used within 72 hours after unprotected intercourse, independent of the time in the menstrual cycle. Although some protection is afforded even when these methods are used within 5 days of unprotected coitus, each contraceptive regimen is substantially more effective the sooner it is used. The contraceptive methods that are available in the United States are either hormonal or mechanical. Hormonal methods include the use of an estrogen–progestin combination, estrogen, progestin, mifepristone (Mifeprex), or danazol (Danocrine). Mechanical methods include use of an intrauterine device (IUD).

A common form of emergency contraception is an estrogen–progestin combination consisting of 0.05 mg ethinyl estradiol and 0.25 mg levonorgestrel (Preven), taken orally in 2 doses 12 hours apart starting within 72 hours of unprotected coitus. However, some data show that emergency contraception is effective if used up to 120 hours after intercourse. Emergency contraception also may be accomplished by taking combinations of other oral contraceptives at 12-hour intervals (Table 41-1). The progestin-only method consists of 0.75 mg levonorgestrel taken orally in 2 doses 12 hours apart. Alternatively, a recent randomized controlled trial has demonstrated that a single dose of 1.5 mg levonorgestrel is as effective as a 2-dose regimen. These progestin-only methods are highly effective and are associated with a lower incidence of nausea and vomiting. U.S. Food and Drug Administration–approved dedicated prepackaged products, designed specifically to be used for emergency contraception, are available by physician prescription; each contains detailed physician and patient labeling. Generic oral contraceptives can be used for emergency contraception if they are taken properly.

Because emergency contraception is effective only during a short window of time, many states have encouraged increased access by enacting legislation to allow pharmacists, operating under written protocols with a physician, to provide emergency contraception directly to customers who request this product. Participating pharmacists first must complete a training program on

TABLE 41-1. Emergency Contraceptive Pills Available in the United States

Trade Name	Formulation	Pills per Dose*
Dedicated products		
Plan B	0.75 mg levonorgestrel	1 white
Preven	0.25 mg levonorgestrel	1 blue
	0.05 mg ethinyl estradiol	
Progestin-only oral contraceptives		
Ovrette	0.075 mg norgestrel	20 yellow
Combination oral contraceptives		
Alesse	0.1 mg levonorgestrel	5 pink
	0.02 mg ethinyl estradiol	
Levlen	0.15 mg levonorgestrel	4 light orange
	0.03 mg ethinyl estradiol	
Levlite	0.1 mg levonorgestrel	5 pink
	0.02 mg ethinyl estradiol	
Levora	0.15 mg levonorgestrel	4 white
	0.03 mg ethinyl estradiol	
Lo/Ovral[†]	0.30 mg norgestrel	4 white
	0.03 mg ethinyl estradiol	
Low-Ogestrel[†]	0.30 mg norgestrel	4 white
	0.03 mg ethinyl estradiol	
Nordette	0.15 mg levonorgestrel	4 light orange
	0.03 mg ethinyl estradiol	
Ogestrel[†]	0.50 mg norgestrel	2 white
	0.05 mg ethinyl estradiol	
Ovral[†]	0.50 mg norgestrel	2 white
	0.05 mg ethinyl estradiol	
TriLevlen[‡]	0.5/0.75/0.125 mg levonorgestrel	
	0.03/0.04/0.03 mg ethinyl estradiol	
Triphasil[‡]	0.5/0.75/0.125 mg levonorgestrel	
	0.03/0.04/0.03 mg ethinyl estradiol	
Trivora[‡]	0.5/0.75/0.125 mg levonorgestrel	
	0.03/0.04/0.03 mg ethinyl estradiol	

*Treatment consists of 2 doses taken 12 hours apart. Use of an antiemetic agent before taking the medication will lessen the risk of nausea, a common adverse effect.

[†]When compared with products containing levonorgestrel, norgestrel was associated with higher rates of adverse effects (Sanchez-Borrego R, Balasch J. Ethinyl oestradiol plus dl-norgestrel or levonorgestrel in the Yuzpe method for post-coital contraception: results of an observational study. Hum Reprod 1996;11:2449–53.

[‡]Dose varies as cycle pack progresses.

Modified from American College of Obstetricians and Gynecologists. Emergency oral contraception. ACOG Practice Bulletin 25. Washington, DC: ACOG, 2001.

emergency contraception, and they may be able to make physician referrals for ongoing care.

A pregnancy test should be negative prior to emergency contraception treatment. Nausea occurs in 30–60% of women who use combination estrogen–progestin for emergency contraception; antiemetics taken within 1 hour before the first dose effectively decrease the incidence of this adverse effect.

No studies have investigated teratogenic effects associated with emergency contraception. Studies of the teratogenic risks of daily oral contraceptive use would predict that an increased risk is unlikely. There are few reports of treatment failure. Menstruation will occur within 21 days in 98% of patients, and more than 50% of patients will have the next menses at the expected time. Patients must seek medical care if they have not menstruated within 21

days of emergency contraception. The effectiveness rate is estimated at approximately 75%, which is less effective than the consistent use of other contraceptives.

Adverse effects such as nausea and vomiting can be severe with high-dose estrogen emergency contraception. Because compliance may be a problem, these agents are used only rarely today for this indication.

Mifepristone, an orally active synthetic antiprogestin with potent antiprogestational and anticorticosteroid activity, is a highly effective postcoital contraceptive that is not commonly used in the United States. It is administered at the time of ovulation, and it acts by delaying endometrial maturation without affecting ovarian hormone production or menstrual bleeding. Given in a single dose within 72 hours of unprotected intercourse, mifepristone prevents approximately 85–95% of expected pregnancies. Adverse effects of mifepristone (eg, nausea, vomiting, and abdominal cramps) are minimal.

Danazol, an androgen derivative, is an effective emergency contraceptive when given within 72 hours of intercourse. However, it is rarely used for this purpose.

Long-acting injectable progestin is released slowly from its intramuscular site. Its effectiveness as a postcoital contraceptive has not been evaluated, so it should not be used for emergency contraception.

American College of Obstetricians and Gynecologists. Emergency oral contraception. ACOG Practice Bulletin 25. Washington, DC: ACOG; 2001.

Glasier A. Emergency postcoital contraception. N Engl J Med 1997;337:1058–64.

Grimes DA, Raymond EG. Emergency contraception. Ann Intern Med 2002;137:180–9.

Grimes DA, Raymond EG, Scott Jones B. Emergency contraception over-the-counter: the medical and legal imperatives. Obstet Gynecol 2001;98:151–5.

Thomas MA. Postcoital contraception. Clin Obstet Gynecol 2001;44: 101–5.

Von Hertzen H, Piaggio G, Ding J, Chen J, Song S, Bartfai G, et al. Low dose mifepristone and two regimens of levonorgestrel for emergency contraception: a WHO multicentre randomised trial. Lancet 2002;360: 1803–10.

42

Simple cyst in postmenopausal patients

A 57-year-old asymptomatic postmenopausal woman has a pelvic ultrasonogram that shows a 3.5-cm left ovarian lesion, as shown in Figure 42-1. The most appropriate next step in management would be

    (A) a CA 125 study
    (B) Doppler flow studies
*   (C) repeated ultrasonography in 3 months
    (D) a computed tomography (CT) scan with contrast
    (E) diagnostic laparoscopy

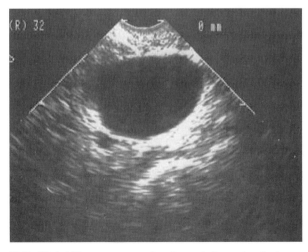

FIG. 42-1. Ultrasonogram showing a left ovarian lesion.

Ovarian cystic masses occur fairly frequently in postmenopausal women. These masses are a cause for concern because the incidence of epithelial ovarian cancer increases in this age group.

Ultrasonographic morphologic parameters of postmenopausal ovarian cysts have been shown to be predictive of the risk of malignancy. Unilocular cysts less than 5 cm in diameter are usually asymptomatic and have a minimal risk of malignancy. Ultrasonographic findings most suggestive of malignancy are papillary projections or solid components of the inner wall of the tumor. Simple cysts without septations, internal papillae, or solid areas have a very low incidence of malignancy. In this case, follow-up ultrasonography in 3 months is the most appropriate option.

Serum CA 125 level has not been shown to be an effective screening tool for ovarian cancer. Data suggest that the CA 125 level is higher than 35 U/mL in only 50% of patients with stage I ovarian cancer. However, CA 125 test results may be useful to help determine the need for surgical intervention if the findings of an ultrasonographic examination are equivocal or suggestive of malignancy. Additionally, CA 125 level is elevated for a multitude of other reasons, such as endometriosis, diverticulitis, and other causes of peritoneal inflammation. Any cancer affecting the peritoneum, pleura, or pericardium will elevate the level of CA 125.

Doppler flow studies of ovarian tumors are being evaluated as an adjunctive method to increase the specificity of vaginal ultrasonography findings. Color Doppler flow studies do not appear to add significantly to predictive ultrasonography findings at this time. Additional studies of smaller ovarian tumors need to be carried out before this method can be recommended as a screening tool in cases like the one described.

A CT scan is a poor imaging modality for assessing cystic ovarian tumors. Ultrasonography is a markedly more effective method.

Diagnostic laparoscopy is not indicated in this case because the findings do not suggest a chance of malignancy. Enlargement of the cyst or a suspicious change in the ultrasonographic parameters during the follow-up period, however, would warrant a diagnostic laparoscopy.

Bailey CL, Ueland FR, Land GL, DePriest PD, Gallion HH, Kryscio RJ, et al. The malignant potential of small cystic ovarian tumors in women over 50 years of age. Gynecol Oncol 1998;69:3–7.

DePriest PD, Shenson D, Fried A, Hunter JE, Andrews SJ, Gallion HH, et al. A morphology index based on sonographic findings in ovarian cancer. Gynecol Oncol 1993;51:7–11.

Levine D, Gosink BB, Wolf SI, Feldesman MR, Pretorius DH. Simple adnexal cysts: the natural history in postmenopausal women. Radiology 1992;184:653–9.

Sassone AM, Timor-Tritsch IE, Artner A, Westhoff C, Warren WB. Transvaginal sonographic characterization of ovarian disease: evaluation of a new scoring system to predict ovarian malignancy. Obstet Gynecol 1991;78:70–6.

43

Initiation of feeding postoperatively

A healthy 25-year-old woman, gravida 1, has undergone an uncomplicated elective cesarean delivery with regional anesthesia for breech presentation. In answer to her inquiry about when she can resume a regular diet, you tell her she may do so

      (A) after she passes flatus
      (B) following a bowel movement
  * (C) immediately
      (D) 48 hours postoperatively after tolerating a liquid diet

A paradigm shift with regard to postoperative feeding has become evident in the surgical literature. The traditional regimen was to give clear fluids on postoperative day 1, followed by dietary advancement only after flatus had been established. The hypothesis that early feeding in the postoperative patient might be well tolerated is based on knowledge that daily postoperative bowel function continues, with absorption of 1–2 L of gastric and pancreatic juices.

Early oral feeding in patients who have undergone uncomplicated cesarean delivery has not been associated with gastrointestinal complaints (eg, nausea, vomiting, or diarrhea) compared with patients who were allowed to sip small amounts of water 12 hours postoperatively and advanced to liquid diets only after bowel sounds were auscultated and flatus was passed. Rapid return of bowel function with substantially shorter mean postoperative time interval to bowel movement in the early feeding group was noted in 1 randomized trial. Thus, early oral feeding after cesarean delivery appeared to be well tolerated by patients, who also experienced shorter hospital stays. No increase in postoperative complications (eg, fever) or hospital readmissions occurred in the early feeding group. Additionally, no significant differences were noted in those patients who were fed early and received general anesthetics compared with general anesthesia patients who were fed only after passing flatus. One study suggested that women who were fed early and whose operations exceeded 40 minutes were more likely to experience ileus symptoms (eg, anorexia, abdominal cramping, or nonpersistent nausea with or without vomiting).

Both the surgical and gynecologic literature point to early feeding of postoperative patients as a viable option after a variety of surgical procedures, including colon surgery. Postoperative morbidity was similar in a group in which patients were allowed to control their rate of oral intake and in a group in which patients received a more traditional fixed postoperative diet. A review of early postoperative feeding in the gynecologic patient found that slow advancement of the diet is probably unnecessary and leads to no increase in demonstrable morbidity. The authors concluded that early feeding did not increase the incidence of aspiration pneumonia, dehiscence, or intestinal leaks. Thus, it is unnecessary to withhold feeding until flatus or defecation has occurred.

Fanning J, Andrews S. Early postoperative feeding after major gynecologic surgery: evidence-based scientific medicine. Am J Obstet Gynecol 2001;185:1–4.

Han-Geurts IJ, Jeekel J, Tilanus HW, Brouwer KJ. Randomized clinical trial of patient-controlled versus fixed regimen feeding after elective abdominal surgery. Br J Surg 2001;88:1578–82.

Horowitz IR. Postanesthesia and postoperative care. In: Rock JA, Thompson JD, editors. TeLinde's operative gynecology. 8th ed. Philadelphia (PA): JB Lippincott; 1997. p. 142–3.

Patolia DS, Hilliard RL, Toy EC, Baker B. Early feeding after cesarean: randomized trial. Obstet Gynecol 2001;98:113–6.

Soriano D, Dulitzki M, Keidar N, Barkai G, Mashiach S, Seidman DS. Early oral feeding after cesarean delivery. Obstet Gynecol 1996;87: 1006–8.

44

Postmenopausal bleeding

A 53-year-old woman had been amenorrheic for 6 months. In the interval, she experienced hot flushes, night sweats, and irritability. She elected to start combined estrogen–progestin therapy, which markedly relieved her symptoms. Now, after 6 months of therapy, she has experienced vaginal bleeding every 4–6 days that requires fewer than 1 pad per day. The most appropriate next step in evaluation of this patient is

* (A) transvaginal ultrasonography
  (B) hysteroscopy
  (C) observation
  (D) vaginal hysterectomy

Postmenopausal uterine bleeding is the most common sign of endometrial hyperplasia and endometrial carcinoma. Age is the greatest independent risk factor associated with hyperplasia or endometrial cancer. In one study, if vaginal bleeding was experienced by a woman older than 70 years who was not receiving hormone therapy (HT), the chance of cancer was 50%. Amenorrheic patients do not require endometrial sampling prior to the initiation of HT. The majority of women are placed on a continuous combined regimen and may have occasional vaginal bleeding during the next 6 months. Approximately 10–20% of patients still may have vaginal spotting at 1 year after initiation of therapy. Patients placed on cyclic estrogen and progestin commonly have 1 short episode of bleeding per month after progestin withdrawal. If unpredictable bleeding occurs, the patient should be reevaluated.

Transvaginal ultrasonography is used as a diagnostic screening tool for endometrial cancer. Endometrial thickness is measured as the distance from the proximal to the distal interface of the hypoechoic layer surrounding the endometrium. A cutoff of 4 mm for symptomatic patients not receiving HT has a sensitivity of 98% and negative predictive value of 99%. Patients who have an endometrial thickness less than 4 mm rarely have endometrial carcinoma. Endometrial thickness greater than 5 mm excludes atrophy but cannot exclude neoplasia.

Some studies have suggested that ultrasonography may be more sensitive than blind endometrial biopsy. Most authors believe a second biopsy is not indicated if thickened endometrium is noted on ultrasonographic examination and the initial biopsy results are normal unless the patient continues to have abnormal bleeding. Endometrial fluid is noted in 12% of asymptomatic older women and

is not considered abnormal. Ultrasonography does not appear to be reliable in patients who are taking tamoxifen citrate (Nolvadex). The apparent thickening of the endometrium in tamoxifen-treated patients has been attributed to changes in the adjacent myometrium.

Of the options, transvaginal ultrasonography would be the best choice in this patient's evaluation. Transvaginal ultrasonography has adequate sensitivity to reassure the patient as long as the endometrium is 4 mm or less in thickness and the patient's bleeding does not continue. Hysteroscopy allows direct visualization of the endometrium and biopsy of any abnormal areas; however, it usually requires sedation and is not indicated as an initial evaluation.

Observation alone is not an acceptable alternative except in the short term after initiation of therapy. Vaginal hysterectomy is not indicated unless intractable bleeding occurs and does not respond to conservative management.

Berek JS, Hacker NF. Practical gynecologic oncology. 3rd ed. Philadelphia (PA): Lippincott Williams & Wilkins; 2000.

DiSaia PJ, Creasman WT. Clinical gynecologic oncology. 6th ed. St. Louis (MO): Mosby; 2002.

Fistonic I, Hodek B, Klaric P, Jokanovic L, Grubisic G, Ivicevic-Bakulic T. Transvaginal sonographic assessment of premalignant and malignant changes in the endometrium in postmenopausal bleeding. J Clin Ultrasound 1997;25:431–5.

Langer RD, Pierce JJ, O'Hanlan KA, Johnson SR, Espeland MA, Trabal JF, et al. Transvaginal ultrasonography compared with endometrial biopsy for the detection of endometrial disease. Postmenopausal Estrogen/Progestin Interventions Trial. N Engl J Med 1997;337: 1792–8.

Shipley CF III, Simmons CL, Nelson GH. Comparison of transvaginal sonography with endometrial biopsy in asymptomatic postmenopausal women. J Ultrasound Med 1994;13:99–104.

45

Pain diagnosis and management

In January 2001, the revised pain management standards of the Joint Commission on Accreditation of Healthcare Organizations (JCAHO) became effective. The single most important indicator of patient pain is

    (A) increased heart rate
*   (B) patient self-report
    (C) support staff assessment of patient pain
    (D) time taken to obtain initial postoperative pain relief
    (E) requirement for intravenous analgesia

Since the 1970s, evidence has accumulated that physicians and nurses do not believe patients when they state they are having pain and that there is a tendency to undermedicate patients because of misconceptions about pain medications, including the risk of addiction. This problem partially results from non–evidence-based information about narcotic administration that has been taught in nursing and medical education programs. Furthermore, several recent studies suggest that many patients do not receive adequate pain control after surgery.

Pain has been declared "the fifth vital sign" by JCAHO. In 1999, JCAHO established guidelines that mandate evidence of pain management, pain treatment, and evaluation of treatment effectiveness in surgical and nonsurgical patient management. The current consensus is that the single most reliable indicator of the existence and intensity of acute pain and any resultant affective discomfort or distress is the patient's self-report.

The Robert Wood Johnson Foundation and JCAHO have collaborated to develop standards and guidelines that serve as a mandate for institutions to develop and implement a process for a pain management program for all patients, including inpatients with acute conditions, ambulatory care patients, and chronic cancer and rehabilitation patients. Standards are evidence based (see Box 43-1).

BOX 45-1

Evidence-Based Standards Required for Recognition and Treatment of Pain in Surgical and Nonsurgical Patient Management

- Patients have a right to pain assessment, pain treatment, and follow-up reassessment of pain.
- Pain treatment should include regularly scheduled drug administration and as-needed drug administration, as well as appropriate patient-controlled analgesic, epidural, or intravenous device.
- Patients should be monitored posttreatment for pain intensity, quality, character, frequency, location, duration, and response to treatment.
- Pain assessment must be charted and documented in writing.
- A plan to teach patients and families that they have a right to pain management must be in place.
- Written pain standards and guidelines are in place in all institutions.
- Methods exist to educate physicians (curriculum in place) and registered nurses (competencies regarding patient-controlled analgesia pumps, assessment, and documentation) regarding standards of care.
- Methods to evaluate pain standards and pain relief are on an area of the chart where vital signs and medications are charted.
- A mission statement exists on pain management and is in standards that include the patient and family bill of rights.
- Patients' rights include information about pain and pain relief.
- Staff is concerned about and committed to pain prevention and management.
- Health professionals respond rapidly to pain reports.
- Patient reports of pain will be believed.
- The patient has a right to state-of-the-art pain management.
- Pain is made visible in the institution by having standards of care, clear expectations, and regular pain monitoring along with vital sign measurement.
- A process is in place for measuring outcomes, such as quality improvement, chart audits, satisfaction surveys, and the use of pain medications.

Modified from Summers S. Evidence-based practice, III: acute pain management of the perianesthesia patient. J Perianesth Nurs 2001;16:112–20.

Joint Commission on Accreditation of Healthcare Organizations. Comprehensive accreditation manual for ambulatory care. Washington, DC: JCAHO; 2000.

Larson L. Treating pain: three models. Trustee 2000;53(7):25–6.

Summers S. Evidence-based practice, II: reliability and validity of selected acute pain instrument. J Perianesth Nurs 2001;16:35–40.

Summers S. Evidence-based practice, III: acute pain management of the perianesthesia patient. J Perianesth Nurs 2001;16:112–20.

46

Paget's disease of the vulva

A 72-year-old woman presents with a well-demarcated pruritic erythematous eczematoid lesion involving both labia. The lesion has a "beefy" appearance with hyperemic areas and a superficial white coating. The gross examination is as shown in Figure 46-1. The findings from colposcopic examination of the cervix and vagina are normal. A biopsy of the lesion results in the diagnosis of Paget's disease. The most appropriate next step in management is

    (A) 5-fluorouracil
    (B) skinning vulvectomy
    (C) clobetasol propionate cream
 * (D) wide local excision
    (E) carbon dioxide laser ablation therapy

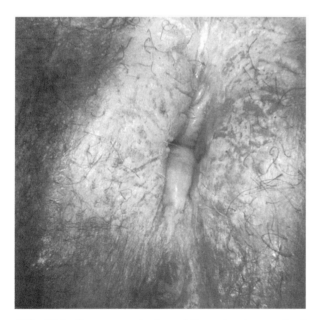

FIG. 46-1. Gross examination of the vulva in a patient with Paget's disease.

Extramammary Paget's disease is an uncommon intraepithelial, usually intradermal, adenocarcinoma that typically occurs in areas rich in apocrine glands (eg, the genitoperineal region and axilla). Extramammary disease makes up 1–2% of primary vulvar neoplasms and is even less common in other sites. Paget's disease of the vulva tends to occur in middle-aged or elderly women. Mean age at diagnosis is 65 years, and the disease has the potential

for local recurrence, dermal invasion, and distant metastasis. Paget's cells, which may arise from intraepidermal cells of apocrine gland ducts or from primitive stem cells of the epithelium, may be found anywhere in the epidermis. Paget's disease also has been reported on the breast, especially around the nipple, and is almost always associated with an underlying breast carcinoma. Malignant in situ or invasive lesions of the genital tract and anus, as well as the lower colon, have been reported in 10–30% of patients with vulvar Paget's disease. After diagnosis, patients should undergo colposcopic evaluation of the cervix, vagina, and vulva, as well as evaluation of the lower colon and anus for evidence of multifocal disease.

On gross examination, Paget's disease appears as an erythematous base, mottled with white hyperkeratotic patches. Symptoms such as pruritus, soreness, and burning are common. Longstanding lesions may be modified by repeated excoriation or superimposed infection, which may delay clinical detection and diagnostic biopsy. Microscopically, large, pale-staining cells are found initially in the basal layer but eventually involve the entire surface epithelium (Fig. 46-2).

Even with surgical therapy, the primary treatment modality for vulvar Paget's disease, the recurrence rate approaches 50%. The most appropriate management is wide local excision with the objective of ruling out an underlying malignancy.

Extramammary Paget's disease may be multifocal, and multiple surgical excisions may be required to control residual and recurrent disease. On rare occasions, wide

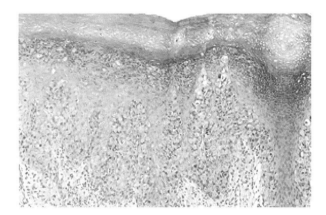

FIG. 46-2. Microscopic examination of the vulva in a patient with Paget's disease. The biopsy specimen shows large, pale cells throughout the epithelium that are particularly prominent near the basement membrane and are consistent with Paget's disease.

local excision and split-thickness skin grafting may be considered in younger women who wish to preserve sexual function.

First-line therapy for Paget's disease would not be 5-fluorouracil, because only short-term remissions have been reported with this drug, and painful ulceratic the treated area are common. Carbon dioxide laser ab tion therapy generally is not recommended, because there is no tissue available to evaluate depth of disease or margin involvement, and the treatment is associated with pain and prolonged healing. In some instances, small recurrences or foci of residual disease may be treated by laser vaporization.

In Paget's disease, the basement membrane is highly irregular, and its rete pegs extend into the dermis to varying depths. Skinning vulvectomy is likely to cut across some of these rete pegs, leading to incomplete resection and the probability of recurrence. The administration of clobetasol propionate is not an appropriate treatment. This medication is used to treat lichen sclerosus, not Paget's disease.

Lloyd J, Flanagan AM. Mammary and extramammary Paget's disease. J Clin Pathol 2000;53:742–9.

Nichols D, Clarke-Pearson D. Gynecologic, obstetric and related surgery. 2nd ed. St. Louis (MO): Mosby; 2000. p. 653–4.

Parker LP, Parker JR, Bodurka-Bevers D, Deavers M, Bevers MW, Shen-Gunther J, et al. Paget's disease of the vulva: pathology, pattern of involvement and prognosis. Gynecol Oncol 2000;77:183–9.

47

Ovary removal at hysterectomy

A 55-year-old woman is scheduled to undergo total vaginal hysterectomy and bilateral oophorectomy for symptomatic uterine prolapse. She is concerned about possible physiologic effects of such surgery. You counsel her that the most common physiologic change after ovarian removal in this situation is

   (A) decrease in insulin resistance
   (B) increase in serum estrone level
   (C) decrease in total cholesterol
 * (D) decrease in serum testosterone level
   (E) decrease in dehydroepiandrosterone sulfate (DHEAS) level

Among women older than 45 years who undergo hysterectomy for benign indications, oophorectomy is frequently recommended to prevent subsequent development of ovarian cancer. Evidence has been growing that the postmenopausal ovary is hormonally active. After natural menopause, the ovaries continue to secrete testosterone. Therefore, bilateral oophorectomy in this case will cause a marked decrease in the serum testosterone level.

Among postmenopausal women, circulating levels of testosterone are 30% lower after surgical menopause, compared with age-matched controls. After natural menopause, estradiol and estrone are derived primarily from peripheral conversion of androgens. Thus, the drop in available androgen precursors with surgical menopause results in a measurable decline in serum estrone and estradiol levels. In contrast, circulating levels of DHEAS, produced by the adrenal gland, are unaffected by menopause or oophorectomy. Table 47-1 shows the blood production rates of androgens.

-1. Blood Production Rates of Androgens*

n	Premenopausal	Postmenopausal	After Oophorectomy
ɛnedione (mg/d)	2–3	0.5–1.5	0.4–1.2
(ng/d)	6–8	1.5–4.0	1.5–4.0
ng/d)	8–16	4–9	4–9
erone (mg/d)	200–250	50–100*	20–70

DHEAS, dehydroepiandrosterone sulfate; DHEA, dehydroepiandrosterone.

*Age-dependent rate.

Based on data from Adashi EY. The climacteric ovary: an androgen-producing gland. In: Adashi EY, Rock JA, Rosenwaks Z, editors. Reproductive endocrinology, surgery, and technology. Vol. 2. Philadelphia: Lippincott Williams & Wilkins; 1996. p. 1745–57; Longcope C. Hormone dynamics at the menopause. Ann NY Acad Sci 1990;592:21–30.

Kritz-Silverstein D, Barrett-Connor E, Wingard DL. Hysterectomy, oophorectomy, and heart disease risk factors in older women. Am J Public Health 1997;87:676–80.

Laughlin GA, Barrett-Connor E, Kritz-Silverstein D, von Muhlen D. Hysterectomy, oophorectomy, and endogenous sex hormone levels in older women: the Rancho Bernardo Study. J Clin Endocrinol Metab 2000;85:645–51.

Lobo RA. Androgens in postmenopausal women: production, possible role, and replacement options. Obstet Gynecol Surv 2001;56:361–76.

48

Use of gonadotropin-releasing hormone agonists prior to hysterectomy

A 42-year-old woman with a uterine myoma of approximately 16–18 weeks of gestation in size presents with heavy irregular vaginal bleeding that has resulted in symptomatic anemia that requires transfusion. In addition, she reports hot flushes and night sweats. An endometrial biopsy shows proliferative-phase endometrium. Conservative therapy is attempted, but fails. Gonadotropin-releasing hormone (GnRH) agonists are being considered for use prior to hysterectomy. The most likely potential result of this therapy is

* (A) reduction in uterine size
  (B) decrease in hemoglobin level
  (C) degeneration of the myoma
  (D) relief of the patient's vasomotor symptoms

Uterine myomas are steroid-dependent proliferations of smooth muscle cells and fibrous connective tissue. They are the most common tumors in the female pelvis and occur in 20–25% of reproductive-aged women. Higher concentrations of estrogen and progesterone receptors have been demonstrated in leiomyomata compared with normal myometrium. In the 10–40% of leiomyomata that become symptomatic, bleeding, pain, and pressure are the most common symptoms.

Uterine leiomyomata account for approximately 30% of hysterectomies in white women and 60% in African-American women. Many of these hysterectomies are performed for menorrhagia. Approximately 75% of such hysterectomies are performed transabdominally, especially if the uterus is larger than 12–14 weeks of gestation in size. Vaginal hysterectomy is associated with lower blood loss, shortened hospital stay, and quicker recovery. Therefore, methods to reduce the size of myomas to facil-

itate vaginal hysterectomy or increase preoperative hemoglobin levels are desirable.

Because of their favorable effects on uterine myomas, GnRH agonists have been used prior to hysterectomy. All GnRH agonists have common effects on myomas, as summarized in Box 48-1. Reduction in size of leiomyomata is the most likely effect of GnRH agonist treatment.

In one study, patients with uteri 14–18 weeks of gestation in size who had been given preoperative therapy with GnRH agonists for 2 months had an 80% chance of having a vaginal hysterectomy. However, women with uterine size larger than 18 weeks of gestation did not experience a sufficient decrease in uterine size to have a vaginal hysterectomy performed.

Early studies demonstrated a preoperative rise in hemoglobin level in patients treated with GnRH agonists. More recent studies have compared therapy with GnRH

Adverse effects of GnRH agonists include hyaline degeneration and focal necrosis in 1–2% of patients. Such adverse effects may be secondary to vasoconstriction of vessels supplying the myomas and are associated with pain and fever in patients with submucosal tumors. If myomectomy is to be performed, the degeneration may cause the plane normally made distinct by the pseudo-capsule of the leiomyoma to be obscured and necessitate piecemeal removal of the leiomyoma. Other adverse effects of GnRH agonists include induction of night sweats and hot flushes in otherwise asymptomatic patients. Therefore, relief of the patient's vasomotor symptoms is unlikely.

agonists plus iron versus iron therapy alone in patients with anemia. Of the patients treated with GnRH agonists plus iron, 74% achieved a hemoglobin level at least 12 g/dL, compared with 46% of patients in the group receiving placebo plus iron, reducing the need for transfusion.

Potential change from midline to low transverse incision by use of preoperative GnRH agonist therapy was studied in a group of 75 premenopausal patients who underwent abdominal hysterectomy. At the time of operation, uterine volumes were smaller, mean hemoglobin levels were higher, and blood loss was decreased in the treated group. Surgeons, who were blinded to treatment modality, elected transverse incisions more often.

Lumsden MA, West CP, Thomas E, Coutts J, Hillier H, Thomas N, et al. Treatment with the gonadotropin releasing hormone-agonist goserelin before hysterectomy for uterine fibroids. Br J Obstet Gynaecol 1994;101:438–42.

Regidor PA, Schmidt M, Callies R, Kato K, Schindler AE. Estrogen and progesterone receptor content of GnRH analogue pretreated and untreated uterine leiomyomata. Eur J Obstet Gynecol Reprod Biol 1995;63:69–73.

Stovall TG. Gonadotropin-releasing hormone agonists: utilization before hysterectomy. Clin Obstet Gynecol 1993;36:642–9.

Stovall TG, Muneyyirci-Delale O, Summitt RJ Jr, Scialli AR. GnRH agonist and iron versus placebo and iron in the anemic patient before surgery for leiomyomata: a randomized controlled trial. Leuprolide Acetate Study Group. Obstet Gynecol 1995;86:65–71.

Stovall TG, Summitt RL Jr, Washburn SA, Ling FW. Gonadotropin-releasing hormone agonist use before hysterectomy. Am J Obstet Gynecol 1994;170:1744–8 [discussion 1748–51].

49

Insomnia at perimenopause

A 46-year-old woman states that for the past 18 months, she has had difficulty getting to sleep. She reports that her menstrual flow is irregular, with bleeding episodes every 30–90 days and no intermenstrual spotting. She has an occasional hot flush, but neither her irregular menstrual flow nor her hot flushes have been disturbing enough to warrant therapy. She consumes 3–5 glasses of alcohol per week and 4 cups of coffee a day, and she smokes a half-pack of cigarettes daily. She has been treated for depression in the past but believes that it is not an issue at present. Her vital signs, body mass index (BMI), and general examination are unremarkable. The best counseling to give her is to tell her that

    (A) insomnia is a common problem, and she should not worry

    (B) the transition to menopause is associated with transient changes in sleep patterns

*   (C) she should consume no alcohol or caffeinated beverages in the evening

    (D) any over-the-counter medication to induce sleep may be helpful

It is estimated that approximately 35% of the adult population in the United States has a sleep disorder. Sleep disorders are one of the most frequent issues that a primary care practitioner confronts. The problem is more likely to be seen in elderly individuals, but it can occur at any age, and there is no gender difference. Sleep disorders can be transient and due to a significant life crisis or illness, or they can be chronic. The latter type is more common and often more associated with medical or psychiatric problems. The use of psychotropic medications, nasal decongestants, alcohol, and caffeine can produce insomnia.

Medical conditions that have been linked with insomnia include osteoarthritis, fibromyalgia, hyperthyroidism, gastroesophageal reflux disease, Alzheimer's disease, certain respiratory diseases, and muscle cramps. Depression is the most common psychiatric illness associated with insomnia and usually involves early-morning awakening, but it also can be manifested by difficulty falling asleep. Anxiety disorders, schizophrenia, sleep apnea, and heavy cigarette smoking are some of the other problems associated with sleep disorders. Individuals who have a chronic illness; who are older than 50 years; and who take multiple drugs, are obese, and have estrogen deficiency are more likely to have insomnia. Perimenopausal women who have difficulty falling asleep have higher systolic and diastolic blood pressures and greater waist-to-hip ratios. Sleep disturbances are more common in perimenopausal and postmenopausal women who do not receive hormone replacement therapy.

The diagnosis is made by gathering a thorough history; no special laboratory tests are needed. Sleep studies (ie, polysomnography) can be undertaken if sleep apnea is suspected, but this step is usually not necessary.

General management includes patient education and lifestyle modification. The patient should be advised to avoid alcohol consumption in the evening, because it could induce sleep disturbances. She should be advised to avoid caffeinated beverages after 5:00 PM or within 6 hours of retiring. In addition, she should be encouraged to avoid daytime napping and aggressive exercise before retiring and to develop a relaxing bedtime ritual conducive to sleep. Avoidance of heavy late-night snacks and reduction of cigarette smoking can reduce insomnia. If the patient's BMI is greater than 25 kg/m^2, weight reduction should be discussed. Hormone therapy will reduce insomnia in perimenopausal and menopausal women who are troubled by hot flushes. If more conservative measures and lifestyle changes are not effective, over-the-counter sleep-inducing medications may be effective for some patients. If the clinician feels that a hypnotic is indicated, a prescription medicine could be more effective. Agents with relatively short action and minimal hangover effect are preferred. Zolpidem (Ambien) is generally well tolerated and should be prescribed with the same indications as any hypnotic agent.

Most over-the-counter sleep aids contain diphenhydramine, an antihistamine that acts by blocking the central histamine-1 receptors. Diphenhydramine is a long-acting agent with adverse effects that include daytime sleepiness, cognitive impairment, and anticholinergic effects, which render it less than ideal for the treatment of insomnia, particularly in older women.

Ancoli-Israel S. Insomnia in the elderly: a review for the primary care practitioner. Sleep 2000;23 suppl 1:S23–S30 [discussion S36–S38].

Dockhorn RJ, Dockhorn DW. Zolpidem in the treatment of short-term insomnia: a randomized, double-blind, placebo-controlled clinical trial. Clin Neuropharmacol 1996;19:333–40.

Jones CR, Czajkowski L. Evaluation and management of insomnia in menopause. Clin Obstet Gynecol 2000;43:184–97.

Owens JF, Matthews KA. Sleep disturbance in healthy middle-aged women. Maturitas 1998;30:41–50.

50

Menorrhagia treated by endometrial ablation

A 38-year-old woman, gravida 2, para 2, presents with a 10-month history of regular but heavy uterine bleeding, which has resulted in anemia. An aspiration endometrial biopsy performed by her referring physician demonstrated proliferative endometrium. The serum thyroid-stimulating hormone level was 3.2 μg IU/mL. She uses condoms for contraception and prefers not to take therapy to manage her bleeding problem. She requests information about endometrial ablation. Of the following statements, the most important one to emphasize is that

    (A) more than 90% of women surveyed are satisfied with the procedure
    (B) the amenorrhea rate is less than 30% after 3 years
  * (C) contraception is still necessary
    (D) endometrial carcinoma has been reported following the procedure
    (E) postablation tubal sterilization syndrome has been reported

Clinicians first described photovaporization of the endometrium with laser in 1981; the procedure was used to treat menorrhagia. Electrocoagulation using the rollerball under hysteroscopic guidance was reported in 1989 and continues to be the standard by which other procedures are measured.

Endometrial resection by hysteroscopy is highly operator dependent. Reported serious acute complications from the procedure include hyponatremia and hypervolemia, which can result in pulmonary edema, cerebral edema, seizures, and death. Early postoperative complications include hematometra, endomyometritis, and cystitis, but their relative incidence is low. Long-term and less frequent complications include endometrial carcinoma and postablation tubal sterilization syndrome. Although the occurrence of pregnancy after the procedure is small, it is critical that this patient continue contraception and not assume that she cannot conceive after undergoing the procedure. Postablation tubal sterilization syndrome was described in 1993 and is associated with tubal sterilization followed by endometrial ablation. The pathogenesis is unclear. Patients present with intermittent vaginal bleeding associated with severe cramping and lower abdominal pain. These patients exhibit marked endometrial scarring, and proximal portions of the fallopian tubes appear swollen to the extent that on gross examination they resemble an early tubal pregnancy. In one study, laparoscopic removal of the tube relieved symptoms in 5 of the 6 patients.

Since 1997, the U.S. Food and Drug Administration has approved 4 devices to conduct endometrial ablation: ThermaChoice (a uterine balloon therapy system containing hot fluid), Her Option (a cryoablative procedure using a specialized patented gaseous mixture therapy), Hydro ThermAblator (a microprocessor-controlled heat saline profusion system), and NovaSure (an intrauterine bipolar conductive metallic mesh system). This new endometrial instrumentation requires less technical skill and carries lower operative risk than rollerball hysteroscopically directed ablation. A comparison of the different devices is shown in Table 50-1.

Menorrhagia, clinically defined as blood loss of more than 80 mL per cycle, is difficult to ascertain from a patient's history. Other indirect historical information, such as cycle length, the number of sanitary napkins or tampons used, or the number of clots passed, is helpful. In phase 2 clinical trials, ThermaChoice and Her Option have been studied with the subjects serving as the pretherapy and posttherapy controls. Two randomized clinical trials have compared rollerball to ThermaChoice ablation. The 3-year clinical trials showed a 93% success rate with ThermaChoice and a 94% success rate with the rollerball using the patients' subjective response as the outcome parameter. The 3-year data were assessed using telephone interviews. Even though patient satisfaction was high for both procedures, the amenorrhea rates for 3 years were roughly 15% and 26%, respectively. Only 1.8% of the patients ranked the menorrhagia as severe, as opposed to 70.3% preoperatively. Less clinical experience is available for Hydro ThermAblator and NovaSure, and more randomized clinical trials are needed. The technology will continue to improve and provide a relatively safe procedure in an ambulatory setting at a reasonable cost.

TABLE 50-1. U.S. Food and Drug Administration–Approved Devices for Endometrial Ablation

Device	Hypomenorrhea (%) PBAC ≤75	Amenorrhea (%) PBAC = 0	Disposable Size (mm)	Depth of Ablation (mm)	Procedure Time (min)
ThermaChoice uterine baloon therapy system	64 E	14.9 E	5.0	5	8
Her Option uterine cryoablation therapy system	67.4 ITT 74.7 E	22.2 ITT 24.7 E	5.5	9–12	20
Hydro thermablator endometrial ablation system	68.4 ITT 77 E	35.5 ITT 40 E	7.8	2–6	10
NovaSure impedance controlled endometrial ablation system	77.7 ITT	36 ITT 41 E	8.0	3.3–5.7	4.2

E, evaluable for follow-up analysis; ITT, intent-to-treat analysis; PBAC, pictorial blood loss assessment chart score.

Roy KH, Mattox JH. Advances in endometrial ablation. Obstet Gynecol Surv 2002;57:790, 792.

Goldrath MH, Fuller TA, Segal S. Laser photovaporization of endometrium for the treatment of menorrhagia. Am J Obstet Gynecol 1981;140:14–9.

Loffer FD. Three-year comparison of thermal balloon and rollerball ablation in treatment of menorrhagia. J Am Assoc Gynecol Laparosc 2001;8:48–54.

Pugh CP, Crane JM, Hogan TG. Successful intrauterine pregnancy after endometrial ablation. J Am Assoc Gynecol Laparosc 2000;7:391–4.

Townsend DE, McCausland V, McCausland A, Fields G, Kauffman K. Post-ablation-tubal sterilization syndrome. Obstet Gynecol 1993;82:422–4.

51
Postoperative cellulitis

A 42-year-old woman has undergone a total abdominal hysterectomy and bilateral salpingo-oophorectomy through a transverse abdominal incision. The surgery lasted 3 hours and was uneventful. She received prophylactic antibiotics. The skin was closed with a subcuticular suture. Her preoperative weight was 92 kg (202.8 lb). She was discharged home on postoperative day 3. She calls you on postoperative day 5 with complaints of incisional tenderness. She is afebrile. On examination, the wound edges easily separate, and a seroma is evacuated. You examine the wound and determine that the fascia is intact with no evidence of cellulitis. The most appropriate next step in management is

> (A) administration of parenteral antibiotics
> (B) a computed tomography (CT) scan of the abdomen and pelvis
> (C) exploration of the wound in the operating room with the patient under anesthesia
> * (D) packing the wound with wet to dry gauze
> (E) approximating the skin edges with staples

Postoperative wound infection continues to be a complication after major gynecologic surgery; its incidence is approximately 5%. Reduction of the risk of infection has focused on the use of meticulous surgical technique and the administration of prophylactic antibiotics. Abdominal hysterectomy is classified as a clean–contaminated procedure, because the bacterial flora of the vagina is in continuity with the operative site during surgery. The Centers for Disease Control and Prevention subdivide incisional infections into 2 types:

1. Superficial infections that involve only the skin and subcutaneous tissues
2. Deep infections that involve the underlying fascia and muscles

Numerous prospective randomized studies and 2 meta-analyses support the efficacy of prophylactic antibiotics in reducing postoperative infectious morbidity and decreasing the length of hospitalization in women who undergo abdominal hysterectomy. Most studies do not identify any particular antibiotic regimen as being superior. The reasons certain individuals develop infection after antibiotic prophylaxis are not clear.

Both local and systemic factors contribute to wound infections. Local factors (eg, the presence of a hematoma or serous fluid collection, necrotic tissue, foreign bodies, and excessive use of cauterization) are more important. Systemic factors include obesity, diabetes mellitus, malnutrition, and systemic disease. The incidence of superficial skin infection is related directly to the length of the surgical procedure. Each additional hour of surgery results in a doubling of the incidence of superficial skin infection. The incidence of postoperative wound infection increases 8-fold when the woman's preoperative weight exceeds 90.1 kg (200 lb). The thickness of the subcutaneous tissue is also a risk factor. In women with more than 4 cm of subcutaneous tissue, the risk of a superficial skin infection increases 3-fold. Factors that predispose the described patient to a superficial wound infection include the length of the procedure, her weight, and the thickness of the subcutaneous tissue.

The first symptom of most wound infections develops during postoperative days 5–10. The initial management of the majority of wound infections consists of opening and draining the wound. The wound usually opens easily following removal of sutures or clips. Rarely is more than gentle pressure necessary to open the incision completely. Purulent material should be cultured to test for aerobic and anaerobic organisms. Once the wound has been opened and drained, initial management involves packing the wound with gauze. Wound packing with wet to dry gauze will effect débridement.

Antibiotic administration is indicated as an adjunct to packing only if there is surrounding cellulitis. Immediately approximating the wound with staples would not be appropriate, because there would not be adequate granulation tissue. Delayed secondary closure of the wound can be considered after granulation tissue begins to develop. Secondary wound closure results in more rapid healing when the time necessary for eventual closure of the wound by secondary intention is taken into consideration. A CT scan is indicated when the practitioner suspects the existence of a deep pelvic infection that involves the fascia or muscles, but it would not be appropriate in this case. Surgical exploration in the operating room is not necessary for this patient, because the fascia is intact and there is no evidence of necrotic tissue or deep infection.

American College of Obstetricians and Gynecologists. Antibiotic pro-phylaxis for gynecologic procedures. ACOG Practice Bulletin 23. Washington, DC: ACOG; 2001.

Droegemueller W. Postoperative counseling and management. In: Stenchever MA, Droegemueller W, Herbst AL, Mishell DA, editors. Comprehensive gynecology. 4th ed. St. Louis (MO): Mosby; 2001. p. 771–821.

Faro S. Postoperative infections. In: Gershenson DM, DeCherney AH, Curry SL, Brubaker L, editors. Operative gynecology. 2nd ed. Philadelphia (PA): WB Saunders; 2001. p. 123–31.

Injuries and fistulae. In: American College of Obstetricians and Gynecologists. Precis: gynecology. Washington, DC: ACOG; 2001. p. 99–106.

Soper DE, Bump RC, Hurt WG. Wound infection after abdominal hys-terectomy: effect of the depth of subcutaneous tissue. Am J Obstet Gynecol 1995;173:465–9 [discussion 469–71].

52

Moderate sedation

While you are performing a hysteroscopy on a woman who is under moderate sedation with mida-zolam (Versed), a nurse reports the patient's blood pressure reading to be 120/70 mm Hg and her heart rate to be 82 beats per minute. The patient has a depressed level of consciousness and has pur-poseful responses only after light tactile stimulation. Your next step in management is to

* (A) reassure the nurse and continue with the procedure
 (B) administer flumazenil (Romazicon) immediately
 (C) administer naloxone (Narcan) immediately
 (D) administer additional midazolam

In January 2001, the Joint Commission on Accreditation of Healthcare Organizations (JCAHO) adopted the American Society of Anesthesiologists (ASA) four levels of sedation and anesthesia (see Box 52-1). The guidelines bring the practice of conscious sedation into the realm of anesthesia in an effort to increase patient safety, because 1) patients can move easily from one level of sedation to another and 2) the response to sedation is unpredictable. Practitioners, therefore, must have appropriate training and education to prepare for emergency situations and be in compliance with JCAHO. They should be able to res-cue a patient who slips into a "deeper than desired" level of sedation, manage a compromised airway, and be pre-pared to handle a compromised cardiovascular system.

The term *conscious sedation* has been replaced with moderate sedation. Although depressed, patients in a state of moderate sedation who respond purposefully to verbal or light tactile stimulation need no airway support, and the integrity of the cardiorespiratory system is main-tained. By contrast, patients in deep sedation respond only after painful tactile or repeated verbal stimulation. Patients under minimal sedation and patients who receive only oral medication or local anesthetics do not fall under JACHO guidelines. Sedation monitoring for these patients is up to the discretion of the health care practitioner.

Practitioners who use moderate and deep sedation for patient comfort must adhere to the guidelines adopted in 2001. A patient who undergoes moderate or deep sedation should have at least a focused physical examination with specific evaluation of the airway. The patient's previous experience with sedative drugs and past medical history must be considered. Informed consent for sedation is nec-essary and should include identification of risks, benefits, and alternatives. Like a patient who will be given tradi-tional anesthetics, a patient who will receive medication for moderate or deep sedation must fast for at least 2 hours if only clear liquids were ingested, and for 6 hours if a light meal was ingested. Careful scrutiny should be given to patients who are obese or have a small neck, jaw abnormality, or small mouth, because such patients pose more difficulty in airway management, especially in an emergency.

In addition to assessing the patient's response during moderate sedation, the practitioner should use pulse oximetry; record the patient's blood pressure at regular intervals, the first before the start of sedation and the last just before discharge; and have an individual available to perform such monitoring. Only during moderate sedation can this individual assist the practitioner with interruptible ancillary tasks of short duration. During deep sedation of the patient, the person monitoring the patient's level of consciousness should have no other responsibilities.

Electrocardiographic monitoring is required for deep sedation but not for moderate sedation unless the patient has significant cardiovascular disease or dysrhythmia is anticipated. An emergency cart with a Yankauer suction device must be in the area. Box 52-2 lists recommended emergency equipment.

Individuals who undergo moderate sedation must be informed about the pharmacologic agents used in cases of an emergency. Combination sedation with a sedative and a narcotic is acceptable but may increase the risks of ventilatory depression and hypoxia. The practitioner must be knowledgeable about the antagonists used to reverse the effects of narcotics and benzodiazepines. Naloxone usually is used to reverse the effects of opioids, and flumazenil is used to reverse the effects of benzodiazepines. Reversal may bring on signs of anxiety and discomfort. The medications should not be administered too rapidly, and the practitioner must be aware that the reversal agent may wear off before the narcotic or benzodiazepine does. Thus, the patient is at risk for resedation. At least 2 hours must have elapsed between the time a reversal agent was administered and the time of discharge. Equipment for the administration of supplemental oxygen must be available. The administration of oxygen is required for deep sedation and should be considered for moderate sedation.

BOX 52-1

American Society of Anesthesiologists Four Levels of Sedation and Anesthesia

1. Minimal Sedation
A drug-induced state in which the patient responds normally to verbal commands. Cognitive function and coordination might be impaired, but breathing and cardiovascular functions remain normal.

2. Moderate or Conscious Sedation
A drug-induced depression of consciousness in which the patient cannot be easily aroused but can respond "purposefully" to verbal commands, either alone or after a gentle touch. Breathing and cardiovascular functions usually remain normal. (The American Society of Anesthesiologists has determined that the familiar term "conscious sedation" should now be known as sedation and/or anesthesia.)

3. Deep Sedation/Analgesia
A drug-induced depression of consciousness in which the patient cannot be easily aroused but responds to repeated or painful stimulation. The patient may need some artificial assistance in breathing, but usually can maintain normal cardiovascular function.

4. Anesthesia
A drug-induced loss of consciousness in which the patient cannot be aroused, even with repeated or painful stimulation. The patient usually cannot breathe without artificial assistance and commonly experiences impaired cardiovascular function.

Data from JCAHO revises standards on anesthesia, EC, and medical staff. Briefings on JCAHO 2000;11(8):1.

BOX 52-2

Recommended Emergency Equipment

Airway Management Equipment
Oxygen source
Suction source
Face masks: infant, child; small, medium, and large adult
Breathing bag and valve set (adult and pediatric)
Oral airways: infant, child; small, medium, and large adult
Nasal airways: small, medium, and large
Laryngoscope handles (tested)
Laryngoscope blades:
  Straight (Miller) no. 1, 2, 3
  Curved (MacIntosh) no. 2, 3, 4
Endotracheal tubes:
  Uncuffed: 2.5, 3.0, 3.5, 4.0, 4.5, 5.0, 5.5, 6.0
  Cuffed: 6.0, 6.5, 7.0, 7.5, 8.0
Stylettes
Surgical lubricant
Suction catheters (appropriate sizes for endotracheal tubes)
Yankauer suction device
Nasogastric tubes
Nebulizer attachment
Gloves
Magill forceps

Intravenous Equipment
Intravenous catheters: 24-, 22-, 20-, 18-, and 16-gauge
Tourniquets
Alcohol swabs
Adhesive tape
Assorted syringes: 1-, 3-, 6-, and 12-mL
Intraosseous needle
Intravenous tubing:
  Pediatric drip (60 drops/mL)
  Pediatric burette type
  Extension tubing
Intravenous tubing: normal saline
3-way stopcocks
Pediatric intravenous boards
Sterile gauze pads
Assorted intravenous needles: 22-, 20-, and 18-gauge

Pharmacologic Agents
Naloxone
Flumazenil
Epinephrine
Atropine
Lidocaine
Glucose (10% and 50%)
Diphenhydramine
Hydrocortisone, methylprednisolone, or dexamethasone
Diazepam or midazolam
Succinylcholine

Reprinted from J Emerg Med, Vol 17, Innes G, Murphy M, Nijssen-Jordan C, Ducharme J, Drummond A, Procedural sedation and analgesia in the emergency department. Canadian Consensus Guidelines. p. 150. Copyright 1999, with permission from Elsevier.

Patients must be carefully monitored in a recovery area prior to discharge. Careful attention must be given to making sure the patient has recovered fully from the sedative medications.

In the case described, the best choice is to reassure the nurse and continue the procedure, because the patient is under appropriate moderate sedation. Naloxone would be administered if the patient had been administered a narcotic. Flumazenil would be given if the patient were oversedated with a benzodiazepine. The addition of oxygen is not necessary because the patient responds appropriately. She does not need additional medication, because it might place her in deep sedation.

Christian M, Yeung L, Williams R, Lapinski P, Moy R. Conscious sedation in dermatologic surgery. Dermatol Surg 2000;26:923–8.

Innes G, Murphy M, Nijssen-Jordan C, Ducharme J, Drummond A. Procedural sedation and analgesia in the emergency department. Canadian Consensus Guidelines. J Emerg Med 1999;17:145–56.

Practice guidelines for sedation and analgesia by non-anesthesiologists. Anesthesiology 2002;96:1004–17.

Recommended practices for managing the patient receiving moderate sedation/analgesia. AORN J 2002;75:642–6, 649–52.

53

Antibiotic-associated diarrhea

A 30-year-old woman is now at postoperative day 15 after a postpartum hysterectomy for postpartum hemorrhage and chorioamnionitis. On postoperative day 9, she required reexploration with bilateral salpingo-oophorectomy for continued abscess collection. She has developed acute respiratory distress syndrome (ARDS) and has experienced diarrhea, which has become bloody over the past 2 days. The tissue culture cytotoxicity assay for *Clostridium difficile* toxin was positive for toxin B from her stool, and you have treated her with oral vancomycin and metronidazole for 5 days. On rounds today, you note that her hemoglobin decreased from 10 g/dL to 7 g/dL overnight, and her rectal bleeding has increased. Results of clotting studies, platelet count, and blood chemistry testing are all normal. After immediate transfusion, the best next step in management is

       (A) a barium enema
       (B) therapy with intravenous immune globulin
       (C) therapy with an oral nonpathogenic yeast *(Saccharomyces boulardii)*
  *   (D) consultation with a surgeon for possible colectomy
       (E) expectant management if vital signs remain stable

The incidence of antibiotic-associated diarrhea varies from 5% to 39%, depending on the antibiotic used. Outpatients have a *C difficile* colonization rate of 3%, whereas hospitalized adults have rates as high as 20–30%. The higher incidence in the hospitalized population is thought to result primarily from destruction of normal protective colonic flora by antibiotic therapy. Only 10–20% of patients with antibiotic-associated diarrhea will have a *C difficile* infection, but the majority of cases of colitis associated with antibiotic therapy will involve the organism. The antibiotics most commonly implicated are clindamycin, penicillin derivatives, and cephalosporins. At-risk patients include patients who have received antibiotics, patients in an intensive care setting, elderly patients, and patients who have had abdominal surgery.

C difficile colitis is a toxin-mediated disease. Recent evidence supports the fact that the toxins A and B released from pathogenic strains of *C difficile* cause fluid secretion, increased mucosal permeability, and marked enteritis when injected into the intestinal lumen of animals. The disease can range from mild diarrhea, which can be treated by discontinuing the antibiotic with or without the addition of cholestyramine, to a severe illness with the patient at risk for anemia, bowel perforation, and death. More morbid patients may develop fever, leukocytosis, and crampy abdominal pain. Some patients with more severe disease will have a distended abdomen from ileus or hypoalbuminemia and ascites as a result of poor gut function.

The diagnosis is made by detection of toxin A or B. The gold standard has been the cytotoxin assay that uses tissue culture because of its high sensitivity and ability to detect minute amounts of toxin B. The turnaround time is 24–48 hours. Another method for detecting the toxin is enzyme immunoassays, which can be completed within hours. However, enzyme immunoassays are not as sensitive as tissue tests, especially with lower levels of toxin B.

The immunoassay must test several stool samples to improve the reliability of the diagnosis.

The first line of treatment generally is to stop the administration of the offending antibiotic. If it is not reasonable to discontinue use of the antibiotic, as in this patient with ARDS, the treating physician should consider changing the antibiotic to one that is less likely to exacerbate the process. The first-line therapy is usually 250 mg metronidazole given 3 times a day by the parenteral, or preferably oral, route. This therapy is very inexpensive. The alternative regimen is 125–500 mg oral vancomycin given 3 times a day. Both these regimens are effective more than 90% of the time. If the patient has a more severe disease, combinations of these drugs should be considered.

Passive immunization with immunoglobulin products has been used successfully to treat a few patients with severe *C difficile* colitis. This patient has severe disease with documentation of toxin B and worsening hematochezia despite double antibiotic therapy. She would be managed best by surgery, which is indicated for patients with severe infection that is not responding to normal treatment. The surgical treatment of choice appears to be total colectomy with preservation of the rectal stump, but some authors support a more conservative colectomy. Indications for surgery include toxic megacolon, acute abdomen, perforation, hemorrhage, and poor response to treatment.

Patients with recurrent infection usually are managed by alternative doses of the antibiotics previously mentioned. Probiotics such as *S boulardii* or lactobacillus strain GG have been used successfully to treat recurrent episodes. Probiotics are biologic agents used to treat infections, especially of mucosal surfaces such as the gut or vagina. Lactobacillus strain GG is a bacterium, whereas *S boulardii* is a yeast. An alternative medication method is the use of enemas with feces from healthy subjects. This method has not been found to be acceptable to practitioners or patients and poses the risk of additional infections in compromised patients. Probiotic therapy is most useful in the prevention of antibiotic-associated diarrhea.

A barium enema or colonoscopy would be contraindicated in this patient because the diagnosis already has been made and her symptoms are worsening. These tests may even be detrimental to a patient who is not improving. They might put her at risk for perforation, especially if she already has developed a dilated colon.

Bartlett JG. Clinical practice: antibiotic associated diarrhea. N Engl J Med 2002;346:334–9.

D'Souza AL, Rajkumar C, Cooke J, Bulpitt CJ. Probiotics in prevention of antibiotic associated diarrhoea: meta-analysis. BMJ 2002;324:1361.

Kyne L, Farrell RJ, Kelly CP. Clostridium difficile. Gastroenterol Clin North Am 2001;30:753–77, ix–x.

Yassin SF, Young-Fadok T, Zein NN, Pardi DS. Clostridium difficile-associated diarrhea and colitis. Mayo Clin Proc 2001;76:725–30.

54

Uterine leiomyoma

A recently married 34-year-old nulligravid woman has a 2-year history of progressively worsening menorrhagia refractory to oral contraceptive therapy. She wishes to become pregnant in the future. On ultrasonographic examination, she is found to have a 7-cm intramural leiomyoma, which causes pelvic pressure. The most appropriate management of this patient is

        (A) administration of gonadotropin-releasing hormone (GnRH) agonist

*   (B) myomectomy

        (C) hysteroscopy with dilation and curettage

        (D) uterine artery embolization

Leiomyomata, commonly referred to as *fibroids*, are the most common solid pelvic tumors and occur in 25–50% of women. They remain the most common indication for hysterectomy in the United States. Many women with leiomyomata are asymptomatic and do not require therapeutic intervention. The most common symptoms are menorrhagia and pelvic pain or pressure. The patient's predominant symptoms and her desire to maintain fertil-

ity or to retain her uterus for personal reasons influence the choice of appropriate therapy.

Myomectomy is the best option for this patient, because it allows her to retain potential fertility. Numerous small studies suggest that after an abdominal myomectomy there is excellent resolution of menorrhagia in approximately 81% of cases, as well as resolution of pelvic pressure. Recurrence rates after myomectomy average approximately 20%. Data suggest that laparoscopic myomectomy has similar efficacy to abdominal myomectomy, with lower morbidity. Operator experience is an obvious prerequisite for this approach.

The use of gonadotropin-releasing hormone agonist has been shown to result in shrinkage of leiomyomata, but the medication cannot be administered long term. Leiomyomata return to their original size within several months of discontinuation of GnRH agonist therapy. Although this therapy would not be definitive in this symptomatic patient, it might be useful in patients closer to the age of menopause. It also might be useful to administer it preoperatively to reduce uterine size and thus facilitate the performance of a hysterectomy. With size reduction, a hysterectomy may be accomplished vaginally rather than abdominally. In addition, a GnRH agonist can be used to reduce bleeding and thus eliminate a patient's anemia prior to surgery.

Thermal balloon ablation may improve the menorrhagia, but it would not alter the patient's symptoms of pelvic pain or pressure. In addition, this procedure is not indicated in patients who wish to retain their fertility.

Hysteroscopy with dilation and curettage may relieve the menorrhagia initially, but it would fail to treat the underlying problem of the intramural leiomyoma.

Hysteroscopic resection is an effective treatment for submucosal leiomyomata, which often result in menorrhagia.

Uterine artery embolization is an increasingly popular alternative to more invasive surgical procedures. Reports suggest that most patients experience significant decreases in menstrual blood loss, in addition to reduction of uterine size due to shrinkage of the leiomyomata. Uterine artery embolization can be performed on an outpatient basis and is associated with lower morbidity than other surgical options. The procedure was first reported in 1995, and a large-scale randomized control trial of the procedure is needed. This procedure is currently contraindicated in patients who desire future fertility.

American College of Obstetricians and Gynecologists. Surgical alternatives to hysterectomy in the management of leiomyomas. ACOG Practice Bulletin 16. Washington, DC: ACOG; 2000.

Droegemueller W. Benign gynecologic lesions: vulva, vagina, cervix, uterus, oviduct, ovary. In: Stenchever MA, Droegemueller W, Herbst AL, Mishell DR, editors. Comprehensive gynecology. 4th ed. St. Louis (MO): Mosby; 2001. p. 479–530.

Goodwin SC, McLucas B, Lee M, Chen G, Perrella R, Vedantham S, et al. Uterine artery embolization for the treatment of uterine leiomyomata midterm results. J Vasc Interv Radiol 1999;10:1159–65.

Klein A, Schwartz ML. Uterine artery embolization for the treatment of uterine fibroids: an outpatient procedure. Am J Obstet Gynecol 2001; 184:1556–60 [discussion 1560–3].

55

Vaginal vault prolapse

An 87-year-old woman, gravida 4, para 4, with hypertension, type 2 diabetes, and known cardiac disease, is referred for management of complete procidentia. She has no desire for sexual activity. She reports urinary urgency and difficulty initiating her urinary stream at the end of the day. She experiences urinary incontinence if she "waits too long" to void. Physical examination reveals complete procidentia, a stage 3 cystourethrocele, and rectocele. No stress urinary leakage is observed during evaluation when the uterus is reduced. Catheterized postvoid residual volume is 300 mL. The most appropriate surgical procedure is

(A) vaginal hysterectomy, anterior and posterior repair
* (B) LeFort partial colpocleisis
(C) cervical amputation with uterosacral ligament plication
(D) vaginal hysterectomy, anterior and posterior repair with sacrospinous ligament fixation
(E) total abdominal hysterectomy with sacrocolpopexy

Because women now live longer and desire to maintain a healthy and active lifestyle, the number of women who present for management of pelvic organ prolapse is likely to increase dramatically. Pelvic relaxation occurs in approximately 50% of parous women, with 15% having symptoms significant enough to warrant surgery.

Uterine prolapse is the result of damage to the vagina and its support systems (ie, endopelvic fascial attachments and the levator muscle plate). Risk factors for uterine prolapse are shown in Box 55-1.

The most appropriate surgical procedure for this patient would be the LeFort partial colpocleisis. The patient is elderly, has significant medical problems, and has no desire for sexual activity. By obliterating the vagi-

na, the LeFort partial colpocleisis corrects total providentia without the need for a hysterectomy. Operating time and blood loss are reduced compared with hysterectomy, and the procedure may be done under local anesthesia with sedation, unlike the other, more extensive reconstructive surgeries.

The LeFort procedure (Fig. 55-1) involves dissecting 2 thin rectangular flaps of vaginal epithelium off the anterior and posterior vaginal wall, extending 2 cm proximal to the cervix to approximately 4 cm from the urethral meatus anteriorly and up to the posterior cul-de-sac posteriorly, avoiding entry into the cul-de-sac peritoneum. The vaginal mucosa is left intact laterally to form drainage canals. Then, beginning at the cervix, the cut edge of the anterior vaginal wall, including any underlying fascia, is sewn to the cut edge of the posterior vaginal wall using interrupted, delayed-absorbable sutures. This procedure gradually inverts the cervix and vagina. Finally, the superior and inferior margins of the rectangle are sutured horizontally, thus obliterating the vaginal canal.

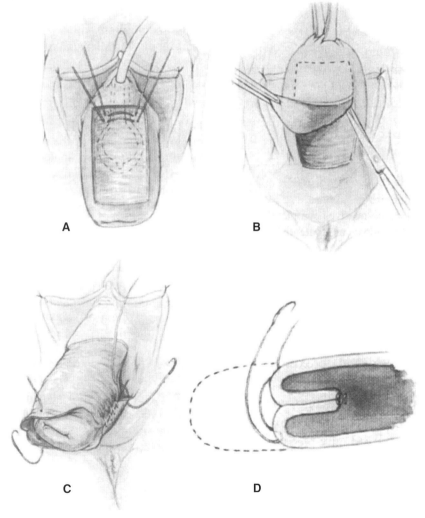

A   B

C   D

FIG. 55-1. LeFort partial colpocleisis. (**A**) The anterior vaginal wall has been removed, and a plication stitch is placed at the bladder neck. (**B**) The posterior vaginal wall is removed. (**C, D**) The cut edge of the anterior vaginal wall is sewn to the cut edge of the posterior vaginal wall in such a way that the uterus and vagina are inverted. (Reprinted from Atlas of pelvic anatomy and gynecologic surgery, Baggish M, Karram M. p. 431. Copyright 2001, with permission from Elsevier.)

A vaginal hysterectomy with anterior and posterior repair would not address the apical defect, which is the primary defect in this patient. The apical defect is best addressed with either a sacrospinous ligament fixation or abdominal sacrocolpopexy. Both of these options effectively treat the apical compartment and are viable options in younger, healthier women. However, they require a substantially longer operative time and have markedly increased morbidity risks such as hemorrhage and neurologic injury. They are not appropriate procedures for this patient. The reported success rates of sacrospinous ligament fixation and abdominal sacrocolpopexy for addressing apical prolapse are 83–95% and 95%, respectively.

Cervical amputation with uterosacral ligament plication (ie, the Manchester-Fothergill operation) is used in women with significant cervical elongation and second- or third-degree uterine descent. Although less invasive than the other choices, it will not provide sufficient support to correct complete procidentia.

Carey MP, Dwyer PL. Genital prolapse: vaginal versus abdominal route of repair. Curr Opin Obstet Gynecol 2001;13:499–505.

Miklos JR, Sze EH, Karram MM. Vaginal correction of pelvic organ relaxation using local anesthesia. Obstet Gynecol 1995;86:922–4.

Norton PA. Pelvic floor disorders: the role of fascia and ligaments. Clin Obstet Gynecol 1993;36:926–38.

Thompson JD. Surgical technique for pelvic organ prolapse. In: Rock JA, Thompson JD, editors. Te Linde's operative gynecology. 8th ed. Philadelphia (PA): Lippincott–Raven; 1997. p. 969–79.

56

Surgical alternatives to hysterectomy

A 39-year-old woman who has undergone a tubal ligation has a 6-month history of menorrhagia refractory to hormonal and nonsteroidal antiinflammatory drug management. She has had 3 vaginal deliveries, and the largest child weighed 4,082 g (9 lb) at birth. A pelvic examination reveals a mobile uterus approximately 10–12 weeks of gestation in size, with good descensus and a gynecoid pelvis. Findings of an endometrial biopsy are normal, and a pelvic ultrasonogram reveals a uterus 10 weeks of gestation in size with intramural leiomyomata and normal ovaries, which confirms the physical examination. The patient desires definitive management with ovarian conservation. The most appropriate surgical management approach for this patient is

      (A) endometrial ablation
      (B) uterine artery embolization
      (C) total abdominal hysterectomy
*   (D) vaginal hysterectomy
      (E) myomectomy

Hysterectomy is the most common gynecologic surgery performed in the United States; with approximately 600,000 hysterectomies performed each year. Leiomyomata are the most common solid pelvic tumors and the leading indication for hysterectomy. Hysterectomy is the definitive treatment of leiomyomata, because it is the only treatment that provides a cure and eliminates the possibility of recurrence. Compared with abdominal hysterectomy, vaginal hysterectomy has lower patient morbidity, cost, and postoperative pain, as well as a quicker return to normal activity. In the United States, however, approximately 75% of hysterectomies are performed abdominally. Contraindications to the vaginal approach are known or suspected uterine adhesions to other pelvic structures, cancer, poor uterine descensus or mobility, significant uterine enlargement, suspected or known adnexal pathol-

ogy, suspected pelvic infection, and significant endometriosis.

Given this patient's physical findings, unless the surgeon has limited experience in vaginal surgery, the initial surgical approach should be vaginal. Numerous techniques exist to remove an enlarged uterus, including uterine morcellation, myomectomy, bivalving, and coring. Conversion to an abdominal hysterectomy is always possible, should it become necessary.

Endometrial ablation, uterine artery embolization, and myomectomy all present the risk of recurrent bleeding and may not definitively manage the bleeding associated with leiomyomata. Endometrial ablation is effective therapy for the control of abnormal uterine bleeding without leiomyomata. Myomectomy should be considered for women who desire future childbearing or who prefer to retain their uterus. Myomectomy traditionally is performed by laparotomy, but both laparoscopic and hysteroscopic techniques may be used, depending on the skill and training of the surgeon and the location of the leiomyomata.

Uterine artery embolization is a relatively new procedure for the management of symptomatic leiomyomas when a patient desires uterine conservation. It is an interventional radiologic technique that includes mapping of the blood supply to individual leiomyomas, followed by the placement of small beads to block this blood supply. Studies suggest a significant decrease in uterine size and bleeding. However, the procedure has risks, including infection, uterine necrosis, bleeding, pain, and ischemic and hypoxic changes, which sometimes require surgery.

American College of Obstetricians and Gynecologists. Surgical alternatives to hysterectomy in the management of leiomyomas. ACOG Practice Bulletin 16. Washington, DC: ACOG; 2000.

Farquhar CM, Steiner CA. Hysterectomy rates in the United States 1990–1997. Obstet Gynecol 2002;99:229–34.

Fylstra DL, Carter JF. Laparoscopically assisted vaginal hysterectomy in a university hospital. J Reprod Med 1996;41:497–503.

Payne JF, Haney AF. Serious complications of uterine artery embolization for conservative treatment of fibroids. Fertil Steril 2003;79:128–31.

Stovall TG. Hysterectomy. In: Berek JS, Adashi EY, Hillard PA, editors. Novak's gynecology. 12th ed. Baltimore (MD): Williams & Wilkins; 1996. p. 727–67.

Wilcox LS, Koonin LM, Pokras R, Strauss LT, Xia Z, Peterson HB. Hysterectomy in the United States, 1988–1990. Obstet Gynecol 1994;83:549–55.

57

Vulvar abscess

A 45-year-old woman with type 1 (insulin dependent) diabetes presents with a history of groin and vulvar pain and swelling for the past 5 days. Examination reveals an erythematous, indurated, fluctuant mass measuring 5 cm × 6 cm that involves the labia majora and extends to the proximal groin and lower abdominal wall. The area is markedly tender. The most appropriate next step in management is

    (A) incision and drainage in the office under local anesthesia
*   (B) incision, drainage, and exploration under general anesthesia
    (C) administration of broad-spectrum antibiotics
    (D) sitz baths 4 times a day

Patients who present with diabetes mellitus, especially longstanding or poorly controlled disease, exhibit a greater frequency and severity of many types of infection. Reasons for this predisposition include ill-defined abnormalities in cell-mediated immunity and phagocyte function associated with hyperglycemia and diminished peripheral vascularization in longstanding disease. Individuals with diabetes mellitus have increased colonization of *Staphylococcus aureus* in skinfolds and nares, which may predispose them to severe soft tissue infections, as in the current patient.

This patient presents with a vulvar folliculitis or Bartholin's gland infection that has progressed to a regional soft tissue infection. The superficial fascial planes of the vulva are continuous with the lower abdominal wall. Because of the decreased vascularity and immune response prominent in longstanding diabetes mellitus, a localized infection of the vulva easily may progress and encompass the ipsilateral or, in more severe cases, contralateral vulva or abdominal wall. Depending

on the aggressiveness of the organism, a major abscess or necrotizing fasciitis may result (Fig. 57-1).

Treatment principles for superficial soft tissue infections include incision, drainage, and aggressive débridement of devascularized tissue, which requires general anesthesia and an operating room setting. With severe infection, the procedure can include removal of wide areas of soft tissue and even fascia, which may require grafting later. Incision and drainage under local anesthesia in the office setting is appropriate for small, superficial soft tissue infections; however, it precludes the aggressive débridement necessary in these infections. Delayed incision and drainage is not appropriate in this case because an obvious fluctuant area is present. This area, as well as the surrounding cellulites, must be opened and débrided. Likewise, treatment with sitz baths or antibiotics without incision and drainage would be inadequate.

Ancillary devices are now available to supplement the customary incision and drainage and follow-up wound

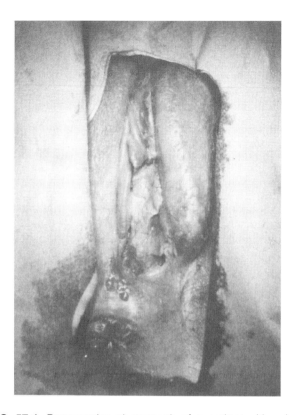

FIG. 57-1. Preoperative photograph of a patient with vulvar and perineal necrotizing fasciitis. Note the asymmetric edema of the labia majora and necrosis of the left labia minora. Further débridement of necrotic tissue was necessary. (Sweet RL, Biggs RS. Infectious diseases of the female genital tract. 4th ed. Philadelphia [PA]: Lippincott Williams & Wilkins; 2002. p. 564.)

care. Products that apply constant suction through a sponge mask have been approved for use; they improve wound cleansing and decrease time to complete wound closure.

Braunwald E, Fauci AS, Kasper DL, Hauser SL, Longo DL, Jameson JL. Harrison's principles of internal medicine.15th ed. New York (NY): McGraw-Hill; 2001. p. 2126–8.

DeAngelo AJ, Dooley DP, Skidmore PJ, Kopecky CT. Group F streptococcal bacteremia complicating a Bartholin's abscess. Infect Dis Obstet Gynecol 2001;9:55–7.

Lentz SS. Use of the vacuum-assisted closure system in management of the gynecologic surgical wound: a case report. J Pelvic Surg 2002;8: 53–6.

Soper DE. Necrotizing fasciitis. In: Faro S, Soper DE, editors. Infectious diseases in women. Philadelphia (PA): WB Saunders; 2001. p. 324–9.

Sweet RL, Biggs RS. Infectious diseases of the female genital tract. 4th ed. Philadelphia (PA): Lippincott Williams & Wilkins; 2002. p. 562–6.

58

Dysmenorrhea

A 42-year-old married monogamous woman, para 3, has had increasingly heavy menses and dysmenorrhea for 1 year. Nonsteroidal antiinflammatory drugs help diminish the symptoms but are now contraindicated because of a recent diagnosis of peptic ulcer disease. The patient smokes 1 pack of cigarettes per day. An endometrial biopsy shows dyssynchronous endometrium. The best next treatment option for this patient is

    (A) 20-μg combination oral contraceptive pills

    (B) ethinyl estradiol

    (C) a copper-containing intrauterine device (IUD) (ParaGard)

*   (D) the levonorgestrel-releasing IUD (Mirena)

Anovulatory bleeding accompanied by menorrhagia is common during the perimenopause, as well as during adolescence. Oral contraceptive adherence rates are higher in healthy adolescents requiring treatment for menorrhagia and dysmenorrhea compared with adolescents without these symptoms. Combination oral contraceptives can decrease anovulatory bleeding in the perimenopausal woman. However, in cigarette smokers older than 35 years, combination oral contraceptives, and patches, rings, and injectable products that contain estrogen are relatively contraindicated.

The copper-containing IUD has been associated with heavier menstrual flow in some users and therefore would not be appropriate for this patient. Use of the levonorgestrel IUD, which releases small amounts of progestin locally within the endometrium, has been observed to result in endometrial suppression. The major change in the menstrual bleeding pattern with its use is an overall reduction in the menstrual volume and number of bleeding days. The mean reduction of menstrual blood loss is approximately 40 mL per month. This reduction often leads to scanty menstrual bleeding, and one third of users experience amenorrhea in 6 months. After 1 year of use, 20% of women who used the levonorgestrel IUD were amenorrheic. Although most women experience extra bleeding and spotting during the first 3–6 months of use, these changes usually are well tolerated with appropriate counseling.

Lahteenmaki P, Rauramo I, Backman T. The levonorgestrel intrauterine system in contraception. Steroids 2000;65:693–7.

American College of Obstetricians and Gynecologists. The use of hormone contraception in women with coexisting medical conditions. ACOG Practice Bulletin 18. Washington, DC: ACOG; 2000.

Pakarinen P, Toivonen J, Luukkainen T. Therapeutic use of the LNG IUS, and counseling. Semin Reprod Med 2001;19:365–72.

Robinson JC, Plichta S, Weisman CS, Nathanson CA, Ensminger M. Dysmenorrhea and use of oral contraceptives in adolescent women attending a family planning clinic. Am J Obstet Gynecol 1992;166: 578–83.

59

Genetic factors associated with endometriosis

A 42-year-old woman who was treated for biopsy-proven endometriosis 20 years ago has a daughter with the same diagnosis. The woman inquires about the likelihood that her second daughter, who is 16 years old, will have endometriosis. Which of the following statements is accurate with respect to the mode of inheritance of endometriosis?

      (A) It is autosomal recessive with variable penetrance.

*   (B) It is polygenic multifactorial.

      (C) It is caused by spontaneous mutations.

      (D) There is no evidence of genetic inheritance.

Since its first description, endometriosis has been found most commonly in patients with a family history of the disease. Specifically, endometriosis occurs with a frequency of approximately 7% in first-degree relatives, compared with a frequency of 1% in the female relatives of the patient's husband. The disease is more severe in women with an affected first-degree relative.

Endometriosis is believed to be a derangement of the immune surveillance system that is transmitted genetically. This derangement is both humoral and cell mediated. Box 59-1 shows proposed systemic and peritoneal immunologic abnormalities in endometriosis.

The cells involved in the development of endometriosis are the B lymphocytes, T lymphocytes, granulocytes, monocytes, macrophages, and natural killer cells. There is increased B cell function. In addition, there are higher levels of complement C3 and C4 in the serum and peritoneal fluid. A decreased cellular-mediated immune response facilitates implantation of ectopic endometrial cells. Peritoneal macrophages release increased quantities of cytokines, prostaglandins, growth factors, and complement components, all of which are associated with peritoneal endometriosis. Levels of cytokines; tumor necrosis factor α; interleukin 1, 6, and 8; monocyte chemotactic protein-1; and interferon are elevated in the peritoneal fluid. Cytokine levels decrease after medical treatment of endometriosis.

Estrogen receptors also play a role in that there is overexpression of estrogen receptor β (ER-β) compared with estrogen receptor α (ER-α) in ovarian endometriomas. It is postulated that a decreased ratio of ER-α to ER-β may well favor the local expression of proinflammatory cytokines in patients with endometriosis.

The Oxford Endometriosis Gene (OXGENE) study has been designed to identify susceptibility genes in endometriosis through linkage analysis. In this international collaborative project, DNA is being collected from families with endometriosis. The aim of the project is to identify susceptible loci and establish a linkage using affected sib-pair analysis. Identification of genes that pre-

dispose women to the disease is the ultimate goal. There does not appear to be a clear Mendelian pattern of inheritance, ie, a pattern of gene loci interacting with each other and the environment to produce the phenotype. The strongest evidence to support a genetic basis for endometriosis comes from 3 studies that have shown a 6- to 7-fold higher risk of endometriosis among first-degree relatives of affected women than among control subjects.

The main candidate genes currently are genes involved in detoxification: cytochrome P-450 (*CYP*), glutathione-

---

BOX 59-1

Proposed Immunologic Abnormalities in Endometriosis

Systemic Abnormalities
- Increased immunoglobulin production
- Increased presence of helper (CD4) cells
- Deficient lymphocyte-mediated cytotoxicity against endometrium
- Embryotoxic serum
- Serum that suppresses natural killer cell activity
- Deficient cellular immunity
- Deficient natural killer cell activity
- Abnormal autoimmune function
- Decreased suppressor cell activity

Peritoneal Abnormalities
- Endometrial stromal cell proliferation
- Increased cytotoxicity of peritoneal macrophages
- Decreased sperm binding to zona pellucida
- Proliferation of lymphocytes
- Increased sperm phagocytosis by peritoneal macrophages
- Increased cytokine levels
- Accentuated cyclic activation of macrophages
- Decreased natural killer cell activity of lymphocytes
- Interleukin-1 receptor antagonist secretion by peritoneal macrophages
- Presence of non–organ-specific autoantibodies

S-transferase (*GST*) and N-acetyltransferase 2 (*NAT2*). Diseases such as diabetes mellitus, asthma, and hypertension do not exhibit Mendelian inheritance patterns and are believed to be multifactorial or polygenic. Endometriosis falls into this category of polygenic multifactorial inheritance.

Environmental factors also play a role, probably by interacting with susceptible genes. In a rhesus monkey model, it was shown that exposure to dioxin or ionizing radiation induced endometriosis in a dose- and time-dependent manner. In a study of humans done in Belgium, a country with high levels of dioxin pollution, dioxin levels were noted to be higher in women with endometriosis than in control subjects. There is no genetic link related to the dioxin effect.

Additional evidence for a genetic basis for endometriosis includes familial clustering of adenomyosis based on magnetic resonance imaging assessment of individuals with karyotypic abnormality *del(7) (q21.2–q31.2)*. In terms of ethnic differences, a higher prevalence of endometriosis has been observed among Asian women than among Caucasian women. In addition, endometriosis is known to be rare in ultraorthodox Jews.

In light of the frequency of occurrence of endometriosis among women, as well as current research in the OXGENE study, it appears that neither a recessive mode of inheritance nor spontaneous mutation is likely.

Coxhead D, Thomas EJ. Familial inheritance of endometriosis in a British population: a case control study. J Obstet Gynaecol 1993; 13:42–4.

Kennedy S. The genetics of endometriosis. J Reprod Med 1998;43: 263–8.

Moen MH, Magnus P. The familial risk of endometriosis. Acta Obstet Gynecol Scand 1993;72:560–4.

Oral E, Arici A. Pathogenesis of endometriosis. Obstet Gynecol Clin North Am 1997;24:219–33.

Simpson JL, Elias S, Malinak LR, Buttram VC Jr. Heritable aspects of endometriosis, I: genetic studies. Am J Obstet Gynecol 1980; 137: 327–31.

Stefansson H, Einarsdottir A, Geirsson RT, Jonsdottir K, Sverrisdottir G, Gudnadottir VG, et al. Endometriosis is not associated with or linked to the GALT gene. Fertil Steril 2001;76:1019–22.

Zondervan KT, Cardon LR, Kennedy SH. The genetic basis of endometriosis. Curr Opin Obstet Gynecol 2001;13:309–14.

60

Human immunodeficiency virus in health care workers

A resident from another specialty is interested in changing programs to obstetrics–gynecology. As program director, you have a junior resident position available. The candidate seems to be acceptable. You offer her a contract, and she subsequently informs you that she tests positive for human immunodeficiency virus (HIV). The most appropriate next step would be to

      (A) withdraw your offer
      (B) welcome her to the department
*   (C) defer your offer pending additional information
      (D) report her HIV status to the state department of health

Because of the widespread risks of HIV infection and development of acquired immunodeficiency syndrome (AIDS), both patients and clinicians are rightly concerned about the risk of spread in the practice of clinical medicine. Physicians who have reason to believe that they are at significant risk of infection should be tested voluntarily for HIV for the protection of their patients, as well as for their personal health. A physician as a patient is entitled to the same rights of privacy and confidentiality as any other patient.

The ethical guidelines involved in testing include autonomy (the right of an individual to self-determination) and beneficence (ie, the obligation of the physician to promote the best interests of the patient).

The risk of clinician-to-patient transmission is extremely low because of routine use of sterile surgical technique and adherence to a policy of universal precautions. Physicians who are infected with HIV should follow standard precautions with regard to patient care. Compliance with risk-limiting procedures is mandatory. These procedures include hand washing, use of protective barriers, and caution in the use and disposal of sharp instruments and needles. Surgical barriers and surgical techniques that limit intraoperative injury further diminish the possible risk of transmission. Clinicians involved in surgical and obstetric procedures always should be aware of the dangers of transmission of any infection, such as hepatitis, tuberculosis, and the common cold—not just HIV infection. The American College of Surgeons has formulated a list of recommendations relative to the surgeon and HIV infection.

All infected physicians must decide which procedures they can perform safely. They should make this decision in consultation with their personal physician, and they may include others, such as the department director, the chief of the medical staff, or the hospital's infectious disease specialists. If physicians can avoid procedures that place patients at risk for infection, they have no obligation to inform their patients that they are HIV positive.

In the scenario described, both the resident and you, as the program director, face difficult challenges. A denial of the position to the resident could be seen as discriminatory, regardless of other circumstances. Deferment of the offer while seeking another candidate raises the same discriminatory concerns. Furthermore, reporting a communicable disease is the responsibility of the diagnosing physician, not the program director. If you were to proceed with the resident's employment and not insist on obtaining further information, you would be remiss in

that you would have failed to safeguard the interests of your patients.

Cain JM. Principles of patient care. In: Berek JS, Adashi EY, Hillard PA, editors. Novak's gynecology. 12th ed. Baltimore (MD): Williams & Wilkins; 1996. p. 21–31.

English DC. Bioethics: a guide for medical students. New York (NY): WW Norton; 1994. p. 161–2.

Human immunodeficiency virus: ethical guidelines for obstetricians and gynecologists. In: American College of Obstetricians and Gynecologists. Ethics in obstetrics and gynecology. Washington, DC: ACOG; 2002. p. 43–7.

Public Health Service guidelines for the management of health-care worker exposures to HIV and recommendations for postexposure prophylaxis. Centers for Disease Control and Prevention. MMWR Recomm Rep 1998;47(RR-7):1–33.

Statement on the surgeon and HIV infection. American College of Surgeons. Bull Am Coll Surg 1998;83(2):27–9.

61

Transurethral incontinence

A 62-year-old woman requests surgery for symptoms of stress incontinence. She complains of severe leakage related to activity, coughing, and sneezing. She had an antiincontinence surgical procedure at the time of an abdominal hysterectomy 10 years ago. Your initial assessment includes a voiding diary, which reveals frequent, small voids. Her physical examination is normal with the exception of hypermobility of the bladder neck. A postvoid residual urine measurement is 30 mL, and urinalysis reveals no blood or inflammatory cells. Before making a recommendation regarding surgery, the single most appropriate diagnostic test is

     (A) cystourethroscopy
     (B) a cough stress test
     (C) complex uroflowmetry
*   (D) complex cystometry
     (E) a methylene blue test

Among women with stress incontinence, 75% will have urodynamic stress incontinence, defined as documented urine leakage with increased intraabdominal pressure in the absence of a detrusor contraction. The remaining 25% with stress incontinence symptoms will have detrusor instability, overflow incontinence, or other causes. Box 61-1 shows terminology for urinary incontinence in women, including symptoms, diagnoses, and tests.

Appropriate diagnosis is paramount prior to surgical intervention, especially for women with recurrent incontinence after previous surgery. In the case described, urodynamic evaluation is indicated to confirm the diagnosis of urodynamic stress incontinence.

Urodynamic testing may include a variety of manometric and physiologic tests. Not all women require uro-

dynamic evaluation prior to surgical management of stress urinary incontinence. Characteristics of women who are most likely to benefit from preoperative urodynamic evaluation include the following:

- Marked concomitant symptoms of urge incontinence
- Abnormal voiding frequency
- Signs and symptoms of possible neurologic disease
- A history of prior antiincontinence surgery or radical pelvic surgery
- A well-supported urethra

Urodynamic testing will most likely benefit women with a history of prior antiincontinence surgery and women with severe incontinence. In other cases, a basic

---

BOX 61-1

Terminology for Urinary Incontinence in Women

Symptoms
Stress urinary incontinence: The complaint of involuntary leakage on effort or exertion, or on sneezing or coughing.
Urinary urgency incontinence: The complaint of involuntary leakage accompanied by, or immediately preceded by, urgency.
Mixed urinary incontinence: The complaint of involuntary leakage associated with urgency and also with exertion, sneezing, or coughing.

Urodynamic Diagnoses
Detrusor overactivity: A urodynamic observation characterized by involuntary detrusor contractions during bladder filling. The diagnosis of detrusor overactivity incontinence is made when incontinence occurs as a result of any involuntary detrusor contraction. (Terms no longer in use include *detrusor instability, motor urge incontinence, reflex incontinence,* and *detrusor hyperreflexia.*)
Urodynamic stress incontinence: Involuntary leakage, observed during filling cystometry and occurring with increased abdominal pressure in the absence of a detrusor contraction. (Term no longer in use is *genuine stress.*)

Urodynamic Tests
Filling cystometry: Measurement of the pressure-to-volume relationship of the bladder during filling.
　Simple cystometry: Measurement with a manometer; no electronic recording of the pressure-to-volume curve during filling is made.
　Complex cystometry: Use of calibrated electronic equipment to record the pressure-to-volume curve during filling.
Urethral closure pressure profile: A graph indicating the urethral closure pressure (defined as subtraction of the intravesical pressure from the urethral pressure) along the length of the urethra.
Abdominal leak-point pressure: The intravesical pressure at which urine leakage occurs because of increased abdominal pressure in the absence of a detrusor contraction.
Uroflowmetry: Measurement of the urine flow rate over time during voluntary voiding.
　Simple uroflowmetry: Measurement made with a stopwatch or mechanical uroflowmeter; no electronic recording of the flow rate.
　Complex uroflowmetry: Use of calibrated electronic equipment to record the flow rate.

Modified from Abrams P, Cardozo L, Fall M, Griffiths D, Rosier P, Ulmsten U, et al. The standardisation of terminology of lower urinary tract function: report from the Standardisation Sub-committee of the International Continence Society. Neurourol Urodyn 2002;21:167–8.

---

demonstration of involuntary loss of urine during stress (ie, a provocative stress test with direct visualization of urine loss), and documentation of a normal postvoid residual urine volume. A screening neurologic examination should demonstrate normal perineal sensory and motor innervation. During the pelvic examination, the surgeon should document urethral hypermobility. Prior to surgery, the surgeon also should address transient causes of incontinence (eg, drug effects and urinary tract infection).

This patient has undergone antiincontinence surgery and has symptoms of urinary frequency. Therefore, urodynamic studies should be performed. In this case, the most important urodynamic study would be cystometry, to exclude detrusor overactivity and to confirm the diagnosis of urodynamic stress incontinence. Other urodynamic studies may include urethral pressure profilometry and determination of Valsalva leak-point pressure, both of which measure urethral function.

Cystourethroscopy might be useful to detect foreign bodies within the urinary tract from prior surgery or to document ureteral patency, but is not as pertinent in this case. Cystoscopy is not routinely performed prior to antiincontinence surgery but is useful in selected cases. A cough stress test is part of a basic office evaluation for incontinence but would not be sufficient in this case for the reasons previously stated. Complex uroflowmetry can be used to investigate voiding dysfunction but would not help to confirm the diagnosis in this case. Finally, the methylene blue test is an office test for fistulae. In cases of suspected vesicovaginal fistulas, methylene blue dye can be diluted in 100 mL of sterile saline and instilled into the bladder through a catheter. A tampon or gauze pack then is placed in the vagina. After 30–60 minutes, the tampon or pack is removed and checked for blue staining, which is indicative of a fistula. This test would not be useful for this patient, because the existence of a fistula is not clinically suspected.

Abrams P, Cardozo L, Fall M, Griffiths D, Rosier P, Ulmsten U, et al. The standardisation of terminology of lower urinary tract function: report from the Standardisation Sub-committee of the International Continence Society. Neurourol Urodyn 2002;21:167–78.

ACOG criteria set. Surgery for genuine stress incontinence due to urethral hypermobility. American College of Obstetricians and Gynecologists Committee on Quality Assessment. Int J Gynaecol Obstet 1996;52:211–2.

Droegemueller W. Postoperative counseling and management. In: Stenchever MA, Droegemueller W, Herbst A, Mishell DR, editors. Comprehensive gynecology. 4th ed. St. Louis (MO): Mosby; 2001. p. 771–821.

Jensen JK, Nielsen FR Jr, Ostergard DR. The role of patient history in the diagnosis of urinary incontinence. Obstet Gynecol 1994;83:904–10.

Lemack GE, Zimmern PE. Identifying patients who require urodynamic testing before surgery for stress incontinence based on questionnaire information and surgical history. Urology 2000;55:506–11.

Weber AM, Taylor RJ, Wei JT, Lemack G, Piedmonte MR, Walters MD. The cost-effectiveness of preoperative testing (basic office assessment vs urodynamics) for stress urinary incontinence in women. BJU Intern 2002;89:356–63.

Weber AM, Walters MD. Cost-effectiveness of urodynamic testing before surgery for women with pelvic organ prolapse and stress urinary incontinence. Am J Obstet Gynecol 2000;183:1338–46.

office evaluation may be sufficient. The evaluation should include careful history gathering to exclude appreciable urge symptoms, documentation of normal voiding habits,

62

Pathophysiology of wound healing

You plan to perform a total abdominal hysterectomy for treatment of symptomatic leiomyoma in a 40-year-old woman. The practice that is most likely to reduce the risk of postoperative infection is

  (A) routine screening for bacterial vaginosis
  (B) administration of supplemental perioperative oxygen
  (C) prevention of hypothermia during surgery
  * (D) administration of prophylactic antibiotics
  (E) preoperative smoking cessation

Surgical site infections occur after approximately 5% of hysterectomies. Host characteristics associated with an increased risk of perioperative infection include diabetes mellitus (especially if glucose levels are higher than 200 mg/dL in the postoperative period), nicotine use, steroid use, and malnutrition (see Box 62-1). Because of entry into the vagina, all hysterectomies are considered clean–contaminated procedures. Perioperative infections are most likely to involve normal vaginal flora, including gram-negative bacilli, enterococci, group B streptococci, and anaerobes. Postoperative infections are increased among women with bacterial vaginosis. Therefore, women with bacterial vaginosis should be treated before undergoing elective hysterectomy. However, the overall impact of routine screening for bacterial vaginosis of asymptomatic patients on posthysterectomy infection has not been demonstrated.

Basic preoperative principles to reduce perioperative infections include preoperative identification and treatment of all infections. Smokers should be encouraged to quit at least 30 days before elective surgery. Nosocomial infections can be reduced by avoiding or minimizing preoperative hospitalization. There may be some benefit to antiseptic baths the night before surgery.

Research has shown that perioperative infections can be reduced with aseptic surgical site preparation. Hair removal from the surgical site should occur immediately before surgery, and shaving should be avoided (electric clippers are preferred).

Prophylactic antibiotics have the greatest role in reducing infection after hysterectomy. Immediately before hysterectomy, the use of a single dose of a broad-spectrum antibiotic is recommended. A second dose should be repeated intraoperatively if the operation lasts more than 3 hours or if the blood loss exceeds 1,500 mL.

Hypothermia—ie, core temperature lower than 36°C (96.8°F)—can occur inadvertently during surgery. Mild hypothermia increases the risk of incisional infections, presumably due to effects on oxygen delivery and leukocyte function. The administration of supplemental oxygen can reduce the risk of surgical wound infections. Surgical drains may be beneficial in some cases; a separate incision is recommended for drain placement. Wound infections are more likely when drains are placed through the primary incision. Closed suction drains are preferred to open drains. All drains become colonized with time, and therefore their timely removal is recommended.

Controversy persists regarding the relative benefits of suturing the vaginal cuff open or closed at the time of abdominal hysterectomy. Proponents of the open cuff cite the potential advantage of drainage of blood or serous fluid from the surgical site. Conversely, the closed cuff might prevent ascending infection in the immediate postoperative period. When prophylactic antibiotics are administered at the time of abdominal hysterectomy, there is no benefit to the open- or closed-cuff technique.

BOX 62-1

Host Factors Contributing to Postoperative Infection

Exogenous
- Antibiotics in use
- Active infection
- Presurgical hospitalization
- Shaving of the operative site
- Inadequate hand washing
- Unclean surgical attire
- Poor surgical technique
- Length of surgery*
- Amount of blood loss*

Endogenous
- Obesity
- Chronic illness (including diabetes)
- Abnormal vaginal flora
- History of repeated infections

*Factors that may necessitate repeated administration of prophylactic antibiotics.

In one prospective randomized study of the open- versus closed-cuff techniques (n = 273), the two groups had similar rates of surgical site infection (7% versus 6%) and other complications (hematoma and vault granulation).

American College of Obstetricians and Gynecologists. Antibiotics and gynecologic infections. ACOG Educational Bulletin 237. Washington, DC: ACOG; 1997.

Colombo M, Maggioni A, Zanini A, Rangoni G, Scalambrino S, Mangioni C. A randomized trial of open versus closed vaginal vault in the prevention of postoperative morbidity after abdominal hysterectomy. Am J Obstet Gynecol 1995;173:1807–11.

Greif R, Akca O, Horn EP, Kurz A, Sessler DI. Supplemental perioperative oxygen to reduce the incidence of surgical-wound infection. Outcomes Research Group. N Engl J Med 2000;342:161–7.

Kurz A, Sessler DI, Lenhardt R. Perioperative normothermia to reduce the incidence of surgical-wound infection and shorten hospitalization. Study of Wound Infection and Temperature Group. N Engl J Med 1996;334:1209–15.

Mangram AJ, Horan TC, Pearson ML, Silver LC, Jarvis WR. Guideline for the prevention of surgical site infection. Atlanta (GA): Centers for Disease Control and Prevention; 1999.

Moller AM, Villebro N, Pedersen T, Tonnesen H. Effect of preoperative smoking intervention on postoperative complications: a randomized clinical trial. Lancet 2002;359:114–7.

63

Recognition of ambiguous genitalia in the newborn

While you are doing rounds in your hospital, you are asked by an associate to come to the delivery room. On arrival, you are told that a term neonate has just been delivered and that the sex of the newborn is undetermined (Fig. 63-1). The mother repeatedly asks if the newborn is a boy or a girl. Your associate asks for your opinion. The most important next step in the evaluation is to order

      (A) testing of serum androgens

*   (B) testing of serum electrolytes

      (C) karyotype determination

      (D) abdominal ultrasonography

      (E) magnetic resonance imaging (MRI)

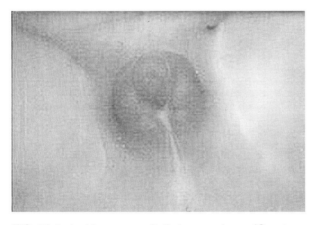

FIG. 63-1. Ambiguous genitalia in a newborn. (Courtesy of Selma Witchel, MD, University of Pittsburgh School of Medicine.)

Abnormalities of external genitalia are uncommon. The optimal management usually requires a team of individuals that initially includes an obstetrician–gynecologist, a pediatric endocrinologist, a psychologist experienced in dealing with intersex disorders, and the support of clerical and nursing staff. The diagnosis of sex often can be made with the use of antenatal ultrasonography. However, although this technique offers a high degree of accuracy, it cannot determine sex with complete certainty. You should inform the patient that a karyotype will identify sex with 100% accuracy. However, other, metabolic issues are more important at this time and will determine the next step in the evaluation.

There are a number of differential diagnoses for ambiguous genitalia, but the most common medical condition is congenital adrenal hyperplasia. Current laboratory and chromosomal analysis make the final diagnosis relatively simple. The key issue, from birth through early life, is the availability of appropriate psychologic counseling for the family and the offspring. As the child develops, a number of issues will need to be addressed.

The main physical finding, besides the general appearance of the exterior genitalia, is the presence or absence of gonadal structures in the inguinal regions. Gonads in the inguinal or scrotal fold are almost certainly testes, because ovaries are not found at these sites. Examination of the phallus, including measurement of the diameter, usually will not provide sufficient sex-differentiating criteria. A stretched penis of less than 2.5 cm in length is 2.5 standard deviations below the mean for an infant at 40 weeks of gestation. A clitoris of a term female infant is less than 1 cm in length. The urethral orifice varies from a mild hypospadias to an opening at the perineal area communicating with a urogenital sinus. A bifid scrotum is usually more obvious and is associated with male gender. The labia can be fused or unfused, with the latter creating more of a diagnostic dilemma in terms of sex assignment. A very gentle rectal examination can be performed, and most clinicians should have sufficient experience to ascertain whether the findings are compatible with the presence of a uterus. In the newborn, the uterus is usually slightly enlarged because of maternal estrogen production.

Elevated levels of dehydroepiandrosterone sulfate and dehydroepiandrosterone can point to adrenal origin. The most common form of congenital adrenal hypertrophy (CAH) causes a deficiency in 21-hydroxylase and a significant elevation in 17-hydroxyprogesterone levels. Elevated 11-desoxycortisol levels can indicate 11 β-hydroxylase deficiency, which is the next most common finding in CAH.

The most important issue related to the immediate survival of the neonate is the status of the electrolytes. There are 2 types of congenital adrenal hyperplasia: salt wasting and non–salt wasting. The salt-losing type of 21-hydroxylase deficiency results in hyperkalemia and hyponatremia. Therefore, baseline electrolyte studies should be ordered immediately. Androgen and karyotype studies can be obtained at the same time but will not have an immediate role in survival. In the nursery, the newborn should be observed closely for signs of adrenal insufficiency, eg, unexplained vomiting and diarrhea that produce dehydration and eventually shock. Often, by the time adrenal insufficiency is noted in a newborn, the infant is very ill and more difficult to treat.

Magnetic resonance imaging will help determine the status of the vagina and internal genitalia. An MRI study is more sensitive and specific than ultrasonography.

Care of the family's emotional issues, particularly taking notice of the parents' mental state, is critical, because they are likely to have substantial fear of the unknown. A psychologist or counselor with specific competence in newborn issues may not be available. After initial diagnosis and early management, follow-up care is usually in the hands of a pediatric endocrinologist. In the newborn, CAH is a complex problem that is usually managed operatively in a tertiary care center and that requires not only attention to endocrinologic and genetic issues but also psychologic counseling.

American College of Obstetricians and Gynecologists. Pediatric gynecologic disorders. ACOG Technical Bulletin 201. Washington, DC: ACOG; 1995.

Evaluation of the newborn with developmental anomalies of the external genitalia. American Academy of Pediatrics. Committee on Genetics. Pediatrics 2000;106:138–42.

Gillis D, Speiser P, Zhou Z, Rosler A. Combined 21-hydroxylase and 11 beta-hydroxylase deficiency: patient report and molecular basis. J Pediatr Endocrinol Metab 2000;13:945–9.

Speroff L, Glass RH, Kase NG. Clinical gynecologic endocrinology and infertility. 6th ed. Baltimore (MD): Lippincott Williams & Wilkins; 1999. p. 339.

64
Premenarcheal pelvic mass

You are called to the emergency department to evaluate a 10-year-old girl who has not yet started menses. Her parents brought her to the emergency room because of abdominal pain. Examination is difficult because of voluntary guarding. Abdominal ultrasonography reveals bilateral solid adnexal masses 10 cm × 10 cm in size. Human chorionic gonadotropin (hCG) level is elevated to 62 mIU/mL, and lactate dehydrogenase (LDH) level is elevated to 137 U/L. The most likely diagnosis is

     (A) endodermal sinus tumor
     (B) immature teratoma
  * (C) dysgerminoma
     (D) theca-lutein cyst
     (E) mature cystic teratoma

Solid or solid and cystic adnexal tumors in the child are usually dysgerminomas or immature teratomas. Dysgerminomas are the most common malignant germ cell tumors, accounting for approximately 50% of all cases. The neoplasm consists of germ cells that have not differentiated to form embryonic or extraembryonic structures, and the majority of patients have stage I disease. Dysgerminomas are bilateral on gross inspection in 10–15% of all cases.

The pathologic diagnosis of dysgerminoma requires a normal alpha-fetoprotein level to distinguish it from endodermal sinus tumor, which may cause elevated levels of this protein. Some dysgerminomas contain isolated gonadotropin-producing syncytiotrophoblastic giant cells, and elevations of hCG are not uncommon in these patients. Dysgerminomas similar to seminomas are associated with elevated levels of LDH, which can be used as a tumor marker. Dysgerminoma is associated with a gonadoblastoma in a small percentage of patients, who usually present with primary amenorrhea, virilization, or developmental anomalies of the genitalia. Chromosomal analysis is important in the treatment of these patients, because the presence of a Y chromosome necessitates bilateral oophorectomy.

Endodermal sinus tumors and immature teratomas are generally unilateral and do not cause elevated hCG levels. Women with endodermal sinus tumors can have increased levels of alpha-fetoprotein. Although immature teratomas are rarely bilateral, an immature teratoma in one ovary

and a mature cystic teratoma in the contralateral ovary may be encountered in as many as 10% of cases.

Theca-lutein cysts, which are detected exclusively in women with significantly elevated hCG levels, result from ovarian hyperstimulation by endogenous or exogenous gonadotropins. Such cysts are usually multicystic and bilateral and contain serosanguinous fluid. Theca-lutein cysts are generally 5–10 cm in diameter but occasionally may be much larger. Treatment is conservative, because these lesions usually regress. Ultrasonography often can assist in the diagnosis.

Mature cystic teratomas are one of the most common ovarian neoplasms. They are bilateral in 10–15% of cases. The cyst lumen contains mature elements reflecting differentiation into tissues normally derived from all 3 germ layers (ectoderm, mesoderm, and endoderm). These benign cystic lesions may contain cartilage, hair, or teeth; hCG levels are not elevated. Ultrasonography may assist in the evaluation. A mature solid teratoma is a rare benign tumor and is virtually always unilateral; hCG levels are normal.

DiSaia PJ, Creasman WT. Clinical gynecologic oncology. 6th ed. St. Louis (MO): Mosby; 2002. p. 351–77.

Hurteau JA, Williams SJ. Ovarian germ cell tumors In: Rubin SC, Sutton GP, editors. Ovarian cancer. 2nd ed. Philadelphia (PA): Lippincott Williams & Wilkins; 2001. p. 371–82.

Talerman A. Germ cell tumors of the ovary. In: Kurman RJ, editor. Blaustein's pathology of the female genital tract. 5th ed. New York (NY): Springer; 2002. p. 967–1034.

65

Acute respiratory distress syndrome

You are treating a patient who weighs 60 kg (132.3 lb) and has acute respiratory distress syndrome (ARDS). The patient is at postoperative day 1 after a total abdominal hysterectomy and bilateral salpingo-oophorectomy for pelvic inflammatory disease unresponsive to antibiotic therapy. She was intubated 30 minutes ago, and blood gas values are as follows:

Blood Gas	Value	Normal Values
Partial pressure of oxygen (P_{O_2})	80 mm Hg	80–100 mm Hg
Partial pressure of carbon dioxide (P_{CO_2})	50 mm Hg	35–45 mm Hg
Hydrogen ion concentration (pH)	7.35	7.35–7.45

The ventilator is set at a tidal volume of 650 mL; forced inspiratory oxygen, 0.5; peak end-expiratory pressure (PEEP), 8 cm of water; and synchronized intermittent mandatory ventilation (SIMV), 12. The respiratory therapist informs you that the inspiratory plateau pressure is elevated at 40 cm of water. Blood pressure is 105/60 mm Hg; pulse rate, 105 beats per minute; temperature, 38.4°C (101.1°F); and respiration, 32 breaths per minute. The next best step in management is to

       (A) place the patient in the prone position
       (B) increase the SIMV from 12 to 20
*   (C) decrease the tidal volume
       (D) start administering intravenous corticosteroids
       (E) decrease the PEEP

The syndrome known as ARDS, formerly called *adult respiratory distress syndrome* rather than *acute respiratory distress syndrome*, as it is today, is a serious respiratory condition. Mortality rates have improved over the past 10–15 years, but the rate of death is still as high as 40%. Common predisposing factors are 1) direct lung injury caused by pneumonia or aspiration and 2) indirect lung injury caused by sepsis or severe trauma with shock. Less common causes are drug overdose, multiple transfusions, and inhalation injury. The syndrome is characterized by the influx of protein-rich edema fluid into air spaces as a result of a "leaking" alveolar capillary barrier. This situation leads to decreased gas exchange. To control the syndrome, it is imperative to eliminate the source of infection by surgical drainage or appropriate antimicrobial therapy, because infection is the usual underlying driving force of the process.

Patients with ARDS have decreased lung compliance, which is manifested by high airway pressure. Patients who require ventilator assistance may have high plateau pressures, which put them at risk for pneumothorax. This patient requires treatment. In the past, tidal volumes of 10–12 mL/kg were recommended, but a large National Institutes of Health–based study has demonstrated a 20% reduction in mortality by switching to tidal volumes of 6–8 mL/kg. The higher the tidal volume, the higher the airway pressure. Therefore, dropping the tidal volume to 360–480 mL is the best first step in the management of this case. This patient's P_{CO_2} value is less of an issue.

Maintenance of PEEP at levels of 5–15 cm of water is important to open and stabilize collapsed alveoli. In addition, PEEP is a mechanism to increase the patient's P_{O_2} without having to increase the fraction of inspired oxygen (F_{IO_2}). Increasing PEEP, however, causes a rise in the inspiratory plateau pressure, an unacceptably high level of which can put the patient at risk for barotrauma. For this patient, decreasing the tidal volume first would be the most reasonable approach, because her PEEP was only 8 cm of water.

Several research trials have investigated the use of the prone position in the treatment of ARDS. The F_{IO_2} and PEEP requirements have been substantially reduced in some patients using this technique. The downside to this approach is that several intensive care unit personnel are required to implement the positioning of the patient because of the risk of dislodgment of the endotracheal tube and intravenous lines. Moreover, because it becomes difficult to observe the patient's face, visual or written communication is impeded. Currently, there are no guidelines to suggest how long patients should be required to maintain the position. For this patient, whose condition is relatively stable with an F_{IO_2} of only 0.5, the prone position would not be recommended.

Increasing the SIMV for this patient would not be recommended. As with the tidal volume, an increase in this parameter lowers the patient's P_{CO_2}. Her spontaneous rate is already above the rate set by the machine. Her P_{CO_2} is relatively high, but permissive hypercapnia has been shown to be well tolerated as long as the pH is higher than 7.25; Pco_2 levels of 65–85 mm Hg are well tolerated. Because dropping the patient's tidal volume theoretically will increase her Pco_2, she should be monitored carefully for the development of respiratory acidosis. If severe respiratory acidosis does develop, it should be managed with sodium bicarbonate therapy.

Corticosteroids have not been shown to be of benefit in the management of early ARDS and may even exacerbate the infectious process. The use of steroids, however, has been demonstrated to be of benefit in patients who are in the later stages of the disease. The mechanism of action is thought to be the reduction of fibroproliferation and inflammatory cytokine release. Practitioners who treat patients with ARDS should make every attempt to keep the Fio_2 as low as possible to lower the risk of oxygen toxicity.

Brower RG, Ware LB, Berthiaume Y, Matthay MA. Treatment of ARDS. Chest 2001;120:1347–67.

McIntyre RC Jr, Pulido EJ, Bensard DD, Shames BD, Abraham E. Thirty years of clinical trials in acute respiratory distress syndrome. Crit Care Med 2000;28:3314–31.

Redding GG. Current concepts in adult respiratory distress syndrome in children. Curr Opin Pediatr 2001;13:261–6.

Ware LB, Matthay MA. The acute respiratory distress syndrome. N Engl J Med 2000;342:1334–49.

66

Smoking cessation strategies

You conduct an annual gynecologic examination on a 36-year-old patient. She has smoked 1–2 packs of cigarettes per day for the past 20 years. She informs you that she smokes the bulk of her cigarettes during her commute to and from work. She notes that she smokes more when she is anxious. She also enjoys smoking after a meal and when out with friends. Her husband is a former smoker. She has tried to quit "cold turkey" without success. She asks you for help to stop smoking. Your best advice for this patient would be to

      (A) carpool with a nonsmoker
*   (B) establish a quit date within 2 weeks
      (C) start taking paroxetine hydrochloride (Paxil)
      (D) use 2-mg nicotine gum

Smoking is the leading preventable cause of death in the United States. It is important for physicians to help patients stop smoking, ideally before a tobacco-related chronic disease develops. For female smokers aged 35–39 years, like this patient, the excess risk of death from all causes decreases by 24% in the first 2 years after smoking cessation and returns to the level of someone who has never smoked after 10–14 years of smoking abstinence.

Among smokers, 70% consistently report that they want to stop smoking. Approximately 30% of smokers attempt to stop in any year, and most of them do so on their own by going "cold turkey," as this patient previously attempted to do without success. Without assistance, only 5–10% of smokers succeed in achieving long-term tobacco abstinence.

In 1996, the Agency for Health Care Policy and Research produced a comprehensive *Smoking Cessation Clinical Practice Guideline* based on a systematic review of treatment literature. An updated guideline was released by the U.S. Public Health Service in June 2000. Data suggest that a wide variety of clinicians can effectively implement these strategies. The 5 major steps to intervention in the primary care setting, known as "the 5 A's," are shown in Box 66-1.

This patient states she is ready for intervention. Research has shown that she will be most successful if she establishes a quit date when her motivation is high. Suggesting that she carpool with a nonsmoker probably is not the most effective strategy to offer at this time.

The U.S. Food and Drug Administration has approved 5 products for smoking cessation treatment. These products include 4 forms of nicotine replacement therapy (nicotine gum, transdermal patch, nasal spray, and inhaler) and a sustained-release form of the antidepressant bupropion hydrochloride (Wellbutrin SR, Zyban). Each product has demonstrated efficacy in randomized double-blind trials of smokers, approximately doubling long-term cessation rates when compared with placebo.

Patients who are highly dependent on nicotine are defined as individuals who smoke more than 1 pack of cigarettes per day, people who smoke within 30 minutes of awakening, and individuals who report that it is diffi-

BOX 66-1

"The 5 A's": 5 Major Steps to Smoking Intervention in the Primary Care Setting

1. *Ask* the patient if she uses tobacco, and document in her medical record her readiness to quit; place a sticker on her file to remind you to ask about smoking status at follow-up visits.
2. *Advise* patients to stop smoking. Deliver clear, strong, personalized messages to quit.
3. *Assess* willingness to stop smoking. Determine what support the patient has, as well as her barriers to quitting (eg, fear of gaining weight or becoming too stressed).
4. *Assist* patients who are willing to stop smoking by doing the following: establish a quit date within 2 wk, provide self-help materials, prescribe smoking-cessation products, refer the patients to smoking-cessation programs if needed, or suggest that the patients start an exercise program to relieve stress.
5. *Arrange* for a follow-up contact to prevent relapse.

Modified from Clinical practice guidelines for treating tobacco use and dependence: a US Public Health Service report. JAMA 2000;283:3245.

cult to refrain from smoking where it is forbidden. Such individuals should use 4-mg nicotine gum, as opposed to 2-mg gum. A lower starting dose (ie, 2 mg) should be considered for persons who smoke 10–15 or fewer cigarettes per day. Because this patient smokes 1–2 packs of cigarettes per day, a recommendation for her to chew 2-mg nicotine gum would not be appropriate.

Paroxetine hydrochloride is approved for use in patients who suffer from anxiety; however, bupropion hydrochloride, an antidepressant with dopaminergic and noradrenergic activity, has been found to be effective for smoking cessation in randomized controlled trials and would be more appropriate to address this patient's smoking problem.

The Agency for Health Care Policy and Research smoking cessation clinical practice guideline. JAMA 1996;275:1270–80.

Clinical practice guidelines for treating tobacco use and dependence: a US Public Health Service report. JAMA 2000;283:3244–54.

Rigotti NA. A 36-year-old woman who smokes cigarettes. JAMA 2000;284:741–9.

67

Initial assessment of sexual molestation

A mother brings her 6-year-old daughter to the emergency department because of a white discharge and vulvar erythema experienced for the past 2 weeks. The child has been hesitant to allow her mother to touch her vulvar area. The mother informs you that recently the child also is reluctant to go near, or be touched by, an uncle who lives with the family. The physical finding most likely to be found in this child is

*   (A) posterior hymenal tear
     (B) vulvar hemangioma
     (C) urethral caruncle
     (D) lichen sclerosus
     (E) labial agglutination

An increase of epidemic proportion has occurred in the annual reports of child sexual abuse. Approximately 85–90% of perpetrators are known to the children, and most perpetrators are related to the victims. This child's recent fear of her uncle should raise a concern about sexual abuse.

Child molestation may involve the gamut from touching or fondling of the child's genitals or touching of the adult's genitals by the child to sexual acts or exposing the child to pornography. Sexual intercourse may involve

oral, genital, or anal penetration or attempted penetration. Unfortunately, the diagnosis of sexual abuse remains difficult to establish in most cases. Methodological problems in studies of the morphologic characteristics of the external genitalia of children have resulted in inconsistencies in the literature regarding physical findings that suggest sexual abuse. Vaginal penetration is difficult to confirm in prepubertal children.

No single criterion is available to establish a diagnosis of sexual abuse. Signs of trauma such as pinch marks, burns, or bite marks on the lower trunk, thighs, buttocks, or genitalia are highly suggestive of, but not definitive proof of, sexual abuse. Abuse may not cause injury, and thus an examination may not detect any physical injury. Children may be seen weeks or months after abuse, by which time most, if not all, injuries have healed. Approximately 25–35% of girls who are identified as victims of sexual abuse have normal-appearing genitalia, and in some studies, only 50% of children had abnormal genital findings that suggested sexual abuse. It is important to perform a physical examination of the genitalia in the supine (frog-leg) and knee–chest position. Visualization of the genitalia and hymen may be improved with low-magnification colposcopy. Photographs of the vulva and hymen should be taken, if possible.

In the absence of obvious signs of trauma, the physical finding most likely to be found in a recently sexually abused child is a posterior hymenal tear or hymenal transection (Fig. 67-1). A deep posterior hymenal notch or

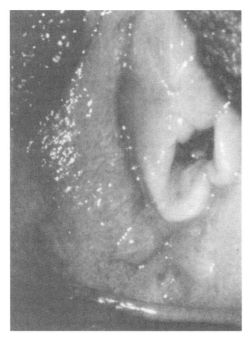

FIG. 67-1. Adolescent hymen showing complete cleft at the 4-o'clock position from prior sexual abuse. (From Evaluation of the sexually abused child; a medical textbook and photographic atlas, edited by Astrid H. Heger, S. Jean Emans. Copyright © 1992 by Oxford University Press, Inc. Used by permission of Oxford University Press, Inc.)

healed tear, an increase in transhymenal diameter, or a deep notch or concavity in the anterior half of the hymen are other findings that should increase suspicion of sexual abuse.

Vulvar hemangiomas are rare benign malformations of blood vessels, from red to brown or purple, and usually 1–2 cm in diameter. Strawberry or cavernous hemangiomas frequently are seen initially in children. Approximately 60% of hemangiomas seen during the first year of life regress spontaneously in size. Most hemangiomas are asymptomatic. Occasionally they become ulcerated and bleed, but they are not associated with sexual abuse.

A urethral caruncle is a small, fleshy outgrowth of the edge of the urethra. It is usually a smooth, benign lesion that may become ulcerated and bleed. Most frequently seen in postmenopausal women, it may be confused with urethral carcinoma but is not related to sexual abuse.

Lichen sclerosus is primarily a vulvar disorder of unknown etiology characterized by thinning of the skin and loss of pigmentation. Approximately 10–15% of cases occur in children. In this benign, chronic condition, shiny, whitish macules coalesce to form sharply demarcated hypopigmented plaques. The urethra, hymen, and vagina are not involved. If left untreated, lichen sclerosus may progress to stenosis of the vaginal introitus, clitoral phimosis, and ulceration of the vulvar epithelium.

Labial agglutination in children is relatively common, and it may persist, if untreated, until estrogenization at puberty. The cause is unknown but probably is related to low levels of estrogen. Local irritation and scratching may denude the thin skin of the labia. With healing, the labia may adhere in the midline. Most children with minor agglutination are asymptomatic, and 50% of cases respond to topical estrogen application. In most studies, labial agglutination was no more common in sexually abused children than nonabused children.

Berenson AB, Chacko MR, Wiemann CM, Mishaw CO, Friedrich WN, Grady JJ. A case-control study of anatomic changes resulting from sexual abuse. Am J Obstet Gynecol 2000;182:820–34.

DeJong AR, Finkel MA. Sexual abuse of children. Curr Probl Pediatr 1990;20:494–567.

Muram D. Child sexual abuse—genital tract findings in prepubertal girls, I: the unaided medical examination. Am J Obstet Gynecol 1989; 160:328–33.

Rimsza ME, Niggemann EH. Medical evaluation of sexually abused children: a review of 311 cases. Pediatrics 1982;69:8–14.

68
Medical abortion

A 28-year-old pregnant woman is at 5 weeks of gestation and is undergoing a medical abortion at home. She calls you at your office to report a temperature of 38°C (100.5°F). The pregnancy termination was initiated 2 days ago with 600 mg oral mifepristone (Mifeprex). Moderate bleeding began today, 1 hour after the patient took 400 µg oral misoprostol (Cytotec). The temperature elevation began shortly thereafter. The most appropriate next step in management is

      (A) a complete blood count
      (B) pelvic ultrasonography
*   (C) the administration of antipyretics
      (D) dilation and curettage (D&C)
      (E) the administration of oral antibiotics

Infectious complications of first-trimester abortion are rare. Surgical abortion is associated with uterine infection in up to 0.5% of procedures done during the first trimester. Sepsis occurred in 0.021% of 170,000 first-trimester surgical abortions performed by Planned Parenthood in New York City. Because it does not involve uterine or cervical instrumentation, medical abortion rarely is associated with endometritis. Most medical abortion studies with more than 500 participants have reported a high efficacy of completed abortion of 95%, with low infection rates of 0.1–0.5%. High efficacy of completed abortion has been noted in studies using standard medical abortion regimens, in addition to alternative regimens that employ low-dose 200-mg oral mifepristone and 800 mg vaginal misoprostol.

A fever or vasomotor response to medication is common and typically thought to be associated with the use of prostaglandin, although this response has been reported after methotrexate or mifepristone administration. The temperature elevation should be short-lived and should resolve spontaneously. Temperature that exceeds 38°C (100.5°F) and persists for several hours despite the use of antipyretics warrants evaluation for infection. In this case, it is reasonable to treat the patient with antipyretics and follow up to make sure the temperature responds. Any patient with persistent pelvic pain in the days after medical abortion should be monitored for infection.

For this patient, there is no need to order ancillary testing (eg, ultrasonography or computed tomography scan). It is too early to diagnose retained products of conception, and a pelvic collection is a less likely cause for this patient's temperature elevation than is a vasomotor reaction to prostaglandin. The patient should be reassured and her symptoms treated at home; if fever recurs, she should be seen in the office. Evacuation of the uterus by D&C would be premature at this time.

Hakim-Elahi E, Tovell HMM, Burnhill MS. Complications of first-trimester abortion: a report of 170,000 cases. Obstet Gynecol 1990;76: 129–35.

Kruse B, Poppema S, Creinin MD, Paul M. Management of side effects and complications in medical abortion. Am J Obstet Gynecol 2000;183:S65–S75.

Lichtenberg ES, Grimes DA, Paul M. Abortion complications: prevention and management. In: Paul M, Lichtenberg ES, Borgatta L, Grimes DA, Stubblefield PG, editors. A clinician's guide to medical and surgical abortion. New York (NY): Churchill Livingstone; 1999. p. 197–216.

Schaff EA, Eisinger SH, Stadalius LS, Franks P, Gore BZ, Poppema S. Low-dose mifepristone 200 mg and vaginal misoprostol for abortion. Contraception 1999;59:1–6.

Spitz IM, Bardin CW, Benton L, Robbins A. Early pregnancy termination with mifepristone and misoprostol in the United States. N Engl J Med 1998;338:1241–7.

69

Risk of deep vein thrombosis with selective estrogen receptor modulators

A 55-year-old white woman has been menopausal for 5 years. She is 1.5 m (5 ft) tall and weighs 47.6 kg (105 lb). Her mother had a total abdominal hysterectomy and bilateral salpingo-oophorectomy at age 45 years, never received hormone therapy (HT), and now at age 75 years has demonstrated osteoporosis and vertebral fractures. The patient has some vasomotor symptoms and severe gastroesophageal reflux disease. A recent dual-energy X-ray absorptiometry scan revealed T-scores of –2.1 spine and –1.5 hip. She does not want to receive HT and, after counseling, elects to begin taking raloxifene hydrochloride (Evista). Of the following choices, the most likely adverse effect associated with raloxifene hydrochloride is

        (A) postmenopausal bleeding
        (B) a decrease in hot flushes and night sweats
        (C) increased low-density lipoprotein (LDL) cholesterol level
*   (D) increased risk of deep vein thrombosis

Although white women are theoretically at greatest risk for osteoporosis, all ethnic groups may experience significant bone loss and subsequent osteoporosis after menopause. As much as 10% of baseline bone mineral content may be lost in the first 10 years after menopause. Further loss results in osteopenia and osteoporosis, and it may eventually lead to vertebral, hip, and other peripheral fractures. The result is significant morbidity and, in the case of hip fracture, increased mortality within the first 3–6 months after occurrence.

Osteoporosis results from an imbalance between the osteoclastic and osteoblastic phases of bone remodeling. Maximum bone mass is achieved during ages 20–25 years in women. Remodeling results in stable bone mass in most women until menopause, when age- and hormone-dependent changes cause a net bone loss and the potential for osteoporosis.

Raloxifene hydrochloride is a nonsteroidal benzothiophene approved for the prevention and treatment of osteoporosis by the U.S. Food and Drug Administration. The drug exerts antiresorptive effects on bone (Fig. 69-1; see color plate). Prevention of future spine fractures has been demonstrated in the Multiple Outcomes of Raloxifene (MORE) Trial. Selective estrogen receptor modulators such as raloxifene and tamoxifen citrate (Nolvadex) were initially evaluated for therapy of advanced breast cancer. Unfortunately, tamoxifen has adverse effects on endometrium that limit its usefulness aside from breast cancer therapy and prevention. Raloxifene does not stimulate breast tissue and has no endometrial or vaginal effects in postmenopausal women. Women who take raloxifene do not experience vaginal bleeding with any greater frequency than women who take placebo.

Use of raloxifene by postmenopausal women does not relieve hot flushes, and a small percentage of users may experience their exacerbation. The incidence of new hot flushes in placebo-controlled studies increased during the first 6 months of raloxifene therapy. After 6 months, the incidence of new hot flushes was not significantly different from the placebo group. Raloxifene improves the lipid profile, and it results in increased levels of high-density lipoprotein cholesterol and decreased LDL cholesterol. Therefore, this patient's LDL cholesterol is unlikely to increase.

Estrogens and raloxifene are similar in being associated with a low, but statistically significant, incidence of deep vein thrombosis (DVT). In an analysis of the extension of the MORE Trial, the authors found an incidence of 1.44 and 3.32 DVT events per 1,000 woman–years for placebo and raloxifene 60 mg/d, respectively. Superficial thrombosis also has been reported to occur more frequently with raloxifene. The greatest risk occurs in the first 4 months of therapy and is similar to the risk expected for HT and tamoxifen use.

Immobilization appears to increase the risk of thrombosis. Therefore, the use of raloxifene should be discontinued 72 hours prior to prolonged immobilization and restarted only after the patient is fully ambulatory.

American College of Obstetricians and Gynecologists. Selective estrogen receptor modulators. ACOG Practice Bulletin 39. Washington, DC: ACOG; 2002.

Boss SM, Huster WJ, Neild JA, Glant MD, Eisenhut CC, Draper MW. Effects of raloxifene hydrochloride on the endometrium of postmenopausal women. Am J Obstet Gynecol 1997;177:1458–64.

Cauley JA, Norton L, Lippman ME, Eckert S, Krueger KA, Purdie DW, et al. Continued breast cancer risk reduction in postmenopausal women treated with raloxifene: 4-year results from the MORE trial. Breast Cancer Res Treat 2001;65:125–34.

Davies GC, Huster WJ, Lu Y, Plouffe L, Lakshmanan M. Adverse events reported by postmenopausal women in controlled trials with raloxifene. Obstet Gynecol 1999;93:558–65.

Delmas PD, Bjarnason NH, Mitlak BH, Ravoux AC, Shah AS, Huster WJ, et al. Effects of raloxifene on bone mineral density, serum cholesterol concentrations, and uterine endometrium in postmenopausal women. N Engl J Med 1997;337:1641–7.

Grady D, Wenger NK, Herrington D, Khan S, Furberg C, Hunninghake D, et al. Postmenopausal hormone therapy increases risk for venous thromboembolic disease. Ann Intern Med 2000;132:689–96.

Walsh BW, Kuller LH, Wild RA, Paul S, Farmer M, Lawrence JB, et al. Effects of raloxifene on serum lipids and coagulation factors in healthy postmenopausal women. JAMA 1998;279:1445–51.

70

Geriatric patient–polypharmacy–drug reactions and interactions

A 79-year-old woman does well until postoperative day 2 after undergoing an abdominal sacrocolposuspension, Burch retropubic urethropexy, Halban culdoplasty, bilateral salpingo-oophorectomy, and posterior colporrhaphy. She now believes that she is in jail and that the nurses are trying to harm her. She is being physically restrained. Before hospitalization, she lived alone in the community, was quite functional, and was able to walk to the store and to care for herself. No new medical problems were identified on a preoperative evaluation. Since surgery, she sleeps deeply and on arousal from sleep is disoriented and drowsy. Mental status testing shows visual hallucinations and perseveration. The most likely diagnosis in this patient is

    (A) paranoid disorder
    (B) dementia
*   (C) delirium
    (D) major depressive episode

This patient has findings typical of delirium, also called *acute confusional state*. The incidence of delirium among surgical patients aged 65 years or older has been reported to be as high as 60%. Because of the high incidence of postoperative delirium, both the patient and her family should be counseled preoperatively to avoid undue concern when confusion occurs.

Known risk factors for postoperative delirium, common features required for diagnosis, and potential intraoperative factors that may predispose this population to the condition are shown in Box 70-1.

The most common cause of delirium that occurs within 24–72 hours of hospitalization is withdrawal from alcohol or benzodiazepines.

Treatment of acute agitation or aggressiveness accompanying delirium should involve a high-potency antipsychotic drug such as haloperidol. Evaluation should include history gathering from the patient's family members, review of the operative records and chart, and physical examination to identify potential risk factors. Fewer than 10% of delirium cases are caused by a central nervous system lesion, and neuroimaging of the brain is of low diagnostic value in the absence of focal neurologic findings or trauma. Particular attention should be directed toward careful review of medications, which are implicated in 22–39% of all cases of delirium. Evaluation should comprise a neurologic examination (ie, the patient's mental status and

psychomotor status), physical examination of major organ systems, and evaluation of vital signs. Potential laboratory tests include a urinalysis to rule out infection, complete blood count with differential, chest radiography, serum chemistry testing, pulse oximetry, electrocardiography, and albumin level testing. Further testing to obtain a diagnosis may include the tests outlined in Box 70-2.

Delirium often is mistaken for dementia or depression. Dementia is associated with global impairment of cognitive function, and the distinction between dementia and delirium may be difficult. Table 70-1 shows the differential diagnosis of delirium and dementia.

Depression is common in physically ill older patients. Criteria for diagnosis of a major depressive episode are shown in Appendix 1. Presurgery information on this patient's baseline status is insufficient to attribute the postoperative acute mental status change to depression. Older patients with depression are at increased risk of postoperative delirium.

Most patients with paranoid disorders, such as schizophrenia, develop symptoms, including a history of eccentric or bizarre behavior and thinking, before they are aged 50 years. Such chronic psychiatric disorders are characterized by disturbances in content and form of thought, perception, affect, sense of self, behavior, and volition. This patient exhibits no preoperative signs that suggest a psychotic disorder.

BOX 70-1

Postoperative Delirium: Risk Factors and Diagnosis

Known Risk Factors for Postoperative Delirium
- Advanced age
- Cardiopulmonary disorders (eg, myocardial infarction, hypotension, and hypoxia)
- Electrolyte abnormalities
- Gastrointestinal or genitourinary disorders (eg, ulcer, bleeding, constipation, and urinary retention)
- Hypoalbuminemia
- Infection
- Polypharmacy (including anticholinergics, opioids, sedative hypnotics, withdrawal, and alcohol use)
- Sensory deprivation
- Overstimulation
- Environmental changes
- Trauma (eg, from falls, fractures, or pain)

Common Features Required for Diagnosis
- Inattention
- Altered levels of consciousness
- Sudden onset and fluctuating course
- Delusions, hallucinations, psychomotor changes, and hypervigilance or increased agitation

Potential Intraoperative Factors That May Predispose This Population to Postoperative Delirium
- Type of surgery
- Hypoperfusion
- Anesthetic drugs, including anticholinergics, barbiturates, and long-acting benzodiazepines
- Metabolic abnormalities
- Cardiovascular complications
- Infection
- Toxicity
- Sensory disturbance before surgery

Adapted from Inouye SK, Bogardus ST Jr, Charpentier PA, Leo-Summers SL, Acampora D, Holford T, et al. A multicomponent intervention to prevent delirium in hospitalized older patients. N Engl J Med 1999;340:669–76.

BOX 70-2

Other Studies to Evaluate Altered Mental Status

- NH_3 level
- Blood cultures
- Drug levels
- Folate level
- Thyroid function screening
- Urinary postvoid residual volume
- Vitamin B_{12} level
- Electroencephalography
- Computed tomography
- Magnetic resonance imaging

Adapted from Delirium. In: American Geriatrics Society and John A. Hartford Foundation. Geriatric curriculum for surgical subspecialties, 2000. New York (NY): American Geriatrics Society and John A. Hartford Foundation; 2000. p. 26.1–26.4.

TABLE 70-1. Differential Diagnosis of Delirium and Dementia

Feature	Delirium	Dementia
Onset	Acute, usually over hours to days	Gradual
Course	Fluctuating over hours	Progressive over months
Duration	Days to weeks	Months to years
Attention	Impaired, very distractible	Unimpaired except if very severe
Orientation	Usually impaired	Often impaired
Memory	Impaired, especially short term	Impaired, especially long term
Perception	Disturbances common	Disturbances not common
Speech	Incoherent	Word-finding difficulties
Sleep–wake cycle	Always disrupted	Often disrupted in severe dementia

Adapted from Inouye SK, Bogardus ST Jr, Charpentier PA, Leo-Summers SL, Acampora D, Holford T, et al. A multicomponent intervention to prevent delirium in hospitalized older patients. N Engl J Med 1999;340:675.

Geriatrics review syllabus. In: Reuben DB, Yoshikawa TT, Besdine RW, editors. A core curriculum in geriatric medicine. New York (NY): American Geriatric Society; Dubuque (IA): Kendall/Hunt Publishing; 1996. p. 183–99.

Inouye SK. Delirium in hospitalized older patients: recognition and risk factors. J Geriatr Psychiatry Neurol 1998;11:118–25, discussion 157–8.

Inouye SK, Bogardus ST, Charpentier PA, Leo-Summer SL, Acampora D, Holford T, et al. A multicomponent intervention to prevent delirium in hospitalized older patients. N Engl J Med 1999;340:669–76.

O'Keefe ST, Chonchubhair AN. Postoperative delirium in the elderly. Br J Anesth 1994;73:673–87.

71

Ectopic pregnancy: evaluation with serum markers

A 25-year-old woman presents approximately 7 weeks after her last menstrual period with spotting and mild abdominal pain. Her serum human chorionic gonadotropin (hCG) concentration is 9,000 mIU/mL. Pelvic examination reveals moderate left adnexal tenderness, and a transvaginal ultrasonogram shows a 2.5-cm mass in the left adnexa with a small amount of fluid in the cul-de-sac. There is no evidence of an intrauterine pregnancy (IUP). A presumptive diagnosis of ectopic pregnancy is made. The patient is treated with 50 mg/m^2 methotrexate sodium. On day 4, her hCG concentration is 12,900 mIU/mL. On day 8, she presents with increased abdominal pain and modest vaginal bleeding. Her abdomen is moderately tender, without rebound tenderness. Pelvic examination again reveals left lower quadrant tenderness. Her vital signs are stable, and her hemoglobin level is unchanged. Serum hCG concentration is 12,000 mIU/mL. Ultrasonographic findings are unchanged. The most appropriate next step in management is

      (A) laparotomy
      (B) laparoscopy
*   (C) repeated administration of methotrexate sodium
      (D) dilation and curettage (D&C)

The incidence of ectopic pregnancy has increased almost 5-fold since 1970. Risk factors for its occurrence include prior pelvic inflammatory disease, history of infertility, and prior tubal surgery. After 1 ectopic pregnancy, the risk of another ectopic pregnancy is increased 7- to 13-fold. The rate of IUP is 50–80%, and the rate of tubal pregnancy is 10–25%.

Early detection of ectopic pregnancy is possible using the sensitive and reliable enzyme-linked immunosorbent assay (ELISA). Currently performed assays will detect hCG concentrations of 20–50 mIU/mL. Urine tests using this assay will detect hCG in the first voided urine at day 21 of the normal menstrual cycle, which is sufficient to detect essentially all symptomatic ectopic pregnancies. Serum hCG concentrations normally increase in a curvilinear fashion and peak at approximately 100,000 mIU/mL. The rise is linear prior to 41 days of gestation. During this time, the mean doubling time for hCG in a normal IUP is 48 hours. A 66% rise in titer will occur within 48 hours in 85% of normal pregnancies. Therefore, a rise of less than 50% in 48 hours gives 99% assurance of a nonviable pregnancy, either intrauterine or ectopic. Failure to increase 15% is predictive of ectopic pregnancy. The hCG discriminatory zone for normal IUPs is approximately 2,000 mIU/mL. At this level, essentially all IUPs should be visible by transvaginal ultrasonography.

Methotrexate sodium, a folinic acid antagonist, was first used for treatment of ectopic pregnancy in 1982. Current outpatient protocols use a single intramuscular injection. A 93% success rate was recorded in a recent series, and success rates by subgroup in the study are shown in Table 71-1. A gestational sac 3.5 cm or larger is a relative contraindication to medical therapy. The patient should discontinue use of vitamins containing folic acid prior to the onset of therapy. A typical methotrexate treatment protocol is presented in Table 71-2.

According to the outpatient protocol, methotrexate sodium is given intramuscularly on day 1, and hCG titers are monitored. The hCG concentrations are measured again on days 4 and 7. If the hCG concentration fails to decrease more than 15%, a second dose of methotrexate sodium is given and follow-up restarted. Once the hCG titer begins falling, testing is repeated at weekly intervals until titers reach 15 mIU/mL. Under this protocol, approximately 20% of patients require a second treatment cycle. Mean time to resolution is approximately 35 days.

This patient demonstrates the so-called separation pain commonly noted during treatment. This pain is thought to

TABLE 71-1. Success Rates of Medical Therapy for Ectopic Pregnancy by Subgroup

Subgroup	Overall Success Cases/Controls (%)	Method Success* Cases/Controls (%)
Total	287/315 (91.1)	287/309 (92.9)
Cardiac activity	35/44 (79.5)	35/40 (87.5)
Size >3.5 cm	9/10 (90.0)	9/10 (90.0)
Cornual	5/6 (83.3)	5/6 (83.3)
Cervical	2/2 (100)	2/2 (100)

* Success after elective withdrawals removed.

Modified from Lipscomb GH. Ectopic pregnancy. In: Ling FW, Duff P, editors. Obstetrics and gynecology: principles for practice. New York (NY): McGraw-Hill; 2001. p. 144. With permission of The McGraw-Hill Companies.

TABLE 71-2. Single-Dose Methotrexate Sodium Protocol

Day	Type of Test or Therapy
0	hCG with or without D&C
1	hCG, liver function, blood urea nitrogen, complete blood count, creatinine, Rh; methotrexate sodium therapy
4	hCG
7	hCG

D&C, dilation and curettage; hCG, serum human chorionic gonadotropin.

For <15% decline between day 4 and day 7 hCG concentrations, repeat methotrexate sodium therapy. For >15% decline between day 4 and day 7 hCG concentrations, follow up weekly until hCG <15 mIU/mL.

Modified from Lipscomb GH. Ectopic pregnancy. In: Ling FW, Duff P, editors. Obstetrics and gynecology: principles for practice. New York (NY): McGraw-Hill; 2001. p. 1144. With permission of The McGraw-Hill Companies.

occur secondary to tubal abortion or hematoma formation as the ectopic degenerates. Pain usually is controlled with ibuprofen. Approximately 15% of patients have pain or other symptoms that require hospitalization or surgical intervention. These symptoms remit after the disappearance of hCG and should not be regarded as failure of therapy.

Repeated administration of methotrexate sodium is the most appropriate therapy in this scenario because of typical separation pain, the decrease in hCG titer of less than 15%, and hemodynamic stability. Laparotomy or laparoscopy would be appropriate after failed medical therapy or with acute abdominal findings. A suction curettage or D&C would be used to differentiate a nonviable IUP from an ectopic pregnancy prior to treatment with methotrexate sodium.

American College of Obstetricians and Gynecologists. Medical management of tubal pregnancy. ACOG Practice Bulletin 3. Washington, DC: ACOG; 1998.

Lipscomb GH. Ectopic pregnancy. In: Ling FW, Duff P, editors. Obstetrics and gynecology: principles for practice. New York (NY): McGraw-Hill; 2001. p. 1134–50.

Lipscomb GH, Bran D, McCord ML, Portera JC, Ling FW. Analysis of three hundred fifteen ectopic pregnancies treated with single-dose methotrexate. Am J Obstet Gynecol 1998;178:1354–8.

Lipscomb GH, Stovall TG, Ling FW. Nonsurgical treatment of ectopic pregnancy. N Engl J Med 2000;343:1325–9.

72

Evaluation of postmenopausal bleeding

A 54-year-old postmenopausal woman who has not used hormone therapy has had persistent spotting for the past 8 months. An endometrial biopsy performed 6 months ago revealed atrophic endometrium. She has continued to spot almost monthly. The most appropriate next step in the evaluation of this patient is

  (A) dilation and curettage (D&C)
  (B) von Willebrand's factor study
* (C) sonohysterography
  (D) pelvic ultrasonography
  (E) magnetic resonance imaging

Postmenopausal bleeding is common. Episodes are likely to increase as more women spend a greater portion of their lives in the postmenopausal years. Although the most common cause is atrophic change of the endometrium, the clinician must rule out endometrial adenocarcinoma. Tissue for histologic analysis may be obtained by the performance of an endometrial biopsy in the office. The results of an endometrial biopsy are clinically equivalent to the findings of a D&C, and an office biopsy is suitable for almost all patients. It costs less and causes less discomfort than a D&C, and it has very low complication rates.

The patient under discussion experienced persistent spotting after a histologic diagnosis of atrophic endometrium. The scenario suggests a cause other than atrophic endometrium. The most likely diagnosis is endometrial polyps.

Sonohysterography is the best next step in the evaluation of this case. A sonohysterogram is obtained by the instillation of a small amount of saline during a transvaginal visualization of the endometrial cavity. It is performed in the office with usually minor discomfort to the patient and negligible risk of adverse effects. The sensitivity of sonohysterography for detection of intrauterine pathologic conditions approaches that of hysteroscopy, and it has a much greater specificity than ultrasonography alone. The efficacy of sonohysterography has been demonstrated in studies of postmenopausal women. A sonohysterogram is useful in detecting endometrial hyperplasia and cancer, because it can demonstrate asymmetric thickening of the endometrial lining. Sonohysterography improves the specificity of information about the location and size of intrauterine lesions such as polyps and leiomyomata. This information may be helpful in planning hysteroscopic surgery.

The traditional D&C procedure is losing its value as a diagnostic tool because it is a blind method that may miss focal pathologic conditions (eg, myomas, polyps, and small areas of endometrial cancer) in 10–25% of cases.

However, a D&C should be performed along with hysteroscopy to improve its efficacy in the detection of pathologic findings.

Screening for von Willebrand's factor is not indicated in this case. Deficiency of this factor is the most common hematologic cause of abnormal bleeding in women, but it is most likely to cause bleeding problems during the reproductive years. Screening for coagulation defects therefore is indicated mainly in younger women with prolonged bleeding, unless there are other clinical signs of a bleeding disorder, such as petechiae or ecchymosis.

Pelvic or transvaginal ultrasonography can diagnose with relatively high sensitivity the presence of polyps, leiomyomata, endometrial hyperplasia, or cancer, which cause thickening of the endometrial lining. The specificity of such ultrasonography, however, is much lower than that of sonohysterography, and its positive and negative predictive values are clearly inferior to those of sonohysterography.

Magnetic resonance imaging is a good technique to determine the extent of pelvic cancer spread and to diagnose leiomyomata and adenomyosis, but not specifically polyps. It is expensive and difficult for many patients to endure. The cost–benefit ratio would not make it an appropriate choice in this case.

Bronz L, Suter T, Rusca T. The value of transvaginal sonography with and without saline instillation in the diagnosis of uterine pathology in pre- and postmenopausal women with abnormal bleeding or suspect sonographic findings. Ultrasound Obstet Gynecol 1997;9:53–8.

Cameron ST, Walker J, Chambers S, Critchley H. Comparison of transvaginal ultrasound, saline infusion sonography and hysteroscopy to investigate postmenopausal bleeding and unscheduled bleeding on HRT. Aust N Z J Obstet Gynaecol 2001;41:291–4.

Laifer-Narine S, Ragavendra N, Parmenter EK, Grant EG. False-normal appearance of the endometrium on conventional transvaginal sonography: comparison with saline hysterosonography. Am J Radiol 2002; 178:129–33.

Schwarzler P, Concin H, Bosch H, Berlinger A, Wohlgenannt K, Collins WP, et al. An evaluation of sonohysterography and diagnostic hysteroscopy for the assessment of intrauterine pathology. Ultrasound Obstet Gynecol 1998;11:337–42.

73

Acute pelvic pain in young women

An emergency department physician requests consultation for a non–sexually active 14-year-old with acute abdominal pain confined to both lower quadrants, but greater in the right lower quadrant. The pain is described as sharp and stabbing, with radiation down the right leg. It has been intermittent over the past 24 hours. The adolescent has taken 800 mg ibuprofen without relief. Menarche occurred 6 months ago, and the patient is currently at the end of a menstrual period. Her physical examination is unremarkable except for the abdominal examination, which reveals decreased bowel sounds and tenderness with rebound in the left lower quadrant. A bimanual examination is difficult because of patient discomfort, but it leads to suspicion of the presence of a mass. Results of tests for human chorionic gonadotropin and sexually transmitted disease are negative. The most appropriate next step in evaluation would be

> (A) laparoscopy
> (B) a spiral computed tomography (CT) scan
* > (C) pelvic ultrasonography
> (D) magnetic resonance imaging (MRI)
> (E) laparotomy

In young women who are being assessed because of pelvic pain, the initial evaluation must distinguish acute from chronic pelvic pain. Acute pain is acyclic and of short duration, in contrast to chronic pain, which by definition is present for 6 months.

The patient's position and attitude should be noted. Patients with significant peritoneal irritation often bend their knees or assume a fetal position. The pelvic examination should include a rectovaginal assessment. Obtaining appropriate cultures is important because of the risk of pelvic inflammatory disease (PID), and pregnancy screening should occur. In patients in this age group, constipation is a frequent cause of abdominal pain, although it usually is associated with chronic abdominal pain.

In this patient, ultrasonography is the most appropriate next step. Ideally, the ultrasonography would be performed with color Doppler flow studies of the pelvis. This diagnostic modality effectively identifies adnexal torsion, with a true positive rate of 87%. When arterial and venous flow are absent, torsion should be strongly suspected. In addition, Doppler findings on ultrasonography that are consistent with torsion include absent or very low velocity (<5 cm/s) arterial flow in the adnexal region. Ultrasonography also can evaluate the appendix. A CT scan of the pelvis can identify the cause of acute pain with a mass or torsion; however, real-time ultrasonography remains the most effective test. Only when the diagnosis is unclear should consideration be given to laparoscopy as the best next step. There is little indication to proceed directly to laparotomy under the clinical circumstances described in this case.

Reported series suggest that untwisting of a torsive adnexa with removal of the predisposing factor (ie, an ovarian cyst) has a high probability of resulting in a functional fallopian tube and ovary. Much of the preservation of the physiologic activity of the adnexa is related to timeliness of surgical intervention, with preservation more common with early intervention.

There have been several explanations for torsion (see Box 73-1). In a series of 87 patients with ovarian torsion, including adolescents, it was noted that the majority pre-

---

BOX 73–1

Causes of Adnexal Torsion

Physiologic
- Increased tubal motility, especially midcycle

Anatomic
- Long mesosalpinx, often with hydatid morgagnian cyst
- Hydrosalpinx free of adhesions
- Ectopic pregnancy

Hemodynamic
- Alterations in ovarian mesenteric vascular supply
- Mesosalpinx venous engorgement

Trauma
- To the abdomen
- From coitus
- From gymnastics

Intraabdominal Pressure Changes
- Coughing
- Defecation
- Hiccuping
- Vomiting

Pregnancy
- Adnexal displacement

sented with peritoneal signs. Other findings included nausea or vomiting (70%), and fever was rare (2%). The pain was usually intermittent, correlating with twisting and untwisting of the adnexa.

Differential diagnosis must include gastrointestinal, urinary, musculoskeletal, and gynecologic problems. One must also consider a possible psychiatric cause for pelvic pain. Acute appendicitis always must be considered, especially if the pain is primarily in the right lower quadrant. Infections involving the urinary tract can present as acute abdominal pain. Both pyelonephritis and cystitis need to be ruled out. Cystitis is more commonly associated with the sexually active adolescent. Other urinary causes include urolithiasis. The pain has a characteristic acute onset and often causes the patient to double over; however, it is primarily located in the flank, although there may be radiation to the lower pelvis. Vomiting and fever are variable. Hematuria usually is noted on urinalysis. Abdominal radiography may identify a calculus.

From the gynecologic perspective, the following conditions should be considered in the differential diagnosis of this patient: mittelschmerz, torsion, acute PID, ovarian cyst, ectopic pregnancy, and endometriosis. Neither MRI nor CT scan would be useful in this case because of the patient's clinical presentation, which suggests torsion.

Economy KE, Laufer MR. Pelvic pain. Adolesc Med 1999;10:291–304.

Houry D, Abbott JT. Ovarian torsion: a fifteen-year review. Ann Emerg Med 2001;38:156–9.

Lee EJ, Kwon HC, Joo HJ, Suh JH, Fleischer AC. Diagnosis of ovarian torsion with color Doppler sonography: depiction of twisted vascular pedicle. J Ultrasound Med 1998;17:83–9.

McGovern P, Noah R, Koenigsberg R, Little AB. Adnexal torsion and pulmonary embolism: case report and review of the literature. Obstet Gynecol Surv 1999;54:601–8.

Mollitt D, Dikler M. The teenage girl. Semin Pediatr Surg 1997;6: 100–4.

74

Screening for cystic fibrosis carrier status

During preconception counseling, a recently married couple ask about the types of testing available to determine the presence of cystic fibrosis (CF) carrier status. You advise them that CF screening has been widely expanded because of new technologies. Testing for carrier status should be offered to

      (A) individuals with a personal or family history of CF
      (B) all Caucasian individuals
      (C) European (Ashkenazi) Jewish individuals
      (D) women with advanced maternal age
*   (E) any individual who plans a pregnancy

Current molecular techniques allow for the elucidation of the structure of DNA and genes. This structural analysis ultimately will result in an understanding of the molecular basis of both normal and pathologic functioning of the human genome. Upwards of 100,000 human genes are being fully characterized. One application of mapping the human genome is the availability of DNA probes for prenatal and preconception diagnosis (Table 74-1). Parental decisions based on the desired attributes of offspring, as well as lifetime risk assessment of specific disease states, present challenges that the obstetrician–gynecologist should keep in mind during preconception counseling.

Symptoms of CF are primarily respiratory and gastrointestinal. Chronic obstructive pulmonary disease leads to bronchiectasis, chronic pulmonary infections, and respiratory failure. The most common finding in the newborn is pancreatic exocrine insufficiency that presents with meconium ileus. Malabsorption and failure to thrive follow in infancy. Cholestasis also may be an initial manifestation of the disease. These conditions ultimately result in high morbidity and early death in affected individuals.

Current therapy relies on aerosolized deoxyribonuclease to act on extracellular DNA from neutrophils found in the sputum to decrease viscosity. Heart–lung transplantation is performed in selected patients. These new modalities are consistent with survival to adulthood in approximately 50% of patients.

Cystic fibrosis is an autosomal-recessive disorder resulting from abnormalities in the transmembrane chloride channel that affects chloride and water transport. The 1,480 amino acid coding region responsible for CF has been sequenced and cloned. More than 1,000 mutations in the gene have been described, more than 200 of which

TABLE 74-1. DNA Probes Available for Diagnostic Use

Gene Probe	Disorder	Application
β-Globin	Sickle cell disease	Prenatal screening
	β-Thalassemia	Prenatal screening
α-Globin	α-Thalassemia	Prenatal screening
	Polycystic kidney disease	Presymptomatic and prenatal screening
Factor VIII	Hemophilia A	Carrier detection, prenatal screening
Dystrophin	Duchenne's muscular dystrophy	Carrier detection, prenatal and presymptomatic screening
CFTR	Cystic fibrosis	Carrier detection, prenatal and presymptomatic screening
Phenylalanine hydroxylase	Phenylketonuria	Prenatal screening

CFTR, cystic fibrosis transmembrane regulator.

Pyeritz RE. Medical genetics. In: Tierney LM, McPhee SJ, Papadakis MA, editors. Current medical diagnosis and treatment 2002. New York (NY): Lange Medical Books/McGraw-Hill; 2002. p. 1657. With permission of the McGraw-Hill Companies.

are known to be associated with clinical abnormalities. The most common single mutation, referred to as F508, accounts for approximately 60% of cases. This mutation is localized to chromosome 7 (7q31.3). This area encodes for the CF transmembrane regulator (CFTR). A 3-base pair deletion at this locus results in the loss of a phenyl-

alanine residue and the subsequent loss of transmembrane regulation of chloride channels. Without CFTR, secretions of the pulmonary and gastrointestinal tracts are extremely viscous. It is hypothesized that in the absence of CFTR, there is inadequate hydration of mucin. The abnormal mucus produced becomes inspissated in the lumina of ductal structures.

Different mutations affect various ethnic groups. Direct gene analysis of groups of mutations therefore can allow for identification of a large proportion of the carrier population within each group. The identification of the most frequent mutations within any specific population has enabled clinicians to offer universal screening.

Previously identified at-risk individuals, such as people with a personal or family history of CF, should continue to be tested. Caucasian European and Ashkenazi Jewish couples are members of high-risk populations that should be tested, with the disease present in 1 in 3,300 births. The carrier frequency in this population is 1 in 29 women (Table 74-2). Couples with advanced maternal age as the sole risk factor also should be offered testing as part of the universal recommendation. Age increases the risk for chromosomal aneuploidy. Older individuals are not specifically at increased risk for mutations resulting in CF.

Carrier identification allows the recognition of pregnancies at risk in an asymptomatic couple not previously identified as being at risk. Such screening could allow for more informed reproductive decisions regarding the transmission of carrier status to future offspring, as well as preconception recognition and consideration of risk.

TABLE 74-2. Carrier Risk and Detection Rate for Cystic Fibrosis in Different Ethnic Groups

Ethnic Group	Carrier Risk Before Negative Test	Carrier Risk After Negative Test	Detection Rate (%)
Ashkenazi Jewish	1/29	1/930	97
European Caucasian	1/29	1/140	80
Hispanic American*	1/46	1/207	57
African American	1/62	1/105	69
Asian American	1/90	NA	NA

NA, data not available.

* This is a pooled set of data and requires additional information to predict risk accurately for specific Hispanic populations.

Note: Residual carrier risk after a negative test is modified by the presence of a positive family history of cystic fibrosis (ie, having a first-, second-, or third-degree relative affected by cystic fibrosis) or by admixture of various ethnic groups. For these specific situations, accurate risk assessment requires standard Bayesian analysis and genetic counseling.

American College of Obstetricians and Gynecologists and American College of Medical Genetics. Preconception and prenatal carrier screening for cystic fibrosis. Washington, DC: ACOG; 2001. p. 25.

Chesnutt MS, Prendergast TJ. Lung. In: Tierney LM, McPhee SJ, Papadakis MA, editors. Current medical diagnosis and treatment 2002. New York (NY): Lange Medical Books/McGraw-Hill; 2002. p. 269–362.

Cohen MB, Balistrera WF. Disorders of digestion. In: Fanaroff AA, Martin RJ, editors. Neonatal-perinatal medicine: diseases of the fetus and infant. 6th ed. St. Louis (MO): Mosby; 1997. p. 1300–1.

Pyeritz RE. Medical genetics. In: Tierney LM, McPhee SJ, Papadakis MA, editors. Current medical diagnosis and treatment 2002. New York (NY): Lange Medical Books/McGraw-Hill; 2002. p. 1645–68.

Rubin BK. Emerging therapies for cystic fibrosis lung disease. Chest 1999;115:1120–6.

75

Acute blood loss

A 48-year-old woman undergoes a total abdominal hysterectomy and bilateral salpingo-oophorectomy for extensive endometriosis. After 3 hours of surgery, the patient develops new-onset tachycardia at 138 beats per minute with blood pressure of 94/58 mm Hg. You anticipate that an additional 10 minutes of surgery will be needed to complete the procedure. She has extensive oozing from the areas of dissection. Estimated blood loss is 1,200 mL. You request that blood be sent for type and crossmatching. The most appropriate treatment is

     (A) to halt surgery and place packs in the pelvis until blood is available
     (B) insertion of a Swan-Ganz catheter
*   (C) initiation of rapid crystalloid infusion
     (D) internal iliac artery ligation
     (E) initiation of dopamine infusion

When unexpected hemorrhaging develops, the surgeon must remain calm in order to provide the leadership and institute the management plan necessary to stabilize the patient. Hemodynamically, unexpected hemorrhaging is significant only when the amount of blood lost is large and the loss occurs at a rapid rate. When the circulating blood volume in a young, healthy woman is reduced by 15–30%, little cardiovascular stress is placed on the body; the ability of the body to compensate for rapid blood loss is generally excellent.

Tachycardia and decreased blood pressure are 2 physiologic responses to the hypovolemia of hemorrhagic shock. Hemorrhagic shock is completely reversible if the circulating blood volume is replaced rapidly. The presence of active bleeding mandates immediate action by the surgeon. The goals of managing a patient who has developed hemorrhagic shock are to replace, restore, and maintain the effective circulating blood volume and establish normal cellular perfusion and oxygenation. Crystalloid replacement of 3 times the volume of blood lost, administered intravenously over 15–30 minutes, should be adequate for resuscitation and should normalize the vital signs as long as the hemorrhage is controlled.

In 1995, the University Hospital Consortium developed guidelines for the use of albumin, nonprotein colloid, and crystalloid solutions, and it recommended that in hemorrhagic shock, crystalloids be the initial fluid resuscitation of choice. Transfusion of packed red blood cells rarely is indicated when the hemoglobin level is greater than 10 g/dL and almost always is indicated when the hemoglobin level is less than 6 g/dL. The need for transfusions for patients with hemoglobin values of 6–10 g/dL is dependent on the patient's physical status, medical comorbidities, and the rate of ongoing hemorrhage.

The fluid preparation selected to replace ongoing blood loss depends on the rate of blood loss and the change in hemodynamic parameters. Crystalloids are rapidly equilibrated throughout the extracellular fluid compartments. Cumulative volumes 3–4 times greater than colloid infusions are necessary to achieve equivalent intravascular volume expansion. Rapid infusion of large volumes of crystalloids has not increased the incidence of cardiopulmonary dysfunction or acute respiratory distress syndrome, or the need for ventilatory support.

Dopamine infusion is not indicated for this patient because her body's adrenergic response to the hemorrhage has resulted in tachycardia. Swan-Ganz catheter placement is not immediately indicated because the hemodynamic changes are due to acute blood loss and volume depletion. If the hemorrhage cannot be controlled or the patient has preexisting cardiac or renal disease, Swan-Ganz catheter placement may be useful if determining the pulmonary artery pressure, pulmonary wedge pressure, central venous pressure, and cardiac output will assist in managing fluid resuscitation. Although bilateral internal iliac artery ligation will decrease the pulse pressure, it will not reduce the blood loss associated with abdominal hysterectomy.

Typing and crossmatching blood for transfusion generally takes 30–45 minutes after the surgeon's request. Because the patient described is hemodynamically unstable, rapid crystalloid infusion will stabilize her more quickly than will temporarily stopping the procedure until blood is available. The surgeon expects that within a short time the surgery and blood loss will be completed. If the surgery will not be completed quickly and the patient is unstable, applying pressure either with instruments, packs, or fingers will temporarily decrease the bleeding while the anesthesia team administers fluids.

Droegemueller W. Postoperative counseling and management. In: Stenchever MA, Droegemueller W, Herbst AL, Mishell DA, editors.

Comprehensive gynecology. 4th ed. St. Louis (MO): Mosby; 2001. p. 771–821.

Levenback C, Lichtiger B, Bui T. Hemorrhage, blood component therapy, and shock. In: Gershenson DM, DeCherney AH, Curry SL,

Brubaker L, editors. Operative gynecology. 2nd ed. Philadelphia (PA): WB Saunders; 2001. p. 132–46.

Pestana C. Fluids and electrolytes in the surgical patient. 5th ed. Philadelphia (PA): Lippincott Williams & Wilkins; 2000. p. 38–56.

76

Ovarian remnant syndrome

Two years ago, a 38-year-old woman underwent a laparoscopic supracervical hysterectomy with bilateral salpingo-oophorectomy for pelvic pain associated with endometriosis. During surgery, extensive pelvic adhesions were found, and postoperatively her symptoms were improved. Six weeks after surgery, she began estrogen therapy. Eighteen months after surgery, she began to report cyclic pain, sometimes exacerbated by coitus. The findings of pelvic examination are unremarkable, as are the findings of imaging studies, including transvaginal ultrasonography, computed tomography scan, and magnetic resonance imaging. The follicle-stimulating hormone (FSH) level is 10 mIU/mL, and the estradiol level is 50 pg/mL. Before surgery, the most appropriate next step is to prescribe

    (A) oral contraceptives
* (B) clomiphene citrate (Clomid or Serophene)
    (C) danazol (Danocrine)
    (D) depot medroxyprogesterone acetate (Depo-Provera)
    (E) megestrol acetate (Megace)

Ovarian remnant syndrome occurs in women who have undergone prior bilateral oophorectomy with or without hysterectomy. In general, incompletely removed functioning ovarian tissue is one of the sequelae of extensive endometriosis, pelvic inflammatory disease, or pelvic adhesions, with or without multiple prior surgical procedures. Chronic pelvic pain results from functioning ovarian tissue encased in adhesions with the surrounding tissue. Symptoms may be present with or without a palpable or radiologically detectable mass. The pain usually is cyclic and exacerbated by intercourse. A finding of premenopausal levels of FSH in the absence of exogenous therapy is useful in establishing the diagnosis.

Clomiphene citrate can stimulate functional ovarian tissue and thus enlarge the ovarian tissue to allow for establishment of the diagnosis. In ovarian remnant syndrome, clomiphene citrate can provide an adjunct to surgery, particularly if the ovarian remnant was not clinically or radiologically detectable. Ovarian remnant syndrome has a recurrence or persistence rate of approximately 10%. Recurrence generally is caused by adhesive disease from multiple prior surgeries and the inability of the surgeon to visualize adequately all the remaining ovarian tissue. By stimulating functioning ovarian tissue so the surgeon can identify it for removal, clomiphene citrate can decrease the rate of persistence and recurrence.

Oral contraceptives, megestrol acetate, and depot medroxyprogesterone acetate will suppress the ovarian tissue. Because the patient described has no palpable or radiologically detectable mass, these agents are not indicated. They may be useful adjuncts in controlling the pain associated with this syndrome, however. Danazol is not indicated, because there is no evidence of endometriosis.

The treatment of ovarian remnant syndrome is surgical excision of the remaining ovarian tissue. The histologic specimen will contain ovarian follicles and stroma. This surgery may require a retroperitoneal dissection to define the relationship of the ovaries to the ureter, bowel, and vagina.

If women with ovarian remnant syndrome are taking estrogen replacement therapy, the dosage commonly prescribed will not suppress FSH to the level found in this patient.

Droegemueller W. Postoperative counseling and management. In: Stenchever MA, Droegemueller W, Herbst AL, Mishell DA, editors. Comprehensive gynecology. 4th ed. St. Louis (MO): Mosby; 2001. p. 479–530.

Kaminski PF, Meilstrup JW, Shackelford DP, Sorosky JI, Thieme GA. Ovarian remnant syndrome, a reappraisal: the usefulness of clomiphene citrate in stimulating and pelvic ultrasound in locating remnant ovarian tissue. J Gynecol Surg 1995;11:33–9.

Kaminski PF, Sorosky JI, Mandell MJ, Broadstreet RP, Zaino RJ. Clomiphene citrate stimulation as an adjunct in locating ovarian tissue in ovarian remnant syndrome. Obstet Gynecol 1990;76:924–6.

Nezhat CH, Seidman DS, Nezhat FR, Mirmalek SA, Nezhat CR. Ovarian remnant syndrome after laparoscopic oophorectomy. Fertil Steril 2000;74:1024–8.

77

Altered mental status after hysterectomy

You are called to evaluate a 45-year-old woman, para 3, aborta 3, on postoperative day 2 of an uncomplicated total abdominal hysterectomy and bilateral salpingo-oophorectomy for hydatidiform mole. The diagnosis of mole was made by dilation and curettage done 1 week prior to the operation. You conclude that she has an altered mental status that was not previously present. Examination reveals no focal, motor, or sensory neurologic deficits. The patient's hemoglobin level is 12 g/dL; leukocyte count, 11,300/μL; blood pressure reading, 108/70 mm Hg; pulse rate, 98 beats per minute; and respirations, 25 breaths per minute. The oxygen saturation is 96% on room air. Serum electrolytes are normal. The pathologist calls you to review the fallopian tube slide (Fig. 77-1; see color plate). The patient has not taken any medications in the past 8 hours. Your next step in management is to order

      (A) magnetic resonance imaging (MRI) of the head
*   (B) intravenous antibiotic therapy
      (C) administration of intravenous steroids
      (D) chemotherapy with EMACO (etoposide, methotrexate, actinomycin D, cyclophosphamide, Oncovin)
      (E) administration of intrathecal methotrexate

Figure 77-1 demonstrates gram-positive rods in a background of inflammation and necrosis. There is no evidence of metastatic gestational trophoblastic disease. Because the patient underwent surgery and has gram-positive rods seen on hematoxylin and eosin stain, the most likely cause of her delirium is severe infection with *Clostridium perfringens*. Septic encephalopathy, with delirium and lethargy, is a common manifestation of sepsis.

Delirium, defined as a state of mental confusion, has been documented in studies to range from 0% to 73% in postoperative patients. Metabolic disorders are one of the more common causes and, fortunately, are reversible in many situations. Box 77-1 shows examples of metabolic disorders that can cause delirium. Rapid correction of hyponatremia can lead to an encephalopathy. Hypercalcemia can cause somnolence, lethargy, and depression, whereas hypocalcemia is associated with irritability. Acidosis with persistent pH less than 7.2, regardless of the cause, results in obtundation and eventual coma. Acute alkalosis can lead to decreased oxygen delivery to

the brain as the oxygen dissociation curve shifts to the left, with resultant ischemia. This sequence of events is especially characteristic of respiratory alkalosis, which is an early manifestation of septic shock. Patients with hypoglycemia have symptoms of confusion, slurred speech, lethargy, and seizures.

The functioning of the patient's cardiorespiratory system, as monitored by vital signs and pulse oximetry, gives clues as to whether the patient is well perfused. This patient's vital signs are relatively stable, and her pulse oximetry findings are normal, which could lead to the erroneous conclusion that sepsis was not the underlying problem. It is critical that the clinician evaluate the patient's medication list to see if it contains an explanation for an altered mental status and make adjustments as necessary. It is also important to determine whether there is a history of alcohol use with signs of withdrawal. A change in surroundings (eg, during treatment in an intensive care unit, where the patient is subject to sensory overload) can precipitate delirium, particularly in the elderly. Life-threatening and other potentially reversible causes, however, must be addressed first. Brain tumors, cerebrovascular accidents, and poisons also should be investigated as possible causes of delirium.

One-way sepsis is thought to cause an altered mental state as a result of an increased blood–brain barrier permeability by endotoxins and cytokines. This condition is postulated to lead to an enhanced effect of cytokines on the brain. In addition, these cytokines can alter regional blood flow by the generation of free radicals and nitric oxide.

BOX 77-1

Metabolic Disorders That Can Cause Delirium

- Dehydration
- Uncontrolled diabetes mellitus or thyroid disease
- Electrolyte disturbances
- Liver disease
- Renal failure

Patients with early septic shock present with tachycardia and an increased cardiac output with decreased vascular resistance. Giving the patient crystalloid or blood can maintain the cardiorespiratory unit in this initial phase. As the infection becomes more severe, the toxins cause myocardial depression, with resultant decreased cardiac output in an already dilated vascular bed. Pressors are indicated at this point to maintain cardiac output and blood pressure. Control of the infection by medical or surgical means before the patient reaches this state is highly advisable. Often multiorgan dysfunction occurs, making recovery much more difficult.

Clostridium perfringens, an anaerobic gram-positive organism, is a leading cause of gas gangrene in humans. It is found normally in the vagina and cervix in as many as 10% of women and rarely causes infection. The bacterium can produce toxins, which can cause tissue damage by attacking lecithin in the cell membrane; the results are a local increase in capillary permeability and intense edema, as seen in myonecrosis. This situation leads to an ischemic environment and, thus, further proliferation of the anaerobic bacterium. Exotoxin produced by the bacterium can cause myocardial depression by inhibiting the calcium pump, and toxin contributes to shock by stimulating the release of platelet-activating factor. The infection can be overwhelming unless quick intervention is instituted. The diagnosis is made by the identification of the organism in a patient who is septic or has evidence of gas in the uterus. If the provider suspects that the patient has the disease but the organism is not identified, the patient should be treated as if the bacterium were identified.

The drug of choice is aqueous penicillin, 20 million–30 million units per day. Alternative medications include tetracycline and erythromycin. Because other organisms usually are involved, gentamicin and clindamycin are recommended. Hyperbaric oxygen treatment is used if the patient can be transported safely to the chamber. Patients who are intubated may pose a logistic challenge.

The use of steroids is not indicated for this patient. Steroids sometimes are used for patients with a protracted course of acute respiratory distress syndrome or in the event of an acute cerebral event. Obtaining an MRI initially would delay the most important aspect of treatment, which is antibiotic treatment for this patient who has had a hysterectomy. Chemotherapy is contraindicated at this time because the patient has sepsis. The EMACO regimen often is used for patients with high-risk gestational trophoblastic neoplasia. Intrathecal methotrexate sometimes is used to treat patients who have documented central nervous system involvement from gestational trophoblastic neoplasia. This patient does not appear to have residual disease, however.

Halpin TF, Molinari JA. Diagnosis and management of clostridium perfringens sepsis and uterine gas gangrene. Obstet Gynecol Surv 2002; 57:53–7.

Naik-Tolani S, Oropello JM, Benjamin E. Neurologic complications in the intensive care unit. Clin Chest Med 1999;20:423–4.

Winawer N. Postoperative delirium. Med Clin North Am 2001;85: 1229–39.

78

Combination hormonal contraceptive methods

A healthy 23-year-old woman who weighs 59 kg (130 lb) asks you for advice on contraception. She has difficulty remembering to take her combination oral contraceptive and is interested in switching to weekly or monthly contraception. You advise her that compared with what she has experienced with oral contraceptives, the symptom she is most likely to experience with use of the weekly ethinyl estradiol/norelgestromin patch (Ortho Evra) is

*   (A) transient breast tenderness
    (B) acne
    (C) headache
    (D) weight gain

Recent studies that have compared either the patch or the etonogestrel/ethinyl estradiol vaginal ring (NuvaRing) with combination oral contraceptives have shown that adverse effects are similar, because they all contain estrogen and progestin. Similar adverse events in the triphasic comparative trial of the patch included headache, nausea, and abdominal pain. Transiently higher occurrences of breast tenderness, which were described as mild to moderate in the patch group, diminished after 2 cycles of use. The patch had no overall effect on body weight gain when compared with placebo. Acne was not specifically evaluated during these trials.

Women who use transdermal contraceptives and who weigh more than 90 kg (198.4 lb) have been reported to experience higher rates of contraceptive failure. It also has been demonstrated that the increased risk of oral contraceptive failure is related directly to increase in body weight. It has been suggested that this increased failure rate may be a consequence of higher metabolic clearance among heavy women.

A comparative study showed similar incidences of adverse events (eg, breast tenderness, weight gain, and nausea). Cycle control with the use of either the patch or the vaginal ring reportedly is comparable to control with the use of combination oral contraceptives. Breakthrough bleeding tends to lessen over time with all combination methods. Thus, patients initiating any hormonal method should be counseled to continue the new method for at least 2–3 cycles if they experience any adverse events.

Bjarnadottir RI, Tuppurainen M, Killick SR. Comparison of cycle control with a combined contraceptive vaginal ring and oral levonorgestrel/ethinyl estradiol. Am J Obstet Gynecol 2002;186:389–95.

Holt VL, Cushing-Haugen KL, Daling JR. Body weight and risk of oral contraceptive failure. Obstet Gynecol 2002;99:820–7.

Sibai BM, Odlind V, Meador ML, Shangold GA, Fisher AC, Creasy GW. A comparative and pooled analysis of the safety and tolerability of the contraceptive patch (Ortho Evra/Evra). Fertil Steril 2002;77 suppl 2:S19–S26.

Zieman M, Guillebaud J, Weisberg E, Shangold GA, Fisher AC, Creasy GW. Contraceptive efficacy and cycle control with the Ortho Evra/Evra transdermal system: the analysis of pooled data. Fertility Steril 2002;77: S13–S18.

79

Perioperative long-term use of warfarin

A 66-year-old woman presents with a pelvic mass. Endovaginal abdominal ultrasonography reveals a large tumor of the left ovary and a small amount of free fluid. The patient desires surgery as soon as possible, but she is at risk for bleeding because she is undergoing long-term warfarin therapy for a history of deep vein thrombosis (DVT). The first episode of DVT occurred 2 years ago and the second episode, 6 months ago. The woman has had numerous pelvic surgeries and is at risk of adhesions. In the perioperative management of anticoagulation in this patient, warfarin is withheld to allow the international normalized ratio (INR) to fall to 1.5. The most appropriate next step is

- (A) preoperative administration of intravenous heparin and postoperative administration of low-molecular-weight heparin (LMWH)
- (B) preoperative and postoperative administration of subcutaneous heparin
- (C) preoperative administration of LMWH and postoperative administration of intravenous heparin
- * (D) no further preoperative treatment and postoperative administration of LMWH

Patients who undergo gynecologic surgery are at risk of developing venous thromboembolism (VTE), including DVT and pulmonary embolism (PE). Patients on long-term anticoagulation therapy are at an increased risk postoperatively for these complications. Complications from anticoagulation therapy are common among gynecologic patients with benign or malignant disease.

In the United States, the following are the most common indications for long-term warfarin therapy:

- Atrial fibrillation
- Presence of a mechanical heart valve
- A history of DVT

Patients who require surgery and are on warfarin therapy present a dilemma, because stopping the warfarin increases the risk of thromboembolism. In recent years, LMWH has emerged as a commonly used prophylaxis for postsurgical thromboembolism, as well as treatment of DVT. It has been found that the administration of LMWH is as effective as therapy with unfractionated intravenous heparin and is not as likely to cause postoperative bleeding. There is no consensus on the preoperative and postoperative management of anticoagulation in patients on long-term warfarin therapy. After warfarin therapy is stopped, it takes approximately 4 days for the INR to reach 1.5 in the majority of patients. Once this value is reached, surgery can be performed. It has been estimated that major surgery increases 100-fold the short-term risk of recurrence of DVT in patients with a history of previous DVT. Therefore, it is imperative to reinitiate anticoagulation as soon as it is deemed safe after surgery, usually 4–6 hours postsurgery.

In patients with a history of VTE, there are several recommendations for preoperative and postoperative antico-agulation, depending on the time interval from the index thromboembolism (Table 79-1).

TABLE 79-1. Recommendations for Preoperative and Postoperative Anticoagulation in Patients Who Are Taking Oral Anticoagulants

Indication	Before Surgery	After Surgery
Acute VTE		
Month 1	IV heparin*	IV heparin*
Months 2 and 3	No change†	IV heparin
Recurrent VTE‡	No change†	SC heparin
Acute arterial	IV heparin	
embolism, month 1	IV heparin§	
Mechanical		
heart valve	No change†	SC heparin
Nonvalvular atrial		
fibrillation	No change†	SC heparin

IV heparin, intravenous heparin at therapeutic doses; SC heparin, subcutaneous unfractionated or low-molecular-weight heparin in doses recommended for prophylaxis against venous thromboembolism (VTE) in high-risk patients.

*Insertion of a vena cava filter should be considered if acute VTE has occurred within 2 weeks or if the risk of bleeding during IV heparin therapy is high.

†If patients are hospitalized, SC heparin may be administered, but hospitalization is not recommended solely for this purpose.

‡The term refers to the condition of patients whose last episode of VTE occurred more than 3 months before evaluation but who require long-term anticoagulation because of a high risk of recurrence.

§IV heparin should be administered after surgery only if the risk of bleeding is low.

This patient has been receiving anticoagulants for more than 3 months since her last episode of VTE, so she does not need preoperative heparin. She should receive postoperative prophylaxis with LMWH as recommended for patients at high risk for VTE until oral anticoagulation has been reestablished, as indicated by an INR of 2.0 or higher. This therapy should be combined with standard methods of mechanical prophylaxis (eg, graduated-compression stockings or intermittent pneumatic compression). Intravenous heparin therapy is an acceptable postoperative alternative in patients whose risk of bleeding postoperatively is low. In this patient with a history of previous pelvic surgeries, the administration of LMWH is the best alternative.

Anderson DR, O'Brien BJ. Cost effectiveness of the prevention and treatment of deep vein thrombosis and pulmonary embolism. Pharmacoeconomics 1997;12:17–29.

Kearon C, Hirsh J. Management of anticoagulation before and after elective surgery. N Engl J Med 1997;336:1506–11.

Rydberg EJ, Westfall JM, Nicholas RA. Low molecular weight heparin in preventing and treating DVT. Am Fam Physician 1999;108:312–34.

Schorge JO, Goldhaber SZ, Duska LR, Goodman A, Feldman S. Clinically significant venous thromboembolism after gynecologic surgery. J Reprod Med 1999;44:669–73.

80

Adnexal torsion in an adolescent

A 16-year-old adolescent presents with a 4-hour history of severe right lower quadrant pain that began shortly after she competed in a gymnastics event. Since the onset of pain, the patient has felt nauseous and has vomited once. Physical examination reveals a pulse of 100 beats per minute and a temperature of 36°C (98.8°F). Abdominal examination shows right lower quadrant tenderness with rebound. Her hematocrit is 36%, white blood cell count is 7,000/µL, and pregnancy test result is negative. An ultrasonogram confirms a diagnosis of adnexal torsion. The next step in management is

    (A) salpingo-oophorectomy
    (B) heparin therapy to prevent embolus
*   (C) untwisting the adnexa
    (D) use of intravenous fluorescein

Torsion of the ovarian or adnexal pedicle is an uncommon surgical emergency caused by rotation of the adnexa on its axis, resulting in arterial or venous obstruction with or without lymphatic obstruction. Torsion of the ovarian pedicle may occur separately from torsion of the fallopian tube, but most commonly the conditions occur together. Adnexal torsion, which makes up 3% of gynecologic operative emergencies, requires prompt surgical intervention to save the adnexa. Patients usually present with acute severe unilateral lower abdominal pain. Two thirds of patients have nausea and vomiting. The preoperative physical examination findings are not specific for torsion, but the twisted adnexa may be detected preoperatively by ultrasonography. Color Doppler ultrasonography may be useful in predicting the viability of adnexal structures by visualizing blood flow within the twisted pedicle.

Ovarian torsion frequently is associated with a cystic or solid ovarian tumor, which may act as a fulcrum to potentiate torsion of the adnexa. Torsion occurs most commonly in young women, typically in their early 20s, and it may occur in postmenopausal women as a complication of benign ovarian tumors. Approximately 20% of cases of torsion occur in pregnancy, often associated with ovaries enlarged by ovulation induction. Many patients have intermittent episodes of pain that resolve spontaneously in the weeks or months prior to the acute episode. All women of childbearing age should have a pregnancy test as part of the preoperative evaluation to exclude the presence of pregnancy or its complications.

Increasingly often, women with ovarian or adnexal torsion are being treated via laparoscopic surgery. Because the majority of cases of torsion occur in young women, conservative surgery is the treatment of choice. With early diagnosis and intervention, conservative surgery is successful in approximately 75% of cases. Prolonged torsion may cause extensive adnexal necrosis, and untwisting may not be feasible.

The next step in management of this patient involves gentle untwisting of the adnexal pedicle, either through the laparoscope or via laparotomy. A cystectomy may be needed, as well as stabilization of the adnexa with sutures to prevent recurrence of torsion. The risk of pulmonary embolus with ovarian or adnexal torsion is only 0.2%, and it is similar when the adnexa is untwisted or removed without untwisting. There is no evidence that the use of intraoperative heparin therapy is of any benefit in prevention of embolization. Untwisting the pedicle is the preferred treatment in patients who wish to preserve fertility, even when the adnexa has a bluish black ischemic appearance. Observation for evidence of improved blood flow to the pedicle after untwisting will assist in decision making regarding the need for removal.

Oophorectomy is performed when torsion of the ovarian pedicle results in a necrotic or gangrenous ovary and the ipsilateral oviduct is viable. Salpingo-oophorectomy is the treatment of choice in instances of severe vascular compromise and a gangrenous or necrotic adnexa.

The use of intravenous fluorescein intraoperatively with subsequent inspection of the untwisted adnexa using an ultraviolet light has been suggested to document vascular integrity. This technique, however, has not been shown to be practical and rarely is used.

Bayer AI, Wiskind AK. Adnexal torsion: can the adnexa be saved? Am J Obstet Gynecol 1994;171:1506–10 [discussion 1510–1].

McGovern PG, Noah R, Koenigsberg R, Little AB. Adnexal torsion and pulmonary embolism: case report and review of the literature. Obstet Gynecol Surv 1999;54:601–8.

Oelsner G, Bider D, Goldenberg M, Admon D, Mashiach S. Long-term follow-up of the twisted ischemic adnexa managed by detorsion. Fertil Steril 1993;60:976–9.

Zweizig S, Perron J, Grubb D, Mishell DR Jr. Conservative management of adnexal torsion. Am J Obstet Gynecol 1993;168:1791–5.

81

Hysteroscopic complications

A 37-year-old woman undergoes a hysteroscopic resection of a 5-cm submucous leiomyoma, which has caused menorrhagia. The distending medium used is a combination 3% sorbitol, 0.5% mannitol. One-half hour into the procedure, you are informed of a fluid deficit of 650 mL. The most appropriate next step in management of this patient is

(A) continue the procedure with close observation of the deficit
(B) discontinue the procedure
* (C) determine serum sodium level
(D) administer furosemide (Lasix)
(E) change the distending medium to 32% dextran 70 (Hyskon)

Potential complications of operative hysteroscopy include bleeding, infection, air embolism, anesthesia-related problems, and complications associated with the use of the distending media. One of the primary risks of hysteroscopic resection of submucous leiomyomata is fluid overload and electrolyte abnormalities related to intravasation of large quantities of distending media. The amount of fluid absorbed is associated with the distending pressure, the number of open vascular channels, and the length of the surgical procedure.

A combination 3% sorbitol, 0.5% mannitol is a hypotonic, electrolyte-free medium with an osmolality of 178 mOsm/kg H_2O. It commonly is used with monopolar current because of its relative nonconductivity. If absorbed in large quantities through vascular channels opened in the endometrium or myometrium, the sorbitol is metabolized rapidly, resulting in intravascular free water. Although mannitol is added for its osmotic diuretic properties, hyponatremia and hypervolemia may ensue. Through osmosis, the free water passes into the extracellular and

intracellular spaces, including brain tissue, causing neurons to swell and lyse. The initial manifestations are nausea, vomiting, headaches, and agitation, followed by the development of hypotension, pulmonary edema, cardiac disturbances, seizures, and eventually coma and death if untreated.

Prevention of these sequelae is paramount and may be achieved by minimizing fluid intravasation. Distending pressures of 60–75 mm Hg, never exceeding 100 mm Hg, should allow good visualization while minimizing intravasation. Fluid balance, as determined by visual calculation or, preferably, by an automated fluid management system, must be assessed every 15 minutes throughout the procedure.

The handling of fluid deficits is outlined in Table 81-1. In this case, with a deficit of 650 mL, a serum sodium level should be determined on an emergent basis and the procedure continued under close scrutiny. If the fluid deficit reaches 1,000 mL, furosemide should be administered and the procedure interrupted until it is known that

TABLE 81-1. Protocol for Monitoring Fluid Deficit with Sorbitol and Mannitol in Operative Hysteroscopy

Deficit (mL)	Action
500	Stat serum Na+, continue procedure
1,000	Stat serum Na+, furosemide 20 mg IV, interrupt procedure until reassured that serum Na+ >125 mEq/mL
1,500	Same as with 1,000 mL
2,000	Stat serum Na+, furosemide 20 mg IV, stop procedure

IV, intravenous; Na+, sodium.

Data from Kim AH, Keltz MM, Arici A, Rosenberg M, Olive DL. Dilutional hyponatremia during hysteroscopic myomectomy with sorbitol-mannitol distention medium. J Am Assoc Gynecol Laparosc 1995;2:241.

the serum sodium concentration is greater than 125 mEq/mL. If the deficit reaches 2,000 mL, the procedure should be terminated.

Severe or symptomatic hyponatremia should be treated with water restriction, diuretics, and hypertonic saline, with a goal of increasing the serum sodium concentration by 1 mmol/L per hour. Changing the medium to 32% dextran 70 would further exacerbate the problem. This high-viscosity fluid acts as a volume expander when absorbed into the vasculature at a ratio of 10:1. For every 100 mL of dextran 70 absorbed, the intravascular volume will expand by about 1 L. This would worsen the degree of hypervolemia and hyponatremia.

Newer technologies, which use bipolar operative hysteroscopes, allow procedures to be performed using isotonic electrolyte solutions such as 0.9% sodium chloride or lactated Ringer's solution. Although volume overload still is possible, the risk of hyponatremia is eliminated. As these instruments are improved and more widely used, the use of hypotonic, electrolyte-free media may become obsolete.

Cofman RS, Diamond MP, DeCherney AH. Complications of laparoscopy and hysteroscopy. 2nd ed. Cambridge (MA): Blackwell Science; 1997. p. 203–11.

Cooper JM, Brady RM. Intraoperative and early postoperative complications of operative hysteroscopy. Obstet Gynecol Clin North Am 2000;27:347–66.

Hysteroscopy and other transcervical procedures. In: American College of Obstetricians and Gynecologists. Precis: gynecology. 2nd ed. Washington, DC: ACOG; 2001. p. 3–7.

Kim AH, Keltz MD, Arici A, Rosenberg M, Olive DL. Dilutional hyponatremia during hysteroscopic myomectomy with sorbitol-mannitol distention medium. J Am Assoc Gynecol Laparosc 1995;2:237–41.

82
Dysmenorrhea

A 20-year-old nulligravid woman presents with a 2-year history of increasing dysmenorrhea. She underwent menarche at 14 years of age. She has regular cycles, is not sexually active, and always has had discomfort with her periods. She has tried oral contraceptives, which give her nausea, and ibuprofen, which relieves her pain but causes symptoms of gastritis. Findings of a pelvic examination are normal. Her previous medical history is noncontributory. She strongly desires medical management before operative intervention. The most appropriate pharmacologic option in the management of this patient is

(A) acetaminophen
(B) naproxen
(C) fluoxetine hydrochloride (Prozac)
* (D) rofecoxib (Vioxx)
(E) aspirin (acetylsalicylic acid)

Primary dysmenorrhea, or dysmenorrhea initiated at the time of menarche, typically refers to discomfort in women during their cycles, without obvious organic pathology. It is thought to result from the production of prostaglandins, especially prostaglandin $F_{2\alpha}$, present in the secretory endometrium. Prostaglandin synthetase inhibitors, such as nonsteroidal antiinflammatory drugs (NSAIDs, eg, naproxen and acetylsalicylic acid, which are cyclooxygenase [COX]-1 inhibitors), have proven efficacy in alleviating these symptoms and usually are recommended as first-line therapy. Side effects associated with NSAIDs include gastritis-type irritation, which this patient has had. Oral contraceptives are also efficacious in the treatment of dysmenorrhea by suppression of ovulation-induced prostaglandin synthesis, but patients may experience nausea with even the low-dose contraceptive pill. Double-blind crossover trials have shown the use of fluoxetine hydrochloride (Prozac) to be effective in alleviating premenstrual symptoms, but not specifically dysmenorrhea. Acetaminophen has minimal antiprostaglandin activity.

On the basis of their reduced potential to injure the gastroduodenal mucosa, COX-2–selective inhibitors were developed as a safe alternative to traditional COX-1 NSAIDs. Prostaglandins are formed by the COX pathway from arachidonic acid; COX-1 is constitutively expressed, whereas COX-2 is inducible and up-regulated in inflammatory conditions (Fig. 82-1).

In vitro studies on human myometrial tissue reveal significant relaxation in human myometrium, with a similar potency in nonpregnant and pregnant tissues. The available data show that COX-2 inhibitors have a favorable safety profile and are as effective as traditional NSAIDs for the treatment of dysmenorrhea with a reduced incidence of gastrointestinal adverse effects except in patients with a recent history of ulcer bleeding. Outcome studies of more than 39,000 patients with osteoarthritis and rheumatoid arthritis found significantly fewer clinically important upper gastrointestinal adverse events with the use of COX-2 inhibitors than nonselective NSAIDs, along with similar efficacy. The COX-2 inhibitors celecoxib (Celebrex) and rofecoxib (Vioxx) have primary indications for the treatment of dysmenorrhea and may be taken once daily. Selective COX-2 inhibitors, as with all NSAIDs, should be used with caution in patients with cardiovascular disease, fluid retention, renal impairment, hypertension, and asthma.

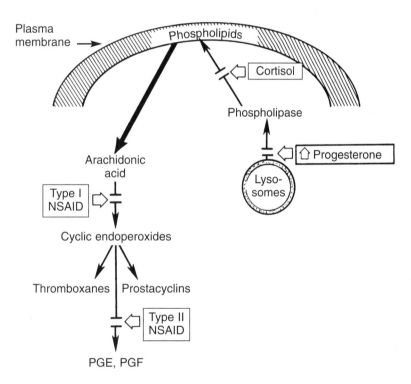

FIG. 82-1. Schematic representation of the formation of arachidonic acid from phospholipid in the plasma cell membrane and subsequent formation of prostaglandins (PGs). Inhibition at various points of the biosynthesis of prostaglandins from phospholipids is shown in boxed captions. NSAID, nonsteroidal antiinflammatory drug. (Reprinted from Am J Obstet Gynecol, Vol 169, Dawood MY, Nonsteroidal antiinflammatory drugs and reproduction. p. 1256. Copyright 1993, with permission from Elsevier.)

Dawood MY. Nonsteroidal antiinflammatory drugs and reproduction. Am J Obstet Gynecol 1993;169:1255–65.

Graham DY. NSAIDS, Helicobacter pylori and Pandora's box [editorial]. N Engl J Med 2002;347:2162–4.

Oviedo JA, Wolfe MM. Clinical potential of cyclo-oxygenase-2 inhibitors. BioDrugs 2001;15:563–72.

Primary and secondary dysmenorrhea and premenstrual syndrome: etiology, diagnosis, management. In: Stenchever MA, Droegemueller W,

Herbst AL, Mishell DR, editors. Comprehensive gynecology. 4th ed. St. Louis (MO): Mosby; 2001. p. 1065–7.

Slattery MM, Friel AM, Healy DG, Morrison JJ. Uterine relaxant effects of cyclooxygenase-2 inhibitors in vitro. Obstet Gynecol 2001;98:563–9.

Vasoo S, Ng SC. New cyclooxygenase inhibitors. Ann Acad Med Singapore 2001;30:164–9.

83

Incisional hernias in minimally invasive procedures

A 27-year-old woman undergoes an operative laparoscopy for removal of a complex, persistent 7-cm left ovarian cyst. After excision, the specimen is placed in an operative extraction bag and removed through a 12-mm horizontal port placed approximately 3 cm superior to the symphysis pubis. The fascial incision requires expansion to accommodate removal of the specimen. The immediate postoperative course is unremarkable. The patient presents 10 days postoperatively and reports suprapubic pressure and pain, especially when standing, but absent when supine. Examination reveals a mass at the lower incision line, which enlarges as the patient stands. The most likely diagnosis is

*   (A) midline ventral hernia without obstruction
    (B) myofascial syndrome
    (C) incision abscess
    (D) midline subfascial hematoma

This patient presents with classic signs and symptoms of a lower abdominal incisional hernia. Symptoms that are observed only when the patient is standing and the lack of other findings or complications indicate a hernia without incarceration or obstruction. A hematoma is unlikely, because the mass is reducible and no superficial ecchymosis is noted. An abscess is unlikely when there is no fever, erythema, or other findings typical of abscess and the area is not fluctuant.

Myofascial syndrome consists of lower-quadrant abdominal pain, usually following a transverse incision caused by entrapment of the ilioinguinal or genitofemoral nerves. It is more common following multiple operations through the same incision. Some authors believe that myofascial syndrome may account for a significant proportion of chronic pelvic pain. One study reported a 14% incidence of myofascial syndrome in patients who had negative laparoscopic findings but a prior abdominal incision. The syndrome would be uncommon in patients with a laparoscopic incision.

As laparoscopic procedures have become more advanced, the frequency of operative complications has increased. The first report of a postoperative laparoscopic hernia was in 1974, when a survey of members of the American Association of Gynecologic Laparoscopists noted an incidence of 21 hernias per 100,000 procedures. Of these hernias, one fifth occurred despite fas-

cial closure. These results subsequently have been confirmed. Overall, the risk of hernias appears to be greater at extraumbilical sites. Laparoscopic hernias occur more frequently with larger operative ports (ie, >10 mm) and ports that have been enlarged by manipulative devices. However, hernias also have been reported after the use of 5-mm ports.

It is recommended that fascial defects larger than 10 mm be closed. Multiple techniques for fascial closure have been devised, especially for smaller ports. Some authors recommend manual closure of the fascia for larger incisions only. It is clear that even with careful closure, not all postlaparoscopic hernias may be prevented.

Applegate WV. Abdominal cutaneous nerve entrapment syndrome. Surgery 1972;71:118–24.

Boike GM, Miller CE, Spirtos NM, Mercer LJ, Fowler JM, Summitt R, et al. Incisional bowel herniations after operative laparoscopy: a series of nineteen cases and review of the literature. Am J Obstet Gynecol 1995;172:1726–31 [discussion 1731–3].

Fear RE. Laparoscopy: a valuable aid in gynecologic diagnosis. Obstet Gynecol 1968;31:297–309.

Kadar N, Reich H, Liu CY, Manko GF, Gimpelson R. Incisional hernias after major laparoscopic gynecologic procedures. Am J Obstet Gynecol 1993;168:1493–5.

Schiff I, Naftolin F. Small bowel incarceration after uncomplicated laparoscopy. Obstet Gynecol 1974;43:674–5.

Steege JF. Persistent or chronic pelvic pain. In: Rock JA, Thompson JD, editors. Te Linde's operative gynecology. 8th ed. Philadelphia (PA): Lippincott–Raven; 1997. p. 645–56.

84

Recurrent bacterial vaginosis

A 27-year-old woman has a 6–8-week history of vaginal odor and discharge. She has tried over-the-counter treatments for yeast, and her family practitioner prescribed a 1-time treatment of oral fluconazole (Diflucan), all without resolution of her symptoms. A physical examination reveals a grayish homogeneous discharge. A saline wet preparation shows a pH of 5.0 and the presence of clue cells. The results of cervical cultures are negative. A 1-time oral course of metronidazole eased, but did not resolve, the symptoms. The most appropriate medical treatment option for this patient is

    (A) doxycycline
    (B) vaginal clindamycin hydrochloride (Cleocin) ovules
    (C) miconazole vaginal cream
  * (D) vaginal metronidazole
    (E) oral clindamycin hydrochloride

Bacterial vaginosis (BV) is the most common cause of abnormal vaginal discharge among women of childbearing age. It develops when the normal vaginal microflora, composed primarily of lactobacilli, is replaced by an overgrowth of *Gardnerella vaginalis*, anaerobes, mycoplasmas, *Prevotella* species, and *Mobiluncus* species. Lactobacilli make lactic acid, which is responsible for the normal vaginal pH of 3.8–4.2. In addition, many lactobacilli produce hydrogen peroxide (H_2O_2), which is toxic to a wide variety of microorganisms. It has been suggested that H_2O_2-producing lactobacilli play a critical role in protecting the vagina against the overgrowth of pathologic bacteria.

The presence of BV has been linked to a number of important genital tract sequelae, such as cervicitis, endometritis, pelvic inflammatory disease (PID), and postoperative infections (eg, postabortal PID, posthysterectomy cuff cellulitis, and post–cesarean delivery endometritis). Furthermore, BV is seen concomitantly in women with *Neisseria gonorrhoeae*, *Chlamydia trachomatis*, *Trichomonas vaginalis*, and human immunodeficiency virus (HIV). Bacterial vaginosis has been found in 10–25% of patients in general gynecologic and obstetric clinics and in up to 64% of patients seen in sexually transmitted disease clinics.

Criteria used to diagnose BV include the following:

- Presence of a milky homogeneous discharge associated with a fishy odor, due to production of triethylamine by the vaginal BV microflora
- pH greater than 4.5
- Presence of clue cells

Figure 84-1 illustrates clue cells on microscopic examination, which are indicative of BV.

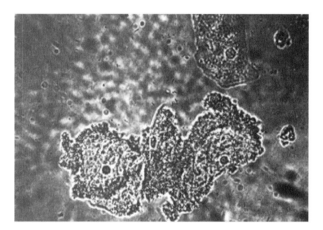

FIG. 84-1. Clue cells indicative of bacterial vaginosis on microscopic examination.

The 2002 Centers for Disease Control and Prevention (CDC) Guidelines for the Treatment of Sexually Transmitted Diseases reflects an update on the treatment of BV based on an evidence-based review of the literature since 1998. The 2002 CDC guidelines for treatment and screening are shown in Box 84-1. The alternative regimens, which include clindamycin vaginal cream, are less effective in treating BV. Clindamycin is a broader-spectrum agent that acts against lactobacilli to decrease the number of these organisms, whereas metronidazole is more sparing of lactobacilli. Doxycycline is the recommended treatment for *Chlamydia cervicitis,* which often causes a mucopurulent discharge. Miconazole cream is a treatment for vaginal yeast infections, which often manifest with vulvovaginal pruritus and show the presence of pseudohyphae or spores on a saline wet preparation.

With recurrent episodes of BV, as with any infectious disease, the question to be addressed is whether this

---

BOX 84-1

Centers for Disease Control and Prevention Recommended Guidelines for Bacterial Vaginosis Treatment

Regimens for Nonpregnant Women

Metronidazole, 500 mg orally twice a day for 7 d
  OR
Metronidazole gel, 0.75%, 1 full applicator (5 g) intravaginally once a day for 5 d
  OR
Clindamycin cream, 2%, 1 full applicator (5 g) intravaginally at bedtime for 7 d

Alternative Regimens for Nonpregnant Women

Metronidazole, 2 g orally in a single dose
  OR
Clindamycin, 300 mg orally twice a day for 7 d
  OR
Clindamycin ovules, 100 mg intravaginally once at bedtime for 3 d

Opportunities for Screening

At preoperative testing before hysterectomy and elective therapeutic abortion
In patients with mucopurulent cervicitis
In patients with other sexually transmitted diseases (especially individuals at risk for human immunodeficiency virus [HIV] infection)
At the time of group B streptococci culture during the third trimester of pregnancy

---

Adapted from Centers for Disease Control and Prevention. Sexually transmitted diseases treatment guidelines. MMWR Recomm Rep 2002;51(RR-06):61–2.

---

occurrence is a relapse or a reinfection. Although no consensus exists as to what constitutes recurrent BV, more than 4 episodes in a year would most likely define recurrent BV. No studies have shown a reduction in rate of infection when antimicrobials have been used to suppress pathogens in male partners. Therefore, the focus in recurrent BV is more on relapse. As a general practice, if the patient fails to respond to an antibiotic administered by one route, she may respond to its administration by another route or to a different agent. It is important to ensure that BV is the correct diagnosis; therefore, active pursuit of other diagnoses is recommended. A suggested therapy for recurrent BV includes a standard regimen of metronidazole for longer periods, as long as 2 weeks.

Agnew KJ, Hillier SL. The effect of treatment regimens for vaginitis and cervicitis on vaginal colonization by lactobacilli. Sex Transm Dis 1995;22:269–73.

Assessment of risk factors for preterm birth. ACOG Practice Bulletin 31. American College of Obstetricians and Gynecologists. Obstet Gynecol 2001;98:709–16.

Hamrick M, Chamblis ML. Bacterial vaginosis and treatment of sexual partners. Arch Fam Med 2000;9:647–8.

Hillier SL. The vaginal microbial ecosystem and resistance to HIV. AIDS Res Hum Retroviruses 1998;14 suppl 1:S17–S21.

Sobel JD. Bacterial vaginosis. Annu Rev Med 2000;51:349–56.

Soper DE. The normal vaginal microbial ecosystem: importance of the diagnosis and treatment of bacterial vaginosis. Ob/Gyn Spec Ed 2002;5: 9–11.

85

Menorrhagia chemotherapy

You are consulted regarding a 14-year-old adolescent with leukemia who is scheduled to receive chemotherapy. Her oncologist wants your recommendation in regard to prevention of menorrhagia during the chemotherapy. The patient is not sexually active and has had heavy, irregular menses since menarche at age 12 years. Examination reveals Tanner stage 4 breast and pubic hair development. Findings of a gynecologic examination are normal. The most appropriate recommendation is

      (A) administration of depot medroxyprogesterone acetate
      (B) administration of continuous oral contraceptives
      (C) expectant management
  * (D) administration of a gonadotropin-releasing hormone (GnRH) agonist
      (E) administration of megestrol acetate (Megace)

Adolescents and women who are undergoing cytotoxic chemotherapy are at risk for heavy menstrual flow due to thrombocytopenia. Excessive vaginal bleeding during bone marrow suppression may necessitate multiple transfusions and increase the patient's distress and discomfort. Gonadotropin-releasing hormone agonists have been used to induce amenorrhea during cytotoxic chemotherapy and bone marrow transplantation. Among thrombocytopenic women who receive a GnRH agonist, amenorrhea is maintained in 73–100%. In general, amenorrhea is expected within 1 month if a GnRH agonist is administered during the luteal phase of the menstrual cycle. Among women who receive cytotoxic chemotherapy, menstrual problems are prevented most effectively if GnRH agonist therapy is begun at least 2 weeks before the onset of thrombocytopenia. Typical maximum duration of GnRH therapy should be 6 months or less because of possible complications from osteoporosis without add-back therapy (ie, estrogen or hormone therapy).

Irregular bleeding and breakthrough bleeding are common with depot medroxyprogesterone acetate, continuous oral contraceptives, and megestrol acetate. In the first year of use, 70% of depot medroxyprogesterone acetate users experience irregular bleeding. Continuous administration of oral contraceptives can maintain amenorrhea for 6–9 months, although high-dose regimens may be required to limit bleeding episodes. With the use of continuous oral contraceptives for 3-month intervals (to reduce menstrual frequency), breakthrough bleeding occurs in 8.5% of women who take high-dose pills (50 µg ethinyl estradiol) and in 36% of women who take lower-dose formulations (30 µg ethinyl estradiol). Megestrol acetate is a progestin used as palliative therapy for carcinoma of the breast and endometrium. When used in continuous fashion for suppression of endometriosis, megestrol acetate results in breakthrough bleeding in 41% of women.

An additional potential benefit of GnRH agonist therapy is the possible preservation of ovarian function and thus fertility. Compared with the other treatments suggested, GnRH agonist is easier to administer during chemotherapy. Among women with thrombocytopenia, intramuscular administration of depot medroxyprogesterone acetate is problematic because of the risk of hematoma formation. Administration of oral contraceptives or oral megestrol acetate is impractical during chemotherapy because of stomatitis, which develops in more than three quarters of bone marrow transplant recipients. Administration of a GnRH agonist can be achieved through multiple routes. In addition, this therapy is not associated with increased risk of venous thromboembolism.

Expectant management is not the best option in this case, because this adolescent has a history of heavy, irregular menses. The risk of severe menstrual bleeding during cytotoxic chemotherapy would be high. It would be appropriate to induce amenorrhea in this patient.

Droegemueller W. Endometriosis and adenomyosis. In: Stenchever MA, Droegemueller W, Herbst A, Mishell DR, editors. Comprehensive gynecology. 4th ed. St. Louis (MO): Mosby; 2001. p. 531–64.

Ghalie R, Porter C, Radwanska E, Fitzsimmons W, Richman C, Kaizer H. Prevention of hypermenorrhea with leuprolide in premenopausal women undergoing bone marrow transplantation. Am J Hematol 1993; 42:350–3.

Kaunitz AM. Menstruation: choosing whether . . . and when. Contraception 2000;62:277–84.

Laufer MR, Townsend NL, Parsons KE, Brody KA, Diller LR, Emans SJ, et al. Inducing amenorrhea during bone marrow transplantation: a pilot study of leuprolide acetate. J Reprod Med 1997;42:537–41.

Pereyra Pacheco B, Mendez Ribas JM, Milone G, Fernandez I, Kvicla R, Mila T, et al. Use of GnRH analogs for functional protection of the ovary and preservation of fertility during cancer treatment in adolescents: a preliminary report. Gynecol Oncol 2001;81:391–7.

Schlaff WD, Dugoff L, Damewood MD, Rock JA. Megestrol acetate for treatment of endometriosis. Obstet Gynecol 1990;75:646–8.

Speroff L, Darney P. A clinical guide for contraception. 2nd ed. Baltimore: Williams & Wilkins; 1996.

86
Chronic pelvic pain

A 34-year-old woman with a long history of chronic vague lower abdominal pain complains of urgency and frequency. Her urinalysis results are negative, and she has no urgency or frequency today. She has been treated in the past for vaginal and bladder infections and reports that results of bladder and vaginal cultures were often negative. She experiences some dyspareunia with deep penetration and notes increased pain after coitus and around menses. She says she has to strain excessively for some bowel movements. A trial of continuous oral contraceptives has not alleviated the pain. She has no history of pelvic surgery or of upper genitourinary tract infection. Physical examination reveals vague suprapubic discomfort, but examination of the abdomen and pelvis discloses no trigger points; her uterus and adnexa are normal. The most likely diagnosis is

      (A) endometriosis
      (B) adenomyosis
      (C) chronic endometritis
      (D) irritable bowel syndrome
*   (E) interstitial cystitis (IC)

The diagnosis and management of chronic pelvic pain presents an ongoing enigma for the practitioner. The source of chronic discomfort may be not only the structures located in the pelvis (ie, the bladder, bowel, fallopian tubes, ovaries, and uterus); referred pain from other areas also may be involved. Most physicians are comfortable diagnosing and managing problems in areas in which they have a greater understanding. The gynecologist is much more likely to recognize endometriosis or chronic pelvic inflammatory process than chronic urinary tract disorders or irritable bowel syndrome. One of the hallmarks of patients with chronic pelvic pain is a prior history of sexual trauma.

Pelvic adhesions are thought to be a frequent source of pelvic pain, but several paradoxes exist. The degree of discomfort may not reflect the amount of adhesive disease present. Asymptomatic chlamydial pelvic infection may produce adhesions without a major systemic illness. Adhesiolysis often is ineffective. It has been demonstrated that lysis of adhesions relieves pain in only 50% of patients.

Referred pelvic pain may originate from the anterior abdominal wall, and if a trigger point can be identified, the pain will be relieved by injecting the area with a local anesthetic. Irritable bowel syndrome is poorly understood and is characterized by spasmodic abdominal pain, bloating, and varying episodes of constipation and diarrhea. It is a functional disorder much more frequently seen in women than in men.

Interstitial cystitis should be included in the differential diagnosis of chronic pelvic pain. Patients with IC have a history of being treated for urinary tract or vaginal infections, and the condition can be exacerbated by menses, coitus, and stress. In 1988, the National Institute of Diabetes and Digestive and Kidney Diseases published criteria for diagnosing IC for research purposes, but the criteria may be too rigid to manage patients in an active clinical setting. Besides urinary tract symptoms, the hallmark of this diagnosis is its chronicity, with a pattern of intermittent flaring interspersed with periods of remission. Urinary frequency is a key historical symptom, but often patients are not aware of the number of times they void per day. Any patient who voids more than 15 times a day should be strongly suspected of having IC. The pathogenesis is thought to be related to the activation of the bladder sensory nerves related to urothelium dysfunction. Tests include a potassium sensitivity test using a dilute solution of intravesical potassium solution. Patients with IC experience urgency, pain, or both in response to this potassium challenge. More than 80% of IC patients will have positive results, whereas only 2% of controls will experience discomfort. Experts are divided on the diagnostic usefulness of cytoscopy to observe the characteristic bladder ulcerations.

The patient should understand that the overall objective of therapy is to reduce the symptoms and improve the quality of life. Although complete remission is desirable, it is not always achievable. Dietary modification (eg, elimination of citrus fruits, caffeinated beverages, alcoholic beverages, and spicy foods) may be helpful. Bladder retraining as the frequency resolves has been found to be effective for some patients. Oral medications have been used with different rationales. Amitriptyline has been hypothesized to stabilize mast cells and has a moderate anticholinergic effect.

Chronic and multimodal therapy often are necessary to keep the IC in remission. Intravesical therapy is considered a second-line management. Gynecologists who are comfortable managing this condition should consider at least a 3–6-month trial of the therapies outlined before a referral should be needed.

Chronic pelvic pain. In: American College of Obstetricians and Gynecologists. Precis: gynecology. 2nd ed. Washington, DC: ACOG; 2001. p. 122–7.

Meyers DL, Aguilar VC. Gynecologic manifestations of interstitial cystitis. Clin Obstet Gynecol 2002;45:233–41.

Parsons CL, Bullen M, Kahn BS, Stanford EJ, Willems JJ. Gynecologic presentation of interstitial cystitis as detected by intravesical potassium sensitivity. Obstet Gynecol 2001;98:127–32.

87

Sexually transmitted diseases

A single 24-year-old woman who has been sexually active since age 16 years presents for discussion of abnormal results of a Pap test obtained by the liquid-based cytology technique; the test revealed atypical squamous cells of undetermined significance (ASC-US). The most appropriate next step in her management is

      (A) 2 additional Pap tests at 4–6-month intervals
*   (B) human papillomavirus (HPV) testing
      (C) cervical cultures
      (D) colposcopy

A National Institutes of Health–sponsored conference recommended evidence-based modification of the current standard of management of HPV-related diseases. Guidelines for the treatment of women with cervical cytologic abnormalities were developed through a multi-step process. The panel reviewed the literature regarding Pap test technology, the new liquid-based cytology, the role of HPV and cervical cancer precursors, and results of the National Cancer Institute–sponsored Atypical Squamous Cells of Undetermined Significance/Low-Grade Squamous Intraepithelial Lesions Triage Study. Input from the professional community at large also was considered. The revisions in the Bethesda system for classification of the results of Pap tests (Box 87-1) and the criteria used by cytologists in rendering cytologic evaluation, as well as the terminology used for reporting cytology results, were released in 2002.

The 2001 Bethesda system describes 2 categories of atypical squamous cells (ASC): 1) ASC-US and 2) atypical squamous cells, cannot exclude high-grade squamous intraepithelial lesions (ASC-H). An algorithm shows acceptable management options (Appendix 2, Fig. 2):

- Immediate referral for colposcopy
- Two more Pap tests at 4–6-month intervals, when using the standard Pap test technique, with referral for colposcopy of any woman with abnormal results of ASC or greater
- Human papillomavirus testing, with referral for colposcopy of any woman with positive results for high-risk HPV type

When the Pap test uses liquid-based cytology media or an HPV test sample is collected at the time of the Pap test and held until the Pap test results are available, "reflex HPV DNA testing" is the preferred approach, because the test can be performed without the need to collect another sample for HPV testing.

A U.S. Food and Drug Administration–approved HPV test is commercially available. Because this patient's Pap test was performed with liquid-based cytology, HPV testing is the preferred next step in her treatment. If test results are positive for high-risk HPV types, the next step would be colposcopy. If the Pap test used standard cytologic methods, repeated Pap tests would be the preferred option. Cervical cultures should be obtained if mucopurulent cervicitis or other clinical indications exist.

BOX 87-1

The 2001 Bethesda System (Abridged)

Specimen Adequacy
    Satisfactory for evaluation *(note presence/absence of endocervical/transformation zone component)*
    Unsatisfactory for evaluation ....*(specify reason)*
        Specimen rejected/not processed *(specify reason)*
        Specimen processed and examined, but unsatisfactory for evaluation of epithelial abnormality because of *(specify reason)*
General Categorization *(Optional)*
    Negative for intraepithelial lesion or malignancy
    Epithelial cell abnormality
    Other
Interpretation/Result
    Negative for intraepithelial lesion or malignancy
        Organisms
            Trichomonas vaginalis
            Fungal organisms morphologically consistent with *Candida* species
            Shift in flora suggestive of bacterial vaginosis
            Bacteria morphologically consistent with *Actinomyces* species
            Cellular changes consistent with herpes simplex virus
        Other nonneoplastic findings *(Optional to report; list not comprehensive)*
            Reactive cellular changes associated with
                Inflammation (includes typical repair)
                Radiation
                Intrauterine contraceptive device
            Glandular cells status posthysterectomy
            Atrophy
    Epithelial cell abnormalities
        Squamous cell
            Atypical squamous cells (ASC)
                of undetermined significance (ASC-US)
                cannot exclude HSIL (ASC-H)
            Low-grade squamous intraepithelial lesion (LSIL)
                Encompassing: human papillomavirus/mild dysplasia/cervical intraepithelial neoplasia (CIN) 1
            High-grade squamous intraepithelial lesion (HSIL)
                Encompassing: moderate and severe dysplasia, carcinoma in situ; CIN2 and CIN3
            Squamous cell carcinoma
        Glandular cell
            Atypical glandular cells (AGC) *(specify endocervical, endometrial, or not otherwise specified)*
            Atypical glandular cells, favor neoplastic *(specify endocervical or not otherwise specified)*
            Endocervical adenocarcinoma in situ (AIS)
            Adenocarcinoma
    Other *(List not comprehensive)*
        Endometrial cells in a woman ≥40 years of age
Automated Review and Ancillary Testing *(Include as appropriate)*
Educational Notes and Suggestions *(Optional)*

Modified from Solomon D, Davey D, Kurman R, Moriarty A, O'Connor D, Prey M, et al. The 2001 Bethesda System: terminology for reporting results of cervical cytology. JAMA 2002;287:2116. Copyright © 2002 American Medical Association. All rights reserved.

Solomon D, Davey D, Kurman R, Moriarty A, O'Connor D, Prey M, et al. The 2001 Bethesda System: terminology for reporting results of cervical cytology. JAMA 2002;287:2114–9.

Solomon D, Schiffman M, Tarone R. Comparison of three management strategies for patients with atypical squamous cells of undetermined sig-

nificance: baseline results from a randomized trial. J Natl Cancer Inst 2001;93:293–9.

Wright TC Jr, Cox JT, Massad LS, Twiggs LB, Wilkinson EJ. 2001 Consensus guidelines for the management of women with cervical cytological abnormalities. JAMA 2002;287:2120–9.

88

Sexual dysfunction as a side effect of selective serotonin reuptake inhibitors

A 45-year-old woman has been treated for depression. She has responded well to a regimen of 20 mg fluoxetine hydrochloride (Prozac) daily and has noted a significant improvement in her mood. She tells you that she would like to continue treatment but that since she initiated therapy, she has had difficulty achieving orgasm. You tell her that the most appropriate treatment for her anorgasmia is

    (A) referral for sexual dysfunction counseling
    (B) the addition of low-dose diazepam to her regimen
    (C) daily vulvar application of 2% testosterone gel
    (D) use of sildenafil citrate (Viagra) prior to intercourse
*   (E) changing her antidepressant to bupropion hydrochloride (Wellbutrin)

Persistent delay or absence of orgasm is a common sexual problem. Approximately 10% of women report lifelong lack of orgasm, and at least 50% report situational or intermittent orgasmic problems. Sexual counseling to treat primary orgasmic dysfunction often is successful. Such counseling involves desensitization of the woman in sexual situations to lessen her anxiety and guilt while enhancing her sexual excitement and pleasure. However, for this patient, who can identify the initiation of an antidepressant as the probable cause for a change in her previously normal sexual function, referral for sexual counseling would not be an appropriate first step.

Physical causes of orgasmic dysfunction may include pelvic or spinal surgery or trauma, as well as neurologic diseases (eg, Parkinson's disease or multiple sclerosis). Current knowledge about the sexual adverse effects of certain medications, such as antihypertensives, is not as well defined for women as it is for men. However, the adverse effects of several psychotropic medications have been documented in women. Tranquilizers such as diazepam are believed to inhibit sexual functioning secondary to antidopaminergic action. Thus, the addition of low-dose diazepam to this patient's regimen would not be appropriate. Antipsychotic medications such as thioridazine hydrochloride (Mellaril) and fluphenazine have been reported to cause orgasmic dysfunction. Antidepressants such as the selective serotonin reuptake inhibitor (SSRI) fluoxetine hydrochloride and others in its class frequently cause decreased sexual desire and inhibit orgasm.

Several steps can be initiated to reduce the sexual adverse effects of SSRIs. The dose can be decreased to the minimum effective level, or the patient can take a "drug holiday" (ie, not take the medication on the day of sexual activity).

Results of small studies of the use of sildenafil citrate and topical testosterone for the correction of sexual dysfunction in women have been inconclusive. Therefore, neither of these options has an established role in treatment for this patient.

Unlike the SSRIs, the antidepressant bupropion hydrochloride can promote positive effects (eg, increases in libido, arousal, and intensity of orgasm). A change in the patient's antidepressant to bupropion would be the best option to reduce antidepressant-induced sexual adverse effects. If her depression does not respond as well to bupropion, an SSRI may be slowly reintroduced so that a combination of SSRI and bupropion is used.

Dell DL. Depression in women. Clin Update Womens Health Care 2002;1:182.

Meston CM, Frohlich PF. The neurobiology of sexual function. Arch Gen Psychiatry 2000;57:1012–30.

Rothschild AJ. Sexual side effects of antidepressants. J Clin Psychiatry 2000;61 suppl 11:28–36.

89

Domestic violence

A 27-year-old woman comes to your office for her annual well-woman examination. During your conversation with her, she becomes tearful and reveals that her current marital relationship is abusive. A common gynecologic report from a patient in this social situation is

(A) menstrual migraines
(B) galactorrhea
* (C) chronic pelvic pain
(D) oligomenorrhea

Domestic violence is a pattern of assault and controlling behavior perpetrated by one partner against the other. Physical violence is usually only a component of abuse that often includes sexual and psychologic attacks, emotional intimidation, verbal abuse, stalking, destruction of property, and social isolation.

In the United States, women are 6 times more likely than men to experience violence committed by an intimate partner. Annually, 2 million–4 million women are beaten by their partners, and 2,000–4,000 die from their injuries. Women report more than half a million rapes, sexual assaults, or both each year; fewer than 20% of these assaults are committed by strangers. Female victims of domestic violence experience an average of 6 violent episodes per year. At least 30% of U.S. women will be a victim of domestic violence at some point.

A previous history of physical and sexual abuse is present in 25–40% of patients with chronic pelvic pain. The basis for the association is not clear, but the trauma of an abusive event may kindle depression or a pain-processing disorder. When determining the medical history of a woman with chronic pain, therefore, it is important to include questions about any history of childhood or adult physical or sexual abuse. The evaluation should include discussion of the patient's past and current sexual relationships.

The interviewer should determine whether the patient is currently sexually active and, if so, whether any pain is associated with sexual relations. It is also important to ascertain how the patient's pain has affected the frequency or enjoyment of sexual relations. Finally, it is important to gain insight into how the patient feels her pelvic pain has affected both her sexual and nonsexual relationships with her partner.

No association has been found between domestic violence and menstrual migraines, galactorrhea, or oligomenorrhea.

American College of Obstetricians and Gynecologists. Domestic violence. ACOG Educational Bulletin 257. Washington, DC: ACOG; 1999.

Association of Professors of Gynecology and Obstetrics. Chronic pelvic pain: an integrated approach. Washington, DC: APGO; 2000.

Geary FH Jr, Wingate CB. Domestic violence and physical abuse of women: the Grady Memorial Hospital experience. Am J Obstet Gynecol 1999;181 suppl 1:S17–S21.

Kyriacou DN, Anglin D, Taliaferro E, Stone S, Tubb T, Linden JA, et al. Risk factors for injury to women from domestic violence against women. N Engl J Med 1999;341:1892–8.

90

Oral medications for migraine

A 27-year-old nulligravid woman has a history of intermittent unilateral pulsating headaches associated with photophobia and nausea at least 1–2 times per month. Her current headache has persisted for 2 days unrelieved by acetaminophen and codeine. Findings of her history, physical examination, and neurologic examination do not suggest an underlying pathologic condition. The most effective oral therapy for the relief of her acute, persistent headache is

      (A) a β-blocker
      (B) a tricyclic antidepressant
      (C) dihydroergotamine (Migranal)
  * (D) a serotonin receptor agonist
      (E) a calcium channel blocker

Migraine is a common idiopathic, chronic neurovascular disorder characterized by episodes of severe headache lasting 4–72 hours without treatment. Typically, the headache is unilateral; throbbing; moderate to severe; aggravated by routine physical activity; and associated with nausea with or without vomiting, photophobia, or phonophobia.

The International Headache Society has established diagnostic criteria for migraine subtypes, the most common of which are *migraine with aura*, known as "classic migraine," and *migraine without aura*, referred to as "common migraine" (see Box 90-1). In several population-based studies in the United States, the incidence of migraine ranged from 1% to 8%. Migraine was more common in whites than in Asian Americans or African Americans.

Several studies indicate that in children, the prevalence of migraine is slightly higher in boys than in girls, but the prevalence becomes higher in women than in men, at a ratio of 3:1. Migraine prevalence is generally highest between ages 35 and 45 in both sexes, and the condition causes patients to miss work and time with their families. A familial or genetic predisposition to migraine has long been recognized.

Many women with migraine report that their headaches are associated with the menstrual cycle, with a substantial increase in the likelihood of migraine around the time of menstruation. A much smaller percentage (7–14%) of women have migraines only during their menses, and these headaches are more likely to be migraine without aura. The timing of increased risk for migraine at menses coincides with the time of estrogen withdrawal, but hormonal levels are not an exclusive trigger.

In 15% of patients, migraine attacks are preceded or accompanied by transient focal neurologic symptoms, which are usually visual (ie, migraine with aura). The median frequency of attacks is 1–2 per month, and the median duration of an attack is 24 hours. At least 10% of

patients have weekly attacks, and 20% have attacks lasting 2–3 days. Pathophysiologically, migraine involves dysfunction of brain stem pathways that normally modulate sensory input. The exact mechanisms are currently unknown.

Treatment of migraine includes pharmacologic and nonpharmacologic therapies. The latter include education

---

BOX 90-1

Modified Diagnostic Criteria for Migraine

1. Migraine without aura
  A. Headaches lasting 4–72 h
  B. At least 2 of the following characteristics:
    • Unilateral pain
    • Throbbing, pulsatile quality
    • Moderate or severe intensity
    • Aggravation by movement
  C. Any 1 of the following:
    • Nausea or vomiting
    • Photophobia or phonophobia
  D. At least 5 attacks fulfilling A–C
2. Migraine with aura
  A. At least 3 of the following 4 characteristics:
    • One or more fully reversible aura symptoms indicating brain dysfunction
    • One or more aura symptoms developing gradually over more than 4 min
    • No aura symptom lasting more than 60 min
    • Headache following aura within 60 min
  B. At least 2 attacks fulfilling A

Modified from Criteria for migraine defined by Headache Classification Committee of the International Headache Society. Classification and diagnostic criteria for headache disorders, cranial neuralgias and facial pain. Cephalalgia 1998;8 suppl 7:1–96.

about the disorder and changes in lifestyle to reduce migraine. Such lifestyle changes include regular sleep, regular meals, exercise, avoidance of stress, and avoidance of dietary triggers.

Drugs for treatment of migraine include medications taken to treat acute attacks and medications taken daily to reduce the frequency of attacks (Table 90-1). Nonspecific pharmacologic treatment for attacks includes aspirin,

TABLE 90-1. Selected Drugs Used in the Acute Treatment and Prophylaxis of Migraine*

Drug Class	Type of Drug	Drug Used, with Dose	Acute Rx for Migraine	Prophylaxis for Migraine
Analgesics	NSAIDs	Ibuprofen, 400–800 mg, orally OTC or Rx	•	•
		Naproxen, 250–500 mg, orally OTC or Rx		
		Indomethacin, 50 mg orally	•	
	Acetaminophen	Acetaminophen, 1,000 mg orally OTC	•	
	Opioids	Codeine, 30 mg orally	•	
	Opiate antagonist	Butorphanol, 1 mg, NS	•	
	Combination analgesics	Esgic, 1-2 tablets orally (butalbital, 50 mg, acetaminophen, 325 mg, caffeine, 40 mg)	•	
		Fioricet, 1–2 tablets orally (butalbital, 50 mg, acetaminophen, 325 mg, caffeine, 40 mg)		
Vasoactive agents	Dihydroergotamine mesylate	Dihydroergotamine mesylate, 1 mg IM, SQ, IV	•	
	Other combination agents	Midrin, 2 capsules orally, then 1 each hour up to 6 capsules (isometheptene mucate, 65 mg dichloralphenazone, 100 mg, acetaminophen, 325 mg)	•	
	5-HT agonists[†]	Sumatriptan, 6 mg SQ, 25–100 mg orally, 20 mg NS		•
		Naratriptan, 1.0–2.5 mg orally		
		Rizaptriptan, 5–10 mg orally		
		Zolmitriptan, 1.25–2.5 mg orally		
	Ergotamine	Ergotamine, 2 mg orally	•	
		Various combinations of ergotamine and caffeine, orally and rectally		
β-Blockers		Propranolol, 80–240 mg orally, once daily		•
		Metoprolol, 50–100 mg orally, once daily		
Antidepressants	Tricyclic antidepressants	Amitriptyline, 25–100 mg orally, once daily		•
		Doxepin, 175–300 mg		
	Selective serotonin reuptake inhibitors	Fluoxetine, 20–80 mg orally, daily (others may be effective)		•
Calcium channel blockers		Verapamil, 80–480 mg, daily		•
		Nimodipine, 30 mg 3 times daily		
Anticonvulsants		Valproic acid, 250–500 mg orally, daily		

DHE, dihydroergotamine; 5-HT, 5-hydroxytryptamine; IM, intramuscularly; IV, intravenously; NS, nasal spray; NSAIDs, nonsteroidal antiinflammatory drugs; OTC, over the counter; Rx, prescription; SQ, subcutaneously.

* Consult the manufacturer or other information for a complete list of therapeutic precautions, contraindications, and drug interactions.

† The maximum to be administered in 24 hours is 2 doses of any formula with at least 2 hours between doses.

• Indicates drug is preferred for tension headache prophylaxis. All drugs listed for migraine prophylaxis may have some efficacy.

Adapted from Kieu A, Saxton E. Approach to the patient with headache. In: Pregler JP, DeCheney AH, editors. Women's health: principles and clinical practice. Hamilton (ON): BC Decker Inc; 2002. p. 722–3.

acetaminophen, nonsteroidal antiinflammatory drugs, opiates, and combination analgesics. Specific treatments include ergotamine tartrate (Ergomar), ergotamine tartrate plus caffeine (Wigraine), dihydroergotamine, and triptans. Analgesics and nonsteroidal antiinflammatory drugs may ameliorate an acute attack, but the response to therapy may vary. These drugs should be taken as soon as the headache component of an attack is recognized and should not be taken for more than 2–3 days a week.

The newest and most effective oral treatment for the relief of acute migraine headache is a class of selective serotonin receptor agonists that activate 5-hydroxytryptamine receptors and are known as triptans. This class of agents should not be confused with selective serotonin reuptake inhibitors. Triptans, which have provided a significant advance in the treatment of migraine, are presumed to work directly on the pathogenesis of migraine by 3 main mechanisms of action:

- Cranial vasoconstriction
- Peripheral trigeminal inhibition
- Inhibition of transmission through second-order neurons of the trigeminocervical complex

Several triptans are available, all with well-established efficacy and safety records, as well as moderate adverse effects such as tingling and paresthesias. Their use is contraindicated, however, in patients with cardiovascular disease. The triptans are administered by several routes, but patients prefer oral formulations, which account for more than 80% of triptan prescriptions. Thus, a serotonin receptor agonist would be the best choice of medication in the treatment of this patient. ·

Patients who have more than 2–3 headaches per month or attacks that are unresponsive to acute-attack medica-tion and that cause significant disability are candidates for preventive therapy. Approximately two thirds of patients given a drug used for preventive therapy will have a 50% reduction in the frequency of headaches. Beta blockers, such as propranolol, are among the first agents used for migraine prophylaxis. Their use is contraindicated in patients with asthma and congestive heart failure. Tricyclic antidepressants, used in prophylactic treatment, may decrease the frequency and intensity of migraine headaches but are not effective in the treatment of an acute attack. Calcium channel blockers, such as verapamil hydrochloride, are widely used in preventive therapy, but not in the treatment of acute attacks. Evidence of their benefits is limited, and adverse effects such as constipation, leg swelling, and atrioventricular conduction disturbance limit their use. Ergotamine and dihydroergotamine are low-cost drugs used for treatment of acute attacks, but their erratic pharmacokinetics, lack of evidence regarding effective doses, sustained generalized vasoconstrictor effects, and high risk of rebound headaches limit their use. Their long-term use should be avoided because of the possibility of tolerance, physical dependence, and chronic daily headaches.

Ferrari MD, Roon KI, Lipton RB, Goadsby PJ. Oral triptans (serotonin 5-HT 1B/1D agonists) in acute migraine treatment: a meta-analysis of 53 trails. Lancet 2001;358:1668–75.

Goadsby PJ, Lipton RB, Ferrari MD. Migraine—current understanding and treatment. N Engl J Med 2002;346:257–70.

Hamelsky SW, Stewart WF, Lipton RB. Epidemiology of headache in women: emphasis on migraine. In: Goldman MB, Hatch MC, editors. Women and health. San Diego (CA): Academic Press; 2000. p. 1084–97.

Silberstein SD. Migraine and other headache disorders. Clin Update Womens Health Care 2002;1:1–59.

91

Endometrial ablation

A 38-year-old woman, para 2, who has undergone a tubal ligation, has a long history of menorrhagia. Her menorrhagia has increased over the past 6 months. Her periods are regular, lasting up to 10 days with heavy bleeding 5 out of 10 days. A recent hemoglobin measurement was 10.0 g/dL. She has a normal-sized uterus. Evaluation of the endometrium with ultrasonography and biopsy had normal findings. She does not desire management with oral medications because she is taking numerous medications for lupus erythematosus and hypertension. She prefers the most conservative approach to management. Of the following management options, the option you would recommend at this time is

      (A) dilation and curettage
      (B) vaginal hysterectomy
*   (C) use of the levonorgestrel-releasing intrauterine device (IUD) (Mirena)
      (D) endometrial ablation

Heavy menstrual bleeding can greatly affect a woman's quality of life. Initial treatment typically involves the use of oral hormonal and nonhormonal therapies. Despite the theoretical advantages of these drug treatments, many women eventually are offered, and undergo, hysterectomy despite its inherent morbidity and time loss from normal activity. As a result of studies on the rates and indications for hysterectomy, less invasive techniques that spare the uterus are being used for the control of abnormal bleeding.

One surgical alternative to hysterectomy is endometrial ablation. Endometrial ablation can be performed by a hysteroscopic technique with electrical energy used to cause necrosis with rollerball, excision, or vaporization of the endometrium. More recently, techniques using thermal therapy or cryotherapy for endometrial ablation without hysteroscopic intervention have been developed.

Endometrial ablation and hysterectomy have been compared in multiple trials, and most studies have shown patient satisfaction with treatment to be similar in the 2 operative groups. However, in studies with follow-up times longer than 2 years, patient satisfaction with endometrial ablation significantly decreased. Endometrial ablation is a less invasive procedure than hysterectomy, but because it still involves surgery, there is inherent risk associated with anesthesia and with the procedure itself (eg, fluid overload, uterine perforation, bleeding, infection, and recurrent bleeding).

Intrauterine devices have been used primarily as a means of contraception. Progestogen-releasing IUDs initially were developed as a means of reducing IUD expulsion by the addition of uterine-relaxing hormones. Studies have shown use of the levonorgestrel IUD to be associated with a significant reduction in menstrual blood loss. After 1 year of use, 20% of women who used the lev-

onorgestrel IUD were amenorrheic. The levonorgestrel IUD has been reported to reduce heavy menstrual bleeding by up to 90% in case studies.

Randomized trials to compare the levonorgestrel IUD with other forms of hormonal management in cases of abnormal bleeding have shown comparable and improved efficacy. Overall, although quality-of-life scores were significantly higher in the IUD groups, some adverse effects, such as intermenstrual bleeding and breast tenderness, were more common in users of the levonorgestrel IUD. Two trials compared use of the IUD with endometrial resection with a 1-year follow-up. Patient satisfaction rates were similar, and significant improvements were described in blood count, serum iron levels, and menorrhagia, as estimated by pictorial chart scores. No significant difference was noted in incidence of dysmenorrhea at 12-month follow-up. In another randomized trial that involved 56 women scheduled for hysterectomy because of ovulatory dysfunctional uterine bleeding, 64.3% of those assigned to IUD use chose to cancel surgery, compared with only 14.3% of the group allocated to their current medical management.

A multicenter trial in Finland randomized 236 women with menorrhagia to use of the levonorgestrel IUD (n = 119) or hysterectomy (n = 117). In the group that received the levonorgestrel IUD, 20% had a hysterectomy, and 68% continued IUD use for 12 months. Of the women assigned to the hysterectomy group, 107 underwent surgery. Health-related quality of life improved significantly in both the IUD and hysterectomy groups, as did other indices of psychologic well-being. There were no significant differences between the groups except that women with hysterectomy had less pain. Overall, costs were 3 times greater for hysterectomy. In this study, the significant improvement in health-related quality of life highlights the importance of treating menorrhagia and the fact that the levonorgestrel IUD was a cost-effective alternative to hysterectomy.

In light of these studies and the patient's desire for the most conservative management and a nonoral hormonal treatment, the levonorgestrel IUD is a viable option for long-term (5-year) treatment of menorrhagia with iron deficiency anemia. Treatment with hysterectomy involves major surgical intervention, and the efficacy of dilation and curettage is inconsistent in the treatment of menorrhagia.

American College of Obstetricians and Gynecologists. Management of anovulatory bleeding. ACOG Practice Bulletin 14. Washington, DC: ACOG; 2000.

Andersson K, Odlind V, Rybo G. Levonorgestrel-releasing and copper-releasing (Nova T) IUDs during five years of use: a randomized comparative trial. Contraception 1994;49:56–72.

Crosignani PG, Vercellini P, Mosconi P, Oldani S, Crotesi I, De Giorgi O. Levonorgestrel-releasing intrauterine device versus hysteroscopic endometrial resection in the treatment of dysfunctional uterine bleeding. Obstet Gynecol 1997;90:257–63.

Hurskainen R, Teperi J, Rissanen P, Aalto AM, Grenman S, Kivela A, et al. Quality of life and cost-effectiveness of levonorgestrel-releasing intrauterine system versus hysterectomy for treatment of menorrhagia: a randomised trial. Lancet 2001;357:273–7.

Kittelsen N, Istre O. A randomized study comparing levonorgestrel intrauterine system (LNG IUS) and transcervical resection of the endometrium (TCRE) in the treatment of menorrhagia: preliminary results. Gynaecol Endosc 1998;7:61–5.

Lahteenmaki P, Haukkamaa M, Puolakka J, Riikonen U, Sainio S, Suvisaari J, et al. Open randomised study of use of levonorgestrel releasing intrauterine system as alternative to hysterectomy. BMJ 1998;316:1122–6.

Lethaby AE, Cooke I, Rees M. Progesterone/progestogen releasing intrauterine systems for heavy menstrual bleeding (Cochrane Review). In: The Cochrane Library, Issue 2, 2003. Oxford: Update Software.

92

Pain management

A 45-year-old woman is being treated for chronic pain secondary to advanced cervical cancer. She currently receives 100 mg of oral morphine every 4 hours. She has required 6 rescue doses of 60 mg each during the previous 24 hours. Her pain medication should be adjusted so that the oral morphine dose she receives every 4 hours with rescue is

    (A) 100 mg with 90 mg rescue
    (B) 120 mg with 60 mg rescue
    (C) 140 mg with 60 mg rescue
*   (D) 160 mg with 90 mg rescue

In its 2001 implementation of pain-related standards of care, the Joint Commission on Accreditation of Healthcare Organizations (JCAHO) pointed out the connection between unrelieved pain and negative physiologic and psychologic effects. These adverse outcomes were generalized from the hospitalized patient to the majority of patients in nearly all health care settings (ie, hospitals, long-term care facilities, surgical centers, mental health facilities, home health services, and ambulatory care centers). Now JCAHO requires that assessments be made of a patient's level of pain on admission and throughout a patient's hospital stay.

Pain is a prevalent symptom in patients with cancer. Pain is experienced by approximately one third of patients who are undergoing active therapy and 70% of patients with advanced malignant disease. Although most patients attain acceptable relief, compelling evidence exists that treatment often is inadequate. In some patients, inadequacy of treatment is due to either refractory pain or noncompliance.

However, far more often it reflects failure of clinical management—most important, underuse of analgesics.

A patient with severe cancer pain generally is given an opioid at a dosage equivalent to 5–10 mg of intramuscular morphine, 15–30 mg orally, every 4 hours (Table 92-1). Patients switched from a higher-dose drug should begin at a dose one half to two thirds the equianalgesic dose of the current medication. The expectation underlying this approach is that a new drug will have relatively greater effects because of incomplete cross-tolerance between opioids. If pain remains severe after the initial dose, the subsequent dose can be doubled.

The preferred approach is the administration of the medication on a fixed around-the-clock schedule with a rescue dose, usually equal to 5–10% of the total daily dose, offered as needed every 1–2 hours for breakthrough pain. This approach allows the patient control over dosing and can be used to estimate the increment required in the fixed dose.

Table 92-1. Dosing Data for Opioid Analgesics

Drug Class	Name of Drug	Approximate Equianalgesic Oral Dose	Approximate Equianalgesic Parenteral Dose
Opioid agonist	Morphine	30 mg every 4 h (around-the-clock dosing); 60 mg every 3–4 h (single dose or intermittent dosing)	10 mg every 3–4 h
	Codeine	130 mg every 3–4 h	75 mg every 3–4 h
	Hydromorphone (Dilaudid)	7.5 mg every 3–4 h	1.5 mg every 3–4 h
	Hydrocodone (in Lorcet, Lortab, Vicodin, others)	30 mg every 3–4 h	Not available
	Levorphanol (Levo-Dromoran)	4 mg every 6–8 h	2 mg every 6–8 h
	Meperidine (Demerol)	300 mg every 2–3 h	100 mg every 3 h
	Methadone (Dolophine, others)	20 mg every 6–8 h	10 mg every 6–8 h
	Oxycodone (Roxicodone, also in Percocet, Percodan, Tylox, others)	30 mg every 3–4 h	Not available
	Oxymorphone (Numorphan)	Not available	1 mg every 3–4 h
Opioid agonist–antagonist and partial agonist	Buprenorphine	Not available	0.3–0.4 mg every 6–8 h
	Butorphanol (Stadol)	Not available	2 mg every 3–4 h
	Nalbuphine (Nubain)	Not available	10 mg every 3–4 h
	Pentazocine (Talwin, others)	150 mg every 3–4 h	60 mg every 3–4 h

Note: Published tables vary in the suggested doses that are equianalgesic to morphine. Clinical response is the criterion that must be applied for each patient; titration to clinical response is necessary. Because there is no complete cross-tolerance among these drugs, it is usually necessary to use a lower-than-equianalgesic dose when changing drugs to retitrate to response.

Cautions: Recommended doses do not apply to patients with renal or hepatic insufficiency or other conditions affecting drug metabolism and kinetics. Refer to clinical practice guidelines for management of pain in infants younger than 6 months.

Adapted from Acute Pain Management Guideline Panel. Acute pain management: operative or medical procedures and trauma. Rockville (MD): Agency for Health Care Policy and Research, Public Health Service, U.S. Department of Health and Human Services; 1992. AHCPR publication no. 92-0019. p. 20.

The patient in this example, who has been receiving 100 mg of morphine every 4 hours and who has required six 60-mg rescue doses during the previous 24 hours, has shown a need for an additional 360 mg per day. It would be reasonable to increase the fixed dose to 160 mg every 4 hours and simultaneously increase the rescue dose to 90 mg, thereby maintaining it at 10% of the total daily dose.

The predictable consequences of long-term administration of opioids include tolerance and physical dependence. This is not the same as addiction, which is a psychologic dependence that manifests itself as drug abuse. It is important to differentiate addiction from tolerance and physical dependence to avoid misinterpretation of patient requests and undertreatment of pain. Tolerance is a physiologic-receptor phenomenon and is inevitable. Patients will develop tolerance to any opioid they take over a long time and will require higher doses. When tolerance occurs, higher doses should be prescribed. Physical dependence is a pharmacologic property that is defined as the development of withdrawal symptoms (eg, sweating, tremors, and tachycardia) after either abrupt cessation of the drug or sudden reduction in dose. Patients should be warned to avoid abrupt discontinuation of opioids, and the dose should be tapered if an opioid is discontinued.

The management of persistent pain in older persons. J Am Geriatr Soc 2002;50 suppl 6:S205–S224.

Quality improvement guidelines for treatment of acute pain and cancer pain. American Pain Society Quality of Care Committee. JAMA 1995; 274:1874–80.

93

Embolization complications

A 27-year-old woman underwent uterine artery embolization for multiple leiomyomata 3 days ago. Prophylactic antibiotics were prescribed. She now presents with uterine pain, tenderness, temperature of 39°C (102.2°F), and leukocytosis. The most appropriate management of this patient is

* (A) observation
  (B) a course of antibiotics
  (C) hysterectomy
  (D anticoagulation
  (E) exploratory laparotomy

With the increasing popularity of uterine artery embolization as a treatment for the leiomyomatous uterus, it is imperative for gynecologists to become familiar with the procedure, the postoperative course, and the potential complications. After the procedure, there may be considerable pain, which may continue for 4–5 days. This pain is expected in the immediate postoperative period, because the blood supply to the leiomyomata has been obstructed. Most protocols involve a postoperative course of narcotic analgesics and nonsteroidal antiinflammatory agents. Antiemetics are routinely prescribed to alleviate postprocedure nausea. Because of early reports of serious uterine infections, most protocols generally include the prescription of prophylactic antibiotics.

The incidence of a flulike postembolization syndrome is approximately 20%. The etiology of this syndrome is not completely understood, but it most likely involves ischemia and an inflammatory response. Signs and symptoms, as in this case, include pain, fever, malaise, myalgia, and nausea. The best management is close observation with appropriate analgesic therapy. Some patients may require hospitalization because of the need for intravenous hydration or parenteral narcotics.

Because this patient received a course of prophylactic antibiotics and the presentation is typical of postembolization syndrome, additional antibiotic therapy is not indicated. Additional antibiotics might be necessary if the clinical course worsens and the patient develops evidence of a severe uterine infection, with symptoms of profuse,

foul-smelling vaginal discharge and signs of peritonitis.

Given this patient's history, a hysterectomy is not needed. A severe uterine infection with necrosis and signs of peritonitis may necessitate the removal of the uterus. In the long term, hysterectomy may be the appropriate option if the patient's original symptoms are not alleviated.

Embolization to treat leiomyomata has not been associated with the development of venous thrombotic events. There have been no reports that dislodgment of the embolization material has resulted in venous thrombosis at another site. The particles used for embolization are approximately 500 μm—50 times the size of a red blood cell—and they do not pass through the capillary circulation to the venous side. The procedure is minimally invasive, and patients are able to ambulate soon after its completion, minimizing the risk of a deep vein thrombosis.

In this patient, exploratory laparotomy would be an appropriate intervention only if signs of peritonitis were observed.

Goodwin SC, McLucas B, Lee M, Chen G, Perrella R, Vedantham S, et al. Uterine artery embolization for the treatment of uterine leiomyomata midterm results. J Vasc Interv Radiol 1999;10:1159–65.

Leung DA, Goin JE, Sickles C, Raskay BJ, Soulen MC. Determinants of postembolization syndrome after hepatic chemoembolization. J Vasc Interv Radiol 2001;12:321–6.

Ravina JH, Herbreteau D, Ciraru-Vigneron N, Bouret JM, Houdart E, Aymard A, et al. Arterial embolisation to treat uterine myomata. Lancet 1995;346:671–2.

94

Postoperative complications

A 43-year-old woman with a history of endometriosis underwent a total abdominal hysterectomy and bilateral salpingo-oophorectomy for a complex pelvic mass. The procedure was difficult because of multiple adhesions, especially in the area of the pelvic side wall. Postoperatively, the patient reported greater-than-expected abdominal pain. Her complete blood count was stable; however, a metabolic profile revealed blood urea nitrogen (BUN) concentration of 34 mg/dL and creatinine concentration of 1.9 mg/dL. Preoperative BUN concentration was 10 mg/dL and creatinine concentration, 0.5 mg/dL. The most likely findings noted on a subsequent computed tomographic (CT) scan of the abdomen and pelvis would be

* (A) ureteroperitoneal fistula
   (B) vesicovaginal fistula
   (C) ureterovaginal fistula
   (D) unilateral hydronephrosis

The close proximity of the urinary and reproductive tracts predisposes the ureters and bladder to damage during surgery for gynecologic disease. Approximately 50–90% of lower urinary tract injuries occur during gynecologic surgery. Ureteral injury may occur in 0.5–2.5% of gynecologic procedures. In 1 study, the incidence of ureteral injury in radical hysterectomy was 1.1%; however, 75% of injuries occur during hysterectomy for nonmalignant disease. Injuries occur more frequently in patients with severe endometriosis, history of pelvic inflammatory disease or pelvic abscess, and uterine distortion by pelvic masses such as leiomyomata.

Prevention of ureteral injury begins with the preoperative evaluation of the patient. Routine intravenous pyelography (IVP) or other studies have not been shown to decrease the incidence of injury. However, if the patient presents with symptoms suspicious for involvement of the urinary tract (eg, hematuria or previous diagnosis of severe endometriosis), an IVP or CT scan may be useful to identify preexisting injury or obstruction. Most experienced gynecologic surgeons do not advocate routine preoperative placement of ureteral stents or catheters. Placement of these devices has not been shown to decrease the incidence of ureteral injury and may damage the intima of the ureter. If use of a stent is indicated because of a difficult dissection or complication during the procedure, it may be placed by open cystotomy or cystoscopy.

Several authors emphasize adherence to strict anatomic principles and "ureteral consciousness" during abdominal surgery to prevent injury. This method includes preoperative assessment of the extent of pelvic disease and urinary tract studies, when indicated. It continues with awareness of ureteral location during the entire operation, especially during dissection in close proximity to the ureter, and it concludes with heightened awareness of the patient's symptoms that may suggest injury during the postoperative period. Intraoperative management must include restoration of anatomy when opening the abdominal cavity and identification of the ureters in their course from the pelvic brim to entry into the bladder. The most likely sites of ureteral injury are listed in Box 94-1.

Some authors advocate the intravenous use of indigo carmine dye with routine cystoscopy after all gynecologic procedures to identify unrecognized injury. In a series of 3,597 major gynecologic operations in which routine cystoscopy was performed, 5 unsuspected ureteral injuries were noted.

If ureteral injury is suspected because of intraoperative findings or the patient's postoperative course, standard contrast studies usually will clarify the diagnosis. This patient presents classic symptoms of a urinoma caused by laceration of the ureter during dissection and subsequent extravasation into the retroperitoneal or peritoneal space. The other diagnoses may be excluded by lack of contrast

---

BOX 94-1

Sites of Ureteral Injury

• Pelvic brim and near the ovarian ligaments
• At the level of the uterine artery
• Proximal to the bladder

Modified from Thompson JD, Wiskind A. Operative injuries to the urinary tract. In: Nichols DH, editor. Reoperative gynecologic and obstetric surgery. 2nd ed. St. Louis (MO): Mosby; 1997. p. 196.

in the vagina and absence of hydronephrosis on CT scan. Vesicovaginal and ureterovaginal fistulae most likely would cause drainage of urine from the vagina, and a significant increase in creatinine concentration would not be expected. Unilateral ureteral obstruction would be associated with a more modest rise in creatinine concentration of 0.8 mg/dL or less.

Angioli R, Penalver MA. Urinary tract injuries. In: Walters MD, Karram MM, editors. Urogynecology and reconstructive pelvic surgery. 2nd ed. St. Louis (MO): Mosby; 1999. p. 177–86.

Holloway HJ. Injury to the urinary tract as a complication of gynecologic surgery. Am J Obstet Gynecol 1950;60:30–40.

Hurt WG. Gynecologic injury to the ureters, bladder, and urethra: prevention, recognition, and management. In: Hurt WG, editor. Urogynecologic surgery. 2nd ed. Philadelphia (PA): Lippincott Williams & Wilkins; 2000. p. 377–86.

Mann WJ, Arato M, Patsner B, Stone ML. Ureteral injuries in an obstetrics and gynecology training program: etiology and management. Obstet Gynecol 1988;72:82–5.

Thompson JD, Wiskind A. Operative injuries to the urinary tract. In: Nichols DH, editor. Reoperative gynecologic and obstetric surgery. 2nd ed. St. Louis (MO): Mosby; 1997. p. 189–229.

95

Benefits of hormone therapy

A 60-year-old woman requests information about hormone therapy (HT). She is interested in the benefits of HT other than those that involve alleviation of vasomotor symptoms, bone preservation, and prevention of vulvovaginal atrophy. You advise her that HT is likely to help protect her against development of

    (A) systemic lupus erythematosus (SLE)
    (B) rheumatoid arthritis
    (C) migraine
*   (D) colon cancer
    (E) gallbladder disease

Many studies have demonstrated the beneficial effects of menopausal HT on vulvovaginal atrophy, vasomotor symptoms, and osteoporosis. Users of HT have an increased risk of breast cancer and stroke. Continuation of therapy with HT is a significant problem. Many women do not fill their prescriptions or discontinue therapy, either because of the medication's adverse effects or fear of cancer, particularly breast cancer.

Hormone therapy is likely to help protect against the development of colon cancer. A meta-analysis of epidemiologic observational studies and a recent prospective randomized trial suggest a 20–35% reduction in risk of colon and rectal cancer in postmenopausal women who have ever used HT. Much of the apparent reduction was limited to current users. Colorectal cancer is the third leading cause of cancer morbidity in women in the United States. A biologic reason for the beneficial effect of HT may be that exogenous estrogen decreases production of secondary bile acids, which are thought to initiate or promote malignant changes in the colonic epithelium. Estrogens also may decrease serum insulinlike growth factor-1 (IGF-1), which is a mitogen that may be needed by colonic cells to progress to malignancy.

Systemic lupus erythematosus is an autoimmune disease of unknown etiology, but evidence implicates sex steroid hormones in its pathogenesis. In a large prospective cohort study, postmenopausal HT was associated with an increased risk for developing SLE, and this risk was related to the duration of hormone use. Moreover, concerns about HT in women with SLE relate to the increased risk of venous and arterial thrombosis in women with this disease. Data are insufficient to recommend the use of HT among women with stable or inactive disease or with no history of thrombosis, nephropathy, or antiphospholipid antibodies.

Hormone therapy has not been shown to prevent the development of rheumatoid arthritis, and randomized controlled trials and prospective cohort studies have shown no beneficial effect of HT on the clinical course or disease markers of rheumatoid arthritis. Women with rheumatoid arthritis, however, frequently have decreased bone mass, and treatment options for osteoporosis in these women should be considered.

In addition to a genetic or familial predisposition, several internal and external factors may trigger migraine headache. Fluctuating or falling levels of estrogen appear to be related to migraine activity, and migraine incidence may increase in the menopausal years. Although the effect of HT on migraine is variable, most evidence suggests worsening of headaches with HT.

The use of HT carries up to a 2-fold increase in risk of gallbladder disease. In a large prospective cohort study, the risk of cholecystectomy appeared to increase with dose and duration of use, and to persist for 5 or more years after stopping treatment. Both the oral and transdermal routes of estrogen administration effect similar changes in bile lipids and cholesterol, and both routes may increase gallstone formation.

Hernandez-Avila M, Liang MH, Willett WC, Stampfer MJ, Colditz GA, Rosner B, et al. Exogenous sex hormones and the risk of rheumatoid arthritis. Arthritis Rheum 1990;33:947–53.

Grodstein F, Colditz GA, Stampfer MJ. Postmenopausal hormone use and cholecystectomy in a large prospective study. Obstet Gynecol 1994; 83:5–11.

Grodstein F, Newcomb PA, Stampfer MJ. Postmenopausal hormone therapy and the risk of colorectal cancer: a review and meta-analysis. Am J Med 1999;106:574–82.

Rossouw JE, Anderson GL, Prentice RL, LaCroix AZ, Kooperberg C, Stefanick ML, et al. Risks and benefits of estrogen plus progestin in healthy postmenopausal women: principal results from the Women's Health Initiative randomized controlled trial. JAMA 2002;288: 321–33.

Sanchez-Guerrero J, Liang MH, Karlson EW, Hunter DJ, Colditz GA. Postmenopausal estrogen therapy and the risk for developing systemic lupus erythematosus. Ann Intern Med 1995;122:430–3.

96
Urinary system physiologic changes in older women

A 77-year-old woman had an uncomplicated total abdominal hysterectomy and bilateral salpingo-oophorectomy. On postoperative day 2, her urine output is 20–25 mL/h and is concentrated, despite the administration of 3 L of 5% dextrose in normal saline intraoperatively, as well as postoperative intravenous fluid administration at 125 mL/h for 24 hours. Preoperative laboratory test results are as follows:

Laboratory Test	Value	Normal Values
Sodium	129 mEq/L	130–150 mEq/L
Potassium	4.1 mEq/L	3.5–5.0 mEq/L
Chlorine	109 mEq/L	96–106 mEq/L
Blood urea nitrogen	15 mg/dL	7–18 mg/dL
Hematocrit, preoperative	38%	36–46%
Creatinine	0.8 mg/dL	0.6–1.2 mg/dL
Bicarbonate	23 mEq/L	23–29 mEq/L

The patient's postoperative vital signs remain stable, hematocrit is within normal limits, and she is afebrile. The patient is becoming increasingly irritable and aggressive, however. She has adequate pain control. The best next step in her management is to

    (A) administer hypertonic saline
    (B) treat the patient with lorazepam (Ativan) for sedation
    (C) order intravenous pyelography
* (D) repeat serum electrolyte testing
    (E) increase intravenous fluids to 175 mL/h

Metabolic disturbances may cause deliriumlike mental status changes. The older patient is at increased risk of changes in body water and sodium levels. Renal functions change with age as creatinine clearance decreases by 1 mL/min per year after age 40 years and the ability to concentrate urine and excrete a water load is diminished. The stress of surgery often induces increases in antidiuretic hormone (ADH), also known as arginine vasopressin, which is involved in the homeostasis of blood volume and osmolarity and conserves water by concentrating urine.

Antidiuretic hormone is produced by the posterior pituitary gland in response to changes in intravascular volume and blood osmolarity. Increased osmolarity that accompanies the administration of a bolus of 5% dextrose or dehydration promotes the release of ADH through hypothalamic receptors, whereas atrial baroreceptors, which detect increases in intravascular volume, inhibit ADH release. Typically, during periods of high ADH production, the kidneys release concentrated urine of low volume. An increase in ADH may markedly affect urine output postoperatively. Stimulation of ADH in older patients is caused by numerous perioperative factors (see Box 96-1).

This patient has 2 risk factors that should alert the caregiver to check electrolyte levels. A preoperative sodium concentration less than130 mEq/L or greater than 150 mEq/L is a strong independent predictor of postoperative delirium. As a result of a significant ADH effect, serum sodium concentration can decrease markedly and cause symptoms consistent with delirium. In addition, as in this patient, the effect can be exacerbated by the intravenous administration of large amounts of 5% dextrose.

Research has demonstrated that vasopressin release is preserved and increased as individuals age. This effect, together with the stress of surgery, aggressive hydration during the procedure, and reduced preoperative sodium concentration, put this patient at increased risk for postoperative hyponatremia.

The most appropriate course of action for this patient would be fluid restriction and close monitoring of serum electrolytes. An increase in intravenous administration of fluids most likely would worsen the patient's condition. Observation alone or with sedative medications (eg, lorazepam) would not address the underlying problem. Intravenous pyelography is not indicated at this time.

BOX 96-1

Causes of Increased Antidiuretic Hormone Production in Older Perioperative Patients

- Decreased circulating blood volume
- Reduction in mean arterial pressure
- Reduction in left atrial pressure
- Anesthesia
- Use of catecholamines
- Angiotensin II
- Atrial natriuretic peptide
- Prostaglandins
- Drugs with β-adrenergic or β-cholinergic properties
- Opiates

Adapted from Flear CT, Gill GV, Burn J. Hyponatraemia: mechanisms and management. Lancet 1981;2:26–31; and Stout NR, Kenny RA, Baylis PH. A review of water balance in ageing in health and disease. Gerontology 1999;45:61–6.

Flear CT, Gill GV, Burn J. Hyponatraemia: mechanisms and management. Lancet 1981;2:26–31.

O'Keeffe ST, Ni Chonchubhair A. Postoperative delirium in the elderly. Br J Anaesth 1994;73:673–87.

Otsuka F, Morita K, Takeuchi M, Yamauchi T, Ogura T, Sekines K, et al. The effects of intrinsic vasopressin on urinary aquaporin-2 excretion and urine osmolality during surgery under general anesthesia. Anesth Analg 1999;88:181–7.

Stout NR, Kenny RA, Baylis PH. A review of water balance in ageing in health and disease. Gerontology 1999;45:61–6.

97

Credentialing for new procedures

As a member of the hospital credentials committee, you review the requirements for credentialing physicians who request privileges to perform a new gynecologic procedure. The most important reason for the credentialing and monitoring of initial procedures by a physician skilled in the technique is to

    (A) protect the attending physician from lawsuits
*   (B) maximize quality of care and patient safety
    (C) protect other medical staff from lawsuits
    (D) protect the hospital from lawsuits

The process of reviewing credentials and granting clinical privileges is one of the most important functions of a hospital medical staff. Every hospital must ensure quality of patient care and patient safety. The credentialing process addresses the Joint Commission on Accreditation of Healthcare Organization's standard that physicians be qualified by training, experience, and demonstrated competence, and be granted privileges commensurate with their individual abilities.

The process of credentialing consists of collecting and verifying information about a practitioner's personal and professional history, licensure and certification, current hospital appointments and privileges, education and training, and references. Information about education and licensure are essential to determine the fitness of the practitioner to provide care. Verification of this information, obtained from the primary source when possible, will substantiate the information on training and education. Information about a practitioner's current hospital membership and privileges helps ensure that each practitioner has sufficient current experience to maintain competence. Data on each practitioner are maintained in a separate credentials file, and there must be appropriate documentation in each hospital of the deliberations of the medical staff, actions taken, and the rationale for the actions.

The procedure of granting privileges enables the medical institution to meet its obligations to the patient, practitioner, and community. The credentialing and monitoring of initial procedures by a physician trained in the technique are important and help maximize quality care and patient safety. The granting privileges should be only for conditions and procedures that the practitioner is qualified to perform. The obligation of the medical staff to the practitioner is to establish and follow credentialing and privileging procedures that afford due process and to avoid discriminatory and trade-restraining practices.

Medical staff members who request initial privileges or privileges for a new procedure must be credentialed in a similar manner. To further ensure that practitioners are capable of managing the condition or performing the procedure for which they have received privileges, the hospital department to which a practitioner is assigned usually requires a period of supervised practice or proctoring. After observation of a defined and consistently applied number of conditions managed or procedures performed, it is determined whether the care rendered has been appropriate and safe. If the care given by the practitioner is deemed satisfactory, the practitioner is granted independent practice privileges.

An attending practitioner who obtains privileges through the credentialing process is not protected automatically from liability in any lawsuits that might allege medical negligence. The credentialing process, however, does protect the institution and medical staff officers from lawsuits that allege negligent hiring, as long as prudence and reason have been exercised in the granting of privileges, due consideration has been given to patient care and safety, and the actions and rationale for hiring have been documented fully and appropriately.

Joint Commission on Accreditation of Healthcare Organizations. 2002 Hospital accreditation standards. Oakbrook Terrace (IL): JCAHO; 2002. p. 295–310.

Peterson JL. Reviewing credentials and granting privileges. Texas Med 1998;94:91–9.

Sloan FA, Conover CJ, Provenzale D. Hospital credentialing and quality of care. Soc Sci Med 2000;50:77–88.

98

Premenstrual dysphoric disease

A 30-year-old woman has a menstrual diary that reports emotional irritability, breast tenderness, and swelling of the extremities. However, she tells you that her primary problem has been difficulty in coping with activities of daily living during the 5 days before menses in each of her 3 prior menstrual cycles. You tell her that the best treatment for her condition is

*   (A) a selective serotonin reuptake inhibitor (SSRI)
    (B) isoflavones
    (C) a progesterone supplement
    (D) the levonorgestrel-releasing intrauterine device (Mirena)

Premenstrual syndrome (PMS) affects approximately 5–10% of women of reproductive age. More than 150 different symptoms have been associated with this condition. Diagnostic criteria for PMS are listed in Box 98-1. The key element in making a diagnosis of PMS is to establish the characteristic timing of symptoms relative to

menses through a symptoms calendar, which the patient is asked to keep for at least 3 cycles.

Women with PMS who have more severe emotional symptoms are said to have premenstrual dysphoric disorder (PMDD) (Box 98-2). Efficacy in reducing symptoms related to PMDD has been documented for

BOX 98-1

Diagnostic Criteria for Premenstrual Syndrome

Premenstrual syndrome can be diagnosed if the patient reports at least 1 of the following affective and somatic symptoms during the 5 d before menses in each of the 3 prior menstrual cycles*:

Affective
Depression
Angry outbursts
Irritability
Anxiety
Confusion
Social withdrawal

Somatic
Breast tenderness
Abdominal bloating
Headache
Swelling of extremities

*These symptoms are relieved within 4 d of the onset of menses, without recurrence until at least cycle day 13. The symptoms are present in the absence of any pharmacologic therapy, hormone ingestion, or drug or alcohol use. The symptoms occur reproducibly during 2 cycles of prospective recording. The patient experiences identifiable dysfunction in social or economic performance.

Modified from Mortola JF, Girton L, Yen SC. Depressive episodes in premenstrual syndrome. Am J Obstet Gynecol 1989;161:1682–7.

BOX 98-2

Research Criteria for Premenstrual Dysphoric Disorder

A. In most menstrual cycles during the past year, 5 or more of the following symptoms were present for most of the time during the last week of the luteal phase, and were absent in the week postmenses, with at least 1 of the symptoms being either 1, 2, 3, or 4:
  1. Markedly depressed mood, feelings of hopelessness, or self-deprecating thoughts
  2. Marked anxiety, tension, feelings of being "keyed up" or "on edge"
  3. Marked affective lability (eg, feeling suddenly sad or tearful or increased sensitivity to rejection)
  4. Persistent and marked anger or irritability or increased interpersonal conflicts
  5. Decreased interest in usual activities (eg, work, school, friends, hobbies)
  6. Subjective sense of difficulty in concentrating
  7. Lethargy, easy fatigability, or marked lack of energy
  8. Marked change in appetite, overeating, or specific food cravings
  9. Hypersomnia or insomnia
  10. A subjective sense of being overwhelmed or out of control
  11. Other physical symptoms (eg, breast tenderness or swelling, headaches, joint or muscle pain, a sensation of bloating, weight gain)
Note: In menstruating females, the luteal phase corresponds to the period between ovulation and the onset of menses. In nonmenstruating females (eg, women who have undergone a hysterectomy), the timing of luteal and follicular phases may require measurement of circulating reproductive hormones.
B. The disturbance markedly interferes with work or school or with usual social activities and relationships with others (eg, avoidance of social activities, decreased productivity and efficiency at work or school).
C. The disturbance is not merely an exacerbation of the symptoms of another disorder, such as major depressive disorder, panic disorder, dysthymic disorder, or personality disorder (although it may be superimposed on any of these disorders).
D. Criteria A, B, and C must be confirmed by prospective daily ratings during at least 2 consecutive symptomatic cycles. (The diagnosis may be made provisionally prior to this confirmation.)

Modified from Diagnostic and statistical manual of mental disorders, 4th ed., Text Revision. Washington, DC: American Psychiatric Association; 2000. p. 774.

several classes of drugs, especially the SSRIs. Two notable examples that have proved to be useful in clinical trials are fluoxetine hydrochloride (Prozac, Sarafem) and sertraline hydrochloride (Zoloft). Daily administration of fluoxetine hydrochloride was superior to placebo in reducing symptoms of tension, irritability, and dysphoria. Low-dose fluoxetine not only was effective but also was associated with fewer adverse effects than fluoxetine at doses used to treat depression.

Daily use of sertraline hydrochloride also was noted to be effective when compared with placebo. A trial that incorporated a late-luteal-phase dosing strategy also documented sertraline to be effective in abating symptoms of PMDD. This intermittent dosing schedule of sertraline may lead to increased compliance. It can be initiated 14 days before the expected onset of menses and discontinued the day menses begins.

No studies have proved consistently that hormone therapy is helpful in treating PMDD. The progestin drospirenone is a spironolactone analogue that possesses antimineralocorticoid and antiandrogenic activity. One preliminary study has compared the use of the combination oral contraceptive ethinyl estradiol–drospirenone (Yasmin) and placebo in patients with diagnosed PMDD. A consistent trend was found in the reduction of symptoms, suggesting that ethinyl estradiol–drospirenone is beneficial in the treatment of PMDD.

No evidence exists to show that isoflavones are useful for the treatment of PMDD. However, isoflavone is a natural soy-based chemical found in estrogen receptors, and thus it potentially could mitigate some of the vasomotor symptoms experienced during menopause. Progesterone has not been shown to uniformly help improve symptoms of PMDD. To date, no published studies have evaluated the effects on PMDD of the levonorgestrel-releasing intrauterine device.

A wide variety of supportive, lifestyle, and dietary supplementation approaches to treating PMDD have been recommended. The approaches supported by literature include aerobic exercise and dietary supplementation. Compared with placebo, calcium carbonate has been noted to decrease the symptoms of PMDD after 2 menstrual cycles. Various botanicals have been demonstrated to have variable results in counteracting the symptoms of PMDD.

American College of Obstetricians and Gynecologists. Premenstrual syndrome. ACOG Practice Bulletin 15. Washington, DC: ACOG; 2000.

Carr M. Selections from current literature: treatments for premenstrual dysphoric disorder. Fam Pract 2001;18:644–6.

Diagnostic and statistical manual of mental disorders: DSM-IV TR. 4th ed. Washington, DC: American Psychiatric Association; 2000. p. 771–4.

Freeman EW, Kroll R, Rapkin A, Pearlstein T, Brown C, Parsey K, et al. Evaluation of a unique oral contraceptive in the treatment of premenstrual dysphoric disorder. J Womens Health Gend Based Med 2001;10:561–9.

Jermain DM, Preece CK, Sykes RL, Kuehl TJ, Sulak PJ. Luteal phase sertraline treatment for premenstrual dysphoric disorder: results of a double-blind, placebo-controlled, crossover study. Arch Fam Med 1999;8:328–32.

Yonkers KA, Halbreich U, Freeman E, Brown C, Endicott J, Frank E, et al. Symptomatic improvement of premenstrual dysphoric disorder with sertraline treatment. A randomized controlled trial. Sertraline Premenstrual Dysphoric Collaborative Study Group. JAMA 1997; 278:983–8.

99

Asymptomatic leiomyoma

A 39-year-old woman, gravida 1, para 1, comes to your office for her routine annual examination. The patient denies any pelvic pain or abnormal uterine bleeding. She states that she has not experienced any pelvic pressure or any urinary or bowel symptomatology. Current ultrasonography reveals a uterus 15 cm × 10 cm × 5 cm suggestive of multiple leiomyomata; her ovaries appear normal. The best next step in her treatment is

   (A) gonadotropin-releasing hormone (GnRH) agonist therapy
   (B) exploratory laparotomy
 * (C) reevaluation in 6 months
   (D) uterine artery embolization
   (E) laparoscopic myolysis

Uterine leiomyomata are the most common disorder observed in reproductive-aged women; they are seen in as many as 50% of women in some studies. These benign tumors also are the most common indication for hysterectomy in the United States. Only 20–40% of patients with uterine leiomyomata report symptoms. The most common symptom is abnormal uterine bleeding. Uterine enlargement may compress adjacent organs, which can cause bowel or bladder problems. Ureteral compression is rare, but it can occur.

In the past, the presence of a uterine leiomyoma in a uterus larger than 12 weeks of gestation size was considered sufficient justification for surgery. However, no data are available to support that position. Sarcoma is rare (2–3 per 1,000 women). A uterus that increases in size more than 6 weeks in 1 year is thought to suggest sarcoma; however, one study of premenopausal women found that sarcoma was no more common in a subgroup of women who experienced a rapidly enlarging uterus than in women whose uterus did not enlarge.

Researchers have attempted to differentiate histologic subtypes of leiomyomata using magnetic resonance imaging (MRI). It is possible that MRI accompanied by selected needle biopsy could identify malignancy, but such an approach is both invasive and expensive. An MRI would not be appropriate for the described patient at this time.

Gonadotropin-releasing hormone agonist has been used to shrink leiomyomata in selected individuals. Shrinkage up to 30–50% of the original size may help facilitate surgery and reduce blood loss. The described patient is completely asymptomatic, however, and no surgery is needed at this time.

Exploratory laparotomy is not indicated. The patient is relatively young and asymptomatic. An ultrasonographic finding of normal ovaries further supports the diagnosis of leiomyoma and suggests that an ovarian lesion is less likely.

Laparoscopic myolysis is a relatively new procedure to destroy the viability of leiomyomata in situ without having to resort to removal. The procedure uses laparoscopy with electrothermy, laser coagulation, or cryotherapy. With this method, multiple holes are drilled into the body of the leiomyoma, and the tissue is damaged with an energy source. The procedure appears to work best in tumors that have demonstrated significant diminution in size after GnRH agonist preparation. This procedure may cause adhesion formation. The frequency and impact of laparoscopic myolysis are unknown at this time, and this procedure would not be the best step for this patient.

In a large multicenter prospective single-arm clinical trial of 586 patients who were undergoing uterine artery embolization for symptomatic uterine leiomyomata with a median follow-up time of 8.2 months, the following important observations were made:

- Ninety-eight percent of women had a successful procedure.
- Uterine and leiomyoma reductions were 35% and 42%, respectively.
- Menorrhagia improved in 83% of patients.
- Pelvic pain improved in 77% of women.
- Forty-one percent of women older than 40 years became amenorrheic.

Uterine artery embolization is expensive and should be used only in symptomatic patients to whom future fertility is not an issue. A prospective randomized clinical trial is needed to study the procedure further.

The most appropriate management for this patient is reevaluation in 6 months to monitor any changes in her symptoms and to assess whether the leiomyomata are changing rapidly.

Ongoing research has indicated therapeutic compounds that block specific growth of leiomyomata, and such compounds may be available for use by practitioners in the future. Cell cultures of leiomyomata and normal myometrial tissue have demonstrated the presence of the following growth factors, which have potential regulatory roles in the proliferation of muscle cells:

- Platelet-derived growth factors
- Heparin-binding epithelial growth factors
- Hepatoma-derived growth factors
- Basic fibroblast growth factors

Experimental compounds are known to inhibit DNA synthesis of normal myometrium and leiomyoma cells. Interferon-α also has been shown to inhibit growth factor–stimulated proliferation in normal leiomyoma cells. These results suggest that future nonsurgical treatments may be available for patients with symptomatic or asymptomatic leiomyomata.

American College of Obstetricians and Gynecologists. Surgical alternatives to hysterectomy in the management of leiomyomas. ACOG Practice Bulletin 16. Washington, DC: ACOG; 2000.

Goodwin SC. Uterine artery embolization for the treatment of uterine fibroids. Fertil Steril 2003;79:136–7.

Nowak RA. Novel therapeutic strategies for leiomyomas: targeting growth factors and their receptors. Environ Health Perspect 2000;108 suppl 5:849–53.

Parker WH, Fu YS, Berek JS. Uterine sarcoma in patients operated on for presumed leiomyoma and rapidly growing leiomyoma. Obstet Gynecol 1994;83:414–8.

Schwartz LB, Zawin M, Carcangiu ML, Lange R, McCarthy S. Does pelvic magnetic resonance imaging differentiate among the histologic subtypes of uterine leiomyomata? Fertil Steril 1998;70:580–7.

Spies JB, Ascher SA, Roth AR, Kim J, Levy EB, Gomez-Jorge J. Uterine artery embolization for leiomyomata. Obstet Gynecol 2001;98:29–34.

100

Rectovaginal fistula

A 38-year-old woman has undergone an emergency total abdominal hysterectomy, bilateral sal-pingo-oophorectomy, and drainage for a ruptured tuboovarian abscess. The surgery was difficult and complicated by a blood loss of 4 units. Her bowel function has not returned. On postoperative day 5, the patient is still unable to take food by mouth, and she has begun to pass watery stool with purulent discharge through the vagina. She has been febrile, with temperatures higher than 38°C (100.4°F) daily. Rectovaginal examination and air insufflation reveal a 4-cm rectovaginal fistula at the vaginal cuff. The most appropriate next step in management is

      (A) expectant management
      (B) abdominal repair of the fistula
      (C) vaginal repair of the fistula
*   (D) a diverting colostomy
      (E) somatostatin therapy

Rectovaginal fistulae are encountered most commonly after pelvic surgery (eg, abdominal or vaginal hysterectomy), obstetric trauma, or episiotomy breakdown. Inflammatory bowel diseases may cause a spontaneous fistula or increase the likelihood of a fistula after gynecologic surgery. Diverticular disease remains the most common nonsurgically related cause of a rectovaginal fistula.

There are many classification systems for rectovaginal fistulae. Depending on their location in the rectovaginal septum, rectovaginal fistulae are classified as low, middle, or high. Low fistulae enter the vagina at the posterior fourchette, and high fistulae enter the vagina at the vaginal apex. Middle fistulae are located between low and high fistulae. Low fistulae generally are caused by surgical or obstetric trauma and usually are repaired with a perineal approach. A colostomy rarely is required. Low fistulae are the most common. High fistulae most commonly are repaired abdominally and require a colostomy. Simple fistulae are defined as fistulae that enter into the distal half of the vagina, whereas complex fistulae enter into the proximal half of the vagina.

Size of the fistula is a factor in determining the need for a colostomy. Fistulae larger than 2.5 cm usually require a protective colostomy, and this patient has a 4-cm rectovaginal fistula at the vaginal cuff. In addition, she has a fever and abscess, so a colostomy should be performed. A smaller fistula not associated with an abscess would not necessarily require fecal diversion. A fistula should be repaired after the inflammation and induration have resolved. A colostomy also may be indicated to assist in resolving inflammation associated with a large fistula.

Indications for colostomy in the treatment of a patient with a rectovaginal fistula include the following:

- A large fistula located near the vaginal apex
- An irradiated pelvis
- A distal obstruction
- Inflammatory bowel disease
- The presence of an abscess

Before a colostomy is performed, it is important to confirm that the fistula links the colon and the upper vagina. A colostomy is not appropriate for an enterovaginal fistula. A barium enema, gastrointestinal series with small bowel follow-through, colonoscopy, or injection of radiopaque dye through the fistula may be needed to identify the bowel segment that communicates with the vagina. Upper vaginal fistulae also may be enterovaginal or sigmoidovaginal.

Expectant management is not likely to be successful in a woman with a large fistula located high in the vagina. Immediate repair regardless of the route is contraindicated in the presence of active infection, which would cause a high breakdown rate in the repair.

Somatostatin or its analogue octreotide inhibits gastrointestinal hormone production, resulting in decreased gastrointestinal fluid output. This agent is beneficial in decreasing the output from an enterocutaneous or enterovaginal fistula. No role for somatostatin is indicated for this patient, however.

Lavery IC. Colonic fistulas. Surg Clin North Am 1996;76:1183–90.

Schrock TR. Rectovaginal fistulas. In: Block GE, Moossa AR, editors. Operative colorectal surgery. Philadelphia (PA): WB Saunders; 1994. p. 429–46.

101

Stress incontinence

A 28-year-old woman, gravida 1, para 1, was delivered, with the aid of forceps, of a 3,855-g (8.5-lb) infant 9 months ago. She expresses interest in future childbearing. She reports symptoms of stress urinary incontinence with sneezing and coughing. She does not wear protection on a daily basis. She is occasionally incontinent of flatus, but not of stool. Physical examination reveals a stage 1 cystourethrocele with a cotton-tipped swab straining angle of 40 degrees. There is good uterine support with no significant rectocele. The next best step in management is

      (A) α-agonist therapy
*   (B) behavioral therapy
      (C) anticholinergic therapy
      (D) laparoscopic Burch retropubic urethropexy

The incidence of urinary incontinence in reproductive-aged women is approximately 25%. Significant risk factors in the development of stress urinary incontinence include vaginal childbirth, forceps-assisted delivery, and aging.

Treatment of urinary stress incontinence includes behavioral, pharmacologic, and surgical therapies. The following factors should be considered in determining the best treatment:

- Age and health of the patient
- Desire for future childbearing
- Associated pelvic floor support defects
- Severity of symptoms

Vaginal delivery in primiparae results in loss of pelvic muscle strength in the immediate postpartum period, although most of the strength may be restored with pelvic floor muscle rehabilitation.

The Agency for Health Care Research Quality has published guidelines on the treatment of urinary incontinence. The agency recommends that the least invasive and least dangerous procedure appropriate for the patient be the first choice of treatment.

This patient is an ideal candidate for behavioral therapy. In the 1940s, Dr. Arnold Kegel described the beneficial effects of pelvic floor muscle strengthening in reducing urinary incontinence by contraction of the pubococcygeal (PC) muscle using a perineometer. Biofeedback assists in muscle strength reeducation by establishing awareness and function of the PC muscle. Improved strength, tone, and reactivity of the PC muscle may enhance the force of urethral closure during increased intraabdominal pressure, thus reducing urinary leakage. In women who lack the ability to isolate the PC muscle properly, Kegel exercises alone may lead to contraction of the gluteal or abdominal muscles, which may result in worsening of the condition.

Biofeedback therapy provides the patient with immediate audio or visual feedback of the muscle activity that occurs during pelvic floor muscle contraction. Vaginal probes or electromyographic sensors are used. Once the patient learns how to contract the PC muscle properly, she can follow a home exercise regimen. Biofeedback therapy is also helpful in the reduction of fecal and urinary incontinence.

Generally, antiincontinence surgery is reserved for women who have completed childbearing. A survey by the American Urogynecological Association in 2000 revealed that 80% of members would postpone antiincontinence surgery in women who have not completed childbearing. In this patient at this time, surgery is best reserved as an option in case conservative therapy fails.

The bladder neck and proximal urethra contain α-receptors that, when stimulated, result in smooth muscle contraction and increased urethral outlet resistance. The administration of ephedrine is effective in women with mild stress incontinence, but it has adverse effects such as hypertension, tachycardia, and palpitations. The effects of long-term ephedrine therapy have not been studied. Alpha-agonist therapy may be helpful for temporary or allergy-related seasonal relief of stress incontinence, but it would not be the best option for this patient.

Anticholinergic therapy reduces detrusor muscle contraction and is used to treat overactive bladder symptoms, such as urinary urgency, frequency, and urge incontinence. This therapy would not benefit the patient with stress incontinence symptoms.

Complex multichannel urodynamic testing is not necessary in the initial evaluation and management of urinary incontinence. However, it may be reserved for cases in which conservative treatment measures fail, cases involving known neurologic disease, or cases with marked mixed incontinence symptoms. Simple office cystometrography is a cost-effective, minimally invasive test that provides helpful information in the initial evaluation and treatment of urinary incontinence.

Burgio KL, Goode PS, Locher JL, Umlauf MG, Roth DL, Richter HE, et al. Behavioral training with and without biofeedback in the treatment of urge incontinence in older women: a randomized controlled trial. JAMA 2002;288:2293–9.

Burgio KL, Robinson JC, Engel BT. The role of biofeedback in Kegel exercise training for stress urinary incontinence. Am J Obstet Gynecol 1986;154:58–64.

Foldspang A, Mommsen S, Lam GW, Elving L. Parity as a correlate of adult female urinary incontinence prevalence. J Epidemiol Community Health 1992;46:595–600.

Kegel AH. Progressive resistance exercise in the functional restoration of the perineal muscles. Am J Obstet Gynecol 1948;56:238–48.

102

Contraception options for a patient with history of thrombosis

A 42-year-old woman, gravida 2, para 1, seeks a surgical abortion in your office. Her last menstrual period was 10 weeks ago. In addition to discussing the surgical procedure, you take the opportunity to discuss her future contraceptive options. She has used progestin-only oral contraceptives and barrier methods unsuccessfully. She is at risk for sexually transmitted diseases (STDs). During her last pregnancy she had a deep vein thrombosis (DVT) that required heparin therapy. You advise her that her best option for contraception is

*   (A) medroxyprogesterone acetate (Depo-Provera) injection
      (B) the rhythm, or calendar, method
      (C) condoms
      (D) an intrauterine device (IUD)

The use of hormonal contraception in patients with medical conditions is one of the biggest challenges to the practicing gynecologist. Estrogen use increases circulating hepatic serum globulins, which activates the blood-clotting cascade and leads to increased risk of venous thrombosis in current users of combination oral contraceptives. European studies have shown that compared with nonusers, current users of oral contraceptives formulated with 35 mg or less estrogen experience a 3- to 4-fold increased risk of venous thrombosis. This risk, in absolute terms, remains lower than the increased risk of venous thrombosis during pregnancy. Table 102-1 shows rates of DVT in oral contraceptive estrogen dose–defined cohorts.

This patient's history of DVT strongly contraindicates the use of any estrogen-containing contraceptive. Package labeling approved by the U.S. Food and Drug Administration (FDA) for progestin-only oral contraceptives is occasionally the same as that for combined estrogen–progestin preparations. For instance, current labeling for norethindrone progestin-only pills no longer lists a history of thromboembolism as a contraindication. Such a history, however, remains listed as a contraindication in package labeling for norgestrel progestin-only pills and for medroxyprogesterone acetate injections. The best evidence has not characterized progestin-only methods as thrombogenic. Thus, progestin-only contraceptives are considered safe for the patient under discussion.

Practitioners should be aware of current non–evidenced-based FDA package labeling that contraindicates medroxyprogesterone acetate use in subjects with a history of venous thrombosis This patient's prior oral progestin pill failure, coupled with the nonthrombogenic nature and higher compliance rates associated with medroxyprogesterone acetate, suggest this choice as the better option.

Because of the marked association of pregnancy with risk of venous thrombosis, use of less reliable methods is relatively contraindicated. Thus, the low contraceptive efficacy of the rhythm, or calendar, method would obviate

TABLE 102-1. Rates of Deep Vein Thromboembolic Disease in Oral Contraceptive Estrogen Dose–Defined Cohorts

Estrogen-Defined Cohorts (µg)	No. Cases	Person–Years (× 10,000)	Rate/10,000 Person–Years
<50	53	12.7	4.2
50	69	9.8	7.0
>50	20	2.0	10.0
All	142	24.5	5.8

Reprinted from Comprehensive gynecology, 4th ed., Stenchever MA, Droegemueller W, Herbst AL, Mishell DR Jr, editors. p. 313. Copyright 2001, with permission from Elsevier.

its use in this scenario. The use of condoms should be encouraged as a way to prevent acquisition of STDs, but it is a less reliable contraceptive option than medroxyprogesterone acetate. The IUD is inappropriate because of this patient's risk for STDs.

American College of Obstetricians and Gynecologists. The use of hormonal contraception in women with coexisting medical conditions. ACOG Practice Bulletin 18. Washington, DC: ACOG; 2000.

Corfman P. Labeling guidance text for progestin-only oral contraceptives. Contraception 1995;52:71–6.

Fahmy K, Khairy M, Allam G, Gobran F, Alloush M. Effect of depomedroxyprogesterone acetate on coagulation factors and serum lipids in Egyptian women. Contraception 1991;44:431–4.

Frederiksen MC. Depot medroxyprogesterone acetate contraception in women with medical problems. J Reprod Med 1996;41 suppl: S414–8.

Trussell J, Hatcher RA, Cates W Jr, Stewart FH, Kost K. Contraceptive failure in the United States: an update. Stud Fam Plann 1990;21:51–4.

Trussell J, Kowal D. The essentials of contraception. In: Hatcher RA, Trussell J, Stewart F, Cates W, Stewart GK, Kowal D, et al, editors. Contraceptive technology. 17th ed. New York (NY): Ardent Media, 1998. p. 211–47.

103

Acute pelvic inflammatory disease in pregnancy

A 27-year-old homemaker with 7 weeks of amenorrhea presents with abdominal tenderness and malaise. Her temperature is 38°C (100.4°F). An ultrasonographic examination confirms an intrauterine pregnancy. At laparoscopy for presumed appendicitis, the fallopian tubes are noted to be erythematous and surrounded by filmy adhesions. The postoperative pharmacologic regimen that should be initiated for this woman includes

      (A) ampicillin, penicillin, and clindamycin hydrochloride (Cleocin)

*   (B) clindamycin hydrochloride and gentamicin

      (C) ciprofloxacin (Cipro), penicillin, and azithromycin dihydrate (Zithromax)

      (D) benzathine penicillin G and doxycycline

      (E) ampicillin, cephalothin sodium, and gentamicin

Pelvic inflammatory disease (PID) is relatively infrequent during pregnancy because of the anatomic changes that occur in the upper genital tract. The diagnosis should be considered when fever and pelvic tenderness occur early in gestation (Box 103-1).

Treatment for both gonorrhea and chlamydial infection should be begun when the clinical diagnosis is made. Because patients infected with *Neisseria gonorrhoeae* often are coinfected with *Chlamydia trachomatis*, dual therapy should be considered as the routine approach in this situation.

A pregnant woman with PID should be hospitalized and treated with parenteral antibiotics because of the higher risk for maternal morbidity, as well as fetal wastage and preterm delivery. The current recommendation under these circumstances is the administration of clindamycin hydrochloride and gentamicin. Use of these antibiotics should be continued for 24 hours after the patient improves clinically. Oral antibiotics then should be given for a total of 14 days of treatment.

Pregnant women should not be treated with tetracyclines or with quinolones. Ciprofloxacin is a synthetic, broad-spectrum antibiotic of the fluoroquinolone class and is not recommended at present for use in pregnancy. In a prospective study conducted by the European Network of Teratology Information Services, investigators examined data on 549 pregnancies with exposure to fluoroquinolones. Fetal malformations of the urogenital

---

BOX 103-1

Clinical Criteria for the Diagnosis of Pelvic Inflammatory Disease

Symptoms
- None necessary

Signs
- Pelvic organ tenderness, leukorrhea with or without mucopurulent endocervicitis

Additional Criteria
- Elevated C-reactive protein or erythrocyte sedimentation rate
- Temperature >38°C (100.4°F)
- Leukocytosis
- Positive test for gonococcal or chlamydial infection
- Ultrasonography documenting tuboovarian abscess
- Laparoscopy visually confirming salpingitis

Modified from Soper DE. Genitourinary infections and sexually transmitted diseases. In: Berek JS, Adashi EY, Hillard PA, editors. Novak's gynecology. 12th ed. Baltimore (MD): Williams & Wilkins; 1996. p. 437.

BOX 103-2

U.S. Food and Drug Administration Risk Categories for Drugs Used During Pregnancy

Category A: Controlled studies in women fail to demonstrate a risk to the fetus in the first trimester (and there is no evidence of a risk in later trimesters), and the possibility of fetal harm appears remote. Vitamin C is an example of a category A substance when its use does not exceed the recommended daily allowance.

Category B: Either animal reproduction studies have not demonstrated fetal risk but no controlled studies in pregnant women have been reported, or animal reproduction studies have shown an adverse effect (other than a decrease in fertility) that was not confirmed in controlled studies in women in the first trimester (and there is no evidence of risk in later trimesters). Examples are azithromycin, clindamycin, ceftriaxone, cefixime, ampicillin, benzathine penicillin G, cephalothin, and spectinomycin.

Category C: Either studies in animals have revealed adverse effects on the fetus (teratogenic, embryocidal, or other) but no controlled studies in women have been reported, or studies in women and animals are not available. Drugs should be given only if the potential benefit justifies the potential risk to the fetus. Examples include ciprofloxacin and gentamicin.

Category D: Positive evidence of human fetal risk exists, but the benefits from use in pregnant women may be acceptable despite the risk (eg, if the drug is needed to treat a life-threatening condition or a serious disease for which safer drugs cannot be used or are ineffective). An example is doxycycline.

Category X: Studies in animals or human beings have demonstrated fetal abnormalities, or evidence exists of fetal risk based on human experience, or both, and the risk in pregnant women clearly outweighs any possible benefit. The drug is contraindicated in women who are or may become pregnant. Isotretinoin is an example of a category X drug.

Modified from U.S. Food and Drug Administration. Pregnancy labeling. FDA Drug Bull 1979;9:23–4; and Briggs GG, Freeman RK, Yaffe SJ. Drugs in pregnancy and lactation. 6th ed. Philadelphia (PA): Lippincott Williams & Wilkins; 2002. p. xxiv.

system and limb reduction defects were found to be associated with administration of fluoroquinolones. The investigators recommended that future studies regarding the safety of fluoroquinolones focus on these more frequently observed defects. Although the investigators did not conclude that exposure to this class of antibiotics was an indication for termination of pregnancy, they recommended that the fluoroquinolones not be used in pregnancy pending further study. See Box 103-2 for antibiotics commonly used to treat PID and the level of fetal risk they pose.

Doxycycline, because it is closely related to tetracycline, is contraindicated during pregnancy. Inhibition of bone growth and dental staining are theoretical outcomes of exposure. However, doxycycline may be used postpartum. Furthermore, the American Academy of Pediatrics considers tetracycline derivatives safe for breastfeeding mothers.

Benzathine penicillin G is recommended specifically for the treatment of syphilis alone. Ampicillin, cephalothin sodium, and gentamicin, although relatively safe to use, would result in an inadequate spectrum of coverage. Likewise, ampicillin, penicillin, and clindamycin hydrochloride would be safe, although this combination also would provide insufficient treatment.

American College of Obstetricians and Gynecologists. Teratology. ACOG Educational Bulletin 236. Washington, DC: ACOG; 1997.

HIV prevention through early detection and treatment of other sexually transmitted diseases—United States. Recommendations of the Advisory Committee for HIV and STD Prevention. MMWR Recomm Rep 1998;47(RR-12):1–24.

Schaefer C, Amoura-Elefant E, Vial T, Ornoy A, Garbis H, Robert E, et al. Pregnancy outcome after prenatal quinolone exposure: evaluation of a case registry of the European Network of Teratology Information Services (ENTIS). Eur J Obstet Gynecol Reprod Biol 1996;69:83–9.

Sexually transmitted diseases treatment guidelines 2002. Centers for Disease Control and Prevention. MMWR Recomm Rep 2002;51(RR-6):1–78.

Soper DE. Genitourinary infections and sexually transmitted diseases. In: Berek JS, Adashi EY, Hillard PA, editors. Novak's gynecology. 12th ed. Baltimore (MD): Williams & Wilkins; 1996. p. 429–45.

104

Asymptomatic bacteriuria in a geriatric patient

A 70-year-old woman is sent to you for consultation regarding positive results of several urine cultures over the past 8 months. During this time, she has not experienced urinary frequency, hematuria, or dysuria despite positive results of cultures. She is generally in good health. The findings of her pelvic examination are normal. Review of laboratory records reveals 3 positive cultures for *Escherichia coli*, 2 for *Klebsiella pneumoniae*, and 1 for enterococcus. The most likely diagnosis is

    (A) interstitial cystitis
    (B) urethral diverticulum
    (C) chronic urethritis
  * (D asymptomatic bacteriuria
    (E) vesicovaginal fistula

Asymptomatic bacteriuria is diagnosed when a urine culture is positive for at least 10,000 colony-forming units (CFU)/mL in the absence of symptoms. This condition is observed among 20% of women older than 65 years. The prevalence increases with age and is higher in women than in men. After menopause, urogenital atrophy favors vaginal colonization with organisms in the *Enterobacteriaceae* family, especially *E coli*. Urogenital atrophy may predispose postmenopausal women to colonization of the urinary tract. Intravaginal estrogen therapy may decrease the number of recurrent urinary tract infections. Oral hormone therapy does not appear to have the same effect.

The diagnosis of interstitial cystitis would be suspected if the patient had long-term bladder pain, especially if the pain were exacerbated by bladder filling and relieved by voiding. Chronic urethritis would be suggested by reports of dysuria, frequency, and urgency in the absence of a positive urine culture. In the case described, the patient is asymptomatic, so neither interstitial cystitis nor chronic urethritis would be suspected.

Treatment of asymptomatic bacteriuria is not indicated in this case. In most cases, bacteriuria is transient. Moreover, the risks of symptomatic infection and upper urinary tract infection are not increased by bacteriuria. Unnecessary treatment may increase the risk of drug resistance, which might limit options for treatment of future infections. Asymptomatic bacteriuria always should be treated in pregnancy, however, because of increased risk of preterm labor, preterm premature rupture of membranes, and pyelonephritis.

In adult women, the cause of recurrent urinary tract infections can be identified in a minority of cases. Causes of recurrent cystitis include vesicovaginal fistulae, incomplete voiding, and obstructed voiding due to severe uterovaginal prolapse. Urethral diverticula can lead to recurrent symptomatic infections, as well as symptoms of dysuria, dyspareunia, and urinary urgency. In some cases, a tender mass is palpable along the urethra. Because this patient is asymptomatic and has normal findings on gynecologic examination, these diagnoses are not likely.

Symptomatic urinary tract infections should be treated with appropriate antibiotics. Among elderly women, symptoms of urinary tract infection may be subtle. Hospitalization should be considered if urosepsis or upper tract involvement is suspected.

Abrutyn E, Berlin J, Mossey J, Pitsakis P, Levison M, Kaye D. Does treatment of asymptomatic bacteriuria in older ambulatory women reduce subsequent symptoms of urinary tract infection? J Am Geriatr Soc 1996;44:293–5.

Brown JS, Vittinghoff E, Kanaya AM, Agarwal SK, Hulley S, Foxman B. Urinary tract infections in postmenopausal women: effect of hormone therapy and risk factors. Obstet Gynecol 2001;98:1045–52.

Kaye D, Boscia JA, Abrutyn E, Levison ME. Asymptomatic bacteriuria in the elderly. Trans Am Clin Climatol Assoc 1988;100:155–62.

Nygaard IE, Johnson JM. Urinary tract infections in elderly women. Am Fam Physician 1996;53:175–82.

Raz R, Stamm WE. A controlled trial of intravaginal estriol in postmenopausal women with recurrent urinary tract infections. N Engl J Med 1993;329:753–6.

Urinary tract infection. In: Wall LL, Norton PA, DeLancey JOL, editors. Practical urogynecology. Baltimore (MD): Williams & Wilkins; 1993. p. 240–54.

105

Breakthrough bleeding, smoking, and oral contraceptives

A 32-year-old monogamous woman who smokes 2 packs of cigarettes per day has been taking oral contraceptives for 2 years. She has not missed taking any pills and reports irregular spotting for 2 months. Findings of cervical cultures and pelvic ultrasonography are normal, and the pregnancy test result is negative. The most appropriate next step is to

      (A) have the patient begin taking depot medroxyprogesterone acetate (Depo-Provera)
      (B) have the patient switch to the ethinyl estradiol/norelgestromin contraceptive patch (Ortho Evra)
      (C) advise the patient to take nonsteroidal antiinflammatory drugs (NSAIDs)
*   (D) provide reassurance and counsel the patient to stop smoking

In oral contraceptive users, breakthrough bleeding most frequently occurs in the first few months of use. The incidence is greater in the first 3 months, ranging from 10–30% in the first month of use to 1–10% in the third month.

The episodes of breakthrough bleeding may be a consequence of progestin-induced decidualization of the endometrium. This endometrium is shallow and tends to be fragile and prone to breakdown and asynchronous bleeding. Thus, in the present patient, use of additional progestin therapy such as depot medroxyprogesterone acetate would exacerbate bleeding. Because oral contraceptive use has been associated with diminished risk of endometrial hyperplasia and carcinoma, ultrasonography or invasive endometrial biopsy is unwarranted. Blood testing is almost always unnecessary.

Smoking also has been reported to affect cycle control adversely in oral contraceptive users. Cigarette use has been associated with a variety of low-estrogen effects.

Because estrogen is required to support the proliferating endometrium, smoking can cause cycle control problems. Thus, an established oral contraceptive user with breakthrough bleeding should consider smoking cessation.

New-onset breakthrough bleeding may be associated with sexually transmitted diseases (STDs), such as chlamydial infection or gonorrheal cervicitis, thus warranting the need to remind oral contraceptive users to use condoms appropriately. Patients must be evaluated for pregnancy, STDs, cervicitis, and oral contraceptive compliance. There is no evidence that use of the combination ethinyl estradiol/norelgestromin contraceptive patch or NSAIDs will diminish breakthrough bleeding.

Oral contraception. In: Speroff L, Glass RH, Kase NG, editors. Clinical gynecologic endocrinology and infertility. 6th ed. Baltimore (MD): Lippincott Williams & Wilkins; 1999. p. 916–7.

Rosenberg MJ, Waugh MS, Stevens CM. Smoking and cycle control among oral contraceptive users. Am J Obstet Gynecol 1996;174: 628–32.

106

Surgical abortion

A 19-year-old woman at 18 weeks of gestation is referred to you because of a fetal anomaly diagnosed by ultrasonography. After counseling, she requests a termination of pregnancy. She had a cesarean delivery with her first pregnancy. Your recommendation for the most appropriate management is

      (A) hysterotomy
      (B) induction of labor with prostaglandins
      (C) induction of labor with oxytocin
 *   (D) dilation and evacuation (D&E)
      (E) administration of mifepristone (Mifeprex)

Various medical and surgical techniques are available for termination of pregnancy (Box 106-1). Selection of an appropriate approach depends on several issues, including gestational age, coexisting maternal health problems, availability, and patient acceptance.

A pregnancy may be terminated by medical, surgical, or combined means. After the decision to terminate a pregnancy, the majority of women find waiting to be an unacceptable burden. Furthermore, surgery shortens the procedure, and when general anesthesia is employed, it will lessen the patient's anxiety.

BOX 106-1

Abortion Techniques

Surgical
- Dilation and curettage
- Dilation and vacuum aspiration
- Dilation and evacuation
- Menstrual aspiration
- Hysterotomy
- Hysterectomy

Medical
- Intravenous oxytocin
- Intraamniotic saline
- Intraamniotic urea
- Prostaglandins E_1, E_2, 15-methyl-$F_{2\alpha}$, various analogues
  - Intraamniotic injection
  - Extraovular administration
  - Vaginal administration
  - Parenteral administration
  - Oral administration
- Antiprogesterone: mifepristone (Mifeprex)
- Various combinations of the above

Modified from Cunningham FG, Gant NF, Leveno KJ, Gilstrap LC, Hauth JC, Wenstrom KD, editors. Williams obstetrics. 21st ed. New York (NY): McGraw-Hill; 2001. p. 871.

Termination of the pregnancy by surgical means may be accomplished transvaginally or abdominally. Surgical procedures require a specialized environment, and availability may be a consideration. Surgical procedures are appropriate for both first- and second-trimester terminations of pregnancy. Dilation and curettage (D&C) is appropriate in the first trimester, whereas D&E is better suited to second-trimester procedures.

When abortion is performed in the second trimester of pregnancy, risks of morbidity increase in comparison with first-trimester abortions. A larger fetus and somewhat thinner uterine walls increase the risks of incomplete evacuation, uterine perforation, and uterine laceration or rupture. These risks exist regardless of the method chosen.

Risk to the patient can be minimized by adequate and atraumatic cervical dilation prior to removing the fetus and placenta. Preoperative use of an osmotic dilator such as a laminaria tent can soften and dilate the cervix prior to termination of pregnancy.

In performing a D&E at 18 weeks of gestation, ultrasonographic guidance can be extremely valuable in minimizing the risks of incomplete removal, uterine perforation, or laceration. Prophylactic antibiotics are used routinely in this circumstance.

The administration of oxytocin and prostaglandins in second-trimester termination are medical regimens used as alternatives to primary surgical approaches. If uterine perforation or incomplete abortion occurs, further abdominal procedures may be needed for correction.

Of the options listed for this patient, hysterotomy would present the greatest risk of morbidity. Medical induction of labor with prostaglandins after a previous cesarean delivery is not contraindicated but carries an increased risk of uterine rupture. An antiprostaglandin such as mifepristone is not an effective abortifacient in the second trimester. A D&E performed by an experienced practitioner is the safest approach of the options given. Prior cesarean delivery is not a contraindication to the use of the other procedures, but multiple uterotonic agents increase the risk of uterine rupture.

American College of Obstetricians and Gynecologists. Antibiotic prophylaxis for gynecologic procedures. ACOG Practice Bulletin 23. Washington, DC: ACOG; 2001.

American College of Obstetricians and Gynecologists. Medical management of abortion. ACOG Practice Bulletin 26. Washington, DC: ACOG; 2001.

Cunningham FG, Gant NF, Leveno KJ, Gilstrap LC, Hauth JC, Wenstrom KD, editors. Williams obstetrics. 21st ed. New York (NY): McGraw-Hill; 2001. p. 869–82.

Goldstein SR, Danon M, Watson C. An updated protocol for abortion surveillance with ultrasound and immediate pathology. Obstet Gynecol 1994;83:55–8.

Paul M, Lichtenberg S, Borgatta L, Grimes DA, Stubblefield PG, editors. A clinician's guide to medical and surgical abortion. New York (NY): Churchill Livingstone; 1999.

107

Acute pelvic pain in postmenopausal women

A 60-year-old woman reports that she has experienced several days of increasing abdominal pain but states that she does not have vaginal bleeding. She has experienced malaise, anorexia, and constipation. On examination, you find that her lower abdomen is diffusely tender, with guarding. She has a palpable tender left lower quadrant mass. The most appropriate diagnostic test is

      (A) diagnostic laparoscopy
      (B) barium enema study
      (C) contrast enema study with water-soluble media
*   (D) computed tomography (CT) scanning

Diverticulitis should be suspected in women older than 40 years who present with lower abdominal pain. The typical presentation includes pain, left lower quadrant tenderness, and fever. A history of diverticulosis may be present. If a mass is present, CT scanning can be useful in the diagnosis of diverticular abscess. Contrast enema studies (with either barium or water-soluble contrast) are most useful for identifying intraluminal lesions. However, these studies may be inaccurate in this scenario, because sensitivity will be low for detection of extraluminal disease and abscesses. Advantages of CT scanning over contrast enema study are shown in Box 107-1. The sensitivity of CT scanning is greater than 70% for acute diverticulitis, and the specificity is at least 75%.

Although laparoscopy or laparotomy may be required to establish a diagnosis in some cases, surgical intervention is usually unnecessary, because 80% of diverticulitis cases will resolve with medical therapy. If there is no evidence of sepsis or peritonitis, the patient can be treated as an outpatient with a clear-liquid diet, rest, and administration of broad-spectrum antibiotics. As symptoms resolve, the diet is advanced, and stool softeners are prescribed. After the acute event subsides, a contrast enema study can be useful to confirm the diagnosis of diverticulosis.

Women with severe symptoms or evidence of intestinal obstruction should be admitted to the hospital for the administration of intravenous fluids and antibiotics. Immediate surgery is recommended if perforation is suspected. Laparotomy also is indicated if the patient has repeated episodes, a persistent tender mass, or progressive symptoms.

BOX 107-1

Advantages of Computed Tomography Scanning Over Contrast Enema Study

- Improved visualization of extraluminal disease
- Ability to drain abscesses at the time of the diagnostic study
- Less patient discomfort
- Ability to visualize adjacent organs

Chronic pelvic pain. In: American College of Obstetricians and Gynecologists. Precis: gynecology. 2nd ed. Washington, DC: ACOG; 1999. p. 122–7.

Diverticular disease. In: Beers MH, Berkow RB, editors. The Merck manual of diagnosis and therapy. 17th ed. Whitehouse Station (NJ): Merck; 1999. p. 318–20.

Farrell RJ, Farrell JJ, Morrin MM. Diverticular disease in the elderly. Gastroenterol Clin North Am 2001;30:475–96.

108

Alternative medication and management of menopause symptoms

A 53-year-old postmenopausal woman is concerned about her hot flushes and is at risk for osteoporosis. Her uterus is in place. She has been prescribed a continuous oral estradiol preparation, which has provided some relief over the past 3 months. She wants to take a natural progesterone preparation and asks your opinion about topical progesterone therapy. The most appropriate advice that you can give her in regard to over-the-counter progesterone creams is that

    (A) they provide endometrial protection
    (B) they are regulated by the U.S. Food and Drug Administration (FDA)
    (C) therapeutic levels of progesterone can be consistently demonstrated
*   (D) they are variable in their effect

Traditionally, progestins have been divided into 3 categories: progesterone, C_{19} norsteroid progestin, and substituted C_{21} progestin (medroxyprogesterone acetate). The C_{19} norsteroid progestins are found more frequently in oral contraceptives and are further subdivided into estranes (eg, norethindrone) and the gonanes (eg, norgestrel). Each of these categories of progestins has been used for hormone therapy (HT). Transdermal progesterone cream can be purchased over the counter and has been popularized based on a small series of patients in an observational study. The claims made for the topical preparation exceed the known impact of prescription drugs already approved. One study showed fewer hot flushes in women who used topical progesterone cream over 1 year than in women using placebo but did not demonstrate any improvement in bone density in the treated group.

A study of the serum and saliva of women who use a high-concentration cream has found progesterone levels that reach a very low luteal range. In some case reports, it has been observed that the application of topical progesterone cream has resulted in unusually high serum progesterone levels. Because topical progesterone preparations are not strictly regulated by the FDA, they may contain varying amounts of progesterone. Such creams should not be recommended as part of an HT regimen to protect the endometrium. Individuals who elect to use topical progesterone cream should be monitored more closely for endometrial hyperplasia with endometrial biopsies, and transvaginal uterine ultrasonography should be obtained on a regular basis.

Extract from the Mexican yam (*Dioscorea villosa*) is the most common ingredient in topical progestin preparations. No metabolic pathway has been identified in *D villosa* to suggest that progesterone can be produced by this plant species. Mexican yam extract is more likely to be estrogenic, because it does contain varying amounts of diosgenin, a plant estrogen. The progesterone activity observed in some wild yam creams is probably a result of the addition of progesterone. Investigators have found added progesterone in many yam creams tested.

In summary, topical progesterone creams have been highly variable in their effect, have some low level of biologic activity sufficient to reduce hot flushes, and have not exhibited a bone-protective effect; they cannot be relied on to reduce endometrial hyperplasia. If the patient chooses to use topical cream after you have given her this information, the status of her bones and endometrium should be monitored carefully.

Cooper A, Spencer C, Whitehead MI, Ross D, Barnard GJ, Collins WP. Systemic absorption of progesterone from Progest cream in postmenopausal women. Lancet 1998;351:1255–6.

Grady D, Ernster VL. Hormone replacement therapy and endometrial cancer: are current regimens safe? J Natl Cancer Inst 1997;89:1088–9.

Leonetti HB, Longo S, Anasti JN. Transdermal progesterone cream for vasomotor symptoms and postmenopausal bone loss. Obstet Gynecol 1999;94:225–8.

109

Adhesion prevention at laparotomy

A surgery colleague calls you to the operating room for your opinion. He has performed a laparotomy for possible appendicitis on a 13-year-old adolescent who experienced menarche at age 12½ years. To his surprise, he encounters a ruptured ovarian cyst. Your visual assessment is that the cyst is benign and is a corpus luteum. Your colleague is concerned about minimizing adhesion formation, which might result in pelvic pain or infertility. The step that most likely will reduce adhesions is to

        (A) use a harmonic scalpel
*   (B) achieve meticulous hemostasis
        (C) leave 500 mL of Ringer's lactate in the peritoneal cavity
        (D) apply a bioresorbent hyaluronic acid–impregnated membrane

Pelvic adhesions can compromise fertility and produce pelvic pain. They are known sequelae of abdominal surgery and are accentuated by the presence of blood in the peritoneal cavity. The true incidence of adhesions following laparotomy to manage a bleeding ovarian cyst is not known. In spite of all of the attempts to minimize adhesions (eg, with barriers, corticosteroids, and other adjuvant therapy), principles of microsurgery consistently have been the cornerstone. These techniques include the following:

- Minimization of tissue handling
- Use of atraumatic instruments
- Avoidance of ischemia
- Avoidance of injuries to the peritoneal surface
- Use of copious irrigation

Hemostasis should be established as meticulously as possible. Because the fibrin deposition that is part of the clotting process serves as a nidus for adhesion formation, leaving a large quantity of physiologic fluid has not been shown to be effective in preventing adhesions. The concept of floating the peritoneal structures to prevent their adhering together is appealing, but the peritoneal fluid is absorbed too rapidly; absorption occurs within hours rather than the 3–5-day window needed for adhesion prevention.

Use of the harmonic scalpel has been helpful in dissecting significant adhesions associated with chronic inflammatory diseases and some cases of endometriosis. It would not be particularly advantageous in this case and would not be the next step when hemostasis is the chief issue that needs to be addressed.

Data concerning the efficacy of bioresorbable membranes are conflicting. One of the more commonly used membranes, Seprafilm, is a mechanical barrier composed of hyaluronic acid and carboxymethylcellulose. In a small prospective study of patients who underwent bowel surgery followed by second-look laparoscopy, researchers concluded that the incidence of adhesions did not differ significantly between the treated and untreated groups. However, the severity of the adhesions appeared to be reduced in those patients in whom the bioresorbable barrier was used. In a comparison of an oxidized regenerated cellulose adhesion barrier (Interceed) with no adjuvant therapy, use of the barrier was associated with a statistically significant reduction in adhesion formation at second look laparoscopy.

Researchers who have studied peritoneal concentrations of interleukin-1 (IL-1), interleukin-6 (IL-6), and tumor necrosis factor alpha (TNF-α) have found a correlation between adhesion re-formation and high concentrations of IL-1 and IL-6, which suggests that the body's control of adhesion formation is cell mediated. The peritoneal fluid should receive more investigative attention in adhesion prevention.

Cheong YC, Laird SM, Shelton JB, Ledger WL, Li TC, Cooke ID. The correlation of adhesions and peritoneal fluid cytokine concentrations: a pilot study. Hum Reprod 2002;17:1039–45.

Kramer K, Senninger N, Herbst H, Probst W. Effective prevention of adhesions with hyaluronate. Arch Surg 2002;137:278–82.

Sawada T, Nishizawa H, Nishio E, Kadowaki M. Postoperative adhesion prevention with an oxidized regenerated cellulose adhesion barrier in infertile women. J Reprod Med 2000;45:387–9.

Vrijland WW, Tseng LN, Eijkman HJ, Hop WC, Jakimowicz JJ, Leguit P, et al. Fewer intraperitoneal adhesions with use of hyaluronic acid-carboxymethylcellulose membrane: a randomized clinical trial. Ann Surg 2002;235:193–9.

110

Adnexal mass in a postmenopausal woman

A 52-year-old white woman, gravida 2, para 2, presents to your office for evaluation of a 3-cm simple right ovarian cyst. She weighs 106 kg (233.7 lb). The patient had requested transvaginal ultrasonography and CA 125 screening because advanced-stage ovarian cancer recently had been diagnosed in her 61-year-old first cousin. There is no other family history of breast or ovarian cancer. The patient's last menstrual period was 4 years ago. She does not smoke cigarettes, and her blood pressure is within normal limits. She does not take hormone therapy, and her CA 125 level was 19. The most appropriate next step in the management of this case is

        (A) computed tomography (CT) scanning of the abdomen and pelvis
        (B) laparoscopy
  * (C) repeat ultrasonography and CA 125 measurement in 3 months
        (D) administration of gonadotropin-releasing hormone (GnRH) agonists
        (E) administration of oral contraceptives

As the use of radiologic modalities such as CT scanning and ultrasonography becomes more prevalent, the incidental discovery of asymptomatic pelvic masses is becoming a common reason for gynecologic consultation. The referred patient may be very anxious because of the fear of cancer. Only very rarely are small cystic ovarian lesions malignant, however. In a review of 440 postmenopausal women with unilocular masses less than 5 cm in diameter, only 3 women had a malignancy.

The 5-year survival rate for women with stage I ovarian cancer ranges from 75% to 90%. For advanced-stage disease, the survival rate drops to approximately 20–40%. The knowledge that stage I disease is highly curable has led to screening strategies to attempt to identify women with early-stage disease. Management of an adnexal mass depends on a combination of predictive factors for malignancy, including age, menopausal status, size of the mass, ultrasonographic features, presence or absence of symptoms, CA 125 levels, and unilaterality versus bilaterality. Benign tumors are generally smooth walled, cystic, mobile, less than 10 cm in diameter, and unilateral. Approximately 95% of cysts less than 5 cm in diameter are nonneoplastic.

In a study to evaluate unilocular cysts of a diameter 10 cm or less in 256 women older than 50 years, 90% of the women had lesions less than 5 cm in diameter, and 49% of postmenopausal ovarian cysts resolved within 60 days. Of the 45 women with persistent lesions who underwent surgery, all had benign lesions, with serous cystadenomas being the most common. No woman in this cohort had a malignancy.

In a study of 250 postmenopausal women with complex cystic lesions less than 10 cm in diameter, 55% of the lesions spontaneously resolved within 60 days. Of the 114 women who underwent surgery, 7 had ovarian

cancer, 1 had primary peritoneal cancer, and 1 had metastatic breast cancer. Thus, postmenopausal women with complex ovarian cysts or women with solid and cystic areas within an ovary had a significant risk for malignancy.

In approximately 50% of women with stage I ovarian cancers, CA 125 levels are elevated, but CA 125 level alone is not a sensitive predictor of invasive disease. The use of CA 125 levels and ultrasonography has not been shown to be effective in population-based screening for ovarian cancer. Because CA 125 levels can be elevated in premenopausal women with a variety of benign conditions, they do not provide a good test to distinguish benign from malignant conditions in this group of women. Currently, the use of 3-dimensional ultrasonography in distinguishing benign from malignant ovarian tumors is being evaluated.

Small unilocular masses in postmenopausal women have a low incidence of malignancy, and these lesions often spontaneously regress in a short time. The use of serial ultrasonography can prevent unnecessary surgery for benign disease. Postmenopausal women with a unilocular mass less than 5 cm in diameter can be reevaluated with repeated ultrasonography. If the cyst regresses, no subsequent treatment is needed. If the mass grows or develops solid components, surgery is indicated. Persistent masses require continued ultrasonographic follow-up.

Although oral contraceptives and GnRH agonists suppress ovarian tissue in premenopausal women, they are not effective in postmenopausal women, because no functioning ovarian tissue remains to be suppressed. Total abdominal hysterectomy and bilateral salpingo-oophorectomy or operative laparoscopy for an asymptomatic radiologically detected mass would be overly aggressive therapies. A surgical procedure is not indicated for this asymptomatic patient because of the low incidence of malignancy and high likelihood of spontaneous regression. A CT scan of the abdomen and pelvis would not add further information in the evaluation of this woman with a 3-cm simple ovarian cyst and normal CA 125 level.

American College of Obstetricians and Gynecologists. Routine cancer screening. ACOG Committee Opinion 247. Washington, DC: ACOG; 2000.

Bailey CL, Uleland FR, Land GL, DePriest PD, Gallion HH, Kryscio RJ, et al. The malignant potential of small cystic ovarian tumors in women over 50 years of age. Gynecol Oncol 1998;69:3–7.

DiSaia PJ, Creasman WT. Clinical gynecologic oncology. 6th ed. St. Louis (MO): Mosby; 2002. p. 259–88.

NIH Consensus Conference. Ovarian cancer: screening, treatment, and follow-up. NIH Consensus Development Panel on Ovarian Cancer. JAMA 1995;273:491–7.

Roman LD. Small cystic pelvic masses in older women: is surgical removal necessary? Gynecol Oncol 1998;69:1–2.

111

Bladder injury repair

A 43-year-old woman, gravida 2, para 2, undergoes a difficult total abdominal hysterectomy for menorrhagia and an 18-week–sized leiomyomatous uterus. Previous surgical history includes a myomectomy followed by 2 cesarean deliveries. During dissection of the bladder off the lower uterine segment, extravasation of urine is noted, and a 3-cm cystotomy is recognized above the trigone. On completion of the hysterectomy, the gynecologist performs a 1-layer cystotomy repair with absorbable suture. The most likely outcome over the next 8 weeks is

   (A) vesicovaginal fistula
   (B) ureteral obstruction
 * (C) a normal postoperative course
   (D) recurrent bouts of cystitis
   (E) intraperitoneal urinoma

Injury to the bladder occurs in approximately 1 in 500 hysterectomies, often in women with a history of prior pelvic surgery, pelvic infection, or endometriosis. Most authors recommend sharp dissection of the bladder with the tips of the scissors pointed downward toward the uterus and cervix. The use of blunt dissection (eg, with a sponge or the operator's finger) is thought more likely to lead to bladder damage. In cases in which the bladder is extremely adherent, it may be opened at the dome. One finger is placed in the bladder and helps delineate the proper plane as sharp dissection proceeds.

Once a cystotomy occurs, it is important to determine the location of the injury. If the cystotomy is near the trigone, it is prudent to place ureteral catheters to ensure that the repair does not compromise ureteral patency. It is also crucial to mobilize the bladder sufficiently for complete evaluation of the extent of the injury. The repair should begin and end beyond the margins of the laceration. There is no clear evidence about the superiority of a 1- or 2-layer closure. The important principles are to use absorbable suture, make sure the closure is watertight, and drain the bladder for 3–5 days. Prophylactic antibiotics should be used during the period of bladder drainage. Sterile milk may be used to test the integrity of the repair. Intraoperative cystoscopy should be performed

after bladder repair. It is likely that this patient will have a normal postoperative course.

Vesicovaginal fistula is an uncommon complication, but hysterectomy is the most common cause in the United States. Fistulae frequently are associated with unrecognized bladder injuries at the time of surgery or figure-of-eight sutures, which cause tissue necrosis between the bladder and the vagina. Any patient who presents with urine leakage should be evaluated carefully for the presence of a fistula. Placement of a tampon in the vagina after methylene blue dye is instilled in the bladder will aid in the evaluation of a potential fistula. Cystoscopy also is helpful to assess the size and location of the injury. Small fistulae often heal with prolonged bladder drainage.

Intraperitoneal urinomas may be seen after laparoscopic bladder injuries. Bladder trauma occurs most commonly if the bladder is not entirely drained prior to the placement of the trocar. The plasma creatinine level often is elevated because of reabsorption of the intraperitoneal urine. Proper bladder drainage and appropriate trocar placement should help avoid this complication.

Recurrent episodes of cystitis and stone formation were observed more commonly when nonabsorbable sutures were used for bladder repair. Additionally, many practitioners advocate cystoscopy after incontinence procedures to ensure that no foreign material, such as a suture, has been placed through the bladder mucosa.

Lacerations at or near the trigone of the bladder are more common with vaginal procedures. Ureteral patency can be compromised by blind suture placement. In these cases, direct visualization is recommended prior to bladder repair. The laparoscope or cystoscope can be inserted through a small opening of the dome of the bladder to allow easy visualization. Transurethral cystoscopy can be performed. If bladder injury is recognized at surgery and properly repaired, the likelihood of complications is small.

Complications of disease and therapy. In: DiSaia PJ, Creasman WT. Clinical gynecologic oncology. 6th ed. St. Louis (MO): Mosby; 2002. p. 473–500.

Harkki-Siren P, Sjoberg J, Tiitinen A. Urinary tract injuries after hysterectomy. Obstet Gynecol 1998;92:113–8.

Injuries and fistulae. In: American College of Obstetricians and Gynecologists. Precis: gynecology. 2nd ed. Washington, DC: ACOG; 2001. p. 99–106.

Olsson JH, Ellstrom M, Hahlin M. A randomised prospective trial comparing laparoscopic and abdominal hysterectomy. Br J Obstet Gynaecol 1996;103:345–50.

112

Hysterectomy practices and quality assurance

As chair of a new obstetrics–gynecology department in a community hospital, you are asked to establish a quality assurance process to monitor hysterectomy practices. The hospital administrators ask you to outline the elements that are most important in developing a thorough review policy. After reviewing the available literature, you tell them that the most important initial step is to

* (A) establish departmental and administrative support for the project
  (B) review American College of Obstetricians and Gynecologists policies on hysterectomy practices, which can serve as a standard of care
  (C) recognize that most quality assurance activities will require a data analyst
  (D) understand that there is variable liability protection for physicians who participate in the peer review process

Measuring the quality of care has been part of the assessment of hospitals by the Joint Commission on Accreditation of Healthcare Organizations for many years. Although there is considerable discussion concerning exactly what represents quality of care, specific objective and measurable clinical indicators do exist (eg, inappropriate diagnosis, undesirable outcome, or excessive cost). The use of clinical indicators or sentinel events that have been agreed on by the department can serve as a reminder that a policy, physician, or hospital practice should come under review. One of the most important first steps in the establishment of a continuous quality improvement indicator process is to identify leadership. This identification requires not only the participation of individuals in the obstetrics–gynecology department but also the support of the executive arm of the medical staff and the hospital administration, because without their firm commitment, the other necessary steps will not be carried out properly. Therefore, establishing this support for the project should be the initial measure to address the continuous quality improvement process.

The American College of Obstetricians and Gynecologists (ACOG) has developed a list of quality indicators

for in-hospital gynecologic practice (see Box 112-1). It should be noted that ACOG does not regard these indicators as a national standard of care. Once quality indicators are identified, a trained data analyst familiar with continuous quality improvement and the hospital's established process should review the information. In this way, only those issues that need departmental action should come up for review in an executive session.

In 1986, the U.S. Congress passed the Healthcare Quality Improvement Act. This act grants immunity from damages under federal and state laws, including antitrust provisions, to health care practitioners engaged in good faith peer review. Most states have adopted this policy in principle, and many have crafted separate legislation. Leadership, with the advice of counsel, should determine the necessary guidelines and policy to provide immunity against the medical liability issues that might arise in each locale.

In general, the continuous quality improvement process involves the primary department, but it also may involve other services found in the hospital that could affect specific practice. For example, in terms of hysterectomy, a number of important issues involve services

BOX 112-1

Gynecologic Quality Indicators

- Unplanned readmission within 14 d
- Admission after a return visit to the emergency department for the same problem
- Cardiopulmonary arrest, resuscitated
- Occurrence of an infection not present on admission
- Unplanned admission to special (intensive) care unit
- Unplanned return to the operating room for surgery during the same admission
- Ambulatory surgery patient admitted or retained for complication of surgery or anesthesia
- Gynecologic surgery, except radical hysterectomy or exenteration, using 2 or more units of blood, or postoperative hematocrit level of <24% or hemoglobin level of <8 g
- Unplanned removal, injury, or repair of organ during operative procedure
- Initiation of antibiotics >24 h after surgery
- Discrepancy between preoperative diagnosis and postoperative tissue report
- Removal of uterus weighing <280 g for leiomyomata
- Removal of follicular cyst or corpus luteum of ovary
- Hysterectomy performed on a woman younger than 30 y except for malignancy
- Gynecologic death

American College of Obstetricians and Gynecologists. Quality improvement in women's health care. Rev. ed. Washington, DC: ACOG; 2000.

done by individuals other than the attending physician (eg, timing of administration of antibiotic prophylaxis, availability of adequate blood banking services, and the need for timely recording of laboratory test results on the patient's chart prior to surgery). Therefore, the continuous quality improvement process must involve not only the primary department but also other service sites in the institution.

Once a problem is identified, there are numerous alternatives, such as observation of a practitioner's skill, proctoring, external peer review, or remediation. Some of these steps may require reporting the practitioner to the state licensing board or the national data registry.

American College of Obstetricians and Gynecologists. Quality improvement in women's health care. Rev. ed. Washington, DC: ACOG; 2000.

Berwick DM. Continuous improvement as an ideal in health care. N Engl J Med 1989;320:53–6.

Institutional responsibility to provide legal representation. In: American College of Obstetricians and Gynecologists. Ethics in obstetrics and gynecology. Washington, DC: ACOG; 2002. p. 48.

Quality assessment and continuous quality improvement. In: American College of Obstetricians and Gynecologists. Guidelines for women's health care. 2nd ed. Washington, DC: ACOG; 2000. p. 40–9.

113

Discussion of a medical error with the patient

A 35-year-old woman undergoes a laparotomy for myomectomy. Six weeks postoperatively, she has a second operation for a suspected pelvic abscess. A sponge is recovered from the cul-de-sac. Postoperatively, the next step you, as the gynecologist, should take is to

    (A) reprimand the operating room supervisor
    (B) review the hospital records of the first surgery
    (C) prepare a report for the medical executive committee
*   (D) discuss the operative findings with the patient
    (E) facilitate a waiver of all financial charges associated with the second surgery

Medical errors occur in the practice of clinical medicine. Unfortunately, health care providers fear that disclosure of errors will damage their careers. Full and immediate disclosure, however, provides the opportunity for patients to understand their clinical situation and may limit liability. The ethical guideline of primary concern is the patient's right to know. Hospitals accredited by the Joint Commission on Accreditation of Healthcare Organizations are required to tell patients when their treatment outcomes vary from anticipated results.

The physician is under obligation to serve the best interests of the patient, regardless of self-interest or institutional conflicts. Thus, the issue becomes one of providing all the information the patient needs to make informed decisions regarding the situation and proposed treatment. Incomplete and flawed disclosures may take many forms (eg, omission, evasion, or obfuscation).

Under the principle of autonomy, which refers to "self" and "governance," the patient deserves to be given an adequate understanding of the situation to be able to make meaningful choices. In the clinical setting, this principle is understood to mean that an individual has the right to personal rule of self free of the influences of others.

An important ethical assumption is that truthfulness best serves the interests of both physician and patient. Patients want the truth even though it may contain facts that elicit anxiety, fear, embarrassment, loathing, and anger.

Several contemporary concerns adversely affect disclosure in clinical practice: fear of lawsuits, "de-selection" by third-party payers, and actions by licensing agencies. These concerns, whatever their merit, cannot be allowed to influence disclosure.

The issuance of a reprimand to the operating room supervisor or preparation of a report to the medical executive committee are secondary concerns. Review of the hospital records from the initial surgery at this juncture is irrelevant. Waiver of the financial charges associated with the second surgery may be appropriate later.

In the scenario presented, the best approach is to accept responsibility and fully inform the patient. Failure to inform the patient promptly may compound whatever negative consequences may result from the error. Ultimately, once they are fully informed, most patients will be able to comprehend the events that occurred. This approach supports the development of trust in the patient–physician relationship, which ultimately may improve care and decrease liability concerns.

The physician also should be aware of the state's medical code in regard to requirements for informing patients of mistakes. Individual states may have requirements for disclosure of errors, even in the outpatient setting.

Boyle RJ. Communication, truth-telling and disclosure. In: Fletcher JC, Lombardo PA, Marshall MF, Miller FG, editors. Introduction to clinical ethics. 2nd ed. Hagerstown (MD): University Publishing Group; 1997. p. 55–70.

Code of Professional Ethics of the American College of Obstetricians and Gynecologists. In: American College of Obstetricians and Gynecologists. Ethics in obstetrics and gynecology. Washington, DC: ACOG; 2002. p. 97–101.

Ethical decision making in obstetrics and gynecology. In: American College of Obstetricians and Gynecologists. Ethics in obstetrics and gynecology. Washington, DC: ACOG; 2002. p. 1–6.

Lo B. Ethical issues in clinical medicine. In: Braunwald E, Fauci AS, Kasper DL, Hauser SL, Longo DL, Jameson JL, editors. Harrison's principles of internal medicine. 15th ed. New York (NY): McGraw-Hill; 2001. p. 5–8.

114

Urge incontinence

You are treating a 60-year-old woman for symptoms of urge incontinence. She has been unable to tolerate controlled-release oxybutynin chloride (Ditropan XL) because of severe dry mouth. The best next step in her management is

(A) propantheline bromide (Pro-Banthine)
(B) tolterodine tartrate (Detrol)
(C) neuromodulation
* (D) biofeedback-assisted behavioral therapy
(E) pentosan polysulfate sodium (Elmiron)

Urge incontinence is a common problem; it is reported by 14% of women. Urodynamic evaluation will demonstrate detrusor overactivity in most women with urge incontinence, although urodynamic diagnosis is not always necessary prior to therapy. Current treatment options include medication, behavioral modification, pelvic muscle physiotherapy, and neuromodulation.

Although there are many medications available to treat urge incontinence, few have been tested in placebo-controlled trials. Anticholinergic medications—eg, propantheline bromide, oxybutynin chloride, and tolterodine tartrate—are among the best studied. The effect of such drugs is mediated by muscarinic receptors within the bladder wall. Oxybutynin also has additional direct effects on the detrusor muscle. However, anticholinergic adverse effects are common with these medications, resulting in a narrow therapeutic window. For example, oxybutynin causes dry mouth, which may lead to discontinuation of this medication by 10–23% of women.

Several newer agents have been developed to reduce the anticholinergic adverse effects. A controlled-release formulation of oxybutynin chloride is available. Tolterodine tartrate, a selective muscarinic agent, is available in conventional and extended-release formulations (Detrol LA). These newer medications have efficacy similar to oxybutynin chloride but are better tolerated, leading to improved compliance. Although the extended-release preparations offer more convenient dosing schedules, they provide no increase in efficacy. A 3.9-mg transdermal oxybutynin patch has been shown in a clinical trial to reduce incontinence episodes significantly without an increase in dry mouth.

In the case described, severe dry mouth has prevented the patient from taking controlled-release oxybutynin chloride. It is unlikely that she would experience reduced xerostomia with either tolterodine tartrate or propantheline bromide. Tolterodine tartrate has a similar incidence of this adverse effect, and propantheline bromide has a higher incidence. Therefore, these options are unlikely to offer significant benefit compared with controlled-release oxybutynin chloride.

Behavioral therapy traditionally has been an important option for the treatment of urge incontinence. Options include bladder retraining, learning behaviors to abort episodes of urgency, and electromyography for biofeedback. In a randomized, placebo-controlled trial, 4 sessions of biofeedback-assisted behavioral therapy reduced incontinence by 80% and was significantly more effective than the administration of placebo or oxybutynin chloride. Overall patient satisfaction was high, and only 14% of women treated with behavioral therapy wanted to try an alternative treatment. In contrast, 75% of women receiving placebo or oxybutynin chloride requested an alternative treatment. In the case described, biofeedback-assisted behavioral therapy would be the most preferable next step in the care of this woman.

Neuromodulation is a relatively new option for the treatment of urge incontinence. Electronic nerve stimulation can be achieved with external or implantable devices. External devices use vaginal or rectal electrodes to provide direct electrical stimulation to peripheral nerves. In contrast, an implantable electronic sacral nerve root stimulation device (InterStim) consists of an electrode and a pulse generator that are implanted in a 1- or 2-stage surgical procedure. This device was approved by the FDA in 1997. The mechanism of action is not fully understood. Among women with urge incontinence, 63% had substantial improvement with implantation of a test electrode. In women with an initial favorable response, 46% became continent with implantation of the permanent device, and another 13% significantly improved from baseline but were not completely continent. Of 96 subjects implanted with a permanent device, 11% underwent removal of the device because of adverse events. Although this is a promising avenue for treatment of urge incontinence, its role is not established at this time.

Pentosan polysulfate sodium is indicated for the treatment of interstitial cystitis. This medication does not have demonstrated efficacy in the treatment of urge incontinence.

Appell RA, Sand P, Dmochowski R, Anderson R, Zinner N, Lama D, et al. Prospective randomized controlled trial of extended-release oxybutynin chloride and tolterodine tartrate in the treatment of overactive bladder: results of the OBJECT Study. Mayo Clin Proc 2001;76: 358–63.

Burgio KL, Locher JL, Goode PS, Hardin JM, McDowell BJ, Dombrowski M, et al. Behavioral drug treatment for urge urinary incontinence in older women: a randomized controlled trial. JAMA 1998; 280:1995–2000.

Dmochowski RR, Davila GW, Zinner NR, Gittelman MC, Saltzstein DR, Lyttle S, et al. Efficacy and safety of transdermal oxybutynin in patients with urge and mixed urinary incontinence. J Urol 2002; 168:580–6.

Gleason DM, Susset J, White C, Munoz DR, Sand PK. Evaluation of a new once-daily formulation of oxybutynin for the treatment of urinary urge incontinence. Ditropan XL Study Group. Urology 1999;54:420–3.

Harvey MA, Baker K, Wells GA. Tolterodine versus oxybutynin in the treatment of urge urinary incontinence: a meta-analysis. Am J Obstet Gynecol 2001;185:56–61.

Robinson D, Khullar V, Cardozo L. Pharmacological management of detrusor instability. Int Urogynecol J Pelvic Floor Dysfunct 2001; 12:271–8.

Siegel SW, Catanzaro F, Dijkema HE, Elhilali MM, Fowler CJ, Gajewski JB, et al. Long-term results of a multicenter study on sacral nerve stimulation for treatment of urinary urge incontinence, urgency-frequency, and retention. Urology 2000;56 suppl 1:87–91.

115

Polycystic ovary syndrome

A 23-year-old nulligravid woman sees you for her well-woman care. Her history reveals 8 years of an oily complexion, irregular menses, and hirsutism. She has been treated intermittently with oral contraceptives. She states that she has had no serious health problems but describes a family history of heart disease. On physical examination, she is mildly hirsute, with a male abdominal wall hair pattern and no clitoral enlargement. Her body mass index (BMI) is 29 kg/m^2, and her serum cholesterol level is 275 mg/dL. She has no evidence of glucose intolerance. The most appropriate next step in her evaluation is to order a

    (A) test of total serum testosterone
    (B) test of serum triiodothyronine (T$_3$)
*   (C) fasting lipid profile
    (D) random 17-hydroxyprogesterone test

This patient presents with a clinical profile compatible with polycystic ovary syndrome (PCOS). Hypothyroidism is seen in a small percentage of patients with PCOS, and it can cause hyperlipidemia. The appropriate screening test for hypothyroidism is an evaluation of serum thyroid-stimulating hormone (TSH), not T$_3$. The serum prolactin level should be determined in any woman who presents with ovulatory dysfunction; elevated levels have been found in a small percentage of patients with PCOS. The patient does not report any concern about infertility during this visit, and she mentioned no galactorrhea.

The laboratory screening test for adult-onset congenital adrenal hyperplasia, specifically a 21-hydroxylase deficiency, measures 17-hydroxyprogesterone. Because of the circadian secretory pattern of this substance, the optimum time to perform this test is between 10:00 AM and 12:00 PM. There is no information in the clinical presentation that she may be at higher risk because she is Hispanic, Slavic, or an Eastern European Jew. The long-standing nature of her disorder makes the presence of a testosterone-secreting tumor unlikely. Although it would

be appropriate to determine a total serum testosterone level, in the context of this question, that test is not the most appropriate next step. Because the patient's reported total serum cholesterol level is elevated, it is appropriate to proceed with a fasting lipid profile.

The current Adult Treatment Panel III guidelines of the National Cholesterol Education Program recommend screening all individuals with a fasting lipid panel, which includes total serum cholesterol, high-density lipoprotein (HDL) cholesterol, low-density lipoprotein (LDL) cholesterol, and triglycerides. In the United States, 120 million persons have total serum cholesterol levels higher than 200 mg/dL, and 60 million persons have levels higher than 240 mg/dL. Individuals with very high cholesterol levels also can present with unusual physical findings (eg, xanthomata around the eyes and other parts of the skin). With the patient's family history of cardiac disease, it is possible that she has heterozygous familial hypercholesterolemia, which is observed in approximately 1 in 500 individuals.

The positive indicators for coronary heart disease are listed in Box 115-1. Levels of HDL cholesterol at

40 mg/dL or less, or LDL levels of 160 mg/dL or more, along with 1 other risk factor, require therapy. The patient's heredity and obesity make more active management of her hyperlipidemia urgent.

General management measures include walking or other cardiovascular exercise 2½ hours per week and weight reduction. Dietary fats should be reduced to approximately 30% of the total calories consumed. Olive oil should be used in preference to other cooking oils or butter. Increased intake of dietary fiber, fruit, vegetables, whole grains, and garlic have been shown to reduce cholesterol. A vegetarian diet, which excludes meat, eggs, or cheese, also may be effective. Minimal daily alcohol use—88.7 mL (3 oz) of red wine—has been shown to increase HDL cholesterol. Even with strict lifestyle management, however, the patient's LDL and HDL cholesterol levels probably would not change by more than 10%. If the patient does not respond to lifestyle measures, statin therapy is indicated.

American College of Obstetricians and Gynecologists. Precis: primary and preventive care. 2nd ed. Washington, DC: ACOG; 2000. p. 162.

Choice of lipid-lowering drugs. Med Lett Drugs Ther 1998;40:117–22.

Executive Summary of the Third Report of the National Cholesterol Education Program (NCEP) Expert Panel on Detection, Evaluation, and Treatment of High Blood Cholesterol in Adults (Adult Treatment Panel III). JAMA 2001;285:2486–97.

116

Office personnel and patient confidentiality

An 18-year-old woman has questions about the treatment you prescribed for vaginitis. As the patient is leaving the office, you overhear your nurse telling the patient not to worry and saying, "The doctor prescribed the same treatment for your roommate." Your most appropriate response is to

      (A) report the nurse to the state department of health

      (B) reprimand the nurse

*   (C) review with all staff the need for patient confidentiality

      (D) interrupt the conversation and deny the nurse's statement

The right to privacy is one of the most basic human rights. It is closely aligned with personal integrity. Privacy includes the right to noninterference and self-determination. Privacy also includes a person's rights to control access to, and distribution of, personal information. *Confidentiality* refers to the means by which a person's right to privacy is recognized and respected.

It is the clinician's duty to protect a patient's right to privacy and to respect the constraints placed on a clinician by confidentiality. The Hippocratic Oath includes the words "whatsoever I shall see or hear in the course of my profession ... I will never divulge, holding such things to be holy secrets." Although the nurse was trying to help the

patient, her actions conflicted with her responsibility to the other patient involved.

The patient's right to privacy and confidentiality forms the basis for trust expected in the doctor–patient relationship. A careless remark, even with the best of intentions, may have unanticipated negative consequences. These adverse outcomes may be intrapersonal or result in legally mandated actions.

All personnel who are involved directly with patient care should respect the individual's autonomy regarding any and all aspects of their medical care. Workers in the indirect provision of care (ie, personnel who work for health maintenance organizations, insurance carriers, and regulatory agencies) have an equal obligation regarding confidentiality of patients' records.

Reporting the event to outside authorities is unnecessary. Directly reprimanding the nurse alone might not correct the situation. Prevention of future compromise of confidentiality is the best policy. The physician should use this occurrence to review with the entire staff the need for patient confidentiality.

Cain JM. Principles of patient care. In: Berek JS, Adashi EY, Hillard PA, editors. Novak's gynecology. 12th ed. Baltimore (MD): Williams & Wilkins; 1996. p. 21–31.

Lo B. Ethical issues in clinical medicine. In: Braunwald E, Fauci AS, Kasper DL, Hauser SL, Longo DL, Jameson JL, editors. Harrison's principles of internal medicine. 15th ed. New York (NY): McGraw-Hill; 2001. p. 5–8.

Marshall MF. Respecting privacy and confidentiality. In: Fletcher JC, Lombardo PA, Marshall MF, Miller FG, editors. Introduction to clinical ethics. 2nd ed. Frederick (MD): University Publishing Group; 1997. p. 41–54.

Reiser SJ. Selections from the Hippocratic corpus: oath, precepts, the art, epidemics, the physician, decorum, and law. In: Reiser SJ, Dyck AJ, Curran WJ, editors. Ethics in medicine: historical perspectives and contemporary concerns. Cambridge (MA): MIT Press; 1977. p. 5–9.

Rules from the principles. In: English DC. Bioethics: a clinical guide for medical students. New York (NY): WW Norton; 1994. p. 29–53.

117

Bowel injury with laparoscopy

A 38-year-old woman, gravida 2, para 2, has undergone laparoscopic resection of extensive endometriosis. The surgery required meticulous sharp dissection. Hemostasis was obtained with electrocoagulation. Surgery was uneventful, and the patient was discharged on postoperative day 1. After discharge she felt well, and her mild postoperative discomfort was controlled with nonsteroidal antiinflammatory drugs. She resumed a regular diet, and her bowels were functioning normally. On postoperative day 4, she developed an acute onset of nausea, vomiting, abdominal pain, and elevated temperature and was rushed to the emergency department. She is diaphoretic with otherwise stable vital signs. Her abdomen is distended, rigid, and tender. The most appropriate management is

      (A) medical therapy with broad-spectrum intravenous antibiotics
      (B) nasogastric tube placement
      (C) laparoscopy
 *   (D) laparotomy

The 2 most common causes of bowel injury during laparoscopy are trocar injuries and electrosurgical injuries. Less commonly, bowel injuries may occur with the insufflation needle and with blunt and sharp dissection. Bowel injury is rare and is reported to occur in 0.2–0.4% of laparoscopic procedures.

Unfortunately, most bowel injuries are not recognized at the time of the laparoscopy. Once postoperative symptoms occur, prompt recognition and treatment will reduce the incidence of sepsis, multiple organ failure, and death. With an unrecognized trocar injury, symptoms usually develop within 12–48 hours. Women who sustain electrosurgical injuries may not become symptomatic until 4–10 days after surgery. By that time, most patients have been discharged from the hospital and have started to resume normal activities. This delayed presentation results from bowel wall necrosis. Symptoms of bowel perforation include increasing abdominal pain, fever, nausea, vomiting, diarrhea, distention, and elevated leukocyte count.

Electrosurgical injury can occur with the use of unipolar current and direct injury or conduction to the intestines because of insulation failure or capacitive coupling. Although it can be difficult to gauge the extent of electrosurgical damage, small injuries identified when they occur may be oversewn. Even if simple oversewing is performed at the time an electrosurgical injury occurs, however, delayed perforation may develop, because coagulation necrosis can extend beyond the visible burn. If an injury appears to be more than 0.5 cm in diameter, resection of the injured area with closure or anastomosis is preferred, depending on the size and configuration of the defect.

Bowel injuries necessitate a laparotomy to assess and repair the damage. Laparoscopy is not appropriate when there is a clinical suspicion of bowel perforation. Nasogastric tube placement, intravenous fluid resuscitation, and administration of broad-spectrum antibiotics are adjuncts to the surgical procedure but cannot adequately treat a bowel injury. They are not sufficient treatment for this critically ill patient. Free air in the abdomen is a common radiologic finding in the immediate postoperative period, and time to resolution varies. Thus, free air is not necessarily helpful in diagnosing a bowel perforation.

Grainger DA. Postoperative care: endoscopic surgery. In: Gershenson DM, DeCherney AH, Curry SL, Brubaker L, editors. Operative gynecology. 2nd ed. Philadelphia (PA): WB Saunders; 2001. p. 66–88.

Vasilev SA. Intraoperative and perioperative considerations in laparoscopy. In: Vasilev SA, editor. Perioperative and supportive care in gynecologic oncology: evidence-based management. New York (NY): Wiley–Liss; 2000. p. 437–70.

118

Advice to a patient on complications of supracervical hysterectomy

A 45-year-old woman is planning hysterectomy for menorrhagia. She asks about the relative risks of supracervical hysterectomy. You tell her that compared with a total abdominal hysterectomy, a supracervical abdominal hysterectomy is associated with increased risk of

    (A) perioperative infection
    (B) intraoperative bleeding
    (C) urinary tract infection
*   (D) postoperative vaginal bleeding
    (E) intraoperative bladder injury

During the first part of the 20th century, because of the high morbidity and mortality of major surgery, total hysterectomy was reserved for women in whom removal of the cervix was specifically indicated. However, as the surgical risks of total hysterectomy declined, it became the standard of care, virtually replacing supracervical (subtotal) hysterectomy.

In recent years, there has been a resurgence in the performance of supracervical hysterectomy. Prior to the advent of cervical cytologic screening and colposcopic evaluation, cervical stump carcinoma occurred in 1–2% of women after subtotal hysterectomy. Cervical cytologic testing allows the surgeon to identify women at increased risk for carcinoma of the cervical stump. Today the incidence of cervical cancer after subtotal hysterectomy is less than 0.2%. This complication is largely preventable through appropriate patient selection and postoperative follow-up with routine cervical cytologic testing.

Advantages of supracervical hysterectomy compared with total abdominal hysterectomy include decreased risks of bladder injuries, ureteral injuries, intraoperative hemorrhage, perioperative infection, and urogenital fistulae. Disadvantages include the possible retention of endometrial tissue in the lower uterine segment, resulting in continued menstruation after surgery. To reduce the risk of postoperative menstrual bleeding, some practitioners advocate cautery of the endocervical canal or coring of the cervical stump in conjunction with supracervical hysterectomy.

The effect of total and subtotal hysterectomy on sexual function remains controversial. Recent studies suggest that sexual function improves after hysterectomy in general. It is not known whether orgasmic function or other aspects of female sexuality are affected differently by various hysterectomy techniques. In a recent randomized controlled trial of total and supracervical hysterectomy, sexual functioning did not change between groups.

Controversy continues to obscure the benefits and risks of total versus subtotal hysterectomy. A woman should be fully informed about, and fully involved in, the decision to remove or retain her normal cervix at the time of hysterectomy for benign disease.

Harkki-Siren P, Sjoberg J, Tiitinen A. Urinary tract injuries after hysterectomy. Obstet Gynecol 1998;92:113–8.

Jones DE, Shackelford DP, Brame RG. Supracervical hysterectomy: back to the future? Am J Obstet Gynecol 1999;180:513–5.

Scott JR, Sharp HT, Dodson MK, Norton PA, Warner HR. Subtotal hysterectomy in modern gynecology: a decision analysis. Am J Obstet Gynecol 1997;176:1186–92.

Storm HH, Clemmensen IH, Manders T, Brinton LA. Supravaginal uterine amputation in Denmark 1978–1988 and risk of cancer. Gynecol Oncol 1992;45:198–201.

Thakar R, Ayers S, Clarkson P, Stanton S, Manyonda I. Outcomes after total versus subtotal abdominal hysterectomy. N Engl J Med 2002;347:1318–25.

Thompson JD, Warshaw JS. Hysterectomy. In: Rock JA, Thompson JD, editors. TeLinde's operative gynecology. 8th ed. Philadelphia (PA): Lippincott–Raven; 1997. p. 771–854.

Van der Stege JG, van Beek JJ. Problems related to the cervical stump at follow-up in laparoscopic supracervical hysterectomy. JSLS 1999;3:5–7.

119

Adolescent abnormal uterine bleeding

A 15-year-old nulligravid adolescent presents to the emergency department with an acute episode of uterine bleeding. Since menarche at age 12 years, she has experienced irregular menses and has been treated for iron deficiency anemia; she has no other history of bleeding diatheses. Six months ago, her thyroid-stimulating hormone level was normal, but her glucose level was mildly elevated. Her body mass index is 35 kg/m². She has fine dark hair on her chin and lower abdominal wall. A rectal and abdominal examination reveals no obvious masses, but the examination is limited because of the patient's girth. Abdominal ultrasonography reports a probably normal uterus, but the examination is limited. Hemoglobin level in the emergency department was 7.3 g/dL, and results of a pregnancy test were negative. The first step in her treatment would be to

    (A) administer intravenous conjugated equine estrogens (CEEs)
    (B) perform transvaginal ultrasonography
    (C) perform dilation and curettage (D&C)
*   (D) obtain coagulation studies
    (E) initiate oral contraceptives

When evaluating an adolescent with heavy bleeding, it is important to consider the possibility of coagulation disorder. In one study, 28% of 79 adolescents seen in a hospital setting for acute vaginal bleeding had a coagulation disorder. Therefore, for this patient, it is very important to exclude the possibility of coagulation disorder at the initial assessment, and before any therapy is instituted. This patient's presentation is compatible with polycystic ovary syndrome; the underlying issue is anovulatory bleeding. Otherwise, this problem is considered a part of a normal physiologic process during the perimenarcheal years. It is attributed to the immaturity of the hypothalamic–pituitary–ovarian axis. Anovulatory bleeding is often synonymous with dysfunctional uterine bleeding and can be excessive. It can result in anemia and the need for emergency care. Blood dyscrasias such as von Willebrand's disease, factor VIII deficiency, leukemia, and idiopathic thrombocytopenic purpura can produce coagulopathy and cause excessive bleeding. Serious systemic diseases, such as renal and hepatic disease, can result in abnormal uterine bleeding, although they are less common causes. Besides obtaining a complete blood count and a pregnancy test, the physician should assess this patient with coagulation studies prior to the initiation of therapy.

High-dose estrogen therapy is appropriate to control acute uterine bleeding. The oral administration of CEE, up to 10 mg/d, or intravenous doses of CEE, 25 mg every 4 hours up to 24 hours, will control bleeding in most adolescent patients. For this patient, administration of CEEs

may be appropriate if a blood coagulation problem can be ruled out.

Few patients will require a D&C to stop the bleeding. Although the option of D&C never should be totally discarded, it is not the appropriate choice at this time. After an acute bleeding episode has been treated, the likelihood is high that it will be a long-term or recurring problem. It can be treated successfully with cyclic progestin therapy or an oral contraceptive. Although that choice is appropriate for long-term management, it is not an appropriate option until the patient's coagulation status is determined.

Cervical or vaginal malignancy, although rare, may cause acute bleeding. The incidence of endometrial cancer in adolescents aged 15–19 years has been reported as 0.1 per 100,000 cases studied. In a report of adolescent endometrial carcinoma, patients experienced 2–3 years of anovulatory bleeding, and all were obese. Because obesity is associated with the conversion of androgens to estrogens, obese patients who are anovulatory may be at risk for developing endometrial hyperplasia and carcinoma.

American College of Obstetricians and Gynecologists. Management of anovulatory bleeding. ACOG Practice Bulletin 14. Washington, DC: ACOG; 2000.

Claessens EA, Cowell CA. Acute adolescent menorrhagia. Am J Obstet Gynecol 1981;139:277–80.

DeVore GR, Owens O, Kase N. Use of intravenous Premarin in the treatment of dysfunctional uterine bleeding—a double-blind randomized control study. Obstet Gynecol 1982;59:285–91.

Stoval DW, Anderson RJ, De Leon FD. Endometrial adenocarcinoma in teenagers. Adolesc Pediatr Gynecol 1989;2:157–9.

120

Physician decision regarding samples from drug companies

A new pharmaceutical product is being promoted for hormone therapy. The drug recently has been approved by the U.S. Food and Drug Administration (FDA). This product would be prescribed to patients in your office. The company representative suggests that you have your patients try a few samples, and he leaves a large supply at your office. On your desk, you find a note from the salesman in which he offers to give you 4 tickets to a professional sporting event if you agree to prescribe the drug to your patients. The most appropriate next step would be to

(A) distribute the product free of charge to your patients
(B) donate the product to a nearby free clinic
* (C) report the salesman's behavior to the drug company and dispose of the product
(D) dispose of the product

The development of drugs and medical devices is an important part of continuous improvement in health care. Manufacturers involved in these endeavors rightfully target physicians and hospitals for medical input. Because of the desire of practitioners and institutions for financial support of various research and educational programs, there is a strong inducement for interaction with industry.

Although physicians always have rendered advice and opinions on clinical affairs on a fee-for-service basis, when financial benefit for the physician becomes the primary purpose of this activity, a conflict of interest is said to have occurred. The acceptance of a gift or the promise of future gifts suggests a conflict of interest.

Physicians have an obligation to seek the most accurate sources of information about new products they may use for their patients' benefit. Advertising and marketing strategies employed by the manufacturer provide insufficient basis for the physician's decision to prescribe a product. If the company has approval of the regulatory authorities, and if the physician determines that the product is beneficial to an individual patient, consideration for its use is warranted.

Physicians have a fiduciary relationship with patients that obligates them to provide for the best interests of these patients. This responsibility always must take prece-

dence over self-interest. Product use always is based on individual patients' needs. In this scenario, in which the free tickets could be seen as an inducement, it is not appropriate to distribute the product. To avoid conflict of interest and promote ethical practice, it is imperative not only to dispose of the product but also to report the offer of the gift to the sales representative's company so it can issue a reprimand. If appropriate, the offer also should be reported to the FDA.

American Medical Association. E-8.061 Gifts to physicians from industry. Chicago (IL): AMA; 2003.

Commercial enterprises in medical practice: selling and promoting products. In: American College of Obstetricians and Gynecologists. Ethics in obstetrics and gynecology. Washington, DC: ACOG; 2002. p. 7–9.

Guidelines for relationships with industry. In: American College of Obstetricians and Gynecologists. Ethics in obstetrics and gynecology. Washington, DC: ACOG; 2002. p. 40–2.

Lo B. Ethical issues in clinical medicine. In: Braunwald E, Fauci AS, Kasper DL, Hauser SL, Longo DL, Jameson JL, editors. Harrison's principles of internal medicine. 15th ed. New York (NY): McGraw-Hill; 2001. p. 5–8.

Mark DB. Economic issues in clinical medicine. In: Braunwald E, Fauci AS, Kasper DL, Hauser SL, Longo DL, Jameson JL, editors. Harrison's principles of internal medicine. 15th ed. New York (NY): McGraw-Hill; 2001. p. 14–9.

Wall LL, Brown D. Pharmaceutical sales representatives and the doctor/patient relationship. Obstet Gynecol 2002;100:594–9.

121

Vulvar intraepithelial neoplasia

A 44-year-old woman presented to your office with a vulvar lump. Physical examination revealed a raised lesion that measured 2 cm by 3 cm on the left labia majus. The gross lesion was completely excised in an ambulatory surgical center. The pathology report revealed vulvar intraepithelial neoplasia (VIN) grade 3 and no evidence of invasive squamous cell cancer. At the 5-o'clock portion of the specimen, there was a positive microscopic margin not suspected of representing invasion. The most appropriate next step in the care of this patient is

      (A) topical administration of 5-fluorouracil
      (B) wide local excision
  * (C) follow-up in 3–6 months
      (D) laser therapy
      (E) hemivulvectomy

After the diagnosis of VIN has been established by biopsy, therapy is performed in an attempt to eradicate the areas that contain the neoplastic changes. Histologic confirmation is necessary to distinguish VIN from condylomatous lesions. Untreated VIN grade 3 can progress to invasive squamous cell carcinoma. Invasive squamous cell carcinoma has been reported in 2–20% of excised VIN lesions. Additionally, VIN lesions can be multifocal, a finding that commonly requires treatment in several distinct and noncontiguous areas. Because VIN is often multifocal, underestimation of the extent of disease is common.

In most cases, conservative therapy involving either local excision or laser ablation is the recommended treatment. Local excision requires only a 2–3-mm margin of excision and removal of the full thickness of the skin or mucosa; because the lesions are usually sharply demarcated, a larger margin is not necessary. In vulvar Paget's disease, the histologic extent of disease can extend beyond the gross lesion.

The risk of recurrence of VIN with a positive margin can be as high as 50%. Therefore, early follow-up is warranted for this patient. It should be noted that recurrence can develop even if the resection margins are negative. Long-term follow-up is necessary for all women with VIN. Adjuvant therapy is not indicated to decrease the rate of recurrence with a microscopically positive margin.

Spontaneous regression has been reported in some women with VIN grade 2 or 3. It has been observed most commonly in young women or women whose disease was associated with pregnancy. The length of time needed for observation of an untreated patient is the subject of debate. Disease that resolves spontaneously generally does so within 6 months.

Topical 5-fluorouracil has been used to treat VIN, but it can cause significant skin reactions. It is not commonly used because of patient preference and lack of compliance due to the adverse effects of the skin excoriation.

Laser therapy to a depth of 1 mm in non–hair-bearing areas and 3 mm in hair-bearing areas is an effective modality to treat VIN lesions. Even in hair-bearing areas, it is uncommon for VIN to be more than 2.5 mm from the surface of the skin. The precision of laser vaporization can be used to treat VIN involving the clitoris, urethra, or perianal region with less risk of disfigurement or loss of function. In addition, large multifocal areas are amenable to laser therapy. The disadvantage of laser therapy is that it may not definitively treat an unrecognized cancer. Thus, before laser therapy is performed, the presence of invasive disease must be excluded. Laser therapy is not recommended as an adjuvant treatment for a patient with a positive margin.

Hemivulvectomy or wide local excision for a microscopic margin is potentially disfiguring. Reexcision in the region of the positive margin would be indicated if there were a question of invasive disease. Women who are cigarette smokers have a higher incidence of recurrence of VIN. Smoking cessation thus should be recommended to decrease the incidence of recurrence.

DiSaia PJ, Creasman WT. Clinical gynecologic oncology. 6th ed. St. Louis (MO): Mosby; 2002. p. 47–50.

Herbst AL. Neoplastic diseases of the vulva. In: Stenchever MA, Droegemueller W, Herbst AL, Mishell DR Jr, editors. Comprehensive gynecology. 4th ed. St. Louis (MO): Mosby; 2001. p. 999–1022.

Jones RW, Rowan DM. Spontaneous regression of vulvar intraepithelial neoplasia 2–3. Obstet Gynecol 2000;96:470–2.

Modesitt SC, Waters AB, Walton L, Fowler WC Jr, Van Le L. Vulvar intraepithelial neoplasia, III: occult cancer and the impact of margin status on recurrence. Obstet Gynecol 1998;92:962–6.

122

Supracervical hysterectomy and sexual functioning

A 42-year-old woman is planning to undergo hysterectomy for symptomatic uterine leiomyomata. She is concerned about the effects of hysterectomy on sexual function. You advise her that among women who undergo hysterectomy, the portion of the procedure most likely to have a negative effect on sexual function is

        (A) removal of the uterine cervix
        (B) removal of the uterine corpus
        (C) shortening of the vagina associated with hysterectomy
*   (D) associated removal of the ovaries

A number of recent studies have provided reassuring results regarding the impact of hysterectomy on sexual function. Among 1,101 women who underwent hysterectomy in 1 study, overall sexual functioning improved after surgery. Specifically, reports of dyspareunia dropped from 19% to 4%, and reports of impaired libido decreased from 10% to 6%. The percentage of women who reported that they engaged in sexual relations increased from 70% to 77%. Poor sexual function after hysterectomy is more common among women who undergo bilateral oophorectomy. Therefore, associated removal of the ovaries is the portion of the planned procedure that is most likely to have an adverse effect on sexual function.

Vaginal length and other vaginal dimensions do not predict postoperative sexual function. Among women who have undergone vaginal hysterectomy or other operations for prolapse, incontinence, or both, change in vaginal dimensions (vaginal length or caliber) has not been found to correlate with sexual function (frequency of intercourse, dyspareunia, vaginal dryness, or overall satisfaction).

Few studies have compared sexual function after total hysterectomy with supracervical hysterectomy. In a recent randomized control trial of total and supracervical hysterectomy, sexual functioning did not change between groups.

Kilkku P. Supravaginal uterine amputation vs. hysterectomy: effects on coital frequency and dyspareunia. Acta Obstet Gynecol Scand 1983;62:141–5.

Kilkku P, Gronroos M, Hirvonen T, Rauramo L. Supravaginal uterine amputation vs. hysterectomy: effects on libido and orgasm. Acta Obstet Gynecol Scand 1983;62:147–52.

Rhodes JC, Kjerulff KH, Langenberg PW, Guzinski GM. Hysterectomy and sexual functioning. JAMA 1999;282:1934–41.

Saini J, Kuczynski E, Gretz HF III, Sills ES. Supracervical hysterectomy versus total abdominal hysterectomy: perceived effects on sexual function. BMC Womens Health. 2002;2:1.

Thakar R, Ayers S, Clarkson P, Stanton S, Manyonda I. Outcomes after total versus subtotal abdominal hysterectomy. N Engl J Med 2002; 347:1318–25.

Weber AM, Walters MD, Piedmonte MR. Sexual function and vaginal anatomy in women before and after surgery for pelvic organ prolapse and urinary incontinence. Am J Obstet Gynecol 2000;182: 1610–5.

123
Müllerian abnormalities

A 14-year-old nulligravid adolescent is brought to your office because she has not begun to menstruate and is experiencing severe chronic lower abdominal pain. According to her mother, the patient underwent breast changes at age 11 years and experienced changes in pubic and axillary hair at age 12 years. For about a year and a half, she has experienced intermittent pelvic pain. The pain has regularity and is most intense between the first and tenth days of the month. The adolescent states that she has occasional bouts of feeling bloated, urinary urgency, and constipation. Her vital signs are normal, and she exhibits Tanner stage IV breast and pubic hair development. The adolescent is frightened and anxious about the pelvic examination. You observe a blue bulge from the introitus. A single-digit rectal examination reveals only fullness in the area of the vagina and pelvis; no discrete mass can be detected. Ultrasonography demonstrates a normal uterus. The next appropriate step in her treatment is to

* (A) schedule an examination under anesthesia and possible hymenotomy
  (B) order intravenous pyelography
  (C) order cystoscopy
  (D) schedule a laparoscopy

Müllerian (paramesonephric) and wolffian ducts coexist in all embryos during a totipotential period of sexual development, which lasts up to 8 weeks. After that time, 1 duct system, müllerian or wolffian, persists and gives rise to the internal genitalia. The paramesonephric ducts migrate from their lateral location to the midline and form a Y-shaped structure that is the anlage for the uterus, fallopian tubes, and upper third of the vagina. The fusion of the müllerian ducts occurs by 10 weeks of gestation. Canalization to create the cavity, cervical canal, and upper third of the vagina is complete by 20 weeks of gestation. The urogenital sinus migrating cephalad is the last structure to form, and abnormalities of this process can result in imperforate hymen. When this anomaly exists, the remainder of the tract above the blockage is usually anatomically normal but distorted by being filled with blood. The bladder is not usually involved.

Magnetic resonance imaging (MRI) is the preferred modality to study upper-tract müllerian anomalies, although neither MRI nor ultrasonography consistently provides definitive information in the presence of hematocolpos, hematometra, or hematoperitoneum. Cyclic, chronic abdominal pain in the presence of normal secondary sex characteristics and a bulge at the introitus strongly indicate the diagnosis of imperforate hymen. Although this space can contain a lot of blood, the condition develops over such a long time that the patient

almost never has symptoms of hypovolemia. Because this condition occurs late in the development of the müllerian system, the renal system is normally formed.

Surgical drainage of the site is relatively simple. A needle aspiration will remove some of the blood, but it will reaccumulate without a hymenotomy. The hymenotomy should be performed in such a way that the newly formed orifice will not scar or compromise the introitus. This condition includes the potential to develop endometriosis. Although the exact incidence and long-term sequelae of endometriosis in this clinical setting are unknown, the physician needs to discuss the situation with the parents. If the clinical severity of the imperforate hymen warrants (eg, the patient has long-term severe lower abdominal pain), laparoscopy should be considered. If endometriosis is present at the time of laparoscopy, it should be staged, and it is medically prudent to consider therapy. The long-term prognosis for patients with imperforate hymen in terms of sexual function and psychologic adjustment is excellent.

Congenital abnormalities of the female reproductive tract. In: Mishell DR Jr, Stenchever MA, Droegemueller W, Herbst AL. Comprehensive gynecology. 3rd ed. St. Louis (MO): Mosby–Year Book; 1997. p. 245–51.

Normal and abnormal sexual development. In: Speroff L, Glass RH, Kase NG. Clinical gynecologic endocrinology and infertility. 6th ed. Philadelphia (PA): Lippincott Williams & Wilkins; 1999. p. 339–47.

124

Tamoxifen citrate (Nolvadex) for breast cancer prevention

A 46-year-old white nulligravid woman who comes to your office is concerned about reducing her risk for breast cancer. Her family history reveals that her mother developed breast cancer at age 59 but is alive and well after treatment. Two first cousins on her father's side had breast cancer after age 50 years. The patient experienced menarche at age 12 years, and her menstrual cycles always have been regular. She describes her breasts as cystic and comments that breast self-examination always has been difficult. Results of yearly mammography have been normal since age 40 years. Her surgical history is significant for tubal ligation and 2 breast biopsies with benign findings. She takes no medications. The most appropriate option for this patient is

* (A) tamoxifen citrate (Nolvadex)
  (B) raloxifene hydrochloride (Evista)
  (C) prophylactic mastectomy
  (D) gonadotropin-releasing hormone (GnRH) agonists
  (E) mammography every 6 months

Tamoxifen citrate is a nonsteroidal compound with both estrogenic and antiestrogenic effects on selected tissues. The Breast Cancer Prevention Trial showed that administering tamoxifen to women at high risk for developing breast cancer was associated with a 49% reduction in the occurrence of invasive breast cancer and a 50% reduction in noninvasive disease. This study was designed as a double-blind, randomized, placebo-controlled trial to test the ability of tamoxifen to reduce the incidence of breast cancer in a high-risk population. A total of 13,388 women were randomized to receive tamoxifen or placebo for 5 years. *High risk* was defined as being older than 60 years or being aged 35–59 years with an increased risk of breast cancer of greater than 1.66% over 5 years, as predicted by the Gail model.

The Gail model is a clinically validated formula that factors in age, number of affected first-degree relatives, age at menarche, age at first live birth, number of previous breast biopsies, and the pathologic diagnosis of atypia or hyperplasia in the biopsy specimen. The model uses these variables to predict the risk for breast cancer in 5 years or life expectancy. A 5-year predicted risk of 1.66% or greater is considered high.

In the Breast Cancer Prevention Trial, women taking tamoxifen had fewer hip, spine, and radius fractures and had no increase in risk of myocardial infarction or angina. The tamoxifen group had increased risk of thromboembolic disease, endometrial cancer, and cataracts. Tamoxifen is likely to prevent estrogen receptor–positive tumors. This study was closed prior to completion because of the obvious benefit of the medication. Unfortunately, because of the early closure of the study, no survival benefit for women who received tamoxifen could be demonstrated. The U.S. Food and Drug Administration has granted approval of tamoxifen for the reduction of the risk of breast cancer in women at high risk for the disease. The medication should be taken for 5 years. This patient has a 5-year predicted breast cancer risk of 3.99%, calculated by the Gail model. Therefore, she meets the criteria for prophylaxis with tamoxifen.

Women with an intact uterus who take tamoxifen should be monitored closely for symptoms of endometrial hyperplasia or cancer and should have a gynecologic examination at least once a year. Patient education should focus on the risks of endometrial proliferation, endometrial hyperplasia, and endometrial cancer. Prompt reporting and investigation of any abnormal vaginal symptoms—eg, bloody discharge, spotting, staining, or leukorrhea—are necessary. If atypical endometrial hyperplasia develops, appropriate gynecologic management should be instituted, and the use of tamoxifen should be reassessed. If tamoxifen therapy is continued, hysterectomy should be considered in women with atypical endometrial hyperplasia. Tamoxifen use may be reinstituted after hysterectomy for endometrial carcinoma in consultation with the physician responsible for the woman's breast care.

Screening tests are not recommended for women who take tamoxifen, because they have not been effective in the early detection of endometrial cancer. Such screening tests may lead to more diagnostic and invasive procedures without any therapeutic benefit to the patient.

The selective estrogen receptor modulator raloxifene hydrochloride (Evista) is chemically related to tamoxifen. In 7,705 postmenopausal women at high risk for osteoporosis treated with 60 mg of raloxifene daily, 120 mg of raloxifene daily, or placebo, there was a significant decrease in the incidence of breast cancer in both the raloxifene groups. Because this study was not designed to monitor the reduction in the risk of breast cancer, the findings must be validated. Currently, the National Cancer Institute is recruiting patients for its prevention 2 trial of tamoxifen citrate versus raloxifene hydrochloride for the reduction in the risk of breast cancer in postmenopausal women. Although the role of raloxifene in the prevention and treatment of breast cancer is under investigation, this drug is beneficial in preservation of bone density and in prevention of osteoporosis. It is an estrogen antagonist in the breast and endometrium. A history of venous thromboembolism is a contraindication to its use.

Prophylactic mastectomy generally is recommended for women at a much greater risk than the patient described. Usually these women have a *BRCA1* or *BRCA2* mutation and a risk of developing breast cancer higher than 50%.

Screening mammography at 6-month intervals will not decrease the incidence of breast cancer. In a middle-aged patient, such as the 46-year-old woman described, screening mammography at intervals of 1–2 years is a subject of debate. Decreasing the interval to 6 months is not recommended. Similarly, the use of GnRH agonists to reduce the risk of breast cancer has not been subjected to randomized studies.

American College of Obstetricians and Gynecologists. Tamoxifen and endometrial cancer. ACOG Committee Opinion 232. Washington, DC: ACOG; 2000.

American College of Obstetricians and Gynecologists. Tamoxifen and the prevention of breast cancer in high-risk women. ACOG Committee Opinion 224. Washington, DC: ACOG; 1999.

Cummings SR, Eckert S, Krueger KA, Grady D, Powles TJ, Cauley JA, et al. The effect of raloxifene on risk of breast cancer in postmenopausal women: results from the MORE randomized trial. Multiple Outcomes of Raloxifene Evaluation. JAMA 1999;281:2189–97.

Fisher B, Constantino JP, Wickerham DL, Redmond CK, Kavanah M, Cronin WM, et al. Tamoxifen for prevention of breast cancer: report of the National Surgical Adjuvant Breast and Bowel Project P-1 Study. J Natl Cancer Inst 1998;90:1371–88.

Hartmann LC, Schaid DJ, Woods JE, Crotty TP, Myers JL, Arnold PG, et al. Efficacy of bilateral prophylactic mastectomy in women with a family history of breast cancer. N Engl J Med 1999;340:77–84.

125

Estrogen and breast cancer

A 52-year-old woman was treated 3 years ago for stage I ductal carcinoma of the breast. She previously had a hysterectomy. The tumor was estrogen- and progesterone-receptor negative. Results of a biopsy of the sentinel node were negative for metastatic disease. The patient visits your office and reports recurrent hot flushes that interfere with her sleep, and chronic vaginal dryness with mild dyspareunia. She drinks alcohol on occasion, smokes one-half package of cigarettes per week, and does not exercise. Clonidine and selective serotonin-reuptake inhibitors have not alleviated her symptoms. She takes no vitamin preparations. She is a slender woman with a body mass index of 20 kg/m². She has questions about estrogen therapy. You advise her to

     (A) obtain a dual-energy X-ray absorptiometry bone study

     (B) obtain *BRCA1* and *BRCA2* gene mutation studies

     (C) use 25-µg vaginal estradiol tablets (Vagifem)

*   (D) use short-term systemic estrogen

Although breast cancer is not the leading killer of women, it is a major cancer that many women are very worried about developing. Studies have shown that women have a much greater fear of developing breast cancer than cardiovascular disease. The 5-year survival rate for localized breast cancer has increased from 72% in the 1940s to 97% in recent decades. Of all women with breast cancer, 65% survive 10 years, and 56% survive 15 years. Many women have relatives or friends who are breast cancer survivors, which may create the impression that the disease incidence is higher than it actually is.

Some studies show that hormone therapy (HT), particularly if used for longer than 5 years, increases the relative risk of breast cancer by 25–30%. However, the majority of studies in which subjects have used estrogen therapy alone do not show an increase in relative risk of breast cancer. Many physicians are reluctant to prescribe HT to women who have had a previous diagnosis of breast cancer regardless of staging, the status of nodes, receptor information, or severity of the patients' menopausal symptoms.

In an observational study of 2,755 women aged 35–74 years who had the diagnosis of invasive breast cancer while enrolled in a large health maintenance organization, the investigators identified 174 users of HT after the diagnosis and therapy. Women in the study were recurrence-free at the time of HT initiation. Users of HT were matched to selected nonusers of similar age, disease stage, and year of diagnosis. Relative risk of breast cancer recurrence in users versus nonusers was 0.50 (95% confidence interval [CI], 0.32–0.85). The relative risk of breast cancer mortality in HT users was 0.34 (95% CI, 0.13–0.91). The investigators concluded that there were lower risks of recurrence and mortality in women who used HT after breast cancer diagnosis than in women who did not use HT. These findings have since been confirmed in other studies.

The ultimate decision whether or not a woman should receive HT after the diagnosis of breast cancer rests with a well-informed patient and her physician. The highest rate of recurrence is within the first 2 years of the diagnosis. This patient appears to be tumor-free after 3 years. The information given about her suggests that she is at risk for osteopenia, if not osteoporosis. A dual-energy X-ray absorptiometry bone study would provide information but is not the correct option.

The use of 25-µg vaginal estradiol tablets may provide symptomatic relief of dryness for this patient. This option typically would not address her hot flushes, though, because of minimal change to her blood estradiol level.

Approximately 5–10% of breast carcinomas are associated with *BRCA1* and *BRCA2* mutations; 85% of women who carry these mutations will develop breast cancer during their lifetime. Women who carry these mutations also have an increased risk of ovarian cancer: a 40–60% chance with *BRCA1* and a 15–20% chance with *BRCA2*. Although this information would be helpful for future consideration, it does not address the most immediate concern.

This patient's symptoms, lifestyle, physical findings, and 3-year posttherapy interval should give the physician sufficient confidence to prescribe short-term estrogen therapy. However, in counseling individuals, it is critical to note that studies are observational and that a prospective randomized control study is the optimum way to determine the relative risk. Finally, it is important to counsel the patient that although she may not increase her recurrence risk by using estrogen therapy, she does not escape background risk. A detailed explanation of the risks and benefits should be documented in the patient's record.

Dew J, Eden J, Beller E, Magarey C, Schwartz P, Crea P, et al. A cohort study of hormone replacement therapy given to women previously treated for breast cancer. Climacteric 1998;1:137–42.

O'Meara ES, Rossing MA, Daling JR, Elmore JG, Barlow WE, Weiss NS. Hormone replacement therapy after a diagnosis of breast cancer in relation to recurrence and mortality. J Natl Cancer Inst 2001;93:754–62.

Peters GN, Fodera T, Sabol J, Jones S, Euhus D. Estrogen replacement therapy after breast cancer: a 12-year follow-up. Ann Surg Oncol 2001; 8:828–32.

126–129

Von Willebrand's disease and other hematologic disorders at menarche

Select the best next treatment option (A–E) for each of the following patients presenting with clinical problems at menarche (126–129).

(A) Splenectomy
(B) Platelet transfusion
(C) Steroids
(D) 1-Deamino-8-D-arginine vasopressin (desmopressin acetate) (DDAVP)
(E) Intravenous conjugated estrogens

C   **126.** A 15-year-old adolescent presents with epistaxis. She has a platelet count of 40,000/μL.

B   **127.** A 12-year-old adolescent presents with menorrhagia, fatigue, pallor, and easy bruisability. Her platelet count is 175,000/μL. Her laboratory workup shows an absence of glycoprotein IIB and IIIA in the urine.

D   **128.** A 21-year-old woman presents with menometrorrhagia and mild anemia. Results of her workup for dysfunctional uterine bleeding are negative. Her platelet count is 200,000/μL. There is a family history of easy bruisability, and the use of oral contraceptives has not reduced the flow.

A   **129.** A 14-year-old adolescent presents at menarche with profuse vaginal bleeding and "tea-colored" urine. She is taking steroids and has symptoms consistent with anemia.

Von Willebrand's disease is the most common inherited bleeding disorder, affecting 3–4 persons per 100,000, or as much as 1% of the population. The disease originally was described in 1924, and it has since been understood that von Willebrand's factor (vWF) is an adhesive glycoprotein actively involved in hemostasis. Patients may present prior to puberty with epistaxis or easy bruisability. Patients with von Willebrand's disease have decreased factor VIII levels. The disease has 3 types, based on decreased quantities of vWF, factor VIII, or both. Types 1 and 3 result in bleeding secondary to reduced levels of vWF protein, whereas type 2 involves qualitative defects in platelet function. Von Willebrand's factor stabilizes and carries factor VIII in plasma, thus mediating adhesion of platelets to the subendothelium at sites of vascular injury. It binds specific platelet membrane glycoproteins and blood clotting factor VIII. Deficiency of the factor results in defects in formation of platelet plugs at the sites of vascular injury. Von Willebrand's factor is synthesized in endothelial cells and megakaryocytes (patient 128) .

The basic screening tests for patients similar to patient 128 include complete blood count, factor VIII, vWF antigen, and vWF–ristocetin cofactor activity. Table 126–129-1 provides a comparison of coagulopathies and their evaluation.

The diagnosis should be suspected in a patient presenting with mucocutaneous bleeding in the presence of a normal platelet count. Epistaxis occurs in 60% of patients, and 40% of patients have easy bruisability and hematomas; 35% have menorrhagia, 35% have gingival bleeding, and 10% have gastrointestinal bleeding.

Treatment in part depends on the subtype (types 1–3). Approximately 75% of patients respond to DDAVP, a synthetic analogue of antidiuretic hormone L-arginine vasopressin. The remaining patients do not respond to DDAVP. Other antifibrinolytic agents, such as epsilon-aminocaproic acid (Amicar), can be administered to prevent clot lysis. These agents carry an increased risk of thrombosis.

Von Willebrand's disease is transmitted in an autosomal-dominant pattern of inheritance. The human von Willebrand's gene has been localized to chromosome 12.

Glanzmann's disease, or thrombasthenia, is a primary qualitative platelet disorder (patient 127). Patients with the disease have severely dysfunctional platelets that fail to aggregate, which results in lack of clot formation. The platelet count is often normal. The molecular basis involves the absence of glycoproteins IIb and IIIa, ie, the fibrinogen receptor necessary for normal platelet aggregation. There are 2 types of Glanzmann's disease (I and II), which reflect complete or partial deficiency of the glycoprotein complex, respectively. When platelet aggregation is absent, the diagnosis is established by determining the presence or absence of glycoproteins using gel

TABLE 126–129-1. Coagulopathies: Their Diagnosis and Management

Disorder	Diagnostic Aspects	Treatment
Von Willebrand's disease	Abnormal levels of APTT, factor VIII, vWF antigen, ristocetin cofactor	DDAVP
Glanzmann's disease	Normal platelet count, abnormal findings on gel electrophoresis or flow cytometry studies	Platelet transfusion
Idiopathic thrombocytopenia	Abnormal PT and PTT, low platelet count	Steroids
Autoimmune hemolytic disorder	Anemia, dark urine	Steroids

APTT, activated partial thromboplastin time; DDAVP, 1-deamino-8-D-arginine vasopressin (desmopressin acetate); PT, prothrombin time; PTT, partial thromboplastin time; vWF, von Willebrand's factor.

electrophoresis or flow cytometry studies. Because the disease is related to platelet dysfunction, the treatment of choice is platelet transfusion.

Idiopathic thrombocytopenia results from increased platelet destruction. Microangiopathic hemolytic anemia, in addition to young, large platelets, is seen on peripheral smear. The diagnosis is suspected when the patient presents with excessive bleeding, and a coagulopathy is established based on abnormal prothrombin time, abnormal activated partial thromboplastin time, and low platelet count (patient 126). It is important that the patient not be taking aspirin products during testing. Treatment is best initiated with intravenous immune globulins and intravenous steroids. The objective of therapy is to shorten the bleeding time by increasing vascular stability and ameliorating the endothelial abnormalities associated with the platelet dysfunction. Platelet survival is increased with the steroid therapy. The exact mechanism of action of intravenous immune globulin G (IgG) is not fully understood. It is believed that the IgG occupies the Fc receptors on the reticuloendothelial cells, contributing to less platelet destruction.

Autoimmune hemolytic anemia is an erythrocyte disorder representing intracorpuscular defects. Inherited genetic mutations, as well as acquired nutritional deficiencies, lead to defects in globin chain and heme synthesis. Abnormal membrane structural proteins or defective intracellular enzymes result in abnormal blood cell function, which leads to hemolysis. Patients primarily present with signs and symptoms of anemia (pallor, weakness, and exercise intolerance or dizziness) but also may have associated abnormal uterine bleeding (patient 129). Symptoms of dark, tea-colored urine secondary to the intravascular hemolysis are noted. Fever and abdominal pain are less common presenting symptoms. Splenectomy is curative in 60–80% of patients. Compatible transfu-

sions of erythrocytes, which can withstand hemolysis, are often difficult to accomplish. Although the administration of corticosteroids and immune globulin therapy have been recommended, splenectomy is the time-honored therapy, because the spleen clears the circulatory system of abnormal red blood cells and is responsible for the ongoing red blood cell destruction. Any adolescent who presents with menorrhagia, especially at menarche, merits inclusion of bleeding diathesis in the differential diagnosis.

The administration of intravenous conjugated estrogens would not be appropriate until a diagnosis is established, and thus would not be the next best thing to do. When administered at 25 mg every 4 hours for as long as 24–36 hours, this treatment is often very useful in controlling the immediate blood loss associated with anovulation.

Dilley A, Drews C, Miller C, Lally C, Austin H, Ramaswamy D, et al. Von Willebrand disease and other inherited bleeding disorders in women with diagnosed menorrhagia. Obstet Gynecol 2001;97:630–6.

Ewenstein B. Von Willebrand's disease. Annu Rev Med 1997;48: 525–42.

Hambleton J. Advances in the treatment of von Willebrand disease. Semin Hematol 2001;38 suppl:7–10.

Lee CA. Women and inherited bleeding disorders: menstrual issues. Semin Hematol 1999;36 suppl 4:21–7.

Mohlke KL, Nichols WC, Ginsburg D. The molecular basis of von Willebrand disease. Int J Clin Lab Res 1999;29:1–7.

Nathan D, Orkin S. Hematology of infancy and childhood. 5th ed. Philadelphia (PA): WB Saunders; 1998.

Nichols WC, Ginsburg D. Von Willebrand disease. Medicine (Baltimore) 1997;76:1–20.

Sadler JE. Biochemistry and genetics of von Willebrand factor. Annu Rev Biochem 1998;67:395–424.

Templeman C, Hertweck SP, Sanfilippo J. Vaginal bleeding in childhood and menstrual disorders. In: Sanfilippo JS, Muram D, Dewhurst J, Lee P, editors. Pediatric and adolescent gynecology. Philadelphia (PA): WB Saunders; 2001. p. 237–47.

130–131
Low urethral closure pressure

For each of the following patients with urinary incontinence (130–131), select the best pharmacologic or surgical treatment modality (A–E).

(A) Oxybutynin chloride (Ditropan)
(B) Anterior colporrhaphy
(C) Burch procedure
(D) Periurethral collagen injection
(E) Sling procedure

E   **130.** A 60-year-old multiparous woman has no midline, paravaginal, or anterior vaginal wall defects. The cotton-tipped swab test strain angle is 40 degrees, the intravesical pressure is 9 cm water with 300 mL of distention with saline, the urethral closure pressure is 12 cm water, and the leak point pressure is 48 cm water. The patient has taken estrogen compliantly for 12 years and has a history of hysterectomy for myomatous uterus 15 years ago.

D   **131.** A 70-year-old multiparous woman has no midline, paravaginal, or anterior vaginal wall defects. The cotton-tipped swab test strain angle is 15 degrees, the urethral closure pressure is 10 cm water, and the leak point pressure is 40 cm water. The patient has been taking estrogen vaginal cream for 6 months and had a hysterectomy and anterior colporrhaphy 20 years ago. She was treated successfully with irradiation for vaginal cancer 7 years ago.

Both patients have intrinsic sphincter deficiency (ISD). This condition is characterized by a low urethral closure pressure (<20 cm water) and a low Valsalva leak point pressure (<60 cm water). It is important to note, however, that the use of these measurements alone to diagnose ISD is controversial. The practitioner must evaluate other historic data carefully before making a diagnosis of ISD. The literature often refers to the condition as a *pipestem urethra*. The following 2 treatments most often are cited in the literature:

1. Placement of a urethral sling at the urethrovesical junction
2. Injection of a periurethral bulking agent, usually collagen

Causes of ISD include radiation therapy to the pelvis, estrogen deficiency, infection, and previous genital tract surgery. To maintain urethral continence, coaptation and compression of the urethra must occur. Coaptation is achieved by a mucosal seal that results from the infolding of the urethra surrounded by the soft, spongy submucosal vascular plexus. Compression occurs because of the actions of the urethropelvic ligaments and the levator muscles on the mid and proximal urethra. Trauma from previous surgery or decreased vascularity from radiation therapy readily interferes with these processes.

Before patients with ISD can be treated appropriately, the condition must be diagnosed correctly. The appropriate urodynamic and urethral pressure profile measurements must be gathered after careful history compilation and physical examination. In addition, it is important to address the simple causes of incontinence (eg, the use of certain medications, estrogen deficiency, and urinary tract infection).

Incontinent patients with a hypermobile urethra (patients who have a strain angle measurement >30 degrees on a cotton-tipped swab test) and a normal urethral pressure profile benefit most from a surgical procedure to correct the anatomic defect in urethrovesical angle. The Burch or Marshall–Marchetti–Krantz procedure has been employed most often to correct this anatomic defect, and this correction is effective. Patients who have a component of ISD, however, will have higher failure rates if the procedure alone is used. The urethral sling provides the best cure rate for these more complicated patients, with a reported success rate of 90%. Unfortunately, patients who receive the sling procedure have a higher rate of postoperative voiding dysfunction, which often requires self-catheterization. One study randomized patients to Burch versus sling procedure and noted no difference in outcome with 3 months of follow-up.

Bulking agents have been used successfully to treat ISD in women with nonmobile urethras. Patients who receive collagen injections may require multiple treatments, and success rates after 1 year can be as high as 80%. Durasphere is a bulking agent approved by the

U.S. Food and Drug Administration within the last decade. It is a gel with small carbon particles suspended throughout; early studies suggest it may be effective longer than collagen. Teflon is used less today because of concerns about migration, embolization, and granuloma formation. Although ISD often is treated by the sling procedure, patients who are older, are debilitated, or have had radiation therapy probably would benefit more from a less invasive procedure. Patients who have had radiation therapy have end arteritis of arterioles, which may contribute to difficulty in healing after surgery. This condition could put the patient at risk for fistula formation or continued incontinence. The sling procedure should be considered in patients who have previously been treated with pelvic irradiation only after failure of bulking injections.

Anterior colporrhaphy has fallen out of favor as a sole procedure to treat the hypermobile urethra in urodynamic stress incontinence. It is used, however, to manage patients who have a midline anterior vaginal wall defect with cystocele, and it often is performed in conjunction with other procedures. If not carefully performed, the anterior colporrhaphy procedure can put the patient at risk for ISD because of suturing close to the urethra.

Oxybutynin chloride is an anticholinergic and smooth muscle relaxant and an excellent agent in the management of patients who have uninhibited detrusor contractions or detrusor instability. Potential adverse effects include dry mouth, constipation, drowsiness, urinary retention, and lactation suppression. Extreme caution must be exercised if the drug is to be administered to patients with glaucoma.

The management of urinary incontinence is complex. Patients should be screened and evaluated carefully. Patients who have undergone previous procedures should be considered for referral to an expert. Scores of procedures have been described to treat various forms of incontinence. The pubic bone sling and tension-free vaginal tape procedures are relatively new, are simple to perform, and have demonstrated favorable results in the treatment of intrinsic sphincter deficiency in recent trials. The tension-free vaginal tape procedure emphasizes support of the mid versus proximal urethra.

Kershen RT, Atala A. New advances in injectable therapies for the treatment of incontinence and vesicoureteral reflux. Urol Clin North Am 1999;26:viii, 81–94.

Partoll LM. Efficacy of tension-free vaginal tape with other pelvic reconstructive surgery. Am J Obstet Gynecol 2002;186:1292–5 [discussion 1295–8].

Portera JC, Summitt RL Jr. Common operations for stress incontinence: selecting the correct operation. Clin Obstet Gynecol 1998;41:712–8.

Rovner ES, Ginsberg DA, Raz S. Why anti-incontinence surgery succeeds or fails. Clin Obstet Gynecol 1998;41:719–34.

Sand PK, Winkler H, Blackhurst DW, Culligan PJ. A prospective randomized study comparing modified Burch retropubic urethropexy and suburethral sling for treatment of genuine stress incontinence with low-pressure urethra. Am J Obstet Gynecol 2000;182:30–4.

132–135

Asymptomatic infection in intrauterine device users

For each patient who is using an intrauterine device (IUD) and who has an asymptomatic infection (132–135), select the best management plan (A–E).

    (A) Remove the IUD.
    (B) Leave the IUD in place and recommend close follow-up.
    (C) Leave the IUD in place and prescribe oral sulfamethoxazole-trimethoprim (Bactrim) for 4 weeks.
    (D) Initiate oral azithromycin therapy and remove the IUD.
    (E) Leave the IUD in place and treat the patient with oral metronidazole (Flagyl).

E   **132.** A 32-year-old woman has had an IUD for 3 years, and the cervical wet mount preparation shows mobile flagellated organisms the approximate size of a white blood cell.

D   **133.** A 34-year-old patient has had an IUD for 4 years and has a cervical wet mount preparation that reveals sheets of white blood cells. The Gram stain shows gram-negative diplococci in pairs.

B   **134.** A 38-year-old woman who has had an IUD for 7 years demonstrates sulfa granules on the Pap test.

B   **135.** A 29-year-old woman who has had an IUD for 2 years is discovered to be human immunodeficiency virus (HIV) positive. All other tests for sexually transmitted diseases (STDs) are negative.

Perhaps the primary reason why IUD use is not more prevalent in the United States is because of the prior concern over risk of upper genital tract infection leading to significant morbidity and potential loss of fertility. Rates of pelvic inflammatory disease (PID) in IUD users have been estimated to be 1–2.5 per 1,000 woman–years of use. The most likely time for contracting the disease is within 20 days of insertion. It has been calculated that a patient will contract PID more often during this time than throughout the additional years of use. The administration of prophylactic antibiotics, especially in low-risk populations, has not been demonstrated to be effective. When established criteria determine that a woman has contracted PID, the device should be removed after appropriate blood levels of antibiotics have been achieved.

An additional concern with regard to IUD use is the risk of ectopic pregnancy as a result of scarring from infection. The copper-containing IUD (ParaGard T 380) has been shown to lower the ectopic pregnancy rate of users compared with the general population without IUDs. The early progesterone-secreting IUDs, however, put the patients at a 30–40% increased risk for ectopic pregnancy in comparison with the general population. The levonorgestrel-releasing IUD (Mirena) has been shown to decrease the ectopic pregnancy rate, rivaling the success of the copper device.

For most practitioners, removal of the IUD in patients with clinical endometritis is the treatment of choice. Women with asymptomatic infections pose a dilemma. It generally is recommended that the IUD be removed after initiation of treatment in patients with evidence of gonorrhea or chlamydial infection. Some small studies have shown that patients with asymptomatic infections can be treated with antibiotics with the device left in situ. Other studies have demonstrated that patients with asymptomatic gonorrhea will develop clinical endometritis soon after insertion of the device. The World Health Organization recommends removal of IUDs in patients with documented purulent cervicitis, such as patient 133.

Asymptomatic HIV-positive patients, such as patient 135, can be allowed to keep the IUD in place with careful clinical evaluation by the health care practitioner. A critical reassessment of the patient's lifestyle is necessary. The sexual partner must be considered, as the patient may transmit the virus. The addition of a barrier method (eg, the condom) should be considered strongly for this group of patients to protect both partners and patients from STDs.

Trichomoniasis is diagnosed in a patient with mobile protozoan organisms on wet preparation (patient 132). She should be educated about her STD risks; removal of the device is not necessary. Metronidazole is a proven and effective therapy. Patients who are asymptomatic and have evidence of actinomycetes on the Pap test should be managed expectantly. The diagnosis of actinomycetic infection by cytologic testing is based on the presence of sulfa granules (patient 134). Some authorities continue to recommend antibiotic treatment (eg, penicillin, doxycycline) with or without removal of the IUD. Evidence against such aggressive therapies is reflected in a study in which the diagnosis could not be confirmed by a second cytologist in almost 20% of cases. In addition, actinomycetes are indigenous in the female genital tract. When cultures are used to detect the organism in women without IUDs, as many as 27% were documented to have the organism present. Furthermore, the presence of the organism did not predict the development of pelvic actinomycosis in patients with or without an IUD. For patient 134, the best answer is to leave the device in place with no intervention. Sulfamethoxazole-trimethoprim is not the drug of choice for this organism.

Grimes DA. Intrauterine device and upper-genital-tract infection. Lancet 2000;356:1013–9.

Lippes J. Pelvic actinomycosis: a review and preliminary look at prevalence. Am J Obstet Gynecol 1999;180:265–9.

Nelson AL. The intrauterine contraceptive device. Obstet Gynecol Clin North Am 2000;27:723–40.

Sinei SK, Morrison CS, Sekadde-Kigondu C, Allen M, Kokonya D. Complications of use of intrauterine devices among HIV-1-infected women. Lancet 1998;351:1238–41.

World Health Organization. Medical eligibility criteria for contraceptive use. 2nd ed. Geneva: World Health Organization; 2000.

136–138

Pulmonary embolus, myocardial infarction, and septic shock

A 37-year-old woman with diabetes mellitus undergoes an abdominal hysterectomy. Twenty-four hours postoperatively, you are asked to see the patient for what she describes as "chest discomfort and difficulty breathing." Match the diagnosis (A–E) with each of the findings described (136–138).

(A) Pulmonary embolus
(B) Septic shock
(C) Musculoskeletal disease
(D) Pneumothorax
(E) Myocardial infarction

A **136.** The patient's breathing is shallow, and she reports chest pain that is "like a knife" and is worse during inspiration. Her pulse rate is 110 beats per minute, respirations are 18 per minute, temperature is 38°C (100.4°F), and pulse oximetry measures 80%. On physical examination, she appears anxious, is pale, and has coarse breath sounds at the lateral margin of the chest, on the right side only. The left side sounds clear.

E **137.** The patient tells you she "can't take a breath" and reports pain in the middle of her back that radiates to her left shoulder. The pain is constant. Her pulse rate is 120 beats per minute, respirations are 12 per minute, temperature is 37.6°C (99.7°F), and pulse oximetry measures 91%. On physical examination, you note tachycardia and an S3 gallop rhythm. Her chest sounds clear.

B **138.** The patient is breathing rapidly and is confused about where she is. Her pulse rate is 115 beats per minute, respirations are 16 per minute, temperature is 36.1°C (97.0°F), and pulse oximetry measures 95%. On physical examination, she appears disoriented and distressed secondary to involuntary shaking. Her skin is moist to the touch. Her lungs demonstrate bibasilar rales.

Clinicians commonly are asked to evaluate patients with symptoms such as "difficulty in breathing" and "chest discomfort." Failure to recognize potentially dangerous conditions—in particular, pulmonary embolus—may lead to serious morbidity and death (Table 136–138-1).

Chest discomfort associated with a pulmonary embolism is believed to be related to distention of the pulmonary artery or to pleuritic irritation due to infarction of an adjacent segment of lung. Pain is sharp, characteristically occurs with inspiration, and may be lateral (patient 136). Dyspnea is an associated symptom, along with palpitations and dizziness due to hypotension. Pulmonary embolism usually results from deep vein thrombosis. In general, thrombi form in the deep veins of

TABLE 136–138-1. Typical Features of Acute Chest Discomfort

Condition	Quality	Location	Associations
Acute myocardial infarction	Pressure, tightness, heaviness, burning	Radiation to arms, shoulders, left side	Dyspnea
Pulmonary embolus	Pleuritic	Lateral	Dyspnea, tachypnea, tachycardia, hypotension
Pneumothorax	Pleuritic	Lateral	Dyspnea, decreased breath sounds
Musculoskeletal disease	Aching	Variable	Worse with movement
Septic shock	Hyperventilation	Variable	Confusion, disorientation

Modified from Lee TH. Chest discomfort and palpitations. In: Braunwald E, Fauci AS, Kasper DL, Hauser SL, Longo DL, Jameson JL, editors. Harrison's principles of internal medicine. 15th ed. New York (NY): McGraw-Hill; 2001. p. 61.

the lower extremities—in particular, in the proximal veins of the iliofemoral system. In the gynecologic setting, thrombi also are commonly found in pelvic and renal veins. Depending on their size and the location from which thrombi embolize, symptoms can range from dramatic hemodynamic compromise to relatively mild dyspnea or mild pleuritic chest pain. Although not diagnostic, the history and the physical examination are extremely helpful in directing initial response (see Box 136–138-1). Patients with pulmonary embolism that is recognized and treated experience a dramatic (as high as 10-fold) reduction in mortality.

Chest symptoms associated with myocardial ischemia are visceral and described as heaviness, pressure, or squeezing (patient 137). These symptoms commonly radiate to the neck, jaw, back, or upper extremity. Patients may report dyspnea. In a woman with diabetes mellitus, symptoms of chest pain may be masked or altered by peripheral neuropathy.

With sepsis, hyperventilation may cause the patient to complain of dyspnea. Confusion, disorientation due to an acute encephalopathy, and focal neurologic signs may be present relatively early in the course of sepsis. Sepsis is also suggested by tachycardia and paradoxical hypothermia (patient 138).

A patient with no signs of obvious trauma may present with a spontaneous pneumothorax manifested by reports of chest pain and dyspnea. Absent breath sounds on the affected side suggest an initial diagnosis of pneumothorax.

Musculoskeletal disease generally is described as aching. Its location may vary. Discomfort tends to worsen with movement.

A working diagnosis will lead to the rapid initiation of possibly lifesaving therapy, but more definitive diagnosis will rely on a combination of diagnostic aids. A careful and thoughtful history and physical examination, in conjunction with observation of the patient, are prerequisites to accurate diagnosis and therapy. Appropriate laboratory and radiologic evaluations (ie, a complete blood count, tests of arterial blood gas and cardiac enzymes, chest radiography, and electrocardiography) complement the history and physical examination.

Spiral computed tomography of the chest has been demonstrated to be an excellent method for confirming

---

BOX 136–138-1

Physical Findings Suggestive of Pulmonary Embolism

- Pleuritic chest pain
- Cough
- Dyspnea
- Edema
- Fever
- Gallop rhythm
- Hemoptysis
- Phlebitis
- Pulmonary rales
- Syncope
- Tachycardia
- Tachypnea

Stein PD, Saltzman HA, Weg JG. Clinical characteristics of patients with acute pulmonary embolism. Am J Cardiol 1991;68:1724.

---

pulmonary embolism, and it is fast replacing ventilation perfusion scintigraphy in clinical application. Helical scanning allows for the visualization of both proximal and segmental emboli. Although it is expensive and requires a large volume of contrast material (with a corresponding increase in likelihood of allergic reaction), some investigators rate its use overall as comparable to pulmonary angiography, long the gold standard in the diagnosis of pulmonary embolism.

Cross JJ, Kemp PM, Walsh CG, Flower CD, Dixon AK. A randomized trial of spiral CT and ventilation perfusion scintigraphy for the diagnosis of pulmonary embolism. Clin Radiol 1998;53:177–82.

Kim KI, Muller NL, Mayo JR. Clinically suspected pulmonary embolism: utility of spiral CT. Radiology 1999;210:693–7.

Lee TH. Chest discomfort and palpitations. In: Braunwald E, Fauci AS, Kasper DL, Hauser SL, Longo DL, Jameson JL, editors. Harrison's principles of internal medicine. 15th ed. New York (NY): McGraw-Hill; 2001. p. 60–5.

Munford RS. Sepsis and septic shock. In: Braunwald E, Fauci AS, Kasper DL, Hauser SL, Longo DL, Jameson JL, editors. Harrison's principles of internal medicine. 15th ed. New York (NY): McGraw-Hill; 2001. p. 799–804.

Stein PD, Saltzman HA, Weg JG. Clinical characteristics of patients with acute pulmonary embolism. Am J Cardiol 1991;68:1723–4.

Wells JL, Salyer SW. Diagnosing pulmonary embolism: a medical masquerader. Clin Rev 2001;11:67–77.

139–141
Urethritis

For each of the following clinical scenarios (139–141), select the best treatment (A–E).

    (A) Cystoscopy with hydrodistention of the bladder
    (B) Acyclovir (Zovirax)
    (C) Urethral dilation
    (D) Azithromycin dihydrate (Zithromax)
    (E) Topical estrogen cream

D   **139.** A 25-year-old woman presents with dysuria and urinary urgency. Symptoms began 2 weeks ago and are exacerbated by intercourse. The results of 2 urine cultures have been negative. Findings of her gynecologic examination are normal, with the exception of tenderness along the anterior vaginal wall.

A   **140.** A 38-year-old woman reports having experienced urinary urgency and pelvic pain for several months. She voids frequently because of pain with bladder filling. Examination reveals no evidence of vaginitis or cervicitis. The findings of urine analysis and culture are normal.

E   **141.** A 4-year-old girl presents with painful urination and spotting of blood in her underwear. Examination reveals erythematous, friable tissue at the urethral meatus. There is no vaginal discharge or vaginal bleeding.

Many conditions can cause urinary tract pain. Acute cystitis is the most common cause of dysuria and bladder pain in young women. However, the differential diagnosis includes urethritis, urethral syndrome, urethral diverticula, interstitial cystitis, presence of foreign bodies, and other conditions.

The diagnosis of acute urethritis should be suspected if urine cultures are negative despite a history of frequency and urgency (patient 139). Urethral tenderness also suggests urethritis. A mass palpable along the anterior vaginal wall suggests a urethral diverticulum. In urethritis, urinalysis may demonstrate pyuria. If pus can be expressed from the urethra, it should be cultured for bacterial pathogens and inspected for *Trichomonas* species. In particular, the Centers for Disease Control and Prevention recommends that all patients with urethritis be evaluated for possible gonorrhea and chlamydial infection and that empiric treatment be initiated as soon as possible. Treatment options include azithromycin dihydrate and doxycycline.

Long-term symptoms of frequent voiding, urinary urgency, and pain with bladder filling suggest the diagnosis of interstitial cystitis (patient 140). Dysuria, dysmenorrhea, and dyspareunia also may be present. Diagnosis traditionally includes cystoscopy with hydrodistention, with the patient anesthetized. After an initial cystoscopic survey of the bladder, the bladder is filled to a maximum pressure of 80–100 cm water. This pressure can be achieved by hanging the fluid 80–100 cm above bladder level. Adequate distention may require occlusion of the urethra with a finger in the vagina. After distention, a second cystoscopic bladder survey typically reveals petechial hemorrhages throughout the bladder. This procedure can be therapeutic as well as diagnostic: After hydrodistention, 60% of women with interstitial cystitis achieve a remission for 4–12 months. Cystoscopic diagnosis is not always necessary before empiric treatment for interstitial cystitis, but it has the advantage of excluding other conditions (eg, urethritis, urethral diverticulum, presence of foreign bodies, and neoplasia). Empiric treatment may be appropriate when the diagnosis of interstitial cystitis is consistent with the patient's history and physical examination. Other treatment options for interstitial cystitis include administration of oral pentosan polysulfate sodium (Elmiron), bladder instillations with dimethyl sulfoxide or heparin, and transcutaneous electrical nerve stimulation.

In young girls, the differential diagnosis of premenarcheal bleeding includes precocious puberty, vulvovaginitis, urethral prolapse, trauma, foreign bodies, and vaginal tumors. An annular protrusion of erythematous tissue at the urethral meatus (patient 141) suggests the diagnosis of urethral prolapse. This condition is thought to occur most commonly in African-American girls and typically is seen before menarche. The most common symptom is contact bleeding. Voiding is not obstructed, although dysuria can occur. Initial treatment includes topical estrogen therapy several times daily for 2 weeks. In refractory cases, surgical excision is necessary.

Acyclovir (Zovirax) can be useful in the treatment of acute infection with herpes simplex. Although women with herpes simplex infection may experience urethritis, the typical presentation includes painful vulvar ulcers. The duration of acute outbreaks can be shortened with antiviral therapy, such as acyclovir, famciclovir (Famvir), or valacyclovir hydrochloride (Valtrex).

Urethral dilation has been used to treat women with urethral syndrome, defined as an idiopathic inflammatory condition of the urethra. Many such cases are now recognized to represent subclinical infections with chlamydia and other pathogens. Urethroscopy may reveal erythema and exudate. Empiric therapies recommended for treatment of urethral syndrome include various antibiotics, antispasmodics, α-blockers, and estrogen (for postmenopausal women). The role of urethral dilation has been questioned because of the absence of any clear evidence of efficacy.

Elder JS. Congenital anomalies of the genitalia. In: Walsh PC, Retik AB, Vaughan ED, Wein AJ, editors. Campbell's urology. 7th ed. Philadelphia (PA): WB Saunders; 1998. p. 2120–3.

Imai A, Horibe S, Tamaya T. Genital bleeding in premenarcheal children. Int J Gynaecol Obstet 1995;49:41–5.

Lemack GE, Foster B, Zimmern PE. Urethral dilation in women: a questionnaire-based analysis of practice patterns. Urology 1999;54:37–43.

Maher CF, Carey MP, Dwyer PL, Schluter PL. Percutaneous sacral nerve root neuromodulation for intractable interstitial cystitis. J Urol 2001;165:884–6.

Parsons CL. Interstitial cystitis. In: Ostergard DR, Bent AE, editors. Urogynecology and urodynamics. 4th ed. Baltimore (MD): Williams & Wilkins; 1996. p. 409–26.

Peeker R, Fall M. Treatment guidelines for classic and non-ulcer interstitial cystitis. Int Urogynecol J Pelvic Floor Dysfunct 2000;11:23–32.

Scotti RJ, Ostergard DR. Urethral syndrome. In: Ostergard DR, Bent AE, editors. Urogynecology and urodynamics. 4th ed. Baltimore (MD): Williams & Wilkins; 1996. p. 339–60.

Sexually transmitted diseases treatment guidelines. Centers for Disease Control and Prevention. MMWR Recomm Rep 2002;51(RR-6):1–78.

Siegel SW, Catanzaro F, Dijkema HE, Elhilali MM, Fowler CJ, Gajewski JB, et al. Long-term results of a multicenter study on sacral nerve stimulation for treatment of urinary urge incontinence, urgency-frequency, and retention. Urology 2000;56 suppl 6:87–91.

Valerie E, Gilchrist BF, Frischer J, Scriven R, Klotz DH, Ramenofsky ML. Diagnosis and treatment of urethral prolapse in children. Urology 1999;54:1082–4.

142–144

Human papillomavirus and cervical cancer

Determine the most likely human papillomavirus (HPV) genotypes (A–D) associated with each of the following clinical scenarios (142–144).

(A) HPV types 16 and 18
(B) HPV types 6 and 11
(C) HPV types 1 and 3
(D) HPV types 12 and 17

A **142.** A 23-year-old woman has a microinvasive squamous cell cervical carcinoma.

B **143.** A 19-year-old woman has vulvar condylomata acuminata and atypical squamous cells of undetermined significance detected on cervical cytologic testing.

A **144.** A 28-year-old woman is human immunodeficiency virus (HIV) positive and has persistent cervical intraepithelial neoplasia grade 3 (CIN 3) following cold knife cone biopsy with negative margins.

More than 100 different types of HPV infection have been isolated and characterized and are caused by double-stranded DNA viruses that replicate within epithelial cells. Identification of HPV subtype is based on the description of the DNA genotype. Hybridization techniques are used to type the HPV DNA. Any new HPV type must share less than 50% DNA homology with any known HPV type.

Of the numerous HPV types, more than 20 have been associated with lesions in the anogenital area. The low-risk HPV types—6, 11, 42, 43, and 44—usually are associated with benign lesions, such as condylomata. Of these HPV types, 6 and 11 are the most common. These lesions rarely progress to malignancy. Despite the separation into low- and high-risk HPV types, women may be infected simultaneously with more than 1 HPV type.

Over the past 20 years, HPV has been established as a sexually transmitted virus that may result in genital neoplasms. Autoinoculation also can occur. The virus can be shed from both microscopic and macroscopic lesions and is highly contagious; ie, 25–65% of sexual partners develop the infection. The high-risk HPV types—16, 18, 31, 33, 35, 39, 45, 51, 52, 56, and 58—are detected in intraepithelial lesions and invasive cancers. Of these HPV types, 16 and 18 are the most common. More than 85% of all cervical cancers contain high-risk HPV; most cervical adenocarcinomas in situ are associated with high-risk HPV. High-risk HPV types also have been associated with preinvasive and invasive vulvar carcinoma.

High-risk HPV infects the cervical epithelium and is found in the intraepithelial precursor lesions. Human papillomavirus DNA is epifocal, extrachromosomal, or nonintegrated. In cancers, the DNA is integrated into the human genome. All HPVs contain at least 7 early genes, $E1$–$E7$, and 2 late genes, $L1$ and $L2$.

Human papillomaviruses carry their genetic instructions within a cellular double-stranded DNA. Infections caused by these viruses generally are not systemic but result in local infections that present as gross or microscopic papillary lesions.

Multiple studies have demonstrated that HIV-infected women have a higher rate of CIN and HPV infection than women who are not immunosuppressed. The severity of CIN in HIV-positive women is related to T cell function; HIV-positive women with CIN have absolute T cell counts approximately one half those in HIV-positive women without CIN. In 1993, the Centers for Disease Control and Prevention included invasive cervical cancer as an acquired immunodeficiency syndrome–defining illness. HPV types 1, 3, 12, and 17 are not associated with anogenital infection.

DiSaia PJ, Creasman WT. Clinical gynecologic oncology. 6th ed. St. Louis (MO): Mosby; 2002. p. 5–11.

Duggan MA, Benoit JL, McGregor SE, Inoue M, Nation JG, Stuart GC. Adenocarcinoma in situ of the endocervix: human papillomavirus determination by dot blot hybridization and polymerase chain reaction amplification. Int J Gynecol Pathol 1994;13:143–9.

Schiffman MH, Bauer HM, Hoover RN, Glass AG, Cadell DM, Rush BB, et al. Epidemiologic evidence showing human papillomavirus infection causes most cervical intraepithelial neoplasia. J Natl Cancer Inst 1993;85:958–64.

Schiffman MH, Brinton LA. The epidemiology of cervical carcinogenesis. Cancer 1995;76:1888–1901.

Sun XW, Ellerbrock TV, Lungu O, Chiasson MA, Bush TJ, Wright TC Jr. Human papillomavirus infection in human immunodeficiency virus-seropositive women. Obstet Gynecol 1995;85:680–6.

Trimble CL, Diener-West M, Wilkinson EJ, Zaino RJ, Kurman RJ, Shah KV, et al. Reproducibility of the histopathological classification of vulvar squamous carcinoma and intraepithelial neoplasia. J Lower Genital Tract Dis 1999;3:98–103.

145–146
Selection of intrauterine device

For the following sexually active women who desire long-term contraception, have negative results on a pregnancy test, and are at low risk for pelvic inflammatory disease (PID) (145–146), select the best management option (A–E).

    (A) The copper-containing intrauterine device (ParaGard T 380)
    (B) The levonorgestrel-releasing intrauterine device (Mirena)
    (C) Tubal sterilization
    (D) Combined oral contraceptives

A   **145.** A 38-year-old woman, para 2, aborta 2, had unprotected intercourse on vacation 4 days ago. Her periods are normal and regular.

B   **146.** A 36-year-old woman, para 3, aborta 3, has anemia from chronic menstrual blood loss. She smokes 20 cigarettes a day and had PID 5 years ago. She has become dissatisfied with the use of condoms and spermicides.

The intrauterine device (IUD) is used for contraception by less than 1% of women in the United States. Although the IUD is characterized as having the highest level of user satisfaction of any contraceptive used by women, it continues to be grossly underused. If used for more than 2 years, it is more economical than oral contraceptives and certainly more economical than tubal sterilization. The IUD has 2 major advantages: It is reversible, and it is effective. Two types are offered in the United States: the copper IUD, available since 1984, and the levonorgestrel-releasing IUD, available since 2000. Failure rates for the copper IUD are 0.8% at 1 year and 2.1–2.8% at 10 years; failure rates for the levonorgestrel IUD are 0.1% at 1 year and 0.7% at 5 years. These failure rates may be compared to those of tubal sterilization, which has a failure rate of 0.8–3.7% at 10 years, depending on the method used.

The IUD is not an abortifacient when used for standard contraception. It acts mainly by exerting adverse effects on sperm. The IUD initiates a sterile foreign body reaction in the uterine cavity, which causes cellular and biochemical changes leading to toxicity to sperm. Women who use IUDs have lower sperm concentration in the uterine cavity after intercourse than women who do not use IUDs. Users of IUDs also have lower fertilization rates, as determined by human chorionic gonadotropin levels. Additionally, users of the copper IUD have lower rates of normally dividing fertilized ova that reach the uterine cavity. The levonorgestrel IUD also acts by making the cervical mucus thick and hostile to sperm because of the release of 20 µg of levonorgestrel per day.

The major concern for IUD users has been PID. Studies before 1980 were potentially flawed because of inaccurate diagnosis of PID and the failure to recognize

and adjust for confounders. Since 1980, it has been recognized that most infections result from insertion through a naturally contaminated vagina. Another finding is that there was little chance of PID among IUD users with no risk factors (ie, no recent endometritis, multiple sex partners, or cervicitis). The PID rate among IUD users has decreased over the years.

The copper IUD has the advantage of approval for a 10-year period. Cramping and bleeding occur more often with this device than with the levonorgestrel IUD. Use of the copper IUD is contraindicated in women with Wilson's disease because of the copper content. A major benefit of this device is its proven off-label use as an emergency contraceptive device, especially for women who want continued long-term contraception. It can be placed 5 days after intercourse at any time in the cycle.

The levonorgestrel IUD is approved for 5 years of use. The major advantages are decreased menstrual flow and improvement of dysmenorrhea. Some patients experience headaches, acne, mastalgia, or amenorrhea; these adverse effects occur in 20% of patients by 1 year of use and in 60% by 5 years. Amenorrhea is a major reason for discontinuing use of the device.

Off-label noncontraceptive uses of the levonorgestrel IUD include management of menorrhagia, treatment of dysmenorrhea, and use for hormone therapy. Women who use this IUD in the menopausal years experience decreased spotting, if it was a problem when using progesterone-containing oral hormone regimens. The levonorgestrel IUD also is used by patients who have been prescribed tamoxifen therapy, because it decreases the likelihood of the development of endometrial neoplasia. Nonmedicated IUDs (eg, the copper IUD) have demonstrated, through case–control studies, the ability to protect against endometrial cancer. Whether this protection is due to interference of a localized response to hormones or to the establishment of an inflammatory reaction hostile to cancer is unknown. It is also not clear whether the levonorgestrel IUD provides better protection against PID than the copper IUD. The mechanism of action may be thickened mucus or decreased menstrual blood flow.

Tubal sterilization would not be a good choice for patient 145 because she is already at risk for pregnancy. Furthermore, tubal sterilization would offer patient 146 no relief from menorrhagia or protection from endometrial cancer. The use of combined oral contraceptives is contraindicated for patient 146 because she is a smoker and for patient 145 because she is at risk for pregnancy. Serial use of emergency contraception is not as effective as routine use of combined oral contraceptives, an IUD, or tubal sterilization. Practitioners also must remember

that although the IUD is superb at preventing pregnancy, it offers no substantial protection against sexually transmitted diseases.

Burkman RT. Intrauterine devices and pelvic inflammatory disease: evolving perspectives on the data. Obstet Gynecol Surv 1996;51: 35S–41S.

Dardano KL, Burkman RT. The intrauterine contraceptive device: an often-forgotten and maligned method of contraception. Am J Obstet Gynecol 1999;181:1–5.

Hatcher RA, Nelson AL, Zieman M, Darney PD, Creinin MD, Stosur HR, et al. A pocket guide to managing contraception. Tiger (GA): Bridging the Gap Foundation; 2002. p. 77–86, 134.

Hubacher D, Grimes DA. Noncontraceptive health benefits of intrauterine devices: a systematic review. Obstet Gynecol Surv 2002; 57:120–8.

Rivera R, Yacobson I, Grimes D. The mechanism of action of hormonal contraceptives and intrauterine contraceptive devices. Am J Obstet Gynecol 1999;181:1263–9.

147–150
Pediatric vulvovaginitis

For each pediatric patient whose history and physical findings suggest a diagnosis of vulvovaginitis (147–150), select the most appropriate therapy (A–F).

(A) Ceftriaxone sodium (Rocephin)
(B) Removal of foreign body
(C) Trimethoprim sulfamethoxazole
(D) Clotrimazole cream
(E) Observation
(F) Mebendazole (Vermox)

C   **147.** A 4-year-old girl who recently returned from a trip to Central America presents with a 2-week history of a purulent bloody vaginal discharge. Examination reveals nonspecific erythema of the vulvovaginal epithelium and absence of a foreign body.

E   **148.** A 10-year-old girl presents with a 2-month history of a white, watery discharge that keeps her vulva moist. There is no associated odor or pruritus. Examination reveals Tanner stage III breast and stage II pubic hair development. Findings of a wet mount are negative for fungal elements or clue cells.

D   **149.** A 9-month-old infant presents with a 3-week history of vulvar irritation. In the past 2 months, she has had recurrent otitis media requiring antibiotic therapy. Examination of the vulva reveals diffuse erythema extending from the labia to the mons, with satellite lesions of erythema along the periphery of the diaper area.

F   **150.** A 5-year-old girl presents with a 1-week history of vulvar and perianal pruritus. Two older siblings, aged 8 and 9 years, also have recently reported perianal pruritus. Examination reveals nonspecific erythema of the vestibular and perianal areas, along with scant mucoid vaginal discharge. Findings of a wet mount are negative for fungal elements.

Vulvovaginitis, the most common gynecologic disorder in the pediatric age group, is seen most frequently in children aged 2–7 years. Physiologic and behavioral factors increase susceptibility to vulvar infections in children. The prepubertal vulva and vagina are exposed to bacterial contamination more frequently in children than in adults. The hypoestrogenic vagina lacks glycogen and lactobacilli, creating a neutral pH that favors the growth of various pathogens. The child's vulva lacks protective fatty tissue and pubic hair, and when a child squats, the lower third of the vagina is unprotected and open. The close proximity of the vagina to the anus, in combination with poor hygiene, increases the likelihood of infection.

The classic symptoms of vulvovaginitis—introital erythema, pruritus, and vaginal discharge—vary from child to child but cause great concern for parents. The quantity of discharge may vary from minimal to copious; the color ranges from white or gray to yellow or green. Other symptoms may include pruritus, pain, and sometimes dysuria. Typically, vulvovaginitis in children involves irritation of the vulva with secondary involvement of the

lower third of the vagina. Vulvovaginitis caused by a foreign body in the vagina usually is associated with a malodorous, purulent, and frequently blood-stained discharge. In such cases, removal of the foreign body is the definitive treatment.

Nonspecific vulvovaginitis accounts for up to 75% of pediatric cases. Cultures typically yield normal flora (eg, lactobacilli, diphtheroids, *Staphylococcus epidermidis*, or alpha streptococci) or gram-negative enteric organisms (usually *Escherichia coli*), and a wet mount shows many white blood cells. Young children with nonspecific vulvovaginitis commonly have symptoms of itching and vulvar erythema for months or years before a gynecologic visit.

Shigellae are an uncommon cause of pediatric vulvovaginitis and are commonly associated with a persistent bloody, purulent vaginal discharge. There is generally no evidence of an intravaginal foreign body that is resistant to topical therapies. Although the cause is usually ingestion of contaminated food or water, many, if not most, cases are not associated with a recent history of diarrhea. Vulvovaginitis associated with *Shigella* species, as in patient 147, is treated with trimethoprim sulfamethoxazole. Ceftriaxone sodium is indicated in the treatment of vulvovaginitis associated with organisms susceptible to a broad-spectrum cephalosporin, but its clinical effectiveness in the treatment of vulvovaginitis caused by *Shigella* species is unknown and, therefore, is not the most appropriate treatment for this condition. Other causes of an odorless bloody discharge may be vulvar irritation (eg, from scratching or masturbation), trauma, precocious puberty, condyloma acuminatum, or, rarely, a tumor (eg, sarcoma botryoides).

Patient 148 has a nonpruritic, nonodorous, white, watery discharge; no fungal elements or clue cells in a wet mount preparation; and evidence of breast and pubic hair development. Thus, this preadolescent exhibits normal physiologic vaginal discharge secondary to estrogenic stimulation. The most appropriate management is observation.

In patient 149, diffuse vulvar erythema with satellite erythematous lesions in the periphery of the diaper area is typical of candidal infection, which may follow antibiotic therapy. The most appropriate treatment in this case is clotrimazole cream.

The differential diagnosis of persistent or recurrent vulvovaginitis includes pinworms, vulvar skin disease, ectopic ureter, and child abuse. In patient 150, whose predominant symptom is vulvar and perianal pruritus, the most likely diagnosis is infection with *Enterobius vermicularis*, especially if siblings have similar symptoms. A single dose of mebendazole is effective therapy.

Emans SJ, Laufer MR, Goldstein DP. Pediatric and adolescent gynecology. 4th ed. Philadelphia (PA): Lippincott–Raven; 1998. p. 75–90.

Koumantakis EE, Hassan EA, Deligeoroglou EK, Creatsas GK. Vulvovaginitis during childhood and adolescence. J Pediatr Adolesc Gynecol 1997;10:39–43.

151–154

Pharmacologic therapy for breast cancer

For each of the following patients (151–154), select the most appropriate pharmacologic therapy (A–D).

(A) Raloxifene hydrochloride (Evista)
(B) Alendronate sodium (Fosamax)
(C) Conjugated equine estrogens and medroxyprogesterone acetate
(D) Conjugated equine estrogens

C **151.** A 55-year-old thin white woman who has been amenorrheic for 2 years presents with marked hot flushes, night sweats, and vaginal dryness.

B **152.** A 65-year-old white woman who weighs 45.5 kg (100 lb) and is 1.5 m (5 ft) tall underwent a 4-vessel bypass last year and has confirmed osteoporosis of the spine.

A **153.** A surgically menopausal 42-year-old white woman has osteoporosis of the spine confirmed by dual-energy X-ray absorptiometry (DEXA). Her mother had osteoporosis and breast cancer at age 49 years. The patient is not troubled by menstrual symptoms.

D **154.** A 55-year-old woman with menopausal symptoms had a vaginal hysterectomy and has been taking 500 mg calcium 3 times a day with 800 IU vitamin D per day. A DEXA scan shows osteopenia in both the spine and the hip.

Hormone therapy (HT) or estrogen therapy (ET) will control hot flushes, night sweats, and other symptoms of menopausal women. Patient 151 apparently has an intact uterus. Therefore, combined HT is appropriate using conjugated equine estrogens and medroxyprogesterone acetate. The patient's major symptoms would not be relieved by either raloxifene hydrochloride or alendronate sodium. The addition of vaginal estrogen would be appropriate for this patient if HT does not relieve vaginal dryness.

Patient 152 has a history of cardiovascular disease and osteoporosis and is not a candidate for either HT or raloxifene hydrochloride. Evidence does not support the use of HT for reduction of cardiovascular risk in this patient with known cardiovascular disease. Venous thromboembolism occurs in 10–40 of 10,000 adults annually. The risk is elevated in patients with a previous history of thromboembolism, recent surgical procedures, immobilization, cancer, lower extremity fracture, or inherited coagulation disorder. Patient 152, therefore, would benefit from alendronate sodium. Postmenopausal women who take alendronate have demonstrated significant increase in bone mass. Alendronate has no known effect on the lipid profile, coronary artery endothelium, or reactivity. Statin therapy may be added if indicated.

Patient 153 most likely would benefit from raloxifene hydrochloride therapy. It has been demonstrated that raloxifene is an appropriate therapy for osteoporosis of the spine. Studies of raloxifene in the fourth year of the Multiple Outcomes of Raloxifene Evaluation (MORE) trial have shown a significant reduction in breast cancer. Use of raloxifene resulted in a 62% decrease in the incidence of breast cancer and a 72% decrease in the risk of invasive breast cancer compared with placebo. Most of the decrease resulted from an 84% decrease in estrogen receptor–positive breast cancer in the raloxifene group. Raloxifene had no effect on estrogen receptor–negative breast cancer or noninvasive breast cancer. The data suggest that selective estrogen receptor modulators such as raloxifene bind to estrogen receptors in the breast competitively to inhibit estrogen-induced DNA transcription. Raloxifene does not appear to increase breast pain or mammographic density compared with ET alone or HT. In contrast to estrogen and tamoxifen, raloxifene was not associated with an increase in endometrial cancer or vaginal bleeding. Raloxifene is not approved by the U.S. Food and Drug Administration (FDA) for the prevention of breast cancer in high-risk women, but it is approved for treatment and prevention of osteoporosis.

Patient 154 has undergone hysterectomy and has menopausal symptoms. Therefore, ET consisting of conjugated equine estrogens would be appropriate for her. Effects of ET alone on the lipid profile are better than the effects of HT. Adequate calcium and vitamin D intake is essential for bone mineral maintenance and should be continued.

Boss SM, Huster WJ, Neild JA, Glant MD, Eisenhut CC, Draper MW. Effects of raloxifene hydrochloride on the endometrium of postmenopausal women. Am J Obstet Gynecol 1997;177:1458–64.

Cauley JA, Norton L, Lippman ME, Eckert S, Krueger KA, Purdie DW, et al. Continued breast cancer risk reduction in postmenopausal women treated with raloxifene: 4-year results from the MORE trial. Multiple Outcomes of Raloxifene Evaluation. Breast Cancer Res Treat 2001; 65:125–34.

Davies GC, Huster WJ, Lu Y, Plouffe L Jr, Lakshmanan M. Adverse events reported by postmenopausal women in controlled trials with raloxifene. Obstet Gynecol 1999;93:558–65.

Delmas PD, Bjarnason NH, Mitlak BH, Ravoux AC, Shah AS, Huster WJ, et al. Effects of raloxifene on bone mineral density, serum cholesterol concentrations, and uterine endometrium in postmenopausal women. N Engl J Med 1997;337:1641–7.

Grady D, Herrington D, Bittner V, Blumenthal R, Davidson M, Hlatky M, et al. Cardiovascular disease outcomes during 6.8 years of hormone therapy: Heart and Estrogen/Progestin Replacement Study follow-up (HERS II). JAMA 2002;288:49–57.

Grady D, Wenger NK, Herrington D, Khan S, Furberg C, Hunninghake D, et al. Postmenopausal hormone therapy increases risk for venous thromboembolic disease. The Heart and Estrogen/Progestin Replacement Study. Ann Intern Med 2000;132:689–96.

Hulley S, Grady D, Bush T, Furberg C, Herrington D, Riggs B, et al. Randomized trial of estrogen plus progestin for secondary prevention of coronary heart disease in postmenopausal women. Heart and Estrogen/Progestin Replacement Study (HERS) Research Group. JAMA 1998;280:605–13.

155–158

Prophylaxis for human immunodeficiency virus

Each of the following clinical scenarios involves a health care practitioner (155–158) who recently tested seronegative for human immunodeficiency virus (HIV) and who now is exposed to body fluids from patients. Select the best management plan (A–F) for each health care practitioner.

> (A) Educate the health care practitioner about universal precautions only.
> (B) Immediately initiate nevirapine (NVP, Viramune) therapy for 3 days.
> (C) Immediately initiate zidovudine (ZDV, Retrovir, AZT) therapy for 3 days.
> (D) Immediately initiate zidovudine therapy for 4 weeks.
> (E) Immediately initiate lamivudine (Epivir, 3TC) and zidovudine therapy for 4 weeks.
> (F) Immediately initiate lamivudine, zidovudine, and indinavir sulfate (IDV, Crixivan) therapy for 4 weeks.

A **155.** A health care practitioner has urine and fecal material splashed in his eyes during examination of an HIV-positive patient with uterine prolapse. He flushes his eyes with water within 40 seconds.

F **156.** A health care practitioner receives a solid-needle injury to the index finger while performing a subcuticular skin closure on an HIV-positive patient with cervical cancer.

F **157.** A health care practitioner is injured with a 16-gauge butterfly needle removed from an HIV-positive patient who has completed intravenous antibiotic therapy.

E **158.** A health care practitioner who is "HIV phobic" is injured with a suture needle while repairing a laceration of an immigrant patient in the emergency department of a big-city hospital. The patient's HIV status is unknown, she refuses an HIV test, and she leaves the area against medical advice.

Health care facilities should and must provide avenues for counseling health care practitioners after HIV exposure. Following recommendations from the U.S. Public Health Service in 1987, universal precautions have been instituted as the first line of defense for the prevention of HIV and other bloodborne infections in health care practitioners. In accordance with these guidelines, all patients are assumed to be infectious. Precautions involve the use of protective barriers such as gloves, gowns, aprons, masks, and protective eyewear. Health care practitioners also should be careful to avoid injuries by needles, scalpels, and other sharp instruments. In addition, health care practitioners with weeping dermatitis or exudative skin lesions should avoid direct patient care.

The precautions are instituted when health care practitioners work with patients' tissue, blood, or body fluids contaminated with blood. Other body fluids for which universal precautions should be instituted are semen, vaginal fluid, peritoneal fluid, amniotic fluid, and pleural fluid. Universal precautions do not apply to saliva, feces, urine, vomitus, sweat, or nasal secretions. Therefore, the health care practitioner does not have to wear a gown when assessing a patient in a routine prenatal checkup. Similarly, health care practitioner 155, who was splashed with fecal matter and urine, does not need postexposure prophylaxis (PEP) to HIV, because the viral load in these fluids is essentially nonexistent. Thus, for this health care professional, education about universal precautions will be sufficient. Exposed areas, including areas with needlestick injuries, should be washed or irrigated.

Health care personnel exposed to HIV-infected blood should consider prophylaxis, which ideally is initiated within 36 hours of the exposure. Animal studies have demonstrated that therapy started immediately is much more effective. However, exposed individuals who present after 36 hours nevertheless should be assessed for treatment. The actual risk of contracting an HIV infection after exposure is determined by the volume of contaminant, the viral load of the source patient, whether deep injury occurred, and whether there was direct injection into a blood vessel. The overall risk for HIV seroconversion after a needlestick during surgery is approximately 0.3%.

Agents used for PEP are divided into 3 classes:

- Nucleoside reverse transcriptase inhibitors
- Nonnucleoside reverse transcriptase inhibitors
- Protease inhibitors (see Table 155–158-1)

Because combination regimens have proved superior to monotherapy regimens in reducing viral loads in HIV-infected patients, combination regimens are used in PEP.

TABLE 155–158-1. Primary Adverse Effects Associated With Antiretroviral Agents

Agent	Primary Adverse Effects and Toxicities
Nucleoside Reverse Transcriptase Inhibitors	
Zidovudine (Retrovir)	Anemia, neutropenia, nausea, headache, insomnia, muscle pain, and weakness
Lamivudine (Epivir)	Abdominal pain, nausea, diarrhea, rash, and pancreatitis
Stavudine (Zerit)	Peripheral neuropathy, headache, diarrhea, nausea, insomnia, anorexia, pancreatitis, increased LFT levels, anemia, and neutropenia
Didanosine (Videx)	Pancreatitis, lactic acidosis, neuropathy, diarrhea, abdominal pain, and nausea
Abacavir (Ziagen)	Nausea, diarrhea, anorexia, abdominal pain, fatigue, headache, insomnia, and hypersensitivity reactions
Nonnucleoside Reverse Transcriptase Inhibitors	
Nevirapine (Viramune)	Rash (including cases of Stevens-Johnson syndrome), fever, nausea, headache, hepatitis, and increased LFT levels
Delavirdine (Rescriptor)	Rash (including cases of Stevens-Johnson syndrome), fever, nausea, diarrhea, headache, fatigue, and increased LFT levels
Efavirenz (Sustiva)	Rash (including cases of Stevens-Johnson syndrome), insomnia, somnolence, dizziness, trouble concentrating, and abnormal dreaming
Protease Inhibitors	
Indinavir (Crixivan)	Nausea, abdominal pain, nephrolithiasis, and indirect hyperbilirubinemia
Nelfinavir (Viracept)	Diarrhea, nausea, abdominal pain, weakness, and rash
Ritonavir (Novir)	Weakness, diarrhea, nausea, circumoral paresthesia, taste alteration, and increased cholesterol and triglyceride levels
Saquinavir (Fortovase)	Diarrhea, abdominal pain, nausea, hyperglycemia, and increased LFT levels
Amprenavir (Agenerase)	Nausea, diarrhea, rash, circumoral paresthesia, taste alteration, and depression
Lopinavir/ritonavir (Kaletra)	Diarrhea, fatigue, headache, nausea, and increased cholesterol and triglyceride levels

LFT, lung function test.

Modified from Centers for Disease Control and Prevention. Updated U.S. Public Health Service guidelines for the management of occupational exposure to HBV, HCV and HIV and recommendations for postexposure prophylaxis. Centers for Disease Control and Prevention. MMWR Recomm Rep 2001;50(RR-11):13.

A 2-drug regimen is used most often, because a 3-drug regimen may be too toxic to merit use after most exposures. Table 155–158-2 shows the recommended PEP after percutaneous injuries. If PEP is initiated and the source is determined later to be seronegative, the therapy can be stopped. The basic PEP regimen generally consists of using 2 nucleoside analogues in several different combinations. The prophylaxis therapy should last for 4 weeks. Monotherapy is no longer recommended.

Health care practitioner 158, who sustained a solid-needle injury while working with a patient of unknown status, can be followed with no PEP or can receive PEP if the source is thought to be at risk for HIV (as is the case for health care practitioner 156). The decision to offer PEP should be based on open and candid conversation between the person exposed and the treating physician. Because health care practitioner 158 was exposed to a patient potentially at risk for HIV who refused HIV testing and the practitioner is concerned about contracting HIV, the best course of action is the basic regimen.

A patient who is HIV positive and has cervical cancer is defined as having acquired immunodeficiency syndrome (AIDS). Because in the case of health care practitioner 156 the patient has AIDS by definition and is HIV-positive, class 2, the 3-drug PEP should be initiated (Table 155–158-2). The regimen usually is defined as the basic 2-drug regimen plus a third drug (eg, lamivudine and zidovudine, plus indinavir) for 4 weeks. Nevirapine is used rarely, if ever, in a PEP regimen because of its potential adverse effects, such as hepatotoxicity, a rash that is difficult to distinguish from Stevens-Johnson syndrome, and acute seroconversion. Health care practitioner 157 is injured with a large-bore hollow needle. In this setting, the 3-drug regimen also is recommended (Table 155–158-2).

Therapy and counseling are best conducted by a team led by an infectious disease consultant. The management can be complex and subject to change, and the adverse effects of the drugs are not negligible. After PEP is administered, follow-up HIV titers should be obtained at

TABLE 155–158-2. Recommended Human Immunodeficiency Virus Postexposure Prophylaxis for Percutaneous Injuries

| Exposure Type | Source Infection Status | | | | |
	HIV-Positive, Class 1*	HIV-Positive, Class 2*	Unknown HIV Status[†]	Unknown Source[‡]	HIV-Negative
Less severe[§]	Recommend basic 2-drug PEP	Recommend expanded 3-drug PEP	Generally, no PEP warranted;however, consider basic 2-drug PEP[‖] if source has HIV risk factors[¶]	Generally, no PEP warranted; however, consider basic 2-drug PEP[‖] in settings where exposure to HIV-infected persons is likely	No PEP warranted
More severe[#]	Recommend expanded 3-drug PEP	Recommend expanded 3-drug PEP	Generally, no PEP warranted; consider basic 2-drug PEP[‖] if source has HIV risk factors[¶]	Generally, no PEP warranted; however, consider 2-drug PEP[‖] in settings where exposure to HIV-infected persons is likely	No PEP warranted

HIV, human immunodeficiency virus; PEP, postexposure prophylaxis.

* HIV-positive, class 1: asymptomatic HIV infection or known low viral load (eg, <1,500 RNA copies/mL). HIV-positive, class 2: symptomatic HIV infection, acquired immunodeficiency syndrome, acute seroconversion, or known high viral load. If drug resistance is a concern, obtain expert consultation. Initiation of PEP should not be delayed pending expert consultation, and because expert consultation alone cannot substitute for face-to-face counseling, resources should be available to provide immediate evaluation and follow-up care for all exposed individuals.

[†] Eg, deceased source person with no samples available for HIV testing.

[‡] Eg, a needle from a sharps disposal container.

[§] Eg, a solid needle and superficial injury.

[‖] The designation "consider PEP" indicates that PEP is optional and should be based on an individualized decision between the exposed person and the treating clinician.

[¶] If PEP is offered and taken and the source is later determined to be HIV negative, PEP should be discontinued.

[#] Eg, a large-bore hollow needle, deep puncture, visible blood on the device, or needle used in the patient's artery or vein.

Modified from Centers for Disease Control and Prevention. Updated U.S. Public Health Service guidelines for the management of occupational exposure to HBV, HCV and HIV and recommendations for postexposure prophylaxis. Centers for Disease Control and Prevention. MMWR Recomm Rep 2001;50(RR-11):24.

6 weeks and at 3, 6, and 12 months if the source is HIV positive or of unknown status. If the hepatitis B and C serologic status of the source patient is unknown, consent should be obtained to assess it.

Bender BS, Bender JS. Surgical issues in the management of the HIV-infected patient. Surg Clin North Am 1993;73:373–88.

Centers for Disease Control and Prevention. Updated U.S. Public Health Service guidelines for the management of occupational exposure to HBV, HCV and HIV and recommendations for postexposure prophylaxis. Centers for Disease Control and Prevention. MMWR Recomm Rep 2001;50(RR-11):1–52.

Flum DR, Wallack MK. The surgeon's database for AIDS: a collective review. J Am Coll Surg 1997;184:403–12.

Patterson JM, Novak CB, Mackinnon SE, Patterson GA. Surgeons' concern and practices of protection against bloodborne pathogens. Ann Surg 1998;228:266–72.

Update: universal precautions for prevention of transmission of HIV and other bloodborne pathogens in health care settings. MMWR Morb Mortal Wkly Rep 1988;37:377–82, 387–8.

159–163
Cervical cancer screening

For each of the following clinical scenarios (159–163), in which all the patients are normal and healthy without symptoms unless otherwise specified, match the appropriate next step in management (A–H).

(A) Perform a Pap test at this visit
(B) Perform a Pap test in 4–6 months
(C) Perform a Pap test in 1 year
(D) Perform a Pap test in 2–3 years
(E) No further need for a Pap test at this or future visits
(F) Perform colposcopy at this visit
(G) Schedule a diagnostic excisional procedure
(H) Schedule a hysterectomy

C **159.** A 19-year-old woman presents for contraceptive counseling and annual testing for sexually transmitted diseases. Her first vaginal intercourse was at age 17 years. She has never had a Pap test.

G **160.** A 34-year-old woman had Pap test findings 4 weeks ago of cervical atypical glandular cells (AGC), favor neoplasia. The results of colposcopy 2 weeks ago were satisfactory, endocervical curettage had normal findings, and cervical biopsy revealed mild cervicitis. The patient is undergoing infertility evaluation.

B **161.** A 32-year-old woman had findings of cervical AGC not otherwise specified (NOS) on a Pap test 3 weeks ago. The colposcopy examination was unsatisfactory (unable to visualize the new squamocolumnar junction completely), findings of the endocervical curettage were normal with the presence of endocervical glands, and findings of ectocervical biopsies were normal.

A **162.** A 71-year-old woman, gravida 2, para 2, who had normal findings on 4 consecutive Pap tests, is taking prednisone for sarcoidosis. Her performance status is good (Karnofsky rating scale 90), and her last conventional Pap test 1 year ago had normal findings.

E **163.** A 48-year-old woman, gravida 3, para 2, aborta 2, had a vaginal hysterectomy for prolapse 1 year ago. Cervical pathology testing revealed cervicitis. Findings of her Pap tests over the past 10 years have been normal.

Two major guidelines have been published concerning cervical cancer screening. The American Society for Colposcopy and Cervical Pathology (ASCCP) sponsored a consensus conference in 2001 that led to the development of guidelines for the management of cases with abnormal findings on Pap tests. The American Cancer Society published guidelines in November 2002 to aid health care practitioners in decisions about the initiation, frequency, and duration of Pap test screening. These guidelines were developed with input from the American College of Obstetricians and Gynecologists and the Society of Gynecologic Oncologists.

One of the changes in the new guidelines concerned when to initiate Pap tests. Screening should begin no later than age 21 or 3 years after the initiation of intercourse, whichever is first in normal, healthy women (patient 159). The rationale was the extremely low incidence of cervical cancer in women younger than 20 years (0 per 100,000 at age 10–14 years, 0 per 100,000 at age 15–19 years, and 1.7 per 100,000 at age 20–24 years for the years 1995–1999). In addition, the regression rates of human papillomavirus infection are 70% for high-risk types and 90% for low-risk types in patients aged 13–22 years.

The screening interval after the initial screen should be every year by conventional cytology or every other year by liquid-based cytology. If a patient has normal findings on 3 consecutive Pap tests, then at age 30 the tests can be spaced to every 2–3 years unless the patient has certain risk factors, such as immunosuppression therapy, diethyl-stilbestrol (DES) exposure, chemotherapy, or positive human immunodeficiency virus status. At age 70 years, with 3 normal Pap test findings and no abnormal test findings in the previous 10 years of screening, Pap testing may be discontinued except in patients at risk, such as patient 162. If a patient older than 70 years has not been screened, the practitioner should try to ensure that she undergoes screening. Patients with a history of cervical cancer should be followed by practitioners who specialize in this disease. Cervical cancer usually is seen only in older women who have not been screened.

Screening of women who have had a total hysterectomy for benign disease, including no cervical intraepithelial neoplasia (CIN), is not indicated if previous Pap test screening findings have been normal (patient 163). If there is a previous history of CIN on the hysterectomy specimen, screening may be discontinued after 3 consecutive negative test results.

The new ASCCP guidelines (Appendix 2) clarify the management of cases with Pap tests with abnormal glandular appearance. Patients with findings of AGC, favor neoplasia, on a Pap test will need a diagnostic excisional procedure to evaluate the cervix, preferably cold knife conization if the colposcopically directed biopsies are discrepant (patient 160). For younger patients, the Pap test finding should be reviewed before proceeding with conization. If the Pap test finding is AGC NOS and findings of colposcopic biopsies are normal, the patient should have a repeat Pap test in 4–6 months (patient 161). Any patient with abnormal uterine bleeding and findings of AGC on a Pap test will need to be evaluated for the presence of an endometrial lesion. If the AGC is thought to be of endometrial origin, the endometrial cavity should be evaluated. On rare occasions, advanced pelvic imaging or laparoscopy may be considered to rule out an ovarian, peritoneal, or fallopian tube carcinoma for patients with unexplained glandular cells found on Pap testing.

American Society for Colposcopy and Cervical Pathology. Management algorithms for abnormal Pap tests. Hagerstown (MD): ASCCP; 2002.

Ries LA, Eisner MP, Kosary CL, Hankey BF, Miller BA, Clegg L, et al, editors. SEER cancer statistics review, 1975–2000. Bethesda (MD): National Cancer Institute; 2003.

Saslow D, Runowicz CD, Solomon D, Moscicki AB, Smith RA, Eyre HJ, et al. American Cancer Society guideline for the early detection of cervical neoplasia and cancer. CA Cancer J Clin 2002;52:342–62.

Wright TC Jr, Cox JT, Massad LS, Twiggs LB, Wilkinson EJ. 2001 consensus guidelines for the management of women with cervical cytological abnormalities. JAMA 2002;287:2120–9.

164–166

Hereditary cancer syndromes

Match the clinical scenario (164–166) with the appropriate diagnosis (A–D).

(A) Sporadic ovarian cancer
(B) Hereditary breast–ovarian cancer (HBOC) syndrome
(C) Lynch syndrome type II
(D) Site-specific ovarian cancer

D **164.** A 44-year-old woman has stage III papillary serous ovarian cancer. Her mother developed ovarian cancer at age 48 years. She has 2 sisters who developed ovarian cancer at ages 41 and 42 years.

C **165.** A 43-year-old woman has stage III papillary serous ovarian cancer. Her father and paternal grandfather had colon cancer in their 40s. Her mother developed endometrial cancer at age 57.

A **166.** A 59-year-old woman has stage III papillary serous ovarian cancer. A maternal uncle developed colon cancer at age 72 years. Her paternal grandmother developed breast cancer at age 67 years. A maternal first cousin developed ovarian cancer at age 63 years.

Epidemiologic studies have described 3 familial cancer syndromes: 1) hereditary breast–ovarian cancer (HBOC) syndrome, 2) site-specific ovarian cancer, and 3) hereditary nonpolyposis colorectal cancer (HNPCC) syndrome, or Lynch syndrome type II. These cancer syndromes are responsible for most cases of hereditary ovarian epithelial cancer.

Hereditary ovarian cancer is defined as follows:

- A woman with 3 or more cases of ovarian cancer in first-degree relatives and 4 or more cases of early-onset breast cancer (before age 50 years)

or

- A woman with 4 or more cases of ovarian cancer in first-degree relatives at any age, including 2 cases of ovarian cancer and 2 cases of breast cancer.

Compared with the lifetime risk of ovarian cancer of 1.6% for the general population, a woman with a single family member with ovarian cancer has a 5% lifetime risk, and a woman with 2 first-degree relatives with ovarian cancer has a 7% lifetime risk. Less than 10% of women with ovarian cancer have a first-degree relative with this disease.

Hereditary breast–ovarian cancer syndrome is characterized by breast and ovarian cancer that develops in multiple family members with onset before age 50. The association between breast and ovarian cancer is supported by data from the Cancer and Steroid Hormone Study; the risk of developing breast cancer may be calculated based on the risk of developing ovarian cancer. When compared with a population risk of 11%, the lifetime risk

for developing breast cancer for a woman with 1 or 2 first-degree relatives with ovarian cancer was 13% and 31%, respectively. A first-degree family history of ovarian cancer in conjunction with a first-degree history of breast cancer greatly increased the breast cancer risk. It has been estimated that HBOC accounts for 85–90% of all hereditary ovarian cancer cases and 30–70% of all hereditary breast cancer cases; 50% of breast cancer cases associated with this syndrome occur before 41 years of age. Papillary serous ovarian adenocarcinoma is the most frequent histologic type.

Site-specific ovarian cancer initially was described as a separate syndrome. Some researchers consider this hereditary syndrome to be a variant of HBOC syndrome. The absence of breast cancer in site-specific ovarian cancer may be a result of chance or of variability in the specific cancer risks within a mutation. This syndrome is responsible for less than 5% of hereditary ovarian cancer.

Lynch syndrome type II, or HNPCC, is predominantly a right-sided colon cancer that usually occurs before age 50 along with cancers of the endometrium and ovary. Lynch syndrome type II is associated with approximately 2% of hereditary ovarian cancer and 5% of colorectal cancer. This syndrome is a result of germline mutations in the DNA mismatch repair (MMR) genes. Mutations in 5 MMR genes result in Lynch syndrome type II.

A gene within chromosome 17, $q12–q2$, was named *BRCA1* for "breast cancer gene number 1." This gene is responsible for approximately half of breast cancer families and for most HBOC families. The chromosomal region *13q12* is named *BRCA2* and is responsible for the remaining breast cancer families and 10–20% of HBOC.

BRCA1 is a large gene encoding a protein of 1,863 amino acids with 24 coding exons. More than 600 different mutations in *BRCA1* have been identified. *BRCA1* is a tumor-suppressor gene, and most of the mutations cause loss of the *BRCA1* protein function. Lifetime estimates for cancer risk for *BRCA1* carriers unselected for family history are approximately 50% for breast cancer and 16% for ovarian cancer.

Each of the ovarian cancer family syndromes has autosomal-dominant transmission of the cancer-predisposing genes. Children of an affected parent have a 50% chance of inheriting a mutated copy of the susceptibility gene.

Claus EB, Risch N, Thompson WD. The calculation of breast cancer risk for women with a first degree family history of ovarian cancer. Breast Cancer Res Treat 1993;28:115–20.

Easton DF, Bishop DT, Ford D, Crockford GP. Genetic linkage analysis in familial breast and ovarian cancer: results from 214 families. The Breast Cancer Linkage Consortium. Am J Hum Genet 1993;52: 678–701.

Schilder JM, Holladay DV, Gallion H. Hereditary ovarian cancer: clinical syndromes and management. In: Rubin SC, Sutton GP, editors. Ovarian cancer. 2nd ed. Philadelphia (PA): Lippincott Williams & Wilkins; 2001. p. 181–200.

Struewing JP, Hartge P, Wacholder S, Baker SM, Berlin M, McAdams M, et al. The risk of cancer associated with specific mutations of BRCA1 and BRCA2 among Ashkenazi Jews. N Engl J Med 1997;3 36:1401–8.

167–170

Abnormal Pap test results

For each of the following clinical scenarios with liquid-based cervical cytology and no gross cervical lesions (167–170), select the best next step in management (A–G).

(A) Repeated cytologic testing in 6 months
(B) Testing for human papillomavirus (HPV) subtypes
(C) Colposcopy and biopsy, if indicated
(D) Loop electrosurgical excision procedure
(E) Colposcopy and endometrial biopsy
(F) Hysteroscopy
(G) Simple hysterectomy

B   **167.** A 25-year-old woman who has had 4 normal findings on annual Pap tests now has findings of atypical squamous cells of undetermined significance (ASC-US).

C   **168.** A 30-year-old woman has cytologic test findings of atypical squamous cells, cannot exclude high-grade squamous intraepithelial lesion (ASC-H).

E   **169.** A 27-year-old woman with abnormal vaginal bleeding has cytologic test findings of atypical glandular cells (AGC).

C   **170.** A 40-year-old woman has a low-grade squamous intraepithelial lesion (LSIL).

The 2001 Bethesda guidelines were developed to assist clinicians in the management of cervical neoplasia. As a comparison with the 1988 Bethesda guidelines, the ASCUS category was revised to be ASC-US, atypical squamous cells of undetermined significance, or ASC-H, atypical squamous cells, cannot exclude high-grade squamous intraepithelial lesion (HSIL). This change was made in an attempt to clarify further whether the cytologist favored a neoplastic or a reactive process. The classification AGUS (atypical glandular cells of undetermined significance) was eliminated and has been replaced with AGC (atypical glandular cells), which is subdivided into atypical endocervical, endometrial, and glandular cells. In addition, the classification AIS (endocervical adenocarcinoma in situ) has been designated as a separate category.

The management of choice for patient 167, who has a single finding of ASC-US, is reflex DNA testing for high-risk subtypes of HPV. Routine colposcopy for patients with a single ASC-US reading has been found to provoke unnecessary anxiety among patients and is not cost-effective. Reflex testing for high-risk subtypes of HPV is preferred now, because 40–60% of colposcopic procedures can be avoided if the patient does not have a high-risk type (Appendix 2, Fig. 1). The low-risk patient can be reassured immediately that she does not have a significant lesion, because high-grade dysplasia and cancer are associated with the high-risk viral types. If the patient is found to have high-risk viral HPV type 16 or 18, she should have immediate colposcopy. The sensitivity of DNA testing for the detection of cervical intraepithelial neoplasia (CIN) 2–3 is at least 83%. The negative predictive value is also quite high. Additionally, if the patient tests negative for the high-risk types of HPV, then the Pap test can be repeated at 1 year instead of at 3–6 months.

When the cervical cytologic finding is ASC-H, as in patient 168, the next best step in management is referral for colposcopy. Approximately 25–95% of patients with this interpretation will have CIN 2–3 detected on biopsy. Up to 10% of patients in the ASC category will have criteria for ASC-H.

Patients who have abnormal vaginal bleeding with AGC, such as patient 169, or patients who have cytologic determination of AIS should have colposcopy and an endometrial biopsy. The diagnosis of glandular cell abnormalities by cervical cytologic testing does not necessarily imply a glandular abnormality detected by histologic testing. Between 50% and 70% of these patients actually will have the diagnosis of CIN 2–3. The symptom of abnormal vaginal bleeding should alert the clinician to the possibility of an endometrial lesion, which can include hyperplasia or carcinoma. A patient older than 35 years with findings of AGC or AIS on cervical cytologic testing should have an endometrial biopsy, regardless of the presence of abnormal vaginal bleeding. The patient who has normal findings on colposcopy and endometrial biopsy may need excisional biopsy of the cervix to rule out small occult lesions of adenocarcinoma of the cervix, because colposcopy findings for glandular disease are not predictive (Appendix 2, Fig. 2). This is especially true for patients with AIS or AGC, favoring neoplasia. If the excision is negative, the diagnosis of neoplasia of the

adnexa must be considered. Consultation with a gynecologic oncologist may be in order.

If the results of cytologic testing is LSIL, as in patient 170, colposcopy with biopsy if indicated is recommended. Although it is well known that many patients with findings of CIN 1 on biopsy will have spontaneous regression of disease, up to 30% with LSIL will have findings of at least CIN 2 on biopsy (Appendix 2, Fig. 3). Reflex testing does not appear to be of much benefit for patients with this classification, because up to 83% of patients in a recent study were noted to test positive for high-risk subtypes of HPV.

Hysteroscopy and hysterectomy are seldom, if ever, used in the initial workup for a patient with abnormal cervical cytologic findings. Colposcopy is always performed prior to these procedures. Certainly, hysteroscopy may be indicated for patients with normal findings on endometrial biopsies. Hysterectomy, except under the rarest of circumstances, is a treatment and not a diagnostic modality.

American Society for Colposcopy and Cervical Pathology. Management algorithms for abnormal Pap tests. Hagerstown (MD): ASCCP; 2002.

Eddy GL, Wojtowycz MA, Piraino PS, Mazur MT. Papanicolaou smears by the Bethesda system in endometrial malignancy: utility and prognostic importance. Obstet Gynecol 1997;90:999–1003.

Human papillomavirus testing for triage of women with cytologic evidence of low-grade squamous intraepithelial lesions: baseline data from a randomized trial. The Atypical Squamous Cells of Undetermined Significance/Low-Grade Squamous Intraepithelial Lesions Triage Study (ALTS) Group. J Natl Cancer Inst 2000;92:397–402.

Solomon D, Davey D, Kurman R, Moriarty A, O'Connor D, Prey M, et al. The 2001 Bethesda system: terminology for reporting results of cervical cytology. JAMA 2002;287:2114–9.

Wright TC Jr, Cox JT, Massad LS, Twiggs LB, Wilkinson EJ. 2001 Consensus guidelines for the management of women with cervical cytological abnormalities. JAMA 2002;287:2120–9.

Appendix 1
Zung Self-Rating Depression Scale

Please read each statement and decide how much of the time the statement describes how you have been feeling during the past several days.

Make check mark (✓) in appropriate column	A little of the time	Some of the time	Good part of the time	Most of the time
1. I feel down-hearted and blue	_____	_____	_____	_____
2. Morning is when I feel the best	_____	_____	_____	_____
3. I have crying spells or feel like it	_____	_____	_____	_____
4. I have trouble sleeping at night	_____	_____	_____	_____
5. I eat as much as I used to	_____	_____	_____	_____
6. I still enjoy sex	_____	_____	_____	_____
7. I notice that I am losing weight	_____	_____	_____	_____
8. I have trouble with constipation	_____	_____	_____	_____
9. My heart beats faster than usual	_____	_____	_____	_____
10. I get tired for no reason	_____	_____	_____	_____
11. My mind is as clear as it used to be	_____	_____	_____	_____
12. I find it easy to do the things I used to	_____	_____	_____	_____
13. I am restless and can't keep still	_____	_____	_____	_____
14. I feel hopeful about the future	_____	_____	_____	_____
15. I am more irritable than usual	_____	_____	_____	_____
16. I find it easy to make decisions	_____	_____	_____	_____
17. I feel that I am useful and needed	_____	_____	_____	_____
18. My life is pretty full	_____	_____	_____	_____
19. I feel that others would be better off if I were dead	_____	_____	_____	_____
20. I still enjoy the things I used to	_____	_____	_____	_____

(continued)

Zung Self-Rating Depression Scale *(continued)*

Key to Scoring

To total the score, add up the numbers that correlate with the patient's response to each statement then divide that number by 80. A score of 0.5 or more may mean the patient is depressed.

	A little of the time	Some of the time	Good part of the time	Most of the time
1. I feel down-hearted and blue	1	2	3	4
2. Morning is when I feel the best	4	3	2	1
3. I have crying spells or feel like it	1	2	3	4
4. I have trouble sleeping at night	1	2	3	4
5. I eat as much as I used to	4	3	2	1
6. I still enjoy sex	4	3	2	1
7. I notice that I am losing weight	1	2	3	4
8. I have trouble with constipation	1	2	3	4
9. My heart beats faster than usual	1	2	3	4
10. I get tired for no reason	1	2	3	4
11. My mind is as clear as it used to be	4	3	2	1
12. I find it easy to do the things I used to	4	3	2	1
13. I am restless and can't keep still	1	2	3	4
14. I feel hopeful about the future	4	3	2	1
15. I am more irritable than usual	1	2	3	4
16. I find it easy to make decisions	4	3	2	1
17. I feel that I am useful and needed	4	3	2	1
18. My life is pretty full	4	3	2	1
19. I feel that others would be better off if I were dead	1	2	3	4
20. I still enjoy the things I used to	4	3	2	1

Zung WW. A self-rating depression scale. Arch Gen Psychiatry 1965;12:63-70. Copyrighted 1965, American Medical Association

Appendix 2

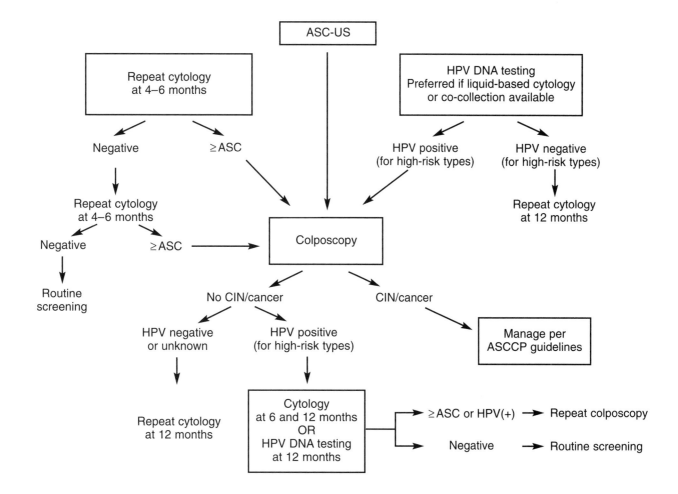

FIG. 1. American Society for Colposcopy and Cervical Pathology (ASCCP) algorithm for treatment of women with atypical squamous cells of undetermined significance (ASC-US) in special circumstances. HPV indicates human papillomavirus. (The Consensus Guidelines algorithm originally appeared in and are reprinted from The Journal of Lower Genital Tract Disease Vol. 6, Issue 2, and are reprinted with the permission of ASCCP © American Society for Colposcopy and Cervical Pathology 2002. No copies of the algorithms may be made without the prior consent of ASCCP.)

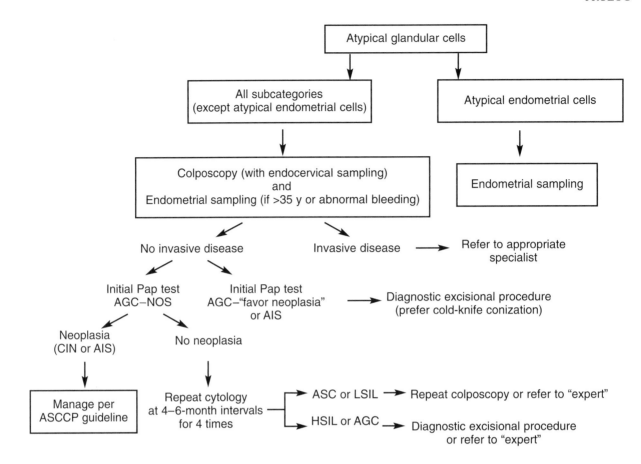

FIG. 2. American Society for Colposcopy and Cervical Pathology (ASCCP) algorithm for treatment of women with atypical glandular cells (AGC). AIS indicates adenocarcinoma in situ; ASC, atypical squamous cells; HSIL, high-grade squamous intraepithelial lesions; LSIL, low-grade squamous intraepithelial lesions; NOS, not otherwise specified. (The Consensus Guidelines algorithms originally appeared in and are reprinted from The Journal of Lower Genital Tract Disease Vol. 6, Issue 2, and are reprinted with the permission of ASCCP © American Society for Colposcopy and Cervical Pathology 2002. No copies of the algorithms may be made without the prior consent of ASCCP.)

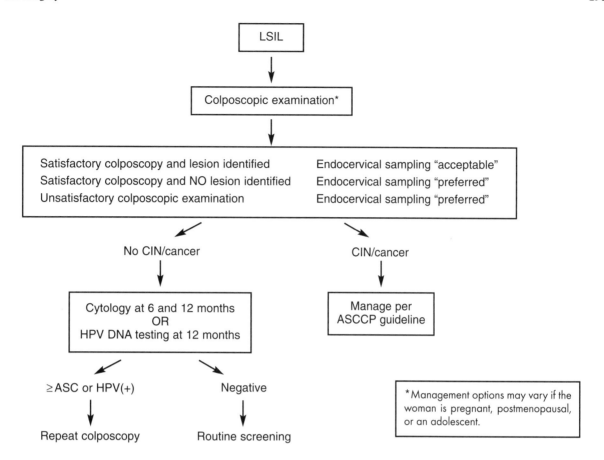

FIG. 3. American Society for Colposcopy and Cervical Pathology (ASCCP) algorithm for treatment of women with low-grade squamous intraepithelial lesions (LSIL). Management options may vary if the woman is pregnant, postmenopausal, or an adolescent. CIN indicates cervical intraepithelial neoplasia. (The Consensus Guidelines algorithms originally appeared in and are reprinted from The Journal of Lower Genital Tract Disease Vol. 6, Issue 2, and are reprinted with the permission of ASCCP © American Society for Colposcopy and Cervical Pathology 2002. No copies of the algorithms may be made without the prior consent of ASCCP.)

Index

NOTE: Numbers refer to questions, not pages.

NOTE: Numbers refer to questions, not pages.

NOTE: Numbers refer to questions, not pages.

NOTE: Numbers refer to questions, not pages.

NOTE: Numbers refer to questions, not pages.

NOTE: Numbers refer to questions, not pages.

NOTE: Numbers refer to questions, not pages.

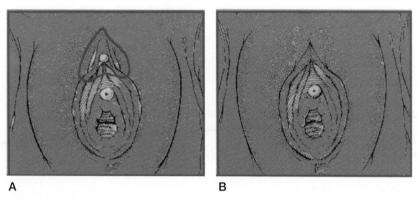

FIG. 10-1. Female circumcision/female genital mutilation, type I: excision of part or all of the clitoris; this type may not be noticed in a hasty examination. (A) Clitoridectomy, drawing of area cut. (B) Clitoridectomy, drawing of healed area. (Copyright © 1999 by RAINBO, Research Action and Information Network for Bodily Integrity of Women)

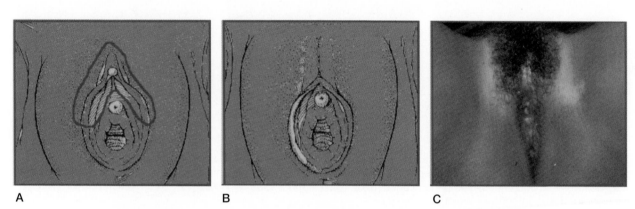

FIG. 10-2. Female circumcision/female genital mutilation, type II: Excision of the prepuce and clitoris together with partial or total excision of the labia minora. (A) Excision, drawing of area cut. (B) Excision, drawing of healed area. (C) Excision healed. (Copyright © 1999 by RAINBO, Research Action and Information Network for Bodily Integrity of Women)

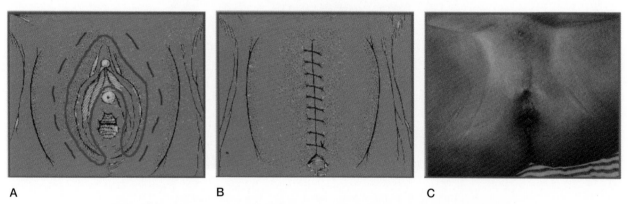

FIG. 10-3. Female circumcision/female genital mutilation, type III: excision of part or all of the external genitalia and stitching or narrowing of the vaginal opening (infibulation). (A) Infibulation, drawing of area cut. (B) Infibulation, drawing of area stitched. (C) Healed infibulation. (Copyright © 1999 by RAINBO, Research Action and Information Network for Bodily Integrity of Women)

1. Apply anaesthesia

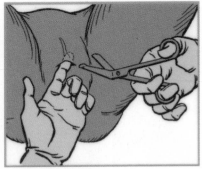
2. Insert 1–2 fingers

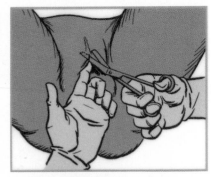
3. Cut with bandagelike scissors avoiding injury to a buried clitoris

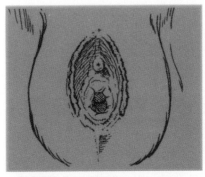
4. Inspect cut edges for bleeding points

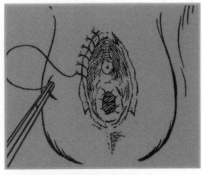
5. Apply hemostatic running absorbable sutures

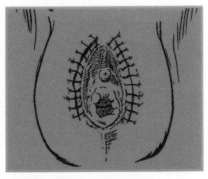
6. Defibulation complete

FIG. 10-4. Six steps for defibulation in cases of circumcision/female genital mutilation. Anesthesia may be local, regional, or spinal, depending on patient's tolerance and assessment of her psychologic state. Flashbacks to original cutting may be traumatic and necessitate general anesthesia. (Copyright © 1999 by RAINBQ, Research Action and Information Network for Bodily Integrity of Women)

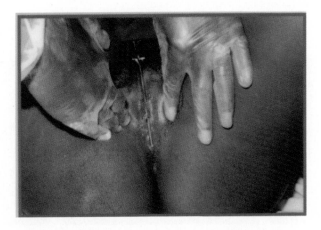

FIG. 10-5. Labia minora infibulation. The labia minora, and not the labia majora, were used to create an infibulation hood of skin over the vulva. (Copyright © 1999 by RAINBQ, Research Action and Information Network for Bodily Integrity of Women)

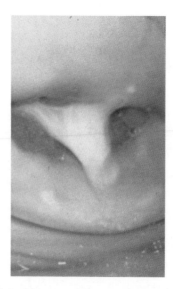

FIG. 30-1. Mucopurulent cervicitis caused by *Chlamydia trachomatis*. (Holmes KK, Mardh PA, Sparling PF, editors. Sexually transmitted diseases. 2nd ed. New York [NY]: McGraw-Hill; 1990. plate 16. With permission of The McGraw-Hill Companies.)

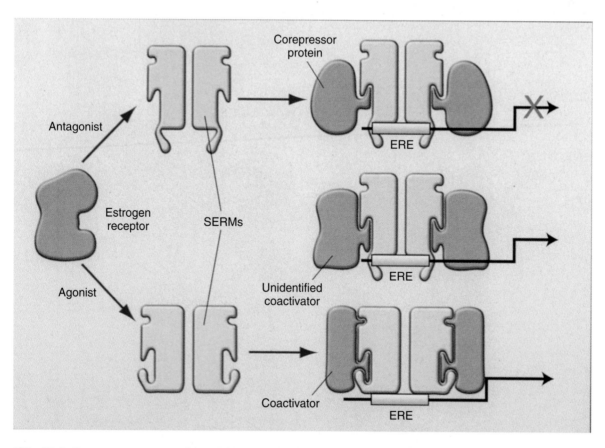

FIG. 69-1. Estrogen-receptor actions. ERE, estrogen response element; SERMs, selective estrogen-receptor modulators (Riggs BL, Hartmann LC. Selective estrogen-receptor modulators—mechanisms of action and application to clinical practice. N Engl J Med 2003;348:620. Copyright © 2003 Massachusetts Medical Society. All rights reserved.)

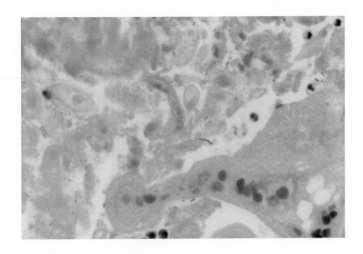

FIG. 77-1. Gram-positive rods with background of necrosis.